ARCHITECTURE
OF THE WESTERN WORLD

ARCHITECTURE
OF THE WESTERN WORLD

Edited and with an introduction
by Michael Raeburn

Foreword by Sir Hugh Casson

Individual chapters by

J. J. Coulton, Michael Grant
Nicola Coldstream, Bruce Boucher
Neil MacGregor, John Maule McKean
Charles McKean

RIZZOLI
NEW YORK

Half title page: Roman stele portraying an architect holding the instruments of his profession.

Title page: The Piazza del Popolo, at Ascoli Piceno in central Italy, is a classic example of Renaissance town planning in its attempt to impose a rational uniformity onto a chaotic medieval commercial centre (which itself was the site of the ancient forum). Clearly demonstrating Alberti's architectural principles, the piazza is dominated by the church and palazzo, while the loggia, built all round it in the early years of the sixteenth century, serves to disguise the irregularities of the older buildings.

© Orbis Publishing Limited
Published in the United States of America
in 1980 by

RIZZOLI INTERNATIONAL PUBLICATIONS, INC.
712 Fifth Avenue/New York 10019

Library of Congress Card Number 80-50659
ISBN 0-8478-0349-x

Printed in Hong Kong by Toppan Printing
Company (H.K.) Limited

CONTENTS

FOREWORD

by Sir Hugh Casson

A view through the gateway into the northern forecourt of Kirby Hall, Northamptonshire, England. Kirby was built largely in the 1570s, but this gate and the façade behind were probably executed in 1638–40 by the stonemason Nicholas Stone the Elder. The broken pediment with a coat-of-arms and the mouldings of the windows on the north façade itself recall aspects of Inigo Jones's architecture as well as designs published by the sixteenth-century architect, Serlio. Kirby has been unlived in since the end of the eighteenth century.

Architecture, it has been said, begins at home. That is the place where we feel at ease, where the roots grow from which we draw our moral and cultural strength. Not surprisingly therefore the beginnings of architecture—like the structural ingenuity of the birds and insects that preceded our own efforts—are usually anonymous, deeply respectful of climate and terrain, firmly practical, but touched always with creative imagination.

These qualities, often overlooked by those historians who are the prisoners of prejudice or dogma, or who prefer (in Rudofsky's phrase) the company of buildings from the Social Register, are eternally valid, as the examples in all shapes, sizes and uses illustrated on the following pages so clearly show. From these we can see and understand that all man-made buildings, whether as humble as a hut or as imposing as a palace, must stand upon the double foundation of function and symbolism; they must be subject first to the parameters of human needs, of climate and current technology (all usually calculable), and secondly to the imagery—physiological, moral, backward- or forward-looking—which is fortunately so difficult to predict, and thus ensures so endless a variety of form.

But this is not all. The articulation of space—the discipline of proportion and geometry; the influences of State and Church, of fashion, privilege or politics—are all elements in the history of architecture which must be analysed and assessed if that architecture is to be fully enjoyed. In such turbulent currents we all need guidance from experts, from scholars who can infuse their learning with perceptive passion, and who can interpret for us in detail the references and sub-codes by which the development of architecture has throughout the centuries been enriched. Such are the experts who contribute to these pages and thus also to our knowledge and after that to our understanding. For in architecture—as in everything else—the more we know, the more we will be rewarded.

In commending most warmly this historical review of the buildings of the western world may I add a warning postscript? Architecture, it must be remembered, cannot properly be appreciated on the printed page, however lively or knowledgeable, nor even in fact by the eye alone. It has to be experienced by all the senses and in all its three dimensions—four indeed if you include (as I would) the dimension of time.

The purpose of this book, therefore, is not just to inform, to delight or even just to open the eyes a little wider to the familiar (and thus so often to the unseen). It is an invitation to all of us to go out and to explore the buildings and spaces that surround us, and to experience them for ourselves as often as we can.

INTRODUCTION

Many of the elements that make up the language of western architecture can be seen in the Chapel of the Three Kings, 1662–4, by Borromini, in the College of the Propagation of the Faith in Rome. The Greek Orders appear in the use of twelve Ionic pilasters to support an entablature that breaks forward over the capitals and curves around the corners. The use of intersecting equilateral triangles to dictate the plan of the chapel, to define the vault and to point the symbolism (Trinity, Three Kings), is derived from Gothic architecture, while the undulating walls and marked diagonals activate the space, enhancing symmetry with movement, beauty with life.

Looking through the pictures in this book, the reader will appreciate the rich variety of buildings within the western tradition, but the variety is less remarkable than the continuity, the essential unity of this tradition. The same architectural forms and the same language of criticism have kept reappearing, to be reinterpreted by succeeding generations. In music the thread leading from antiquity was broken, and Renaissance musicians had to reconstruct what they believed the system of the ancients to have been; but in architecture not only was there a living tradition of building and many actual survivals of classical architecture, there was also a theoretical work preserved intact from the ancient world. This was the treatise *On Architecture* written in retirement by the Roman military engineer and architect Vitruvius Pollio.

The ideas Vitruvius expressed and the terms he used still form, even today, the basis for much architectural theorizing and controversy. In the first place he recognized that there are three different requirements of a building: that it should be structurally sound (*firmitas*), that it must have a practical function (*utilitas*), and that it should be beautiful (*venustas*). Separate histories could be, and have been, written about each of these three aspects, but the authors of this book will show how the final form of a building depends on all three, though at different times one strand, the technological, the social or the aesthetic may be dominant. Our aim is to enable the reader to enjoy more fully the experience of looking at buildings, being in them and moving through them, by a better understanding of the language of architecture.

Vitruvius' book is in many ways maddening, but it does provide a constant thread through architectural history. It was written principally about Greek architecture, and the parts devoted to architecture rather than military engineering are translated from works by Greek theorists, which Vitruvius did not fully understand. He muddled together ideas from different sources, even when they contradicted each other, but it is in part his very obscurity, his openness to reinterpretation, that has ensured his survival. The most important themes that derive from his book are the definitions of the classical Orders (see p. 43), theories of proportion based on a modular system, on simple geometry and on the human body, and aesthetic definitions relating to harmony and proportions such as 'disposition', 'distribution', 'symmetry' and 'eurhythmy'. Over fifty manuscript copies of the book have survived from the Middle Ages, and it seems certain that it was used as a textbook by medieval architects, largely for the geometrical ideas it contains.

In the early Renaissance Brunelleschi and Alberti compared Vitruvius' rules with existing ruins of Roman buildings, and Alberti's influential treatise *De Re Aedificatoria* was more or less a rewriting of Vitruvius. Alberti is scathing about some of the Roman architect's stupidities, but the spread and development of Renaissance architecture would have been unthinkable without his theoretical basis. Even in the mid-nineteenth century a progressive thinker and architect like Gottfried Semper was able to start his book *Der Stil* with a discussion of symmetry and eurhythmy, and Le Corbusier's *Modulor*, published in 1950, is an attempt to create a new, more flexible scale of proportions based on the human figure, to supersede the Vitruvian system codified by the Renaissance.

Treatises and theoretical works have been only one means of handing on architectural ideas, and the medium of transmission has often dictated the eventual form. The most obvious source of ideas is the actual study of other buildings, then the study of models and of two-dimensional representations, finally the adoption of rules or systems. The rules of proportion developed by the Greeks, like the often complex systems of geometry developed in the Gothic period, were used principally for practical purposes. Where there were no fixed standards of measurement, rules were likely to prove a far more effective means of accurate communica-

tion than drawings or models, except for the design of details. The extraordinary unity of the Greek temple form from the western Mediterranean to the Turkish coast must be due very largely to the widespread diffusion of these rules of proportion. The development of two-dimensional representation of groundplans and elevations was also extremely important, though as a medium of transmission it has often proved unreliable. In particular, it has often concentrated developments on the exterior form of buildings, since the interior space is so much more difficult to represent, but new ideas that could be represented by simple drawings have often been most influential.

During the Middle Ages geometrical rules and drawings of details were both used; but with the invention of printing many more architectural treatises became widely available, and much lively and often wildly inappropriate detail, especially in northern Europe and in Spanish lands, can be attributed to unsophisticated copying from these books. Where faithful copying would—and elsewhere did—produce a sterile architecture, the misunderstandings and accretions often produced new authentic local styles. From the middle of the eighteenth century books began to be produced which illustrated not just the prevailing style of the time, but the styles of all periods and all peoples, and the museum mentality of the nineteenth century classified, sub-classified

and multiplied examples. The architect was bewildered, but the painstaking illustrations ensured that whatever pattern he followed he could follow correctly, at least so far as the exterior was concerned. The development of photography has, if anything, increased confusion. The idealized black-and-white photographs of pioneering Modern Movement buildings sometimes led to imitations that have misjudged almost every factor – the siting, the spatial concept, the colour, the scale, even the materials. At the same time, the extensive publication of photographs, plans, drawings and specifications in periodicals has speeded up the communication of new ideas between architects; but new developments and new movements have followed each other with such speed that the revolutionary architect has found his ideas superseded sometimes even before they have reached full development. Mies van der Rohe, for example, one of the real pioneers of the Modern Movement with his Barcelona Pavilion (known universally from photographs—see p. 262—but how many of the architects influenced by it ever saw the building itself?) and other works of the 1920s and 30s, turned in his post-war years in America to an increasingly sterile formalism and perfectionism. The pace of change was such that neither Gropius nor Frank Lloyd Wright was able to produce late works of a significance to compare with their pre-war buildings.

These illustrations demonstrate ways in which two-dimensional representations of architecture have been important in solving technical problems; in disseminating designs; in influencing taste; and to add weight to theoretical argument. All show variations on the Greco-Roman tradition.

Left: The drawings in Villehard de Honnecourt's architectural notebook (see p. 108) illustrate the practical geometry of the medieval architect. Among diagrams showing how measurements should be made and how stones should be cut are (third row) his drawing of a bridge constructed of short timbers and the plan of a cloister illustrating the Vitruvian technique of quadratura: harmonious proportions are achieved by using the length of a half-side as the measure for the half-diagonal of the inner square, making it exactly half the area of the large one, with their sides in the ratio of $1 : \sqrt{2}$.

Right above: This 'Doric' door and window appear in Le Muet's version (1645) of Palladio's 'First Book of Architecture', though not in Palladio's original. The Italian

Renaissance architects, by adapting details found in classical buildings and applying them to modern interior and exterior design, created the classical language of western architecture.

Right below: The well preserved ruins of the 'Temple of Minerva Medica' in Rome, c.AD250, showed Renaissance architects some of the spatial possibilities as well as the structural techniques of the ribbed dome over a centrally planned building (see p. 129); while Piranesi's 'Vedute', published from c.1750 on, appealed to the more archeological interest in ancient buildings that was embodied in the Neo-classical style.

Far right above: Increasingly scholarly study of classical architecture continued through the nineteenth century; this plate from Gottfried Semper's 'Der Stil' (1860-63) shows the use of colour in a moulding of the 'Theseion' at Athens. Semper wanted to get away from the slavish copying of old styles, and by analysing the formative elements to find a new style that was appropriate to his own time.

THE ARCHITECT

The role of the modern architect is in many ways different from that of the architect in the past, although the essential triangular relationship of patron-architect-constructor remains unchanged. Vitruvius demanded of the architect that he should have both imagination and training and that, as well as understanding both the practical and theoretical aspects of construction, he should be versed in letters, drawing, the use of geometrical instruments, optics, arithmetic, history, philosophy, music, medicine, law and astronomy. There is something here of the self-assertion of the military engineer aspiring to be an artist, and some of the reasons he gives for needing this breadth of knowledge are rather surprising: music, for instance, is necessary primarily to make sure that both ropes of a catapult are under equal tension, so that it will shoot straight, but also to judge theatre acoustics, where reverberators known as *echeia* were used. Most Roman architects were probably trained as engineers and they received less social recognition than architects in ancient Greece. There the names of many architects have been preserved, and it seems that they were often responsible for the design and for supervising the various contractors, and that they were given the credit for the authorship of the buildings. In Roman times, and even more in the Middle Ages, the architect was moved firmly from his place as an artist—trained in the Liberal Arts—to a place as a technician—trained in the Mechanical Arts. Buildings of these periods are more often assigned to their patron than to their architect, and in some cases the patron took a leading role in the supervision of the construction. The roof of the abbey church at St Denis (1140s), needed timbers over 10 metres (35 feet) long for the tie-beams, and Abbot Suger, patron of the building, when informed by his master carpenters and his foresters that such long timbers were unobtainable near at hand, himself led a search through the woods. 'Towards the first hour we found one timber adequate to the measure. Why say more? By the ninth hour or sooner, we had, through the thickets, the depths of the forest and the dense, thorny tangles, marked down twelve timbers (for so many were necessary) to the astonishment of all. . . .'

However, the names of many of the medieval master builders are known to us, and details of payments made to them show that they were very highly regarded. They were in a real sense architect-engineers, masters of their craft, but the idea of the artist as such did not exist then. The scale of the great cathedrals, abbeys and castles was such that the master builders seldom saw their plans fully carried out, and there was clearly no sense of their plan being in itself a work of art, to which nothing could be added and from which nothing could be taken away. Throughout the Middle Ages the individual building was often treated more like a whole complex, with plans being modified and modernized as it grew, the whole subordinated to a concept, sometimes worked out for that specific building, sometimes applicable to a whole category of building. Study of the medieval building industry reveals a wonderfully complex social structure, with the workmen, when times were good, indulging in all kinds of restrictive practice, with the master masons or architect-engineers winning rich rewards and earning great respect for their work, but not the artist's laurels. The final accolade went to the ecclesiastical, municipal, noble or royal patron and to the Church, the township, the dynasty or the Crown.

It was in Italy, before the Renaissance,

that the change began to take place. The painter Giotto was in 1334 appointed master mason to the cathedral and city of Florence, and he designed the *campanile*— Giotto's tower. By the middle of the following century the humanist style was established in Italy and the architect was established as an artist. From now on many of the artist-architects had no specific architectural training at all, certainly not through the craft-guild system of the Middle Ages, although in places where the Italian Renaissance style was not yet adopted architectural work was

Left: The fifteenth-century timber roof in Cawston, England, is richly decorated with tracery panels and carved figures of angels.

Right: The bridge at Coalbrookdale, England, 1779, showed both architects and engineers the structural possibilities of iron.

Below: Lay brothers building the church at Schönau in the fifteenth century under the supervision of the master mason with his rule and square. They are shown quarrying and transporting stone, using a crane to position a block of masonry, mixing cement, carving mouldings, and resting from their labours.

still in the hands of surveyors and of master masons. Many of the earliest English books on architecture were designed for use by surveyors and illustrate the mathematical instruments they needed, but it was the proliferation of architectural literature that made it possible for the amateur to design buildings. The same basic knowledge was now in the hands of gentleman-amateur and literate mason, builder or carpenter alike.

The architect-engineer had not vanished, and it should be remembered that of the three greatest virtuosi of the Baroque, two—Borromini and Guarini— were trained in the Gothic tradition, and the other, Balthasar Neumann, was a military engineer. Neumann's Vierzehnheiligen (1742–72) (see p. 178), was completed in the same decade that the iron bridge at Coalbrookdale (1779) was erected, cast by Abraham Darby III and designed by the architect T.F. Pritchard. For the second half of the eighteenth century saw a new and unprecedented development. The British industrial revolution brought into being a new class of building—industrial architecture. This could not be catered for by the traditional methods used for dwellings, nor did it call for a display of gentlemanly architecture, so it was the engineers themselves who stepped into the breach. Although when K.F. Schinkel, the German architect, visited Britain in 1826 it was the work of the engineers which impressed him far more than the work of the architects, in the whole nineteenth-century cult of the Middle Ages the idea of the medieval architect-engineer was not revived. On the contrary, the Gothicists were largely responsible for the myth of medieval architecture springing in a parallel immaculate conception from the self-effacing hand of the anonymous brother or lay craftsmen. The actual metre-wide gap between the hotel and the train-shed at St Pancras Station in London (see p. 215) perfectly represents the irreconcilable gap between engineers and architects. The amateur architect still survived through the nineteenth century, but, increasingly, official restrictions, the rewards of speculative building and the new guild system of professional bodies killed off not only the amateur architect but also the master builder designing the houses he built in traditional local styles.

In the present century the architectural profession has grown in numbers to the extent that there were by 1975 over 25,000 registered architects in Britain, handling some £3,300 million worth of building work, and more than 60,000 practising architects in the USA. An important part of the engineering industry is also engaged in construction. On a humbler level, hardly any building job can be undertaken without an architect to supply drawings to obtain the necessary official permissions. If we look back at the education Vitruvius recommended for an architect, it is not so inappropriate: knowledge of letters, according to the Roman architect, was required to keep good records; philosophy to improve the architect's character and keep him free from avarice; law to understand the regulations concerning light, noise, drainage and water supply, to be able to draw up fair contracts and to avoid litigation; medicine to be able to take considerations of climate and health into account; optics and music were required for knowledge of lighting and acoustics; history to justify by precedent the designs adopted; while drawing, geometry (surveying) and arithmetic (calculating) are self-explanatory; astronomy was only required for clock-makers. It is a far cry from the *homo universalis* of the Renaissance.

And after all that, is the architect to be an inventive artist, responsible for the renewal of our environment? Of course there is a confusion. The term is too broad that covers the man who executes drawings for rows of pseudo-vernacular suburban houses and the man masterminding the planning of a new airport, a new national theatre or even a new metropolis. Yet at the same time many great contributions to the history of architecture have been made by men who did not even go by the name of architect. At the present there is a particularly strong feeling for architecture in which the architect has not played a dominant role, for buildings which are 'organic', for those which are not conformist, which show an imaginative handling of space, which relate to their natural or urban environment and to their social function. Greater interest is being shown in architecture of all kinds outside the main western tradition and, especially, in the local indigenous building styles of western Europe.

Vernacular architecture, architecture without architects, is not easy to define, or, rather, it is hard to draw a clear line between the vernacular and the main architectural tradition; to draw a distinction between 'architecture' and 'mere building' begs the question. It might perhaps be compared to folk music. In its more primitive forms it does not conform to any of the rules, the basic premises of mainstream architecture (in music the diatonic system), but it can react upon it, in a period receptive to its qualities, in a most fruitful way and is itself changed and influenced by general stylistic developments. Its most significant feature, which could at least suggest a definition, is that the contribution of the individual, whether his name is known or not, is always less than the overriding features of the local style. A building whose individuality transcends this local style has already moved away from the essence of the vernacular. The factors which give vernacular architecture its form are social organization, climate, available materials and available skills in using them. Formal and decorative traditions will certainly play their part, but similarities in forms used in different areas where no question of influence can arise suggest that this is a secondary consideration. It would be impossible in a short space to give an indication of the detailed development of any of the hundreds of separate local traditions in the western world, each derived from its own particular circumstances, but in discussing the materials used in building they will be related where possible to vernacular usage.

Right: F.L. Wright combined the skills of architect and engineer. Each of the dendriform columns of the Johnson Wax Building (1936–9) at Racine, Wisconsin, USA, was designed to carry a load of 12 tonnes (12 tons), but Building Code regulations laid down that their diameter should be four times the 23 cm (9 in) of Wright's design. One column was erected and loaded with gravel and cement to demonstrate its structural soundness. Wright described his finished colonnade as creating 'the sense of physical weight dissolved in space'.

Far right: The form of this simple modern building, the studio at Charterhouse school, Surrey, England, by James Dartford, 1958, demonstrates its structural system: the pillars of the concrete frame are exposed in the walls of the lower storey, and the brackets supporting the cantilevered upper storey are plainly visible, while the wide expanses of window indicate that the walls do not bear the load of the building.

STRUCTURAL SYSTEMS

The physical stability of a building depends on the materials used and the structural system adopted. Rough masonry walls need to be thick, and the roof system they support has to be based on a beam which exerts pressure straight downwards through the walls (top left).

The cruck (top centre), the simplest type of wooden frame, is formed of two curved supports which meet at the point of the roof, the opposing weight of each one holding the other one up.

In the box frame (top right) the main posts are not independent self-supporting members, but with the main beams form a rigid frame which absorbs the internal stresses within it.

The stone arch relies for stability on the form and weight of its wedge-shaped voussoirs, each one transferring its own weight and the weight it supports to the one below it. Where the arch springs from the pier, part of the weight of the voussoirs pushes outwards and the walls need to be very strong to resist this lateral thrust.

The inventiveness of Gothic engineers reduced the volume of the solid wall, creating a rib-cage of slender piers and arches which support the vault and the glass-filled walls. The flying buttresses lean on the walls, counter-balancing the lateral thrust of the vault.

In the steel and reinforced concrete frame (far right, bottom) the functions of support and protection are entirely separated, the outside non-load-bearing walls being made up of glass and infill panels. This more specialized application of building materials leads to greater economy in their use.

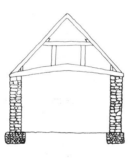

Masonry walls support a roof truss of wood, itself a simple frame structure, clad with tiles or thatch. The strong tie-beam increases the stability of the walls.

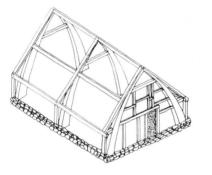

A simple cottage formed of three crucks. The rest of the frame of roof and walls is supported on these crucks, and the spaces between are filled with wattle and daub.

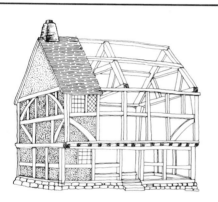

A jettied upper storey in a box frame improved the stability of the main beams, as pressure was exerted on them beyond the points at which they were supported from below.

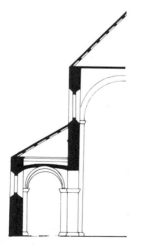

Cross-section of a Romanesque church (Würzburg), showing the thick containing walls of solid masonry (shaded) and the supporting structure of piers and arches.

The Gothic masonry frame (Reims) avoids the lintel, a form in which the weight of stone makes it relatively weak; thus the vertical emphasis is a structural necessity.

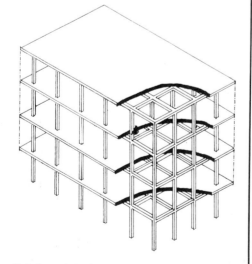

Reinforced concrete is strong as both beam and column, but is especially effective if used to form a continuous frame with rigid joints, supporting floors, roof and glass walls.

BUILDING TECHNOLOGY

To view the history of architecture simply as a branch of the history of technology must lead to a distortion of values, but it is nevertheless impossible to appreciate the work of architects without at least a basic understanding of the properties of building materials, the physical laws which govern the stability of a building and the means by which it can stand up to climate and weather.

The vast majority of buildings consist of walls surrounding an interior space or spaces, with some sort of roof as a covering. The materials of which the building is made serve two functions—to support the structure and to enclose the space. Where the building meets the ground there is generally an intermediate layer built down into the ground as a foundation, and on the soundness of this the ultimate stability of the building may well depend. The foundation serves to transfer the load of the building to the geological substructure on which it rests. A careful examination must first be made of the terrain, which may need reinforcement to prevent subsidence, and the type of foundation is then determined by the structural system of the building and by the nature of the ground. Normally, if a building is of solid-wall construction, the foundation will follow the line of the wall and be dug deep enough to rest on absolutely firm ground. In the case of a frame construction, where the load of a building is concentrated at certain points around the base, the foundation will often be in the form of piles driven deep down into the substructure, although wooden-framed buildings are also built on continuous stone or brick foundations. Where the ground is soft or marshy the foundations may be built as a complete layer, like a raft (sometimes supported on piles), beneath the whole building, to distribute the load evenly without it resting on a solid basis. Many of the buildings of Venice are supported on a special form of raft foundation. The Greeks and Romans generally devoted much care to foundations, and in the Middle Ages a journeyman had to 'know from the height of any wall how thick it should be and how to make the foundation accordingly', although many medieval buildings, York Minster among them, stand on very inadequate foundations.

Masonry has generally been used to build solid walls, which both carry the whole load of the building in themselves and also provide the protective envelope to the interior. As long as the material they are made of will resist crushing forces, and they remain vertical and not subject to lateral forces, masonry walls will remain stable. If covered by a vault exerting lateral forces (pushing the wall outwards at the top), the wall will need to be supported by buttresses or by greater thickness. The greatest danger of instability in a masonry wall is that of buckling outwards, and the beams of floors and ceilings may often add stability by acting as tie-beams and by helping to transfer the load of the building vertically down the walls. Openings in a solid wall may be either straight-topped on the post-and-lintel principle—although in a heavy

Far left: Ballochmyle Railway Viaduct, Scotland, by John Miller, 1847, under construction. Stone arches are very strong, but during building the voussoirs must be supported on wooden centring until the central keystone is placed in position, and the sides must be buttressed if the arch is not to collapse outwards. Here, two of the small arches have been completed, and the centring has been moved to start work on the other side. The design of centring for wide arches has always presented a challenge to the engineer (whether for stone, steel or concrete arches), particularly where the same structures are reused for repeated arches.

Left: Arcaded apse of the eleventh-century ruined church of Val des Nymphes, Drôme, France. The stonework shows clearly the construction of arch and semi-dome and also the distortion caused by the lateral thrust.

Below: The simplest method of constructing a stone dome, requiring no centring, is to build circles of decreasing size on top of each other, as shown in the roofs of these traditional houses in Apulia, southern Italy, known as 'trulli'.

wall the lintel will be subject to great pressure at its centre—or arched, in which case much of the pressure will be transferred to the walls on either side of the opening. Relieving arches built into the masonry above an opening have often been used to relieve a lintel or a true arch of much of the weight pressing on it, and they were used by the Romans, as in the Pantheon, to strengthen the walls themselves.

Frame or skeleton construction has its origins in wooden architecture, but it was adapted for building in masonry in the Gothic period, and the nineteenth and twentieth centuries have seen the development of the iron frame (with glass), the steel frame and the skeleton of reinforced concrete. In a building of this kind the enclosing walls are not load-bearing and the load is dispersed into a framework of members, some under tension, others under pressure, the whole producing a complicated equilibrium of forces. Theoretically the members transmitting the forces have generally been thought of as one-dimensional, so that frame constructions are typified by their linear character. In an exposed wood-frame building this is emphasized by the contrast between the wooden members and the infill material used between them, and in Gothic masonry by the shafted piers and the ribs of the vaulting. The iron and glass galleries and railway sheds of the nineteenth century

and the early steel-framed skyscrapers clearly demonstrate their lattice of lines, while twentieth-century architects have taken particular pleasure in showing that the outer walls are not carrying the main load of the building, and they have raised their buildings on *pilotis* (piles like stilts), cut a horizontal swathe of window along the whole side of a wall, and around a corner too, or made all the walls of glass, revealing the framework which supports the building inside. Frame construction is normally far more economical of materials than mass construction and it offers a much more flexible range of technical possibilities, but it also makes greater technical demands on architects, engineers and builders.

Surface construction is the use of very thin materials as structural elements rather than for cladding or filling in. It is a recent technique and is used principally in concrete shell constructions for roof forms although stressed-skin structures of sheet material or wood are not uncommon now. The material is used in an essentially two-dimensional way, treated as if it had no thickness. Visually, surface construction is characterized by emphasis on the shaping of the surface itself.

The problem of covering a building has provided a far greater challenge to architects than that of constructing the walls. The simplest form of roof is that based on the post-and-lintel principle: a rigid triangular frame rests on the top of the walls, providing both a flat ceiling and a pitched roof to give protection from the weather. It will be of frame construction supporting

a protective cladding. This method is common to most vernacular buildings, but its application to large buildings is limited by the length of timber available, and wood was—until around 1800—the only material from which a roof of this kind could be constructed. This method also meant that no space higher than the top of the walls could be incorporated into a large interior. Ingenious methods were devised for roofing wider areas without the need for long timbers and for raising the ceiling height by means of wooden trusses, but an alternative method had existed, at least for masonry buildings, from an early period. This was the vault, with its derivative the dome. In essence the vault is an arch extended in depth to cover the area of a building and, apart from the difficulties of actual construction, this simple barrel vault produces a lateral thrust which requires the walls to be buttressed. The development of stone vaulting and the corresponding system of buttressing, both ultimately adapted to the technique of skeleton construction in masonry, is the supreme achievement of the Gothic architects. It remained unchallenged until the nineteenth and twentieth centuries, when engineers were able to cover huge areas with vaults of iron and glass and, subsequently, of reinforced concrete.

The Romans showed tremendous skill and imagination in their construction of domes. The Pantheon dome (p. 74), with an inner diameter of 43.5 metres (142 feet), is of special interest for the fact that it was formed as a monolithic structure of

concrete, and therefore, unlike a masonry dome, it exerts no outward pressure, but rests on the walls like a lid. Where domed coverings occur in primitive structures, they are normally formed by corbelling the masonry inwards row upon row until they meet in the middle. The construction of domes has always been considered one of the great feats of the architect and many ingenious methods have been used to overcome the technical or aesthetic problems that they cause.

Modern techniques of construction have multiplied the possibilities for covering buildings, with the use of thin concrete shells, of flexible membranes, of space frames and of suspended constructions, and it is now perfectly possible for a building to have masonry (solid, three-dimensional) foundations, a frame (linear, one-dimensional) construction, and to be roofed with a surface material (two-dimensional). This flexibility has been made possible by the fullest exploitation of available materials, and all the structural systems described are dependent on the properties of the materials used.

BUILDING MATERIALS

Materials used in architecture have been chosen for their physical properties, their availability and cost. What is ready to hand has, naturally, been the first to be chosen, and the most widespread material over the whole of our area has been wood. The most important characteristics of wood are its strength in relation to its weight and its elasticity; it is resistant to both tension and compression and is well

Far left: These granaries at Goms in the Swiss Alps show softwood used in a post-and-plank construction. The stone discs were incorporated to prevent rats from climbing the posts and infesting the stores.

Left: The Drew Garrison house, 1698, at Dover, New Hampshire, USA. The long walls were constructed of solid hewn logs with boards attached to them at the gable ends (the windows are a later addition). Log construction was a common vernacular form in well forested areas and was often used by early settlers in North America.

Below: The wooden frame, in which some members are in tension – that is acting as ties, was used extensively for timber roofs, for centring and scaffolding, and also as the basic structure for many complete buildings. The sixteenth-century guild hall of the slaughterers in Hildesheim, West Germany (now destroyed), had a wooden frame with five stages of jettying at the gable ends.

able to withstand combined pressing and bending forces. These qualities make it suitable for use as a post, beam or tie. However, as an organic material it is perishable and combustible. There is also a limit to its length. One naturally thinks of wood as a material to be used for the frame of a building, but it is also often used, in the form of weatherboarding or shingles, as a cladding material, and can be used, as plywood or as a laminate, as a surface material particularly suited for roof and ceiling construction. Nevertheless, it is in frame construction that its greatest importance lies.

The geographical influence on vernacular styles can be seen most effectively in the variety of timber buildings. In England and France the wood that was preferred in the Middle Ages was oak. It is a hard wood, very strong, but also heavy; it weathers extremely well and indeed, if left exposed, it hardens with age. It was used in true frame constructions, the two basic types being the cruck frame, shaped like a letter A, and the box frame covered by a roof. These underwent great elaboration in every kind of architecture during the Middle Ages. The typical half-timbered house shows the wooden frame with the spaces filled in with wattle and daub, lath and plasterwork, or brickwork. Sometimes the timber frame was plastered over or covered with weatherboarding. In Scandinavia and the Alpine lands softwoods were more common, and these were often used either in the form of horizontal logs built up into walls or in post-and-plank construction. Apart from these differences, many varieties of roof shape were developed, those in areas where deep snow-falls were expected being unmistakable with their deeply overhanging eaves. Sometimes the roof was steeply pitched, but often the pitch was shallow and the snow was then expected to rest throughout the winter and the construction was firm enough to allow for this. Wooden buildings were based on either brick or stone foundations, or on a ground sill resting on these foundations, or on wooden piles. The wooden house has remained the commonest rural house in North America, generally faced with clapboard or shingles, and the climate of the southern states of the USA has led to a characteristic variant with a colonnaded veranda running the full length of the house.

Vast quantities of wood were required during the Middle Ages, and some areas suffered severe deforestation, as wood was also used extensively for shipbuilding and iron-smelting as well as for building. An average timber-frame house required wood from some twelve oaks, and for important buildings whole areas of the forest were destroyed. The shortage of wood led architects and carpenters to devise ways of building up more complex structures with shorter timbers. The tie-beams spanning the nave of the old basilica of St Peter's in Rome were 23 metres (75 feet) long and the corner posts of the timber lantern of Ely Cathedral were 18 metres (60 feet) high, but timbers such as these had to be extremely thick and therefore also very heavy. In order to build two- or more-storeyed buildings the system of jetties was used. The joist beams were cantilevered out over the wall plate, and the walls of the higher storeys were built out beyond those below. In the streets of a city like Paris the upper storeys of the houses would sometimes almost meet

across the street. The medieval architect Villehard de Honnecourt also gives a description and diagram showing 'how to make a bridge over water with twenty-foot timber' (see p. 10).

Development of timber structures has continued, from Philibert de l'Orme's method of providing a curved timber frame for arches and domes by bolting together short planks staggered in alternate layers to the nineteenth-century balloon frame (see p. 234) and the sophisticated laminates of the present day. The Finnish architect Alvar Aalto made particularly imaginative use of wood both in interiors and exteriors, and wood has played an important part in the interiors of Frank Lloyd Wright and many followers of the 'organic' tradition of architecture.

The materials used for building with solid walls are taken from the earth: mud, turf, brick and stone. Mud, turf and cob (mud and straw) buildings have seldom survived, but it is clear that where wood was not used these were in general the commonest materials for vernacular architecture. The walls of such buildings were unjointed, but the characteristic of masonry in stone or brick is that the individual units are jointed to form a cohesive structure, and the stability and resistance to weather will depend on the quality of the jointing. Normally mortar is used to cement the units, although dry stone walls do occur in some localized areas. Because openings in a solid wall will reduce its strength, there are generally fewer windows in masonry buildings than in frame constructions. Few primitive stone buildings have survived, although

Above: Brick-built salt warehouses of the sixteenth to eighteenth century on the river Trave at Lübeck, West Germany.

Far right: In his headquarters building, 1920–25, for the Höchst Dye and Chemical Works near Frankfurt, West Germany, Peter Behrens used vivid colours burned into the bricks to create a dazzling effect. The material and its treatment, with the joints emphasized, were intended to express the industrial character of the building, while the colouring referred to the company's activity. The half-square shape of a brick is also used as a design module, and every feature of the building incorporates dynamic contrasts between squares set parallel or at an angle to the main axis of the hall.

Right: The nineteenth-century brick bottle ovens or kilns at the Gladstone Pottery, Staffordshire, England.

the beehive *trulli* of Apulia built of rough-hewn stone are an extraordinary exception, but stone has remained in most parts of Europe the most highly prized material for monumental architecture. Again geographical conditions have played an important part, and the architecture of different localities is characterized by the colour and texture of the local stone. However, the forms of the buildings vary much less than is the case with wooden architecture.

The techniques of stone working had already been mastered by the ancient Greeks, and they normally dressed the stone after completion of the construction. Apart from their technical proficiency, the Greeks exploited the expressive qualities of stone as a medium for architectural carving and sculpture. The Roman introduction of the masonry arch into formal architecture enormously widened the scope for building in stone or brick. As has often been the case since, bridges demonstrated special virtuosity in techniques that then became a part of the language of architecture. In northern Europe it was not until the twelfth century that stone began to be used to any great extent in domestic building, and that same period saw the development of the Gothic style, which in its various forms throughout Europe exploited the structural, the expressive and the decorative qualities of stone to the fullest possible extent, adapting the most obviously three-dimensional of building materials to an essentially linear system of construction.

Stone varies greatly in its qualities, going from flint and very hard granites, through marbles, which take a fine polish,

sandstones ranging in colour from pale cream to rich iron-reds, some soft, others of great hardness, volcanic stones such as tufa, to the many varieties of limestone —of which the famous stone of the Île de France and of Caen in Normandy provided the material for many of the great Gothic cathedrals. French stone was exported to England over a considerable period of time, and was used for the Tower of London, for Westminster Abbey, Canterbury Cathedral and many other important buildings, although the cost of transport—mostly by water—was high and could more than treble the price of the stone at the quarry. Naturally enough, in vernacular building stone was used only when it was available on the spot, and the expertise required to work stone meant that even in stone-producing areas it was

used less frequently than timber, where this was available also.

The Romans built extensively with bricks, usually making them serve as a permanent formwork for concrete, and bricks were also used by medieval masons, but primarily as a substitute for stone in areas where stone was not to hand. In north-east Germany in particular a very fine brick style was developed in the twelfth century, and in eastern England brick began to be an important building material in the fourteenth century, although vernacular houses of brick were not common for another 300 years. From around 1700 the production of bricks in northern Europe was increasingly industrialized and during the nineteenth century thousands of brick terraces were built in towns, and brick was one of the main materials used in railway and other industrial architecture. It is still one of the most important building materials today, though often as cladding rather than for the actual structure. Brickwork need not be the monotonous repetition of the standard element, but is capable of many decorative variations and can also be effective on a monumental scale.

Until the nineteenth century wood, stone and brick were the main structural materials of architecture, although a number of other materials were often used in building. Roofing materials were important in determining the final appearance of a building, and in vernacular buildings often conditioned the pitch of the roof. Slate roofs, for instance, generally had a lower pitch than tiled roofs. Thatch, where suitable material was available, was widely used, as it provided good insulation, and its lightness made it suitable for use where walls were poorly constructed. Where good weather protection was required, the walls themselves were often rendered or covered with a cladding material. Here again climate and local natural resources played a large part in determining the forms and materials used. Wooden boarding was always typical of North America, but elsewhere the material most widely used, and particularly in urban buildings, was plaster or stucco. Decorative plasterwork has been common in rural architecture since the Middle Ages, but stucco, often patterned in imitation of stonework, covers literally millions of houses in towns throughout the western world. Where masonry is not displayed naturally in the interior of buildings, wood and plaster have remained the most important materials, and both are able to support a wide variety of decorative styles.

The combination of iron and glass came into its own as a structural medium in the nineteenth century, but both materials were used extensively in earlier building work. Iron had been used since antiquity as a material for binding together masonry (though bronze, which is less easily corroded, was preferred) and it played an essential part in the construction of many buildings, from Brunelleschi's dome of Florence Cathedral to Soufflot's Panthéon in Paris. Glass was

Below: Thatched farmhouse, c.1570, at Gutach, Black Forest. In the Alps and surrounding areas the roof of the house assumed a special protective and symbolic importance, and a celebration of dedication would often take place on completion of the wooden roof-frame. Thatch is light and strong and provides good insulation over the huge area of such roofs.

Right above: In North America wood remains the most important building material, and shingles covering roofs or cladding walls have been used frequently on vernacular houses. In the late nineteenth century the vogue for the 'Shingle Style' produced a number of pseudo-vernacular buildings on a grand scale. This fine house at Mount Desert, Maine, was designed by W.R. Emerson in 1879.

Right below: Ceramic tiles have been used in many places and periods as cladding for floors and for interior and exterior walls. The tradition goes back to the ancient Near East, and tilework flourished in Portugal, Spain and Holland. The chimney (now demolished) of this Dutch farmhouse at Goede, Zeeland, is covered with a panel showing the embarkation of troops for a sea-battle in 1799 as well as earlier tiles.

becoming too dense) and the pieces of glass were usually formed by blowing rather than by casting, as had been normal in the Roman period, thus enabling larger and stronger panes to be made. Nevertheless, throughout the Middle Ages 50 cm² (8 sq in) was around the maximum size of panes. By the Gothic period these panes were joined together with leading to form panels which were contained in stone tracery, each panel being a maximum of around 0.2 m² (2 sq ft) in order to remain rigid. The development of the Gothic window, which was fundamental to the whole Gothic style, was made possible by the techniques of carving traceried and mullioned windows and by making strong leaded glass panels.

first used for windows in Roman times, probably in the form of bulls-eye panes set in wooden framework. With its use of the arch in solid-wall construction, Roman architecture developed the possibilities of the window, which is an essential light-conducting element in any architecture that is giving importance to internal space. Window openings would normally have been covered with shutters, but filling them with translucent material did become established practice with the Romans. Glass windows were common in the great Baths, and glass or selenite was also sometimes used in houses and blocks of flats. In Ravenna, the Byzantine capital of Italy, windows were filled with thin panes of translucent alabaster. Here, in fact, glass was used for the decoration of the interior, as the mosaics that fill the walls were made up of tiny *tesserae* of glass. Glass had been used increasingly in wall mosaics since the first century AD, and these mosaics make use of the special quality of glass, which reflects from its face, from its back surface and also from interior imperfections; the *tesserae* were often laid at an angle to the picture surface to exploit this effect. When lit through the honey-coloured alabaster windows at Ravenna, this deeply reflecting quality of glass gives the mosaics a quite extraordinary intensity.

During the Middle Ages windows in secular buildings were generally filled— if at all—with animal membranes (like parchment) or with oiled linen, but from at least the eleventh century the development of stained glass went hand in hand with the development of Christian architecture. The glass was normally coloured in the making (although red was often overlaid on white glass to prevent its

Thomas More in *Utopia* (1516) still describes windows filled with screens of fine linen cloth treated with oil or amber as an alternative to glass in the houses of his ideal city, but glass was used increasingly during the sixteenth century for large houses, though always in small units. Hardwick Hall (1590–96) shows the full development of glass technology applied to a private house in the late sixteenth century. One hundred years later Wren was able to have panes as large as 74 cm × 53 cm (29 in × 21 in) in the Queen's Drawing Room at Hampton Court, and these produce a strange variety in a façade which otherwise uses smaller panes.

From the beginning of the Industrial Revolution in Britain, and with the construction of the cast iron bridge at Coalbrookdale, it was the marriage of iron and glass that lent a new structural material to the architect's repertory. At this same time industrial production of glass allowed its use in virtually all domestic housing, and the early nineteenth century saw the development of the glass-filled bow front to shops as well as the great arcades (see p. 221). The role of iron and later steel and of glass in the architecture of the last two hundred years is dealt with fully later in this book, but it is worth remembering that—with the exception of bricks—they were the first materials to be extensively prefabricated for use in architecture, and that the skyscraper and the non-loadbearing curtain wall, which have dictated the form of so much twentieth-century architecture, depend on these materials, whose structural use in architecture is comparatively recent.

Concrete was used as a structural material by the Romans (see pp. 67ff), the concrete dome of the Pantheon being one of the triumphs of Roman engineering. The great advantage of concrete was that it absorbed many of the internal stresses inherent in the construction of vaults and domes of masonry. However, it was not until the development of reinforced concrete from the mid-nineteenth century that concrete again became an important material in architecture, yet it is now by far the most widely used of all building materials. The fact that concrete can be reinforced with steel depends on the coincidence that both have the same coefficient of expansion; if this were not the case, the material would obviously be unstable in any change of temperature. By becoming, effectively, a unified material, it is able to combine the resistance of concrete to crushing with the tensile strength of steel, so that a beam of reinforced concrete can absorb far more of the stress within itself than would be possible with either just masonry or plain steel. In order to do this effectively it is important that the steel reinforcement

occurs within the concrete member where it will best absorb the stresses that will be applied. Because the function of the reinforcement is to provide tensile strength, cables (sometimes held in ducts or sheaths) which are placed under tension (stretched) either before or after casting the concrete can give greater strength with more economical use of materials than unstressed steel rods. This pre-stressed concrete has been particularly useful in long-span structures such as bridges. Concrete is adaptable for use in virtually all climates, but needs to be clad in extremely hot and wet conditions.

Although concrete can be used for simple post-and-lintel construction, continuous frame construction with rigid joints creates a monolithic structure, enabling better distribution of stresses and greater participation of the whole structure in carrying localized loads. The concrete frame permits a wide variety of basic forms including the simple cantilever. Linear structures based on concrete ribs are derived from the concrete frame. The development of essentially two-dimensional concrete structures based on the slab or shell derives from the work of engineers and in particular of the Swiss Robert Maillart (1872-1940). Maillart's bridges, one of the most potent influences on the exploitation of concrete in building, extended the use of concrete slabs cantilevered out in single spans with astonish-

ing economy and elegance, and he also pioneered the use of the mushroom column, which does not support the floor as a post supports a beam, but as an integral part of the structure, the slab having active reinforcement throughout. Concrete panel construction and thin concrete shells, which allow great freedom of form, particularly in roofs, are derived from the active structural use of the concrete slab. In shell structures the rigidity given by the form of the double curve has led to this being often preferred.

This line of development shows the strength that concrete can give in a structural context, the strength through form, but concrete can also be used for its sculptural qualities, and in the work of the Expressionists, in some of the work of Le Corbusier, and in an extreme degree in the German Atlantik wall (see p. 267), concrete shows strength through mass. In addition, concrete precast in the factory has enlarged the scope of prefabrication, while the versatility of this material has been shown most recently in high-rise

architecture in many ways, but in periods of innovation in engineering architects' needs have themselves often been the conditioning factor in exploiting the possibilities of materials to the fullest extent—whether it was the Romans in masonry and concrete, the high Middle Ages with their skeleton structures in stone, timber and glass, the nineteenth century with the great sheds of glass and iron, or our own century with reinforced concrete.

REPRESENTATION IN ARCHITECTURE

The reason architecture is of such interest to the social historian is that every building tells a story. Architecture, like the other visual arts, is representational, and its subject matter is the function it is required to fulfil. This will be both practical and symbolic. The most obvious practical function for a building is its use as a dwelling, and its form will vary according to the social group it is designed to house. The houses and cottages in a village, a villa, a farmhouse, a castle, a monastery, a country house, a town palace, a row of terrace houses, an apartment block, are primarily dwellings, but they represent very different kinds of social organization. In a similar way representative forms have been evolved for many other building types, from the Christian church to the sports stadium.

Vernacular houses belong, by definition, to a common type, and their most distinctive features are those which represent their most important functions: the door, the hearth (which dictates internal organization and is therefore manifested on the exterior by windows as well as chimney), and the roof. Look at any child's drawing of a house, or think how these features are used in figures of speech relating to the home—indoors, a roof over our heads, hearth and home. By working variations on the basic forms which represent these functions, the architect can begin to express the meaning of the individual building he is designing, and by relating it also to current style or fashion he is able to make a clear and exact statement about his intentions and about the intentions or pretensions of his client. The choices he makes on such matters as scale, height, materials (local or imported), style (conservative or innovatory), decoration (rich or plain), will allow either the utilitarian or the symbolic function to predominate—but in every building the language of form embodies a meaning.

It is possible to go beyond this purely

buildings which have been constructed with a load-carrying structural core of concrete, housing all services, the floors being cantilevered out from it.

Other materials have also been used to suggest new structural forms, including the so-called minimal structures of Frei Otto (see p. 277) and others—great membrane tents supported by poles and cables—and also buildings which are themselves suspended from a central core.

Cable suspension has been used most effectively by Kenzo Tange in Japan (see p. 246) to support roofs. Finally, the space-frame of Buckminster Fuller (see p. 276) is based not on any novel application of materials, but on a structural principle that allows internal forces so to be absorbed that the domes can be constructed of virtually limitless size.

As has been seen, the development of technology has affected the history of

Left: Elaboration of the key symbolic features of a building is often most telling when it is part of an established tradition. In the palaces built for the new nobility after 1700 particular emphasis was given to the door and windows of the main front, as a reflection of the wealth or power of the owner. This unfinished granite façade, gloriously masquerading as a pelmeted and curtained ballroom, was built c. 1750 by an unknown Spanish architect at Vila Boa de Quires for a Portuguese grandee.

Right: The characteristic early American house consisting of a single room with central chimney was taken as a starting point by F.L. Wright in his Malcolm Willey House in Minneapolis, USA, which has an open plan with the hearth as a focus. A deliberate exercise in economy, the house cost only $10,000 in 1934.

Below: The stave church at Heddal, Norway, built during the twelfth and thirteenth centuries, is distinguished by its fantastic roofline.

architectural language and produce 'programme architecture', which is in a more literal sense representational. For example, the church of the early Middle Ages (particularly in the Byzantine world) was certainly intended to depict the heavenly Jerusalem, and the gold ground of the mosaics and richness of decoration were used to enhance this image. Sometimes the depiction has been even more obvious, generally with disastrously banal results

(would Ledoux's projected *Architecture parlante*—see p. 204—really have transcended this?), though occasionally, as in the marine style of Manueline Portugal or some of the more extravagant fancies of the German Rococo, the naivety of the treatment brings it off. But this is a byway, for the symbolic language of architecture is much more powerful.

The architect's choice of his models and the way he imitates or emulates them

are particularly telling. Where local rivalry has been strong, there has been a tendency for competition to be concentrated on one type of building, either taking the form to its limits, as in Gothic spires and vaults, or in skyscrapers, or striving for perfection within a very narrow range, as in classical Greek temples. Such rivalry can produce great variety within a formula, but there will generally be a lack of creative direction, and it thus tends to crystallize a building type. Pioneering originality is, understandably, characteristic of groups or individuals pressing for wide-ranging changes in periods of instability, rejecting both current taste and current ideals. The twentieth-century Modern Movement is the most obvious example, but early Renaissance architecture has this same revolutionary character. Yet the Renaissance was also a movement of revival, and it is one of the remarkable features of western architecture that its history has been punctuated with revivals and with revivals of revivals. The varying, but unmistakable, significance attached to these shows how meanings have been expressed.

When Charlemagne wanted consciously to recreate the Roman Empire with its new capital at Aachen, the design of his minster there was based on the plan of San Vitale at Ravenna (Justinian's capital), and indeed he brought columns to Aachen from Ravenna and from Rome itself. The originality of the Renaissance took the form of a revival of Roman architecture applied to Christian buildings. This conformed with the marriage of

the fashionable demands of their clients went to the Italian or the Flemish pattern books and produced fireplaces based on a triumphal arch or covered their façades with strapwork and grotesques. In this way styles began to lose their existing meanings and to acquire new ones as they became absorbed into the vernacular tradition. Architecture possesses a living language and its stylistic features and characteristics are always ready to be infused with new meanings. Only in the nineteenth century, with its mania for classification, were the architectural styles defined so categorically that they often became capable of little other than banal expression.

The marriage of form and function was taken at that time to mean the symbolic association of practical use with an appropriate historical style, yet this same conjunction was used by the pioneers of the Modern Movement with the catchphrase

Christianity and humanism proposed by the theologians and philosophers, which was eagerly taken up by the Roman church. For this very reason Renaissance styles were avoided by the reformed churches of northern Europe, and this reaction led to the extreme puritan view, which rejected all religious art. The vernacular Bible and Lutheran hymns (often based on folk tunes) replaced the visual imagery, and, where they could, iconoclasts tore down the images. The Counter-reformation, on the contrary, made every use of visual effects, particularly those that could suggest a metaphysical dimension. Comparison of Catholic and Protestant churches in the Low Countries (see pp. 162–3) shows how powerfully architectural language was used in the seventeenth century.

English Neo-Palladianism of the seventeenth and eighteenth centuries provides another example of the clear but changing meanings expressed in architectural forms. The style of Burlington and Kent was based on that of Inigo Jones, based in turn on Palladio, whose work was an interpretation of the buildings described by Vitruvius. For Jones, in the Banqueting House in Whitehall for example, the Roman style was adopted as the style fitted to the absolutist pretensions of the Stuart king, but for the Whig gentry of the eighteenth century Palladianism represented all the virtues of the Augustan age and so joined them in fellowship with those country gentlemen of antiquity, Pliny, Lucretius, Virgil and Horace. Meanwhile, local builders who wanted to pander to

Left above: The mixture of styles in Henry Austin's building at New Haven, Connecticut, USA, 1848-9 – Oriental? Spanish? Romanesque? Italian? – does not immediately suggest the railroad station. Although there are many superb examples of railway architecture, the opportunity was missed of giving a recognizable symbolism to railway buildings as such, and it was left to the engineers who designed the engine sheds to develop a new building type.

Left: The enormously high dome (121 m, 396 ft) of San Gaudenzio, Novara, Italy, built over the sixteenth-century church and beside the eighteenth-century campanile, was begun in 1841 by Alessandro Antonelli, whose technical feats in masonry invite a comparison with the virtuosity of Gustave Eiffel's steel structures. The form of his dome quite clearly represents a symbolic attempt to outdo the dome of St Peter's, Rome—and all other domes—and this is surmounted by a spire, which piles Gothic on top of Classic, topped by a gilded figure of Christ.

Above: The covered stand of the modern sports stadium offers instant recognition, its functional symbolism as evident as that of the church in the past. In Eduardo Torroja's Zarzuela race-track of 1935, near Madrid, the roof, formed of a series of hyperbolic paraboloids in a bold concrete shell construction, is cantilevered out to cover the stand.

'Form follows Function' to mean something altogether more utilitarian.

In the materialist climate of the twentieth century the feeling has grown that the role of the building is to accord totally with the practical requirements of the social life it protects and to reflect these requirements in its form and in its expression. The revival of interest in vernacular architecture is, of course, directly associated with this view. Just as this should—and in the hands of a master can—produce the most humane architecture, so it is only too easy for the form of the dwelling to dictate the pattern of life it should be reflecting—even the kind of comfort to be enjoyed. The spectre of the machine which should be the servant and has become the master is too familiar for us to feel comfortable any longer with Le Corbusier's ideal definition of a house as a 'machine for living in'. One encouraging characteristic of the past decade is the architect's increasing preoccupation with the lives as they are lived of the people who will use his buildings, whether they are his clients or not. It was Philibert de l'Orme, the French Renaissance architect, who wrote: 'It is much better for an architect to make mistakes in decoration, proportion and façades than in practical matters. Badly designed buildings make the people who live in them miserable.'

The basic forms of buildings which are not for living in were, like dwellings, originally dictated by their use. The forms of Greek or Roman temples, or of Christian churches, relate to the rituals performed there. Other places of public assembly, for commerce, administration, work, sport or performance, were given their shape because of the way people using them would relate to one another and to the building. Ease of vision or hearing, accessibility, the life patterns of people in general, dictated a form, which, once found, became a new pattern, a basis for the elaboration of further modes of expression by following or departing from the norm. It is astonishing how few distinct building types there were before the nineteenth century and what a wide variety exists today. Ironically, architectural language has been impoverished rather than enriched by this. The uniformity of Modern Movement architecture before the mid-century and the increasing formal mannerism since then has left us without any special features that distinguish buildings of different types. One of the very few to be established as an instantly recognized type is the stadium or sports centre, perhaps because it is here that what is to the majority the most real of all the community functions in today's world is performed.

The modern insistence on a form which expresses useful function has been matched by an insistence on a form which truthfully expresses structure and materials. The moral message of this truthfulness to nature has been preached so forcibly that it seems heretical to question it—until one realizes that it has been used to attack, or defend, so many contradictory points of view. Age seems to dignify even the pretentious and the obvious sham, and buildings that the moralist would utterly condemn are charming in the eyes of the romantic conservationist. Adolf Loos described Vienna as the city of Potemkin, referring to the film-set wooden façades erected by Catherine the Great's lover to impress his Empress; not only were the buildings of the Vienna Ringstrasse built in borrowed styles, but even the carved stonework turned out to be stucco. It is ironical that these same buildings, like the Houses of Parliament in London or the Opéra in Paris, have become the popular symbols of the city they grace—or betray. Yet deliberate lying is less common than flattery, too ready a desire to please. Borrowed styles applied inappropriately with the naive charm of those builders who copied from the pattern books can be malapropisms rather than lies. Baroque *trompe l'oeil* presented theatrical illusion; while the cinemas of the 1930s were fantasies, making no pretence to reality. The great eclectic buildings of the nineteenth century were themselves often acts of homage to the past rather than claims to pretension.

The strict moralist would have none of this. The French theorist M.-A. Laugier (1713–69) insisted on the correct—the natural—use of the column: that is to support a beam; a column should never support an arch, and the pilaster is against nature and anathema. Decoration unhallowed by ancient Greek usage is utterly to be condemned: 'Because the fripperies of Arabesque [i.e. Gothic] architecture were the taste of Europe for several centuries, are they any the less reprehensible? Because the extravagances of Chevalier Borromini won the approval of all Rome and are still copied there with affectation, are they any more tolerable? It is essential for the success of the Arts to allow nothing that is not founded on principle; otherwise there is no rule except caprice. . . . There is only one way to suppress capricious innovation, to lay down a fixed principle to which the architect is forced to conform and the consequence of which will be directly to condemn his capricious ideas.' (It is worth noting that Laugier has an entry in his index: 'Prejudice, is not origin of beauty'.) Laugier's principle was that architecture should be natural, which meant derived from Greek architecture, because that was based on the most natural form of building, from which architecture originated.

The young Goethe's criticism of Laugier is nearer the point. He ridiculed Laugier's notion of the origin of architecture, pointing out that houses are built of walls, not columns, and that Laugier dictates what we ought to need because our real needs cannot be justified according to his principles. For Goethe truth is needed, not a system, for true art derives from unity of conception: 'If it makes its impression from its own, unique, inner, independent sensibility, untroubled by, ignorant even, of everything foreign to it, then whether it is born of rough savagery or educated sensitivity it is integral and alive.' But views of every colour could be quoted, all based on truth to nature, which give moral justification to just about any kind of architecture. Certainly the sterility of monumental Neo-classicism as advocated by Laugier can be matched by the acres of raw concrete (*béton brut*), stained and streaked by urban pollution—but morally pure and desirable—in any big city.

The virtue of integrity is undeniable. Although it was used here by Goethe to defend the Gothic (German) against the Classical (French and Italian), its application is much wider. Integrity, wholeness, implies unity within itself, and this means a visual and spatial relationship between inside and outside (though it is not necessary to take too narrow a view of this). Integrity also implies a relationship between a building and its environment, and here the evident use of local materials may be of great benefit, although to insist on this may frequently be to ignore the

Ornament and Crime (see p. 252), did not condemn decoration as such; he only saw it as inappropriate for the sophisticated taste of his own time. He himself preferred things plain, but he realized that this would have been as incomprehensible to a man of the fifteenth century as it would be to his shoemaker if he were to ask him to make a pair of perfectly plain shoes without the decoration on which he prided himself. Loos was disturbed by architects' continuing search for a style, by which, he said, they meant a kind of ornament.

STYLE

The notion of style began to be developed in the early nineteenth century, and for the next hundred years it obsessed not only architects but critics, theorists and historians of architecture as well. Earlier revivals, including the Renaissance, had been viewed as revivals of ancient traditions, superior to the work of immediate predecessors; the seventeenth century saw a fragmentation of architecture, but each tradition was sufficiently self-contained for the architect not to be faced with any great stylistic choice; the eighteenth century saw a widening of the repertory, with the introduction of all kinds of exoticism, but critics were concerned primarily with questions of taste, and later of morality. Yet by 1828 the German Heinrich Hübsch could write a book on church architecture with the title *In What Style Should We Build?* The nineteenth century developed the concept of style,

These photographs of Palladio's Villa Barbaro (1565-80) at Maser, Italy, show how different are the visual images obtained in moving around and through a building, although the unity of conception, which makes up the architect's personal style, are evident in each view. The characteristically rhythmic spatial progressions (elaborated in the central hall by Veronese's trompe-l'oeil paintings) define this even more than the eloquent use of classical language and detail.

functions of cladding materials both as protection and as decoration.

Economy of materials and rational expression of the structure, two thoroughly Neo-classical virtues, are likely to contribute to the integrity of a building, but we must distinguish between illusion—used in the seventeenth century to convey metaphysical reality—and sham. Nor should these virtues outlaw decoration and ornament. Adolf Loos, in his essay

using the word to indicate the general characteristics of a particular time and place, deriving from the materials and technical resources available. Even in the work of William Morris or Gottfried Semper this could easily appear to be historical determinism, although Semper insisted that form (style) was a manifestation of the 'idea', which must be in harmony with material resources, but not determined by them. Adolf Loos, writing in the early twentieth century, attacked the self-conscious attempts of the Sezession and Werkbund movements in Germany and Austria, pointing out that it is superfluous to try and 'create a style of our time'; it could not be held that 'every period has had its own style, but ours alone has been denied one'.

The word style originally means handwriting, and handwriting cannot just be put on like a glove; nor, as determinist critics tended to do, should one mistake the hand for the handwriting. The hand is as it is because of many different external events, some dating from the remote past, but it is the hand guided by an original and independent mind that produces the personal handwriting, the style. Rules, traditions, conventions have never confined the original artist, any more than they have enabled the second-rater to produce works of genius. Throughout the history of the western tradition of archi-

Above: In 'The Architect's Dream' (Thomas Cole, 1840) the architect contemplates the peerless and Brobdingnagian exemplars of the past. In which style will he build?

Right: Adolf Loos, most polemical of architectural moralists, showed in his Vienna apartment (1903) that comfort—even cosiness—and good taste were compatible.

Far right below: Laugier's frontispiece shows the origin of architecture in Nature, where the very trees demonstrate the primacy of post-and-beam construction.

Far right above: The beauty of this church (San Michele, Lucca, Italy, begun 1143) confounds the moralist's criticisms that its façade bears little relation to the body of the building and that the decorative columns have no real structural function.

tecture it has been the interplay of originality and tradition that has produced those buildings which have the emotional power to move and excite us, and the symbolic or representational power to make a strong statement—artistic, political, social or religious.

One modern school of architecture and criticism rejects entirely the concept of rules in its concern for 'organic' architecture. This is architecture whose external forms are governed first by usage, then by structure and materials in relationship to the people for whom it is built and to its

environment. Symmetry and all *a priori* decisions are rejected; thus tradition is rejected too. When carried out with discipline, as in some of the work of the hero, Frank Lloyd Wright, this new ideal cannot be faulted, but it is no more of universal application than the other ideal systems of the past, being a new variation on the concept of natural architecture. Whether a lack of rules is more likely to lead to freedom or licence (caprice Laugier would have said), whether rules are more likely to produce discipline or sterility can be debated.

The rules formulated in the Renaissance period did not stultify the development of architectural forms, any more than medieval geometry had done. It is true that the buildings of both Alberti and Palladio differed from their publications, but Bramante, the most 'correct' of the Renaissance architects, still used the language of Roman architecture as a living language offering scope to the imagination of the architect. This classical language could still be used as a living language right up to the nineteenth century by architects of the originality of Soane or Schinkel, and even in the present century Lutyens felt that the mantle of the ancient Greeks had fallen on him when he worked in Doric. The current trend, however, is against rules, and the language of contemporary architecture is reflected both in the language of criticism and in contemporary taste. It is our concern today for the people for whom buildings are designed (not, in most cases, the people who commission them), our concern for the environment, our rejection of the austerity of pure functionalism, our preference for organic structures, that condition our attitude to both past and present architecture. We see symmetry, the Cartesian grid, a super-human scale, as characteristics of totalitarian architecture which offer easy solutions to the commercial speculator. The modern heroes are the architects who broke the rules: the Greek and medieval architects, for whom the rules were not *a priori*

preconceptions but a method of applying their practical experience; Brunelleschi, Michelangelo, Borromini, each of whose enrichment of the classical language was wholly personal; Telford, Bogardus, Eiffel, Maillart, engineers whose work transcended the petty arguments about style; Morris, the town-planner Camillo Sitte, Sullivan, Wright, who reacted against the schematization of imposed planning, looking for outward growth from the central cell of a living organism. We show our appreciation for vernacular architecture, including the 'industrial vernacular' of the nineteenth century, and indeed for the naive application of historicist styles that characterizes 'Victoriana'. Some of our heroes were abominated in the past, and we need to look objectively at the ways our own views are coloured to understand what has been meant in the past by architecture that should be true to nature or whose form should follow its function. The current view is shown in this sentence from a recent architect's manual: 'It is not surprising that nature should provide the best examples of fully developed materials and structural forms, so we must continue to seek other primitive and natural antecedents for future solutions to our more sophisticated environmental problems.'

ARCHITECTURAL SPACE

Modern thinking has conditioned our aesthetic response to a building (Vitruvius' *venustas*) as much as it has coloured our view of its practical and representative function. We see the chief medium of the architect as space, and yet the concept of architectural space is a comparatively modern one. From classical antiquity right up until the nineteenth century aesthetic theory was based on proportions and on the rhythmic disposition and arrangement of the elements. The space was defined by the linear measurements, and it was to the harmony of these that attention was directed, although the Pythagorean system, which underlies both classical and medieval architecture, gave to the *harmony* of linear measures a more abstract unity than the mere definition of pleasing volumes or voids.

The Austrian art-historian Alois Riegl was the first, just before 1900, to look at the history of architecture from the point of view of the interior space of buildings, and more recently the concept of space-time, derived from the ideas of Einstein and Minkowsky, has been applied to architectural space. We can now see space not as a static contained void, but as a positive element in a dynamic relationship with the observer. Every building contains space and is contained within a wider space; it exists to be moved through and to be moved round, and this movement involves space and time. Time is as much a dimension of architecture as it is of music. Further, paradoxically, our perception of this dynamic space, with its implication of the dimension of time, is immediate.

It may be thought anachronistic to discuss the architecture of the distant past in terms of this modern concept of dynamic or active space, but it is used as a description for an aspect—the fundamental aspect—of architecture that has always preoccupied architects. The buildings themselves leave us in no doubt of this. It is also an essential basis to any language that can relate to both contemporary architecture and the architecture of the past. How do we perceive architecture? It is an experience that relates very little to our perception of a photograph of a building, an experience that has defied any means of mechanical reproduction

and therefore retains its unique impact, which for music, painting, even sculpture has been partially destroyed by recordings, radio, television and colour reproductions. As we approach a building we are aware that it affects the space immediately surrounding it, exercising an influence rather like a magnetic field. Depending on its situation we may gain an impression of the whole volume of the building or we may see only a part or one face. It may reveal itself suddenly or it may be the focus of directed planning. We can pass it by, we can—if it is permitted and possible—walk round it, or we can, if we want to go inside it, move towards what we recognize to be the entrance. Already we shall have gained from the building some knowledge about its size and scale, its function, its structure and materials, and we shall have formed various expectations about the interior. Once inside we shall be aware—almost simultaneously—whether it is a simple or a complex space, what direction we are expected to move in, how large it is, how light it is. Other impressions will follow very quickly, but it is clear that our brain is transferring the evidence of our eyes into impressions that do not relate simply to what we see in two dimensions. Our perception of what encloses the space comes *after* our first perception of the space itself. In the end this is not only our first impression, but also our most important impression, and it is the relationship of the space, interior and exterior, to the surfaces and members which define it that is the chief aesthetic concern of the architect. The final part of

this essay is therefore devoted to the means the architect employs to control this relationship.

It is the physical space that is defined by the surrounding walls; what the observer actually perceives is modified by the light and by the viewpoint of the observer. This conceptual space is the active space—the magnetic field—which conditions the observer's impressions of the building, his relationship to the building. In a simple house the space will be divided into a few rooms, but it will be unified by the overall singleness of pur-

Above left: The round church, evenly lit, with an inner colonnade supporting the upper walls, creates static but harmonious internal space. The disruption caused by the diametrical arcade on giant Corinthian columns in San Stefano Rotondo, Rome, is barely suggested by the photograph.

Above centre: An internal staircase gives the architect an opportunity to create directed movement within an interior; spiral staircase at Chambord, Loir-et-Cher, France, c. 1530.

Above right: Light, colour, illusionist painting and wayward sculptural decoration make the space of a Baroque church (Vierzehnheiligen, West Germany, 1742-72 by Balthasar Neumann) expand beyond the walls that define it, pitting appearance against reality.

Left: The gigantic, superhuman scale, the heavy horizontal beams, the strongly emphasized central axis, produce an oppressive, dominating space, intimidating – and empty; Great Hall of the Brussels Law Courts, 1866–83, built by Joseph Poelaert.

pose. The main focus on entering will be the hearth, the main element determining movement the staircase. The exterior will, as we have seen, reflect closely this internal arrangement. In this century Wright designed his private houses using exactly this arrangement. Le Corbusier in the Villa Savoye (see p. 259) and other private houses worked with even greater fluency, doing without the central focus (*focus* in Latin actually means a hearth) and creating a real 'promenade' architecture, spaces to move through. The 'open plan' should be a natural consequence of

central heating and modern structures, but it lacks familiar points of orientation, offers little privacy and is still only rarely adopted. In a complex structure, where the space is divided up, the architect can condition the sense of progression and sense of direction. In the château of Versailles the long corridors, the great state rooms, even the immense avenues in the gardens, forced the courtier to follow a long ritualistic path around the central focus which was the Sun King. Deviation from this path was out of the question. In the new National Theatre in London, by contrast, the arrangement is so flexible that it is hard to find an entrance, and, once inside, there is no sense of orientation or direction, so that one is left with a sense of bewilderment.

This sense of movement and direction imposed on the observer is just as much a part of a unified space. In any western Catholic church, but more particularly in pilgrimage churches, there is a strong directional pull towards the altar, where the sacrifice is performed, or towards the main shrine. The architect has a number of ways of emphasizing this: he can make the altar a strong focal point by decorating that part of the church more elaborately or by allowing it to be lit more brightly, and he can emphasize the path towards it by the rhythmic repetition of elements, such as arcades.

However, there is also a sense in which the movement implicit in a spatial arrangement does not involve physical movement by the observer. In a Gothic cathedral there is a strong sense of movement

upwards, and in a Baroque interior there may often be a sense of the space overflowing its boundaries and expanding outwards. This dynamic space is created by emphasizing the elements of tension in the structure, by implying almost that there is a disequilibrium only just held in check. The emphasis on vertical elements (those that are opposed to the force of gravity) without corresponding horizontal elements, the use of undulating walls, the dramatic use of light, the use of decoration to dissolve the solidity of wall surfaces, these are all means of creating movement in space and making a conceptual space which is larger than the physical space. In the western tradition this has been used particularly to give a mystical, metaphysical dimension to architecture.

The reverse of this, the enclosing space, is characterized by the solidity of walls, by a structure whose mass and weight is stressed by horizontal emphasis, and by rigid symmetry. It betrays a fear of instability and disorder and has almost always been used on a large scale as consciously dominating architecture.

An equation of the physical space and the conceptual space has been attained where a sense of perfect equilibrium is conveyed by the building. This was perhaps most successfully achieved by Renaissance architects in their development of the centrally planned church as an expression of the harmony of the human and the divine. A circular building displays perfect symmetry, and there is thus no change of viewpoint as the spectator moves round in it. The space is static.

Similarly, the round arch (and its derivative the hemi-spherical cupola) typifies a perfect resolution of vertical and horizontal forces. It is an extraordinary sensation being inside a building like Bramante's chancel of Santa Maria delle Grazie in Milan, for the space is not in passive equilibrium, but appears actively almost to support the walls that define it. The sculptor Giacometti said that it is like being inside an eggshell. The effect of disturbing an equilibrium of this kind can be seen in the early Roman church of San Stefano Rotonda. This round church was originally composed of three concentric circles, but during the twelfth century a supporting arcade was built across the diameter of the building, which disrupts the original spatial concept and creates an extraordinarily exciting effect.

The exterior space, the magnetic field set up by the outside form of a building, can also be handled in a number of different ways. In the first place it can

Left: The fortified walls of Conway Castle, Wales, blankly confront the external space.

Left below: One of Palladio's finest achievements was to create intermediate space of great refinement by means of loggias and balconies. The skyline too is broken by statues and finials, so that the building (Palazzo Chiericati, Vicenza, begun in 1550) merges with the surrounding space.

Below: Rosselino's piazza at Pienza, Italy, 1460–63 (see p. 150), unites the façades of the surrounding buildings to make a formal enclosed space. His planning also exemplifies ways of manipulating external space without imposing a rigid plan: the siting of the cathedral apse high above the road; the neatly laid out garden behind the Piccolomini Palace; and the integration of new buildings into existing street lines.

Right: The glittering glass walls of the skyscrapers on New York's Avenue of the Americas soften the impact between these vast buildings and the surrounding space.

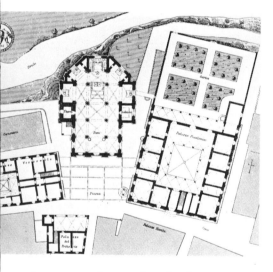

form part of an enclosed urban space, a precinct or piazza. This may be dynamic, like Michelangelo's piazza on Capitoline Hill (see p. 152), or static; it may have a strong dominant focus or it may be an organic unity composed of various elements, a space to be moved through. The piazza can derive its shape from the activities that are to take place there, or this may be imposed as part of a formal plan. But whether or not an elevation of a building is used to define an urban space in relationship to other buildings, any building influences the space around it. What form this influence takes depends on the scale of the building and the form of the exterior walls. A small building can be apprehended more or less as an object enveloped by the surrounding space, whereas a very tall or a very large building

confronts the space where it meets walls and roof. Because these walls and roof are themselves symbols of the interior space, great emotional and aesthetic force is given to the actions of approach to a building, apprehension of its interaction with the external space, movement into the building and apprehension of the internal space. A building constructed for protection, like a castle or prison, will make as uncompromising a confrontation as possible, separating abruptly exterior and interior. But where this separation is not called for means will be adopted to soften the impact of the walls. Two examples of this are the use of windows or of glass and the use of colonnades. Windows suggest the interpenetration of outer and inner space, while colonnades create an intermediate space between exterior and interior. The

Greeks used colonnades to humanize the approach to their buildings, although they were not concerned to manipulate internal space. The Roman Pantheon showed for the first time on a monumental scale the possibilities of internal space, but this was entirely enclosed, the only opening being the circular *oculus* in the roof. It was the development first of the arcade, then of the window combined with vaulting, that led to the creation of unified internal space, first fully achieved in the great Gothic church.

It has to be by his treatment of the walls and roof themselves that the architect controls space. Rhythm and movement, harmony and balance are created by structural or sculptural treatment, by articulation, by the use of colour and the manipulation of light. These all depend

upon the balance between solid and void. A structural treatment will generally reduce the solids as much as possible, treating them as representing linear (or recently more complex) forces. Such treatment will offer the architect the greatest chance for the display of virtuosity, particularly in his treatment of the roof or vault. Handling the solids in a more sculptural way will enable the architect to bring out the expressive qualities of his materials and his architectural forms. Architects of the Baroque period, particularly, used the sculptural treatment in their buildings to create spatial excitement.

By articulation is meant the elaboration of surfaces to establish the function—structural, symbolic or decorative—and relationship of various parts, and so to demonstrate the logic of a structure. The use of the Greek Orders to establish hierarchy on a façade, the use of rustication or the emphasizing of important structural elements like the keystone of an arch are ways of aiding clarity. In architecture with strong linear qualities (the fifteenth century, for example—whether in late Gothic or the work of Brunelleschi—or Art Nouveau) linear decoration has emphasized this. Colour and texture can also have a dynamic effect on articulation. Where an architect has wanted to create spatial ambiguity, articulation or the lack of it can be used to promote this aim. At the same time, extraneous decoration simply overlaid on

a structure, by concentrating attention on the surface itself, can turn a dynamic space into a sterile void.

Symmetry and strong emphasis on a central axis are very powerful weapons in the architect's armoury, since they can create an architecture which dominates its surroundings and the people who inhabit it. At the same time symmetry is one way—though not the only one—to create equilibrium and harmony. This will depend very much on the scale. The Parthenon, which is related (perhaps consciously) to the human scale, produces a miraculous sense of harmony and perfection. However, when imitated on a vast scale, as in some Hellenistic temples, it dwarfs the onlooker; and when reduced in scale to an ornamental temple in an eighteenth-century garden, it takes on the character of a doll's house.

Perhaps most important of all is the architect's use and manipulation of light and colour. Without light space cannot be seen, and control of light enables the architect to model the space itself rather than the surrounding walls. Effects of coloured light were used with increasing boldness from Hagia Sophia in Constantinople and the alabaster-windowed churches of Ravenna to the great Gothic churches with their expanses of stained-glass windows. The architects of the early Renaissance strove for bright, even lighting, and from the time of Palladio the

dramatic possibilities of light began to be exploited. There is an element of the theatrical in Palladio's architecture, an exploitation of the illusionism of perspective, and this was developed in the seventeenth and eighteenth centuries. The set pieces of Bernini and of the Asam brothers (see pp. 169, 176), or the *trompe l'oeil* ceilings brought to perfection by Andrea Pozzo, depend for their success on the manipulation of light. The interiors of Borromini's churches take this to a higher level still. The undulating walls, which merge light into shade, set the whole interior space in motion, and the observer is not, as in theatrical architecture, just an observer of the action, but becomes enveloped in the space. In the eighteenth century glass, curved walls, mirrors, illusionist painting, all transmitted or reflected light and helped to dissolve the solidity of walls, while in this century electric lighting and the glass curtain wall have allowed the control of light and the definition of space to be separated completely, giving the maximum interpenetration of interior and exterior space.

CONSERVATION

The twentieth century has made so many fundamental changes to western architecture that it may be argued that the unified western tradition came to an end with the introduction of new materials and methods and the abandonment of the last vestiges of the Greek Orders. It is true that the pioneers of the 1920s wanted to discard much of the past, but since 1945 increasing concern has been felt, among architects too, for historical buildings and historical environments. The need has been felt for a closer link with the past, not through the imitation of old styles, but through a sense of real continuity. In this architects have taken the lead. The work of Giancarlo De Carlo in Urbino and the very different efforts to care for the whole social and physical fabric of Bologna in recent years are unmatched and obvious examples. Yet it would be wrong to ignore the fact that the movement for architectural conservation is also the result of the alienation felt towards much recent architecture.

Throughout history the buildings which survived were those for which a use could still be found as society changed. Those that were particularly revered were not exempt from alteration and modernization; this was indeed essential if they were to remain living buildings, not museum pieces. Therefore an effort of historical imagination is required to conjure up not only the

Left: This detail from Dürer's watercolour of a wire-drawing mill (c. 1494) shows the unplanned development of medieval buildings in a rural landscape at a time of industrial growth in the late Middle Ages. No efforts of conservation can hope to recreate a complex such as this except as a museum object.

Right: The medieval market piazza in Lucca, Italy, preserves, like a fossil, the shape of the Roman amphitheatre (second century AD) into whose walls the houses were built.

Below: These old houses built up against the Tour Saint-Romain of Rouen Cathedral, France, were pulled down long ago. Changes in society and in fashion have always been a greater destructive force than either natural disaster or structural failure. Yet restoration and conservation have often been incompatible; purism must be tempered with an awareness both of social patterns and of architectural quality.

society of the past, but also the building in its original form. Town buildings have been especially subject to change and destruction for the past 150 years, because of the valuable space they occupy; unlike pictures, they cannot be stored in a basement until fashion changes again. Moreover, whether as part of a planned environment or as a result of organic growth, each individual building will have related to those around it. Yet even in a world dependent on road traffic, urban environment and buildings must be representative of the life actually to be led there, so that the dilemma today is a real one: when old buildings have become inadequate or inappropriate, should they be restored and fitted for a new use, should they be removed and replaced, or should they be incorporated into a new scheme? Where new buildings are to be built, what restrictions should be imposed on architects?

Too often we have had the worst of all worlds. The pressure to preserve everything has led to the preservation of mediocre buildings while fine buildings occupying more valuable sites have, nevertheless, been wantonly destroyed. Increasing restrictions are being imposed on architects, which are so inhibiting as to destroy at the outset any chance of successful architecture, yet economic power has been able to force through appalling desecrations of historic town centres. It would almost have been better to have had a free-for-all. The new Truman brewery in London (see p. 278) is an encouraging sign, for here, as often in the past, old architecture has been incorporated into an entirely new spatial concept, without making any compromise.

We have to realize that as society changes the architecture which reflected that society becomes obsolete, and at the present rate of social change obsolescence comes fast. Only a tiny proportion of the buildings standing today still have much the same practical and symbolic function as they did seventy years ago. Churches and palaces, even farms, private houses, schools and railway stations have to fit into an entirely different structure of society. Yet in the past the architect's work had always to be considered in a very long view. The growth of medieval churches or castles was, like the growth of towns and villages, organic. The dome envisaged by Arnolfo di Cambio at the end of the thirteenth century for Florence Cathedral was planned and executed in the fifteenth century by Brunelleschi. None of Brunelleschi's own work has survived untouched, very little of Michelangelo's, and yet where the spatial concept survives the genius of the architect is seen.

There is no doubt that some buildings lose most or all of their value as architecture once they have ceased to perform their original function, but great architecture, like great music, is capable of reinterpretation, and it will affect the observer even in incomplete or unauthentic versions. Good buildings will be defined by subsequent use and should be 'open' forms able to adapt to changes in taste and in society that fall wholly outside any kind of rational planning. In this way they transcend the time-bound conditions of their creation.

GREEK ARCHITECTURE

The epithet 'timeless' has probably been more often applied to the architecture of Classical Greece than to any other. The great temples seem to have a perfection that lifts them completely out of the context of their own time. Indeed, the elements of Greek architecture have been subject to constant re-interpretation throughout the history of western architecture. It is this that makes it a convenient starting place in this book. Although it did not develop in total isolation from the architecture of earlier times and other places, the beginning of Greek architecture as it is usually pictured—temples with beautifully dressed stone columns and forms obeying tightly defined conventions—is very much a new birth.

After the decline of the sumptuous Bronze Age civilization of Mycenaean Greece during the twelfth century BC, Greece went through a period of poverty and isolation. Building continued, of course, but it was vernacular not monumental, using only the locally available materials of wood, mud brick and thatch; the intention to impress was apparently lacking. During the eighth century BC, however, there were many rapid and dramatic changes. Contact with the civilizations of the Levant was renewed and colonies were founded on the coasts of Sicily and southern Italy. Sanctuaries were established which drew dedications from all over the Greek world. Graves, too, which form our best indication of wealth and population, became more numerous, more richly endowed, and more impressively marked. At the same time a new interest developed in the surviving monuments of the Bronze Age, and in the stories associated with them. Homer's Iliad and Odyssey, revered almost as a bible by later Greeks, were probably composed during this century.

It is not surprising, then, that the characteristic form of the Greek temple also emerged in the eighth century BC. Earlier temples had been small and hardly distinguishable from houses. In fact the functional requirement in the temple of a normal Greek cult was easily satisfied; it was not a place for congregational worship, since the animal sacrifices which formed the major part of the ritual took place at the altar outside. The temple building was simply the house of the divinity, holding his cult statue (if there was one) and the more precious dedications. Thus a room that could be securely closed was all that was strictly necessary.

Dawn view of the Propylaia (437–432 BC), gateway to the Akropolis at Athens, with the little Temple of Athena Nike (c.425 BC) on its lofty bastion to the right. Typically Greek are the impeccably fitted masonry, the crisp, clear forms, and the use of architectural sculpture.

From quite early in the eighth century, however, there is clear evidence of a new desire to impress. Some temples, such as the first Temple of Hera at Samos, were made larger than the bare minimum required. While difficulties with roofing kept them narrow, their length ran up to 30 metres or so (about 100 feet). At some stage in the life of this temple at Samos, probably still in the eighth century, a portico was added round all four sides of the long hall, or cella. The portico may have had some structural or functional advantages, but it seems likely that its main purpose was intended to recall the splendours of the Bronze Age palaces, long since collapsed, but described in epic poetry. Whatever its original aim, however, a portico round a closed hall, or cella, became the characteristic type of Greek temple, and this established Greek architecture from the start as an architecture of columns.

So far, the materials and techniques of Greek architecture were still vernacular, and there is no real evidence that its posts and beams were similar to later Doric and Ionic Orders in any special way. The development of monumental forms and techniques took place in the seventh century, and an important stimulus was probably provided by the renewal, from about 660 BC, of Greek contact with Egypt, where a continuing tradition of monumental architecture could provide visiting Greeks with both formal and technical ideas. But the Greeks had already evolved their distinctive temple type, and rarely borrowed ideas wholesale from elsewhere.

In mainland Greece the most advanced area seems to have been around Argos and Corinth, where temples built partly of dressed stone date from before the middle of the seventh century. During this transitional period, however, wood and mud brick continued in use, and an important role was played by terracotta—more durable and elaborate than the vernacular materials, but more familiar to the Greeks than dressed stone. Terracotta remained standard for roof tiles, but otherwise dressed stone had replaced it by the early sixth century.

In addition to technical change there was a major formal innovation as the idea of an architectural Order was born—one that was to influence much of later western architecture. The structural system of posts and beams came to be articulated into an arrangement of clearly defined elements, each with its fixed form. The earliest and most austere was the Doric Order, used in mainland Greece and the Greek colonies in Sicily and Italy. It seems to have been developed in the mid-seventh century, and quickly reached a stable convention, so that—although different in proportion and detail—every element in the façade of the Parthenon (447–432 BC) had already been seen in the Temple of Artemis at Kerkyra (Corfu; c.600–590 BC), one of the earliest all-stone temples. The Ionic Order, at home in the Greek cities east of the Aegean, did not reach an established form before the mid-sixth century, and even when established allowed for more elaboration and variation than the Doric.

The tradition explaining the Doric Order as a sort of fossilization of vernacular wooden architecture goes back to the Roman architect Vitruvius in the first century BC, but in wood it makes an unnaturally heavy and complex structure. Present evidence suggests that it was composed within a comparatively short period in the mid-seventh century by builders who drew on a variety of sources. These included not only traditional woodwork, but also surviving Bronze Age monuments like the Lion Gate at Mycenae, and perhaps Egyptian architecture. The earliest surviving remains are the painted terracotta metopes from the Temple of Apollo at Thermon (c. 630 BC), but they do not *prove* the use of the full Doric Order. The full Order, however, certainly appears in the earliest all-stone temples soon after 600 BC. Thus by the early sixth century the Doric temple was fully developed in both form and structure.

Top left: The Lion Gate, the entrance to the royal citadel of Mycenae. It was built in the mid-thirteenth century BC, though it remained visible throughout antiquity. The symbolic column between heraldic lions was probably one source for the invention of the later Doric column, but like all Mycenaean and Minoan columns, its shaft tapers from top to bottom.

Below: Reconstruction of the Temple of Artemis at Kerkyra (Corfu), c.600–590 BC. Although only the foundation trenches survive in place, fragments are preserved of all the upper parts of the temple, including a central portion of the sculptured pediment (gable) which shows the Gorgon Medusa.

Right above: The Doric temple at Segesta in Sicily, built in the late fifth century BC. Although unfinished and lacking the inner cella building, it shows the kind of temple for which the Orders were developed.

A Greek technical writer of the third century BC described the progress of architecture as an empirical search for satisfying form. The development of Greek temple architecture had little to do with either structure or function. Nor was it much concerned with internal space; since the main rituals took place outside, the exterior form dominated architects' thinking. There they adhered to rigid convention, intelligently refined but never radically changed, which is specially characteristic of Greek architecture, and justifies its armoury of technical terms. It is most evident in the Doric temples of mainland Greece, where a simple line of development can be traced from early sixth-century temples through the Temples of Apollo at Corinth (c. 540 BC) and Aphaia at Aigina (c. 500 BC) to the Temple of Zeus at Olympia (c. 470–457 BC).

Among the general relationships, the length of plan, inherited from pre-monumental temples, tends to be reduced in relation to width and the columns become

THE GREEK ORDERS: DORIC IONIC AND CORINTHIAN

The most influential creations of Greek architecture were the architectural Orders, Doric, Ionic and (later) Corinthian. These conventional systems of columns and beams were developed for the characteristic Greek temple, with its one-storeyed, surrounding colonnade, but they were later modified for use in a much wider range of situations, and although not strictly functional, their flexibility and expressive forms ensured their lasting popularity.

Right: Corner of a Doric temple, showing the usual low-pitched gable or pediment. The rhythm of the grooved triglyphs of the frieze is taken up in the details of the architrave below and the cornice above.

Below far left and left: The Ionic and Corinthian Orders.

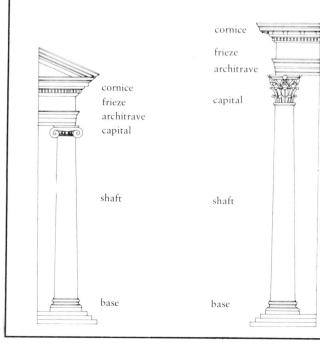

cornice
frieze
architrave
capital

shaft

base

cornice

frieze

architrave

capital

shaft

base

more slender and the entablature lighter. The succession of profiles given to the Doric capital is characteristic of the development in detail. These vary from the spreading outline of the earliest Doric capitals to the stiffer, taller, early fifth-century profile, which seems to react slightly to the load above, but without giving way to it. Similarly the reduplicating rhythms of the Doric entablature, with the triglyphs of the frieze set twice as close as the columns, and the plank-like mutules above set twice as close as the triglyphs were made more explicit (hardly by accident) when, from the mid-sixth century, all mutules were given the same width. Strong colours, notably red and blue, were used to strengthen these rhythms, and to enhance the decorative mouldings.

The maintenance of strict conventions over a considerable area and period is of technical as well as aesthetic interest. It seems to have been achieved by using rules of proportion, which were probably used as a means of transmitting design rather than architectural drawings. Given the austere lines of a mainland Doric temple, a comparatively small number of rules could encapsulate a complete temple design more accurately than any but the most precise drawing, allowing it to be

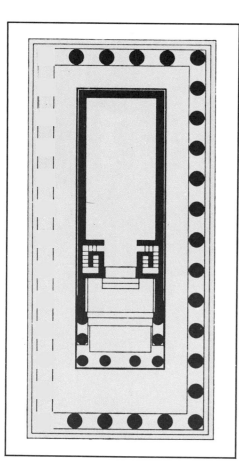

Above left and above centre: The Temple of Athena (or 'Ceres') at Paestum, south of Naples, Italy, c.510 BC. It has an abnormal cornice and mouldings.

Below left·Mature Doric Temple of 'Concord' at Akragas (Agrigento) in Sicily, c.430 BC.

Right: Interior of the Temple of Aphaia at Aigina, c.500 BC. The two-storeyed inner colonnades helped to support the roof timbers.

passed from one architect to another and embodied in temples of different sizes. It is usually hard to tell just what rules were used. Some evidence suggests that the main dimensions were initially related to each other, with the smaller dimensions derived from the larger, working in the order of construction of the building. But the actual dimensions used might be modified by rounding them out to the nearest convenient number of feet (various foot standards were used in different periods and parts of the Greek world). Thus the Temple of Zeus at Olympia has columns twice as high as the distance between them, and the capital width is half that distance; these ratios were presumably consciously chosen. But the width of the grooved triglyphs, usually one fifth of the column spacing, is here rounded out to the nearest quarter foot.

Against this background of strict convention in mainland Greece the architecture of the Greek colonies of Sicily and southern Italy seems strikingly original. These cities were at their most prosperous in the sixth and early fifth centuries and many of their temples are well preserved. The main lines of both the normal temple plan and the Doric Order are unchanged, but in both respects there are general departures from mainland practice as well as individual differences from building to building. Thus in western colonial temples there is a marked emphasis on the front of the cella building, a feature shared with Etruscan and, later, Roman temples, but lacking on mainland Greece; and this emphasis is variously achieved. The Doric Order has a general tendency to

decorative elaboration, partly due to influence from Ionia. More specifically, in the Temple of Athena at Paestum (the so-called Temple of Ceres), a carved moulding replaced the customary severe band along the top of the architrave, and within the Doric outer colonnade there was an Ionic porch to the cella. Neither of these features occurs in Sicilian temples, but they might be original in other ways, for instance in the addition of a second row of columns behind those of the façade but in front of the porch of the cella building. During the fifth century, however, this freer attitude to architecture in the western colonies disappeared, to be replaced by the stricter canons of mainland architecture, as can be seen in the second Temple of Hera (the so-called Temple of Neptune), also at Paestum.

PUBLIC BUILDINGS

Temples were not for congregational worship, so there was no equivalent to a regular Sunday Service. In most cases an annual festival in honour of the divinity was held, attracting a wide spectrum of society, often composed of people from beyond the immediate city confines. But smaller sacrifices might occur more often, and personal dedications could be made at any time. These cults were not run by a priestly caste; with some exceptions priesthoods in Greece were regarded as public offices to be undertaken, like other magistracies, by laymen. It was the city-states that commissioned temples and although they shared the same culture, values and divinities, they were fiercely independent politically. Piety to the gods was an acknowledged virtue and pious dedications had to be seen, so winning esteem for the dedicator as well as the god. Temple building thus enhanced the city's prestige, and with it the individual citizen's sense of his own worth. This explains the almost exclusive concentration on temple building during the first two centuries of Greek monumental architecture, and it remained important even when cities came to feel that their status also depended on their secular buildings.

The organization of public building is best known from Athens, where a democratic constitution generated public records. There, at least from the fifth century on, any public project had to be discussed and passed by the Assembly, which would appoint an annually changing supervisory committee and architect, unless they were already nominated for some related project. The committee then hired workmen directly and was responsible to the Assembly for the proper execution of the project.

In a large commercial city like Athens there was no shortage of skilled labour: citizens, foreigners and slaves worked side by side at the same jobs. But not all cities could count on such a permanent labour force, and many found it convenient to make a contract for a specific job, which had to be completed before full payment was made. This system was also advantageous to cities lacking a fully developed administrative structure, for if a building project were divided into a few large contracts, then the man responsible for administering it would arrange his own supply of labour, materials and equipment. In the sixth century, when public administration was simpler, it may have been common practice to let whole projects to a single person, but this

associated the project closely with the contractor in a way that was later found unacceptable; the prestige of a public project should belong to the city, not to a single man or family.

Nevertheless, the dual motive of piety and prestige, operating through an individual, was important in financing public building. A city could rarely cope with large non-recurrent expenses and so, while it might refuse offers to pay for a whole building, it often relied on private contributions towards a project. As for architects, pay was hardly a great attraction, for they received only about the same rate as skilled workmen. Either they were simply skilled craftsmen, as some scholars believe, or else they were attracted by the prestige associated with a large community venture, and the payment was an

Below left: The unfinished north-east wing of the Propylaia at Athens, 437–432 BC.

Below: Monument of the Haterii, c. AD 100; heavy-duty crane on a Roman funerary monument. Such cranes probably came into use during the Hellenistic period, but simpler versions were known from at least 510 BC.

Right: Rough-faced masonry on the fourth-century frontier fort at Eleutherai, north-west of Athens.

honorarium like that paid to other officials.

In spite of their common feeling of Greekness, Greek cities had no more qualms about fighting each other than had the Christian kingdoms of the Middle Ages, and among the most important and expensive buildings required by a Greek city were its fortifications. Mud brick was often used for the upper part of the walls, but from the sixth century onwards many cities were surrounded entirely by a massive wall of carefully dressed stone, among the most impressive examples of Greek building technique to have survived.

CONSTRUCTION

Methods of construction used in Greek monumental architecture changed little after 600 BC. Blocks of stone were laid without any cement, and relied on their weight and carefully fitted joints for stability. Metal clamps and dowels were used in the most important buildings or where there was a special need of them. Coursed masonry was commonest in free-standing buildings; in the most careful work the blocks are all uniform, with a completely regular system of joints. With fortification walls and terraces, on the other hand, the facing was often built of polygonal blocks, sometimes with curving

joints. The pattern of joints might be brought out by tooling, and the face left either smooth or rough, making possible a wide range of relief and elegance, even in a plain wall.

One special feature of Greek masonry is that it was normally laid with an allowance of stone beyond the intended face, and the whole wall was dressed down only when the building was complete. This not only avoided accidental chipping of the finished face, but also meant that the whole wall could be dressed to a continuous plane. For the same reasons, columns, which were normally built up from several separate drums, were only fluted after erection, when the building was virtually complete.

Great care was usually taken with the foundations of a building. A sloping site would be massively terraced, and special precautions are recorded for temples built on soft ground.

The chief technical problem lay in transporting and lifting heavy blocks of stone. In an ordinary temple the architraves from column to column might weigh over ten tons, and such blocks presented no special problem. In the mid-sixth century, however, several colossal temples about 50 by 100 metres (165 × 330 feet) were built in Ionia, apparently in

rivalry with each other, and these involved blocks weighing up to 40 tons. Some at least of these blocks were rolled from the quarry to the site and there hauled into place up temporary ramps. Cranes were certainly used from the late sixth century onwards, however, thus dispensing with the need for mass labour. The change is well illustrated by two Doric temples of similarly colossal size in Sicily: the Temple of Apollo at Selinous (c. 530–460 BC), designed as a normal temple enlarged, required architrave blocks weighing 40 tons—more than a simple crane could handle; and the Temple of Zeus at Akragas (c. 500–460 BC), which had half-columns projecting from a continuous wall, allowing the architrave to be built up from comparatively small blocks, none of which weighed more than 14 tons. When, in the fourth century, a new generation of colossal temples was started, it seems that cranes of larger capacity must have been developed.

Almost all Greek architecture is based on the post-and-lintel system (that is, on horizontal beams carried by vertical supports), and this seems to be as true of the wooden roofs as of the stone colonnades. The study of theoretical mechanics hardly began before the third century, so there is no evidence of a theoretical understanding of structure and little sign of empirical knowledge either. There was probably some general realization that a beam's strength lies in its height rather than its thickness, and occasional architects appreciated that the greatest strain comes at the middle of a beam. But there is no sign of concerted experimentation like that devoted to form and proportion.

In addition to the simple beam, the Greeks knew of the double cantilever, with two arms balancing each other on either side of a central support; they used it only rarely, but then with sophistication. They also knew and used a number of other methods of spanning an opening in masonry: corbelling, where successive horizontal courses each project out beyond the one below until the opening is bridged; pairs of opposed slabs rising from the two sides of the opening to meet in the middle; and the true arch, with radiating joints. None of these played an important role in buildings, however, and they were rarely employed for spans of over 6 metres (20 feet), which could easily be bridged by a timber beam. Their chief use was in tombs, bridges and fortifications where the massive supports they required could be easily provided, and where the usual wooden roof structure was not sufficiently durable. The surprising neglect of the arch, known certainly from the fifth century, is probably due to the Greeks' ignorance of its true capabilities, to their unwillingness to modify their beloved Orders, and to the difficulty of constructing any but the simplest vault in accurate, dry-laid masonry.

Although Greek architects were competent technically, they apparently did not devote much attention to technical improvement. As we have seen, few Greek buildings involved the creation of large interior spaces; it was the refinement of exterior form which they regarded as their true job.

THE GOLDEN AGE

The great buildings of Periklean Athens mark both a culmination and a turning-point in this process of refinement. In 480 BC Athens had been sacked by the Persians. The city walls were hastily rebuilt in 479 BC, but the ruined temples were probably left as a reminder of barbarian impiety until about 450 BC when peace was made with Persia, and Athens, at the head of a league which was in fact an Empire, had at her disposal the annual tribute of her 'allies'.

The main elements in the programme of

construction that followed were the Parthenon, built on the site of a temple already begun in about 488 BC, and the Propylaia, a new monumental gateway to the Akropolis. Other buildings were also erected during Perikles' supremacy, some at his own instigation like the new Hall of the Mysteries at Eleusis, while others formed part of no concerted programme.

The Parthenon (447–432 BC) was obviously meant to be the grandest temple in Greece. It can hardly be coincidence that its columns were exactly the same height as those of the Temple of Zeus at Olympia, at that time the most prestigious temple in mainland Greece. But in addition it was wider, longer, built out of marble as no large Doric temple had been before, and was more richly endowed with sculpture than any other temple. Sculptured pediments were already used in the early sixth century, but many large temples had no sculptural decoration. The Parthenon had two sculptured pediments, 92 sculptured metopes, and a continuous frieze—the famous Panathenaic procession—running all round the cella building.

Another special feature of the Parthenon was its refinements, those slight variations from the expected straight lines, verticals and uniform repetitions. The platform from which the columns rise, for instance, curves slightly upwards in the middle of each side; the corner columns are 4 centimetres ($1\frac{1}{2}$ inches) thicker than the others; and all the columns slope slightly in-

Above: The famous Parthenon frieze ran round the outside of the inner building of the temple.

Right above: The Parthenon seen from the Propylaia.

Right: Model of the Akropolis in Athens, dominated by the Parthenon, 447–432 BC, with the Propylaia, 437–432 BC, below right, and the Erechtheion, c.420–405 BC, below left.

Below: Reconstruction of the interior of the Temple of Apollo at Bassai, 430–400 BC; there may have been just one Corinthian capital at the far end. The frieze here ran round the inside of the inner building, and the Ionic capitals were specially modified for a view-point such as this.

trived forecourt at the head of a monumental ramp, with the main façade facing the visitor, set off by smaller façades placed at right angles on either side. The Propylaia is in fact the earliest instance in Greek architecture of a coherent complex with several elements formally combined into a harmonious whole. The wings behind these lesser façades were not actually identical, and many scholars believe that an originally symmetrical scheme had to be modified because it encroached on neighbouring sanctuaries; luckily, however, there is no real reason to suppose that Mnesikles, the architect, started out with needless symmetry as his only thought.

A common feature of Periklean architecture was the combination of the Doric and Ionic Orders; sometimes, as in the Propylaia, with columns of both types used side by side; sometimes, as in the Parthenon, with features from one order taken over into the other. Athenian influence almost certainly caused the spread of this idea to the Peloponnese, for it first appears there in the Temple of Apollo at Bassai (c. 430–400 BC), which is said to be another work by Iktinos. This temple, now standing remote in the Arcadian mountains, has an unremarkable Doric exterior; but the inside is articulated by short spur walls ending in Ionic half-columns of most curious design; and at the far end, where the colonnade ran behind the cult statue as in the

wards. Although modern scholars debate the effect of these and other refinements, ancient authors unanimously agree that their intention was to counter certain optical illusions which might make a truly regular building look irregular. As with architectural sculpture, the refinements also occur in earlier and subsequent buildings, but never in such profusion as in the Parthenon.

The architect of the Parthenon was Iktinos, who was probably assisted by others, but the magnificent gold and ivory cult statue of Athena, 12 metres (40 feet) high was sculpted by Pheidias. As a friend of Perikles he oversaw all Perikles'

projects, we are told, so it is not surprising that special attention was given to the inside of the Parthenon, where the cult statue stood. It demonstrates the first change in cella design for about 150 years. Instead of the usual two straight rows of columns forming a corridor almost blocked by the cult statue, the cella of the Parthenon had a spacious horseshoe of columns continuing round behind the Athena so as to frame and enrich the space where it stood.

This interest in space is also found in other Periklean buildings, notably the Propylaia (438–432 BC). Here, however, the space was outside, a carefully con-

Parthenon, the Ionic capitals were replaced by Corinthian ones, with their double ring of acanthus leaves and spiralling tendrils. This is the earliest known use of a form which to the Greeks was simply a variant of Ionic, but which to Roman and Renaissance architects was a separate order, and the most popular of them all. The use of Ionic at Bassai inspired a fashion for this 'foreign' order in the Peloponnese over the next century and a half, but the treatment was in detail abnormal.

The main centre of Ionic was east of the Aegean in Ionia, as the name suggests, although Athens made substantial contributions to its development. Sadly, little is known about early Ionic temples, for all the great sixth-century temples which established the conventions of the Order are poorly preserved, and the history of Ionia in the fifth and early fourth centuries was one of successive foreign dominations which did not encourage architecture. However, it is clear that Ionic conventions were less strict than Doric ones, and throughout the sixth century there was, for instance, considerable variation in the moulded base of each column.

In Asia Minor the Ionic Order had no frieze at first; instead a row of blocklike dentils separated the architrave from the cornice; but in Ionic buildings on the islands of the Cyclades and the Greek mainland, the dentils were replaced by a continuous frieze, usually sculptured, as for instance in the Erechtheion at Athens (c. 420–405 BC). It was not until the late fourth century that frieze and dentils appeared together, as they do in Roman and later versions of the Order. The Erechtheion also shows the first fully developed examples of the Attic-Ionic base, accepted by most later architects as standard, and the beautifully carved mouldings which are a feature of Ionic, each with a traditional decoration echoing its profile.

However, architects in Ionia did not accept these mainland ideas for some time, and the Ionian, or Asiatic, convention is well shown by the Temple of Athena at Priene (c. 350 BC), which although small was influential. Even in the sixth century the cella building and columns were more tightly related to each other in Ionic temples than in Doric, but at Priene the whole plan is based on a uniform square grid, to which both columns and walls conform. The same rational conception can be seen in the colossal Temple of Apollo at Didyma (begun c. 300 BC), with its double row of columns round a cella which was always meant to be unroofed, for it contained the Sacred Grove of Apollo. The tall, closely spaced columns at Didyma demonstrate the gracefulness of Ionic, even on this huge scale; but the temple took about 500 years to build, and was never properly finished.

The architect at Priene, Pytheos, wrote a book on it, and wrote another on his work at the world-famous, but poorly preserved Mausoleum at Halikarnassos. This in itself was nothing new—Iktinos had done the same for the Parthenon, and the practice went back to the mid-sixth century. All these works are lost but are referred to by Vitruvius, so that we have some idea of their content. Thus it appears that, whereas earlier books had been largely practical, Pytheos discussed theoretical matters, such as architectural education and the defects of the Doric Order. This interest in theory was taken further by the systematic ideas on Ionic of the subsequent Ionian architect, Hermogenes, quoted by Vitruvius. Where before it was based rather on traditional convention, there seems to have been a strong

GREEK DECORATED MOULDINGS

A characteristic feature of Greek architecture is the repertoire of mouldings used to articulate the various parts of a building; for instance the Ionic architrave was normally crowned by an ovolo (2). Simple concave and convex mouldings had been used in Egyptian architecture, but the Greeks evolved a wider range, and used them more freely. Each different profile was usually associated with a conventional decorative pattern, the design of which reflected the profile. In Doric architecture these patterns were normally painted, but in Ionic they were carved as well, adding greatly to the general richness of effect. In adopting the Greek mouldings, Roman and later users of the classical Orders preferred profiles based on arcs of a circle to the more flowing Greek curves, and often broke the close relationship between profile and decoration.

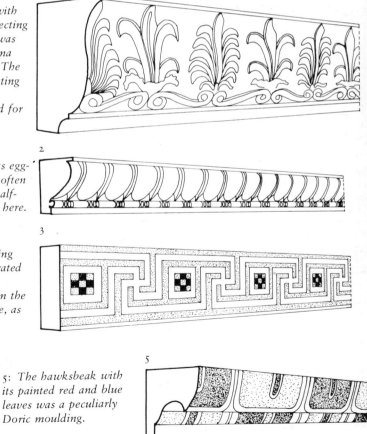

1: The cyma recta, with its concave part projecting beyond the convex, was often used for the sima (gutter) of a temple. The decoration of alternating palmettes and lotus flowers was also used for flat bands.

2: The ovolo with its egg-and-dart decoration often ran above a small, half-rounded astragal, as here.

3: A slightly projecting band might be decorated with one of several patterns, among them the maeander and square, as in this example.

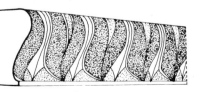

4: In profile the cyma reversa is the opposite of the cyma recta (1). Its leaf and dart reflects the double curve.

5: The hawksbeak with its painted red and blue leaves was a peculiarly Doric moulding.

Above: Roman wall-painting using perspective, from Boscoreale, c.50 BC, probably based on Greek theatrical scenery of the second century BC.

Top: The Erechtheion seems a conscious contrast to the near-by Parthenon. Complex rather than unified, Ionic rather than Doric, its effect depends not on solemnity but on elegance. The graceful maidens each held a sacrificial bowl, and the vertical folds of their skirts echo the fluting of the columns.

tendency to reduce architecture to a theoretical system from the fourth century onwards; there may also have developed a more systematic technique of design.

It is at least arguable that Greek buildings in the sixth and fifth centuries were designed without detailed and accurate drawings, and that the strict conventions and rules of proportion took their place as the tools of design and the means of communication between architects. But there is no doubt that by the first century BC plans, elevations and perspectives were a normal part of architecture, and skill in drawing may already have been expected by the fourth-century Pytheos. The development of a theory-based architecture would certainly be easier if drawings were used, and the increasing range of monumental building would also require them. For the same reason, a new system of proportion was apparently developed in the last three centuries BC, in which every element was derived, not from some other part of the building, but directly from a module, so that each element measured a whole number of modules. This method would make the use of the Orders in widely varying contexts much easier, and was adopted by Renaissance and later theorists.

CIVIC ARCHITECTURE

By the fourth century BC temples were no longer the only buildings required from Greek architects, but their long period of pre-eminence meant that a monumental effect was inseparably associated with the Orders, now applied to other buildings. Civic architecture in a monumental style developed first at Athens, presumably because of the increasingly complex administration needed by the first democracy. At Athens, the agora—the administrative centre of a Greek city as well as its market—already had some public buildings (mostly unpretentious) by the end of the sixth century, and by the end of the fifth the south and west sides were lined with public buildings—council chamber, record office, law-courts, and stoas, which were long, narrow halls with a colonnade forming one long side. Stoas were regarded by the Greeks as the most satisfactory type of building for general public use. They provided ready shelter from sun or rain, a space for meetings or markets, or an area for just strolling and gossiping. They also presented a suitably colonnaded façade to the outside world and were a useful element in town planning.

Since the conventions of stoa design were developed in Athens, the outer

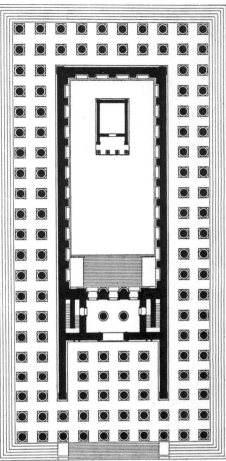

colonnade was usually Doric, even in Asia Minor, but the inner columns, which had to be taller to reach the roof beams, exploited the conventionally more slender proportions of Ionic. In addition to stoas, a courtyard surrounded by porticoes of the same character formed the basis of a number of public building types—the gymnasium, for instance, with its spacious exercise court and rooms opening off it for changing, for washing, and for lessons; or the hotel, with guest-rooms looking on to a central court.

Another important building type was the theatre. Greek drama was closely connected with religion, and at Athens, where the conventions of both tragedy and comedy were developed in the mid-fifth century, drama formed part of the annual festival of Dionysos, the wine-god. The classical theatre building, developed there in the late fifth century, was centred around a circular orchestra, where the chorus, an essential element in classical drama, performed. On one side rose the horseshoe of stone seating, which always made use of a natural hillside for support; on the other was a simple scene-building, with a low stage. Later theatres had a more substantial scene-building with a higher stage, but the original conception was

retained, simple but elegant, and acoustically excellent. Theatres were of course unroofed, and there was seldom a need to house a large crowd under a roof. Where this need arose, the result often seems unsatisfactory, as in the Hall of Mysteries at Eleusis, where the roof was supported on a grid of 42 columns, which must surely have blocked many people's view of the rites. It is only in some later council chambers, as at Miletos, that we find an impressive, unobstructed space.

Thus a system of structure and form developed for temples came to be used for a wide range of other buildings. The structural system was not seriously modified, although materials like mud brick might be acceptable for secular buildings long after they were obsolete for temples.

But more important changes were required in the Orders. In stoas and similar porticoes there was no special reason for lofty columns, so the scale was often small. Access was vital in these public buildings, however, and since by standard temple conventions small columns would be closely spaced, a new convention was developed to provide a more open colonnade, by putting three instead of two triglyphs and metopes above each column spacing. Similarly, whereas temples were

by nature one-storeyed, it was sometimes found desirable to have one portico above another, as in the Stoa of Attalos at Athens, and this too involved new modifications to the conventional forms.

More generally, the desire to elaborate buildings which were in effect mere boxes led to the use of the Orders as decoration. This had been done to a small extent in the sixth and fifth centuries (as, for instance, at Bassai), but was much more common in the fourth century and later. A good example is the Council Chamber at Miletos (c. 170 BC). Here there is no upper floor inside, but the outside is divided into two, with a plain wall below and Doric half-columns above, giving something of the effect of a large temple set on a high podium; similarly, the inner wall surface is articulated with flat pilasters. In this way the application of the Orders to a new range of buildings created a much more flexible system for later borrowers. If Greek architecture had stopped with the Parthenon, it is doubtful whether it would have been so influential.

DOMESTIC ARCHITECTURE

Houses were among the last buildings to be given monumental status, and their

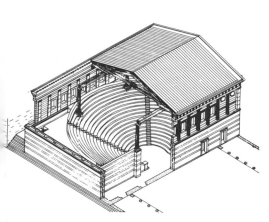

Above left and far left: The Temple of Apollo at Didyma, c.300 BC–AD 200, designed by Paionios of Ephesos and Daphnis of Miletos. The plan shows the coherent arrangement of columns and walls.

Above: The theatre at Epidauros, c.300 BC.

Left: The Council Chamber at Miletos, c.170 BC. It had a span of 15.90 m (52 ft).

Below: Model of the agora at Athens. Apart from the large building in the centre and the temple of Ares below it, it is largely in its Hellenistic form, bordered by long colonnaded stoas.

treatment was for long informal and vernacular, having little effect on other architecture. We have seen how in the ninth century BC both temples and houses usually consisted of just a single room, but whereas temples were characteristically free-standing, the growing density of settlements in the eighth century meant that houses clustered tightly against each other, and although they might be regular and commodious, as at Zagora on Andros, they often consisted of a single room for all domestic purposes. Changes in the pattern of living during the eighth century led increasingly to the provision of separate rooms for different purposes, and an open court became an important element, too.

Most later houses similarly consisted of several rooms opening on to a courtyard. Some favoured schemes of room arrangement can be distinguished, but their significance is often uncertain, and in many cases the exigencies of a cramped urban site led to a highly irregular plan. Where the site was unrestricted, houses were usually rectangular, like the house between Athens and Eleusis built in the late fifth century, and a row of rooms often ran along the north side, facing south through a portico on to a courtyard beyond, so as to catch the winter sun. It is notable how little difference there is between this, a typical prosperous farmhouse, and houses of the same period in the north Greek city Olynthos, where a new quarter was laid out on a grid plan, so allowing regular houses. Most inhabitants of a normal Greek city got their living from farming, so a city house required most of the facilities of a farmhouse.

Houses were commonly built of mud brick, with wooden posts where necessary, and tiled roofs. There is a certain amount of dressed stonework at Olynthos, and the main reception room, used by the men of the family and their friends for dining in, often had painted plaster walls and a simple mosaic floor. But the general impression is of severe simplicity, and even prestige-hungry aristocrats obviously did not expect their status to be judged by their houses. For most, a house was little more than a place in which to sleep. The inward-looking arrangement of rooms around a court meant that houses made little impact from the street, and each house was treated as a separate entity, usually owner-occupied, so that there was no question of several being designed together to form a unified composition, even in the planned area at Olynthos.

More luxurious houses became fashionable in the fourth century and were characteristic of the ensuing Hellenistic period, when Greek culture spread over a vast area of the Middle East, and this enlarged domain was divided into autocratic monarchies like that of the Ptolemies in Egypt. Greater interest in domestic architecture may have been caused, in part, by the fact that the city-states had effectively lost their independence. Important decisions were taken elsewhere and prominent citizens, no longer able to satisfy themselves by active identification with their community, could concentrate on their individual surroundings and social life. In addition, wealthy men would naturally try to imitate the luxurious palaces of the new royalty.

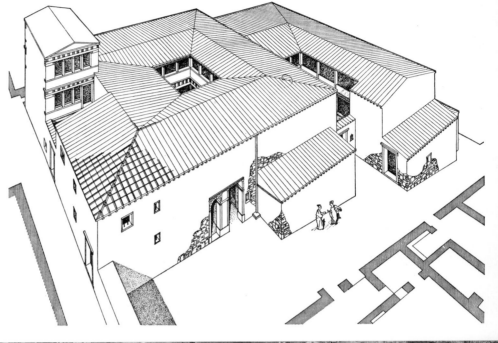

Left: Reconstruction of the House of the Comedians (centre), with its two neighbours, built c.125 BC on the tiny island of Delos in the Aegean.

Left below: View over Delos. Its important sanctuary of Apollo was the chief religious centre for the surrounding islands within the Cyclades group; but during the second century BC it became a wealthy free port, an entrepot for merchants from Italy to the Levant. This brief period of secular prosperity was ended by violent destructions in 88 and 69 BC, so leaving one of the richest collections of late Hellenistic houses.

Below: Reconstruction of a late fifth-century country house between Athens and Eleusis, with rooms on three sides of a courtyard and a simple portico facing south.

None of these palaces survive in good preservation, but many rich houses do, often spreading over several hundred square metres. As before, the intention to impress involved the use of the Orders. In some houses, the main dining-room was treated as a miniature Doric temple, dominating the whole house, although other rooms still clustered round the court in front. More commonly, as at Delos, the court itself became the main element, framed by imposing colonnades which formed a unified front to the rooms opening off it. Mud brick or rubble might still be used for walls, but there was much more dressed stone than at Olynthos, and wall-paintings and floor mosaics were more ambitious.

Even these more elaborate houses were still inward-looking, however, and were not developed into an impressive element in the general fabric of the city. While legislation covered disputes over party-walls and mutual rights, questions of housing rarely entered town planning.

TOWN PLANNING

The need for some kind of town planning arose early. The Greeks began to establish colonial cities in Sicily and southern Italy in the eighth century, and the necessity to control land-holding in the new cities, and probably also to give each settler an equal share of land, must have been a strong inducement to divide the land into rectangular blocks by a regular street pattern. The semi-regular plan at Megara Hyblaia in Sicily belongs largely to the seventh century, but its main lines probably go back to the foundation of the colony in about 730 BC. Completely regular grid plans certainly go back to the sixth century, and remained the only formal street system used by the Greeks.

In established cities this regularity could not be imposed, and there the first step in town planning was the demarcation for public purposes of specific areas within the city. Thus the limits of the agora at Athens were probably established around 600 BC, and from the late sixth century were marked by inscribed stones which engagingly read: 'I am the boundary of

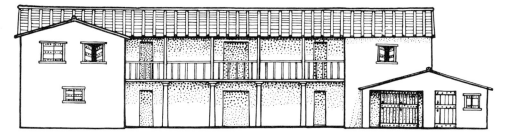

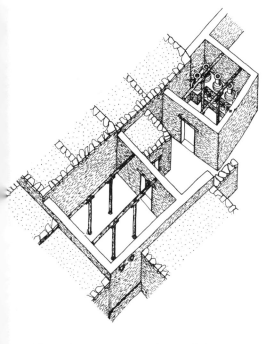

Above: Reconstruction of an eighth-century house at Zagora on the island of Andros. Originally consisting of a single large room, it was quickly extended by the addition of a substantial storeroom across the courtyard.

Right: Private house on Delos, with mosaic floor and marble columns.

Above: The sanctuary of Apollo at Delphi, with its mainly sixth-century buildings set out along a winding road which leads up to the great temple and its altar.

Left: Reconstruction of the akropolis at Pergamon. Apart from the Temple of Trajan (top left) the design dates from the reign of Eumenes II (196–159 BC).

Right above: Designed by Theodoros of Phokaia, in the early fourth century BC, the Tholos at Delphi was the first of several round buildings erected at about this time. Its function is uncertain.

Right: Reconstruction of the sanctuary of Asklepios at Kos. The lower terrace, third century BC, is less symmetrical than the upper one c.150 BC.

the agora.' Improved water supply also received early attention, but in contrast to later Greek cities a classical city had few public facilities, and little concern for the formal arrangement of buildings within a sanctuary or public place.

Ideas on the setting out of public areas, and their size and proper relation to each other, were probably the chief contribution of Hippodamos of Miletos, the earliest Greek name in town planning, for of his work at Athens' port of Piraeus, probably in the 470s BC numerous marker stones survive, defining road alignments, harbours and agora. Remarkable provision for future growth can be seen both here and also at Miletos, refounded at about the same time, for there the area initially set aside for the agora was not fully developed for over 300 years. Hippodamos also set out the colony of Thurii in southern Italy and so forms a link with the regularly planned cities of the Roman world.

The philosophers Plato and Aristotle also had ideas on the proper allocation of space for public purposes, but Plato particularly was concerned more with a static, ideal city than with a real, developing one. One suggestion made by these philosophical theorists which was applied, however, is the separation of trade from civic business by the provision of a separate commercial agora. This can be seen at Priene, some two centuries later, where a small area for selling fish and meat lay just outside the main agora.

Priene presents the clearest picture of the facilities considered appropriate to a small or medium-sized city of the last few centuries BC. Although quite steeply sloping, the streets form a regular grid within

the irregular wall line. The agora is formally framed by stoas with shops behind. Nearby stand the council chamber and civic offices with the stadium and gymnasium below and a theatre on the slopes above.

These elaborate facilities, so different from those of late fifth-century Athens, went hand in hand with increasingly developed administration in the Hellenistic period. Many cities now had a permanent architect to look after their public buildings and fortifications. Officials had control of the agora and gymnasium, officials kept the streets clean and prevented encroachment on them, and more direct legislation controlled life in the cities.

The other important development in

later Greek town planning was a growing interest in the way buildings were related to each other, particularly in sanctuaries and agoras. In a largely sixth-century sanctuary such as Delphi, the siting of each building was a separate matter, decided on grounds of convenience, prominence, or even a desire to slight a neighbouring building. The result might be functional, picturesque, and, because of the basic uniformity of style, even harmonious; but already by the fourth century Greek architects were too aware of the actual spaces contained within a sanctuary or agora to be satisfied with such an informal appearance. Thus at Olympia in the fourth century a conscious effort was made to define the sanctuary area more formally and regularly.

Even so, the buildings in mainland Greece are still viewed as separate, solid entities, partly independent of the space they define. But if we look across to the agora at Miletos, or Priene in Ionia, we find the porticoes have become subservient to the space, bending round corners and merging into each other without any simply conceived mass of their own.

In some ways this change of attitude was part of the same Ionian rationalization that affected temple plans, and it is characteristic of this stage in the development of planning that there is no special emphasis on the axis of a space, no insistence on an axial approach to draw the visitor into the formal pattern. It is hardly before the second century BC that axial symmetry appears in large-scale

planning; that may have been due partly to a new familiarity with Egyptian architecture, where vast symmetrical complexes were common, and partly to a new understanding among architects working for autocrats that architecture could be used to dominate men. A specimen of this new formality is the upper terrace of the sanctuary of Asklepios at Kos (c. 150 BC) with its temple, still thoroughly conventional, but placed axially within a framing horseshoe of stoas, and approached along the axis from a rather earlier and less symmetrical terrace below.

A further innovation, perhaps learned from Egypt, was the conception of the street as a monumental avenue, where previously it had been a mere line of communication. Unlike Priene, Alexandria, founded in 331 BC by Alexander the Great, was dominated by a main avenue, said to have been over 30 metres (100 feet) wide. Few streets elsewhere could match this width, but a main avenue much wider than the traffic required was a feature of several Hellenistic cities. The final stage of this transformation, reached in the first century BC, was the addition of porticoes to form the colonnaded street which is such an impressive feature of Greek cities of the Roman period.

The city which gives us the best idea of the imposing effects achieved by Hellenistic planners is Pergamon, set on a hill rising 275 metres (900 feet) above a surrounding plain in north-west Asia Minor. It became the capital of a small but proverbially rich kingdom during the third century BC, and its main buildings belong to the first half of the second century. A steeply rising theatre seems to articulate the upper part of the city; below it is a long stoa-lined terrace, and a series of broader terraces is set fanwise above it, with the agora, the great Altar of Zeus, the Sanctuary of Athena, and a terrace later occupied by a temple in honour of Trajan (AD 117–38). The entire arrangement is irregular, and partly determined by the site, but its effect is too measured to be accidental. Each terrace, constituting its own clearly defined space from within, forms a distinct part of a larger composition when seen from the distance. A visitor approaching from the sea to the west would first view the city as a whole, with terrace rising upon terrace to the Temple of Athena, then pass by each stately complex on his climb to the royal palace at the top. It is this kind of dominating architecture which so influenced Roman architects of the first century BC.

PRIENE: A GREEK CITY

The city of Priene in western Asia Minor was moved to a new site near the mouth of the Maeander in about 350 BC, and unlike most of its neighbours it did not prosper under the Roman Empire; so most of its buildings belong to the last four centuries BC. The main streets run east-west, along the hillside, while the cross-streets are often just flights of steps, for the site rises 70 metres (225 feet) from the stadium to the theatre, and a further 280 metres (900 feet) to the akropolis above. Unlike that at Athens, the akropolis which dominates Priene was just a defensive strong point; the main sanctuary of the city, that of Athena, occupies a much lower eminence near the middle of the city. Below and to the right of the sanctuary of Athena is the rectangular open space of the agora, with the fish- and meat-market just to the left. The fortification wall along the lower edge of the site is also used to retain a terrace for the stadium and gymnasium, while the theatre takes advantage of the steeper slopes of the upper part of the city.

Above: The Ionic columns of the Temple of Athena (c.350 BC) with the cliffs of the akropolis behind.

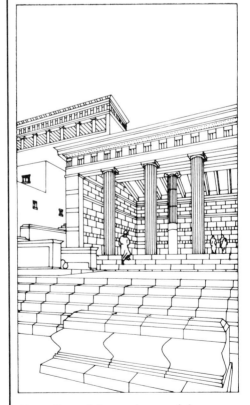

Above: Part of the north stoa of the agora, with the stoa of the sanctuary of Athena above it. In the foreground is one of several altars in the agora which, like other Greek public places, had minor cults attached.

Below: House 33, the largest house in the city, occupied nearly half a block. As usual, the main rooms face south onto the courtyard, and the street façades are virtually blind.

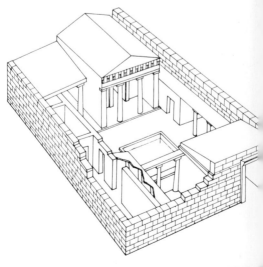

Right: The theatre, with the flood-plain of the Maeander in the distance. The front row of seats with backs was reserved for special dignitaries. The theatre was also used for meetings of the political assembly.

Below: Reconstructed perspective of the whole city. The residential areas are divided into uniform blocks of c.47 × 35 m (160 × 120 ancient feet), but the houses vary in size, with between three and ten houses (usually four) to each block.

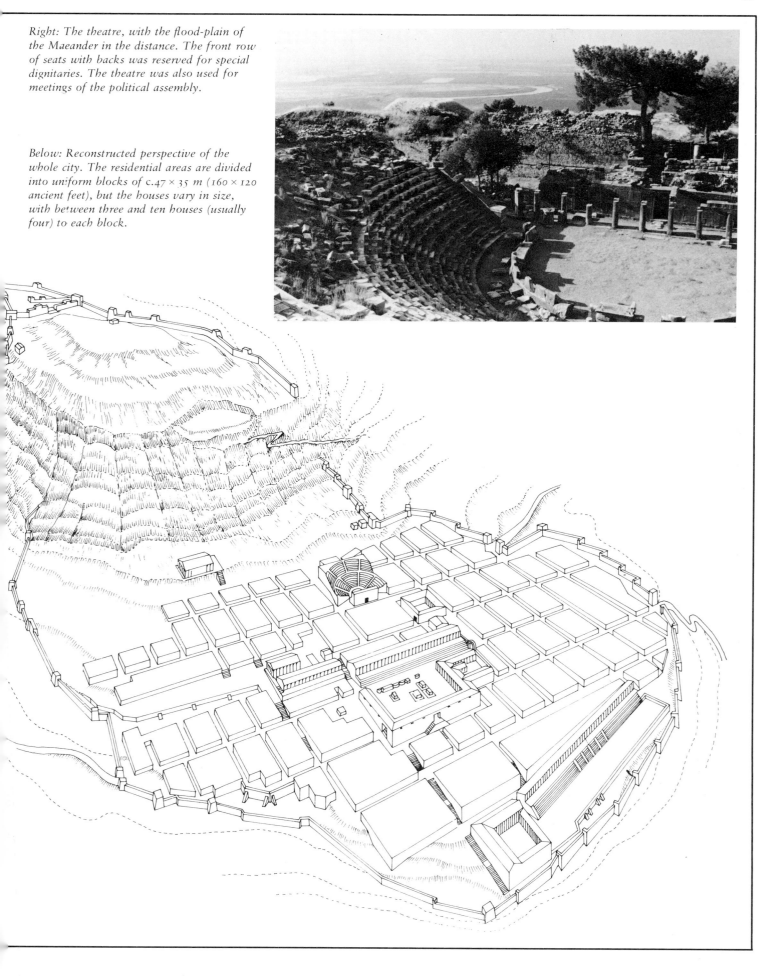

ROMAN ARCHITECTURE

Architecture was outstanding among the Roman arts and was inextricably entwined with most of the others. It was, above all, a social art, giving the people of the Roman Empire benefits which no community had ever achieved before. Many of the outward forms of Roman architecture are clearly taken over from the Greeks, and it was through Rome that these became the common language of a great part of the tradition of western architecture. Vitruvius, who wrote in the reign of Augustus (31 BC–AD 14) and whose work was to become the Renaissance architect's Bible, based the ten books of his *De Architectura* largely on the works of Hermogenes and other well-known architects, mostly Greeks, who had propounded the Greek theories of proportion.

For the Roman historian, Vitruvius' dependence on Greek writers is frustrating, since he tantalizingly neglects the important buildings that were being erected in his own time. Part of his book Vitruvius did, however, base on his own experience, but this was experience as an engineer in the military sphere rather than work as an architect. Not unlike I.K. Brunel in the nineteenth century, he was equally at home in either field, and his career reminds us how very close the discipline of engineering was to that of architecture in the Roman world. It is often difficult to draw a firm line between them, and the most striking of all their achievements, the creation of roads, shows us how construction and military engineering came together.

From a very early date a Via Latina ran to the south, following an island route. But the famous Roman high road, the Via Appia, which offered an all-weather route from Rome to Capua in Campania, was much more scientifically constructed from the outset. This 212-kilometre (132-mile) stretch was built by, and named after, one of Rome's first identifiable statesmen, Appius Claudius Caecus, who in 312 BC held the office of the censorship, which concerned itself, among other things, with public works, including roads.

The Arch of Titus (died AD 81), probably erected by his brother Domitian. The triumphal arch is the antithesis of Roman social architecture because of its uselessness: it serves the community only by glorifying the monarch. It has, nevertheless, exercised great influence on European design. The Arch of Titus stands at the highest point of the Sacred Way, where processions could pass under it. On either flank they would see reliefs representing the principal moments of the triumph Titus celebrated in AD 71 with his father Vespasian and his brother over the Jews. Here the Goddess Rome is seen leading his triumphal chariot, while Victory, accompanied by Honour and Courage, places a wreath upon his head.

Many hundreds of years later the Via Appia was still being admired. Constructed of smooth, sharp-hewn, uncemented blocks, it was wide enough for two carriages to pass abreast. It was planned and brought into being in the middle of a great war against the Samnite mountain tribes of central Italy, and was primarily designed to serve the troops—just as its prolongation in 244 BC to Brundusium (Brindisi) created a starting point for the eastern campaigns of the following century. For Roman roads were, above all, military roads. Trade, Romanization, and personal travel were secondary considerations to begin with, though over the centuries they attained great importance. And, later, it was the Roman roads (from which thousands of milestones still survive today) that enabled Christianity to spread throughout the Empire.

Majestic road planning was based on long-distance surveys of impressive accuracy. In open territory roads ran with that famous straightness, while in broken country they kept to high ground, avoiding narrow valleys which might endanger marching armies. Normally the roads consisted of a number of layers: a foundation of large stones was overlaid by smaller stones and gravel, the surface being either cobbled or paved with large blocks which, in Italy, usually consisted of basaltic lava (*silex* or *selce*). But even with

a slighter surface, the substructure was still solid enough to serve as a lasting base, rendering expensive upkeep unnecessary. For drainage a convex curve or camber at the edges, generally led down into side ditches or gutters. Tunnels, like those of the Etruscans at an earlier date, carried roads through hillsides, and bridges brought them across rivers; the first partially stone-built bridge at Rome was the Pons Aemilius (179 BC).

One of the principal military purposes of the roads was to link together the 'colonies'—towns officially settled either by the citizens of Rome or by those of other Latin towns—so that they could serve as Roman instruments of war. Excavations have revealed that the planning of these towns was often very regular—much more so than that of Rome itself, which remained haphazard until Nero (AD 54–68) tried to replan it. Cosa (Ansedonia) on the Tuscan coast is a good example. Despite controversy about the origins of this regular type of design, it seems to derive from the 'gridiron' arrangement adopted and evolved by the Greek town planner Hippodamos of Miletos, who introduced this formula to the Greek cities of southern Italy in the fifth century BC. Keen interest has also been aroused by a variant of this scheme constructed during the same century at Etruscan Marzabotto (near Bologna), and

the extent of the debt the site owes to Greek influence is still uncertain. But this chess-board town planning appealed to the Roman military mind, which had already surprised the world by its regularly designed camps. Another encouragement to symmetry may have been religious, originating in the augur's division of space for ritual observations.

CIVIC AMENITIES

One of the most characteristic features of a Roman town was its forum, a central open space surrounded by buildings, in which the population crowded and circulated, talked and shouted, conducting

Below: Roman roads in Europe during the third century AD.

Right above: General view of Thamugadi in Numidia (Timgad, Algeria). It was originally planned as a camp for ex-soldiers by Trajan in AD 100.

Bottom centre: The Fabrician Bridge in Rome, constructed by Lucius Fabricius, curator of roads, in 62 BC.

Bottom far right: Part of the road between Antioch and Beroea (Aleppo) in Syria, 6 m (20 ft) wide and constructed of hewn blocks of limestone.

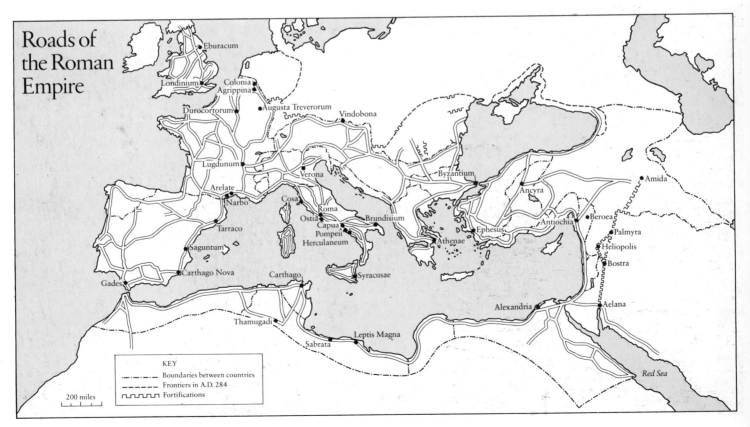

Roads of the Roman Empire

KEY
—·—·— Boundaries between countries
— — — — Frontiers in A.D. 284
⊓⊔⊓⊔ Fortifications

200 miles

their official, religious, commercial and private affairs. The Republican statesman Cato the elder (234–149 BC), who wanted people to get on more quietly with their work, said that the Forum of Rome ought to have been paved with small sharp stones to prevent them from lounging about; but he was trying to deny what had become an irremovable institution. Its origins are mixed, going back to the old Italian marketplace with its rows of shops, to the rectangular agora developed in Greece, and to the Etruscan type of temple which had access only to the front where there was always an open space. A combination of these three formulae can be seen in the fine forum at Pompeii of the second century BC.

Another feature of Roman town planning was its marvellous provision of water. Once again the pioneer was Appius Claudius, who constructed his Aqua Appia to bring water to Rome from the hills in the early fourth century BC. But the modern image of an aqueduct as a series of arches does not apply to this earliest version, for it consisted of subterranean tunnels and owed much to the elaborate drainage-channels with which the Etruscans had criss-crossed the countryside. Then, after another aqueduct, the Anio Vetus (272 BC), had begun to make use of short elevated bridges, much longer arch-

ed sections appeared for the first time along the Aqua Marcia (144 BC). Two and a half centuries later, the capital was served by eight aqueducts totalling over 480 kilometres (300 miles) in length. Their yield was almost doubled by Frontinus (c. AD 30–104) who wrote an account of his work on the water supply of Rome, of which he was in charge, assisted by a staff of slaves called *aquarii*.

'The water of none of these aqueducts', declared the second-century physician Galen, 'is evil-smelling, harmful, filthy or hard.' Yet the water courses were mostly made of masonry, because cast iron was unknown and lead or bronze costly; besides, although lead was very often used for piping within towns, it could be poisonous, as Roman specialists knew, and as the conditions of skeletons has confirmed. However, masonry construction, at least until the most sophisticated methods were available, meant that the channels were not permanently water-tight, and needed constant repair.

These aqueducts of Rome provide that great succession of continuous arches, made of the native volcanic tufa, which so many European painters have admired in the Campagna. For the finest storeyed water-bridges over rivers, one must go to Nemausus (Nîmes) in France and Segovia in Spain. At Nîmes the mighty Pont du

Above: The Pont du Gard, built across the gorge of the River Gardon in southern France in 19 BC by Marcus Agrippa.

Right above: Reconstruction of the second-century BC Temple of Jupiter at the north end of the Forum of Pompeii, Italy.

Right: Aerial view of the enormous Baths of Caracalla (AD 211–217) at Rome, which comprised not only a bathing establishment but an entire community centre providing numerous entertainments and cultural amenities.

Gard, about 250 metres (825 feet) long, had to carry the water nearly 50 metres (160 feet) above the stream, and meet pressure at its base from a seasonally variable current. The arcades of the three superimposed tiers vary in thickness, because the lowest had to find the best foundation points in the river, while the highest had to minimize the wind stress and create the fall required by the channel. Such were the practical aims of the Pont du Gard, yet it is one of the many Roman buildings in which engineering is elevated to an art. However, the hydraulic qualities of this and most other aqueducts were cautious and conservative. They avoided the pressure systems with which Greek theory was familiar and aimed at a simple gravitational flow assisted by gentle falls of level, about six metres in every hundred. This was because the manpower needed to undertake this comparatively simple work was cheap and abundant, while the transport of water over obstacles was costly to install and maintain. Nevertheless, pressure systems were also occasionally employed, for example in the four aqueducts which brought about 75,000 cubic metres of water (2,700,000 cubic feet) daily to Lugdunum (Lyon) in France. Here the water was channelled up as well as down the sides of three valleys, carried by a multiplicity of lead pipes (more than 12,000 tons of them) so that the pressure should not become dangerous.

The water thus lavishly poured into the cities went into their public reservoirs, of which a rectangular open example can be seen at Bauli (Bacoli) near Neapolis (Naples), and an enclosed, arcaded and barrel-vaulted counterpart exists at Constantinople. The water was public property, and after public buildings had been supplied, individuals (unless they tapped it illegally, as was often done) could have

capacity service of water-supply and drainage and heating, the last of which was fed through hypocausts (hollow spaces) beneath the floor and through ducts embedded in the walls. Windows of glass and selenite (crystallized sulphate of lime) were also introduced, at a time when these were still rare in private houses. But the principal architectural and engineering marvels of the baths were the central halls, which could be enormous; the very large church of Santa Maria degli Angeli at Rome, for example, is the central hall of the Baths of Diocletian (c. AD 300), but the remains of vaulted and domed specimens over three centuries earlier can be seen at Pompeii, as well as at Baiae, the other side of Naples.

These sumptuous halls, in their developed form, broke away from the totally vertical and horizontal post-and-lintel formula of Greek architecture. They were held up, not on colonnades supporting architraves, but by gigantic arches, rising direct from massive piers; these, it is true, had classical columns or pilasters attached to them, but this was merely the superimposition of non-functional surface decorations. The swelling curves embodied in arches, vaults, domes and niches—to which surface ornamentation was technically irrelevant—were the features of Roman architecture which made it fundamentally different from its Greek models, and original in the highest degree. And the great bath-halls, where humidity (and, in the warmer rooms, temperature

what was left over (*aqua caduca*) through pipes laid at their own expense. Thus, by imperial times almost every Roman house had a water supply, even if private, sewered sanitation followed far behind.

Much more attention, however, was paid to public lavatories, which, like public fountains, were supplied from the reservoirs. Vespasian (AD 69–79) shocked the fastidious by taxing these latrines; but they continued to increase in number, until by the third century AD there were 144 at Rome. The many surviving examples in other cities, with their rows of 30 or 60 marble seats, show an absence of any desire for privacy. The large underground sewers which flushed the public conveniences—and often received the sewage of private houses too, notably at Eburacum (York) and at Sabrata in North Africa—frequently drew their water from the outflow of the public baths.

The baths, because of their leading role in Roman architecture and social life alike,

are of the first importance. Their ancestors were the hydrotherapeutic establishments of the Greeks, and, early in the first century BC, Hellenized Campania was the first part of Italy in which they appeared: at Pompeii, Herculaneum and elsewhere. These pioneer public baths were the forerunners of the enormous thermal establishments of Rome. Those of Agrippa, Nero, Titus and Trajan have vanished, but great masses of masonry belonging to the Baths of Caracalla and Diocletian are still extant. They are enclosed in vast precincts and, unlike their predecessors, are symmetrical in plan, being designed for an enormous range of social activities. Their scope had begun to expand in this way as a result of the merging of two Greek institutions, the bath and the wrestling school (*palaestra*), and thereafter all manner of entertainments and cultural activities were added. The hot rooms (*caldaria*) and sweating rooms (*laconica*) were fitted to an unseen, high-

Left above: An arch inside the Baths of Caracalla. This building shows the concrete-cored architecture of the Romans at the time of its fullest development.

Left below: The hot room (caldarium) of the Forum Baths at Pompeii, restored AD 3–4. Such rooms, heated from behind the walls and under the floor, required fire-proof instead of wooden ceilings, and it was consequently in this type of structure that south Italian and Roman architects developed the science of concrete-based vaulting.

Right: The Yerebatan Saray at Constaninople (Istanbul), fifth century AD; one of many such enormous underground vaulted cisterns in the city.

as well) required hard vaulting rather than flat wooden roofs, became particularly important media for such methods and forms. They were made possible by the most revolutionary and socially decisive of all Roman technical discoveries: concrete.

CONCRETE AND BRICKWORK

Roman concrete, at its best, was 'pit sand' (*pozzolana*), a clean, finely pulverized, chocolate-red, volcanic, sandy earth. This was mixed in a kiln with limestone reduced to quicklime and then poured over an 'aggregate' of chips or waste of stone, marble or pumice, carefully selected, heavy or light, depending on its purpose. The result was a compact,

monolithic, highly cohesive mass which set very hard, even under water. For over 2,000 years, until the discovery of Portland cement in the nineteenth century, it was far the best binder material that had ever been known. And it exerted no lateral thrust, so that a dome made of concrete was as solid as a lid; when the Romans added buttresses it was because they were over-cautious, preferring to test their materials by experience rather than experiment.

It is possible to hunt in the dim past for the origins of concrete; but it had begun to appear, in a clearly recognizable form, in the walls of Italian houses of the fourth, third and second century BC. Thus, at early Pompeii and Cosa and Ostia, the mud or sun-dried clay house walls con-

tained crushed limestone and were coated by limewash or plaster or, in later years, small rubble as well. Similar developments also occurred in Greece, but it was in Italy that the future of concrete lay. Recent excavations have pushed back the date of its decisive evolution to as early as 193 BC, the year of the construction of the Aemilian Portico at Rome (restored 174 BC). This market-hall on the Tiber consisted of four parallel aisles crossed by barrel-vaulted transepts which were supported on a forest of arches. The entire structure, provided with stepped floor levels to adjust to rising ground, was of concrete covered by the irregularly shaped stones which were used for wall-surfacing at the time. The arches were made by pouring liquid concrete over timber frame-

ROMAN VAULTING

Owing to their discovery of concrete, the Romans built mighty vaults that would have been inconceivable to the Greeks, and the progress of this exciting technique from simple barrel or tunnel construction to the superbly soaring cross-vaulted naves, aisles, apses and domes of huge buildings such as the imperial baths and the Basilica of Maxentius (Constantine) – precursors of the ribbed vaulting of Gothic architecture – can be studied from their surviving remains and ground plans. Ostensibly, the Romans retained the traditional Greek post-and-lintel vertical and horizontal architectural forms, but they became increasingly non-functional, the columns evolving into little more than superficial attachments to the massive piers that supported the vaults.

Right: Barrel, or tunnel, vault under construction and (far right) detail of a section of one of the brick and concrete ribs.

Right: Cross, or groin, vault, showing the position of the ribs.

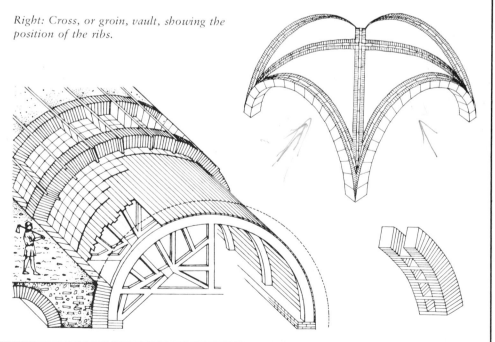

its final form, the three lowest composed of arch-bearing piers. They display engaged columns, yet once again the essential constructional units are not the columns but the massive concrete-cored piers and arches and barrel-vaults. Among the innumerable smaller duplications of the formula throughout the Roman Empire (right down to third-rate stations on Hadrian's Wall) those in Nemausus (Nîmes) and Arelate (Arles) still lay stress on the rhythmical pattern of the old, Greek-style columns; those of Verona and Pula less conservatively reduce the pilasters to very shallow relief, thus stressing the pattern of the non-Greek arches instead and fully exploiting the functional grandeur of the concrete medium.

The same sort of formula triumphs over extraordinary difficulties of terrain in the Markets of Trajan (AD 100–12), situated behind his forum in Rome. Trade on a substantial scale was a somewhat late starter in the history of Rome; the city had depended to an overwhelming extent on the proceeds of agriculture. But the great harbours Claudius and Trajan constructed at Ostia, and the 'Piazzale delle Corporazioni' there, in which floor mosaics in over sixty small rooms advertise the guilds (*collegia*) of merchants, shipwrights and overseas clients, tell a new kind of story. (So does Petronius with his description of Trimalchio, the self-made millionaire.) The *Pax Romana* had by this time brought, if not capitalism developed on modern lines, at least some large scale inter-regional commerce and industry.

An elaborate market precinct was built at Lepcis Magna in North Africa under Augustus, but Trajan's Markets at Rome developed the formula with remarkable skill to fit the greater needs of the capital. Constructed in terraces up the artificially steepened slopes of the Quirinal Hill, and accessible at three different levels, the complex comprised more than 150 shops and offices and a spacious market-hall. At the lowest level a conspicuous feature is the concave hemicyclical façade, corresponding in an almost baroque pattern to

works or centrings, which were then removed. Earlier Greek and Etruscan arches, relatively unambitious, had been made without concrete, as were the arches of early Roman stone bridges and aqueducts; but the new medium made it possible to attain previously unimaginable dimensions and variations. Moreover, concrete was soon used for many other purposes. The channel through which water flowed in the Aqua Marcia was lined with a thick cement of lime and pounded terracotta, and concrete was increasingly used for the bases of temples and the bindings of road pavements. But, as has been said, it was above all in the great bath-halls, with their special humidity and temperature requirements, that the medium found superb expression. In general, the barrel vault, a longitudinal extension of the round arch, was the basic structural unit, and this was often lightened by 'coffering', or sunken panels built up in reverse on the wooden centring in which the concrete was poured.

The arch played an equally important role in the construction of amphitheatres, which can be seen as essentially two theatres placed end to end. At first they were made of wood, and the earliest surviving stone example is at Pompeii (*c.* 80 BC). Rome followed suit 50 years later and then achieved the climax of the form in the Flavian Amphitheatre, opened in AD 80. This astonishing building, later known as the Colosseum, which has so greatly influenced the architects of Europe, measures 189 metres by 152 metres (620 feet by 500 feet), and could accommodate about 50,000 spectators. The travertine-faced exterior, with its blend of solidity, grandeur and grace, is four storeys high in

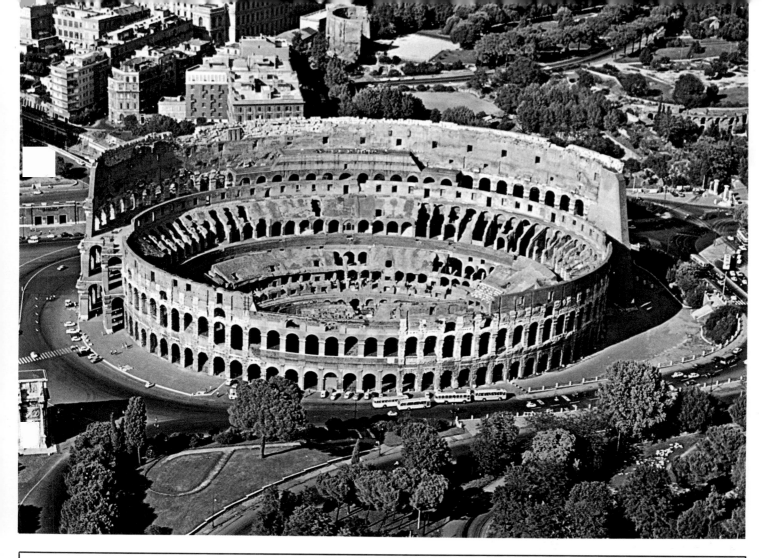

ROMAN ARCHES

It is possible to find Greek and Etruscan forerunners to the arch, the drainage channels (cuniculi) of the Etruscan states being prominent among them, but its exploitation was a Roman achievement. Nearly every Roman concrete arch (or wall) that was intended to be seen was faced with brick. Most of the bricks extended only 12 or 15 centimetres (5 or 6 inches) into the concrete behind them, but every sixth or seventh reached right through to the back, thus forming boxes which kept the concrete in position.

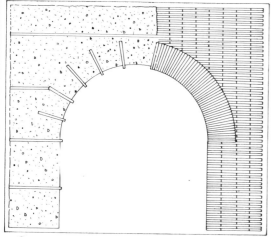

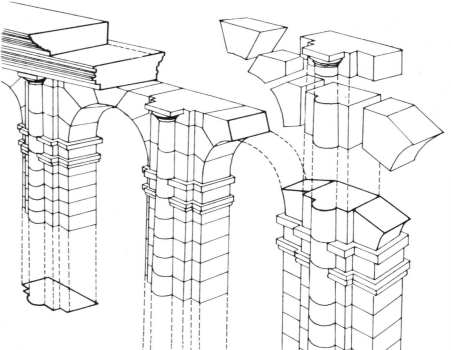

Above: Diagram of the portico of the Forum Holitorium (Vegetable Market) at Rome, c.25 BC. The round arches are framed in the traditional vertical-horizontal classical entablature and (Doric) columns, which now, however, only play a decorative, non-functional part – the formula which was later to create massive masterpieces such as the Colosseum

the convex curve of the adjoining Forum of Trajan. Both buildings were designed by Apollodorus of Damascus (*d.* AD 129), one of the relatively few Roman architects whose name has become renowned. The Markets were constructed of concrete faced with brick, of which a durable, kiln-baked, flat variety, possessing great heat-resisting qualities, had now been evolved.

At their best the bricks used by the Romans were a wonderful material, responsible to a considerable extent for some of their greatest architectural successes. In Greece, until the time of Alexander the Great (356–323 BC), bricks had been unbaked and sun-dried, but thereafter baked bricks (*cocti lateres*) had come into use, reaching a high degree of excellence under the Romans, progressively increasing in thickness, and laid with great accuracy and equality of size, with very close joints. 'In some cities', reported Vitruvius, 'we may see both public works and private houses and even palaces built of brick.'

Augustus boasted that he had found a Rome of brick and left it marble: but the brick was still there underneath. Its appearance as a facing on the surface of buildings was one of the decisive innovations of Roman architecture. At first, in about 80 BC, it had been used as a frame for 'reticulate'—small facing blocks of tufa in the shape of truncated pyramids set in concrete with the square base outwards.

In the second century AD brick appears by itself on the surfaces of buildings. In the Markets of Trajan, for example, it is allowed to display its own attractive qualities, though pieces of stone, such as the Roman travertine, were added at local points to provide variety.

A further innovation had already been tried experimentally, and was now to become habitual: the centring of the vaults, into which the concrete was poured, was no longer planking to be subsequently removed, but a permanent funnel of tiles. This reduced carpentry to a minimum and thus speeded up construction.

The Markets of Trajan were the splendid forerunner of the *Gallerie* of the Italian cities of today; and their focal point was a market-hall, with two superimposed rows of six shops opening off it on either side. Measuring approximately 28 metres by 10 metres (92 feet by 32 feet), it was much smaller than its early predecessor, the Aemilian Portico, built three centuries before. On the other hand, its interior was not broken up by a con-

THE MARKETS OF TRAJAN

The Forum of Trajan (AD 100–12), designed by the imperial architect Apollodorus of Damascus, was the latest, most splendid and most complex of the Fora added to the original Forum Romanum by a number of emperors in turn. Trajan's Forum comprises an approximate rectangle 182 metres (200 yards) long and 120 metres (130 yards) wide, created by cutting back, to a considerable depth, a massive hillside including the lower slopes of the Quirinal Hill. From west to east, the Forum included the Temple of Trajan, which has now vanished; a Greek and Latin library, and, between them, Trajan's Column, which celebrated his conquest of Dacia (Rumania) and which still stands; then the apsed hall of the Basilica Ulpia with its internal colonnades; and finally the large, colonnaded open space of the Forum itself, containing, as its centre-piece a great equestrian statue of the emperor, and flanked to north and south by semi-circular recesses or exedrae. The northern exedra shaped a curved façade for the Markets of Trajan which lay beyond and above.

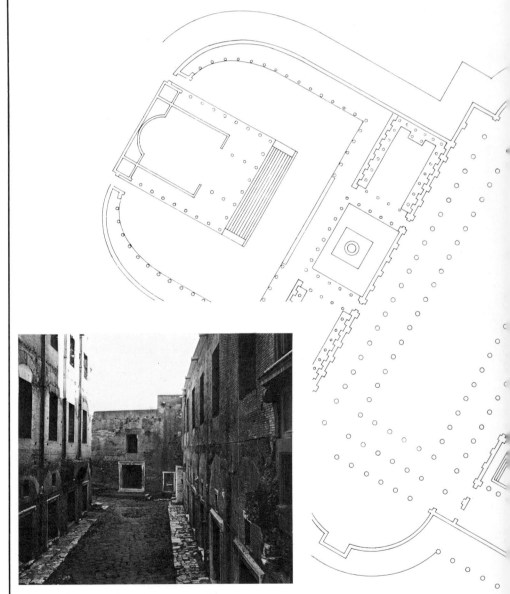

Above: The street (later Spice Street, Via Biberatica), lined with strongly built travertine-framed shop fronts – originally crowned by balconies – and flanked on the left by the three-storeyed frontage of Trajan's market-hall (at the north end of the plan); the third storey is partly restored.

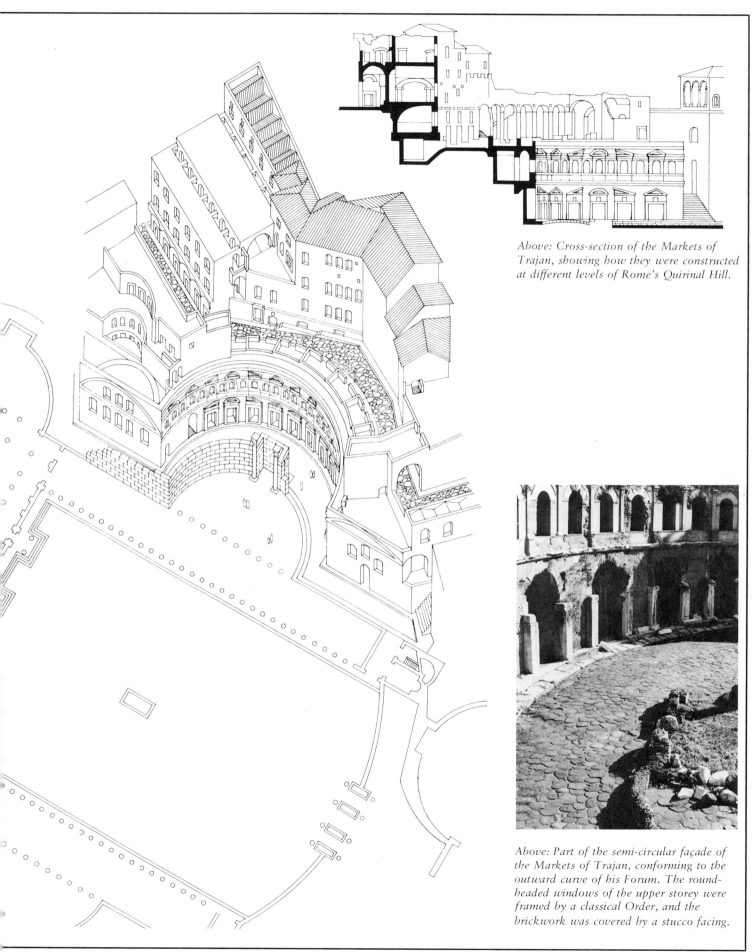

Above: Cross-section of the Markets of Trajan, showing how they were constructed at different levels of Rome's Quirinal Hill.

Above: Part of the semi-circular façade of the Markets of Trajan, conforming to the outward curve of his Forum. The round-headed windows of the upper storey were framed by a classical Order, and the brickwork was covered by a stucco facing.

glomeration of arches, but consisted of a single cross-vaulted rectangular space, reminiscent—in a more utilitarian fashion —of the great halls of the imperial baths. The same device, used during the final phases of the ancient world, was adapted to another highly characteristic sort of Roman meeting-place, the basilica.

BUILDING TYPES, SECULAR AND SACRED

The basilica had already existed, according to another formula, for half a millennium. It was a type, or rather various types, of building which served as law-court, commercial centre and social meeting-place combined. The name 'basilica' is Greek, suggesting the audience-rooms of Greek kings, and there is something of Greek peristyles and colonnaded piazzas in these Italian halls. But they are different, and architecturally original, resembling Greek temples turned inside out, with the now internal colonnades dividing the interior into a nave and aisles. The columns were surmounted by architraves and supported brick walls rising to a flat wooden roof over the nave; these walls could be perforated by windows, since the roofs over the aisles were lower. The first known basilica, built at Rome by Cato the elder in 184 BC, has not survived; the earliest extant example is at Pompeii (c. 120 BC). In later times, the best known

Top: The Basilica at Pompeii, which would have been the centre of the city's commercial and judicial life, dates back to the second century AD.

Above: The temple at Nemausus (Nîmes) in southern France, known as the Maison Carrée. It was built in the time of Augustus between 19–12 BC and AD 1–2.

Right above: A reconstruction of the Basilica of Maxentius (or Constantine), built in Rome in AD 306–12. The huge vaults were directly carried by the concrete piers.

Right below: The three surviving terminal spans of the shorter nave and aisles of the Basilica of Maxentius. The vaults are deeply coffered.

were the Julian and Aemilian basilicas and the Basilica of Trajan. All were built in Rome, and all three adjoined fora, the first two flanking the Forum Romanum, and the last the Forum of Trajan, as did their smaller counterparts in provincial towns, such as Lepcis Magna.

The use of concrete had substituted arches and arcades for the columns of the earliest basilicas; there were long rows of these arches, yet still the roofs were not vaulted but were flat and made of timber.

At the very end of the pagan epoch, however, the architect of the mighty Basilica of Maxentius (AD 306–312), or the architect who then altered and completed it under Constantine the Great, made full use of the properties of concrete. The interior nave and aisles were divided into only three huge bays, supporting the roof, now vaulted, on four massive concrete-covered piers—a great contrast to the 74 columns of the Basilica Julia, which had only been one-third as large. Such a building was rather like one of the great bath-halls seen detached and in isolation.

And even today, after earthquakes and plunderings, the three immense terminal spans of the shorter sides of this Basilica Nova, as it was justly called, still stand, although the columns which adorned them, but which were no part of the essential structure, have vanished.

This was the grandest of the secular meeting-places of the Empire, capable of receiving under its vaulted roof a large swathe of the population. But a pre-eminent social purpose was also served by the temples of the gods. The usual Roman temple, though sharing with its Greek models their traditional post-and-lintel vertical and horizontal column and architrave, nevertheless differed from it in essential respects because of variants introduced by the Etruscans, from whom Rome had originally learnt about such constructions. In particular, the Etruscan and Roman temple generally stood on a foundation or podium some three metres (ten feet) high. It did not face outwards on all four sides like Greek temples, but had a strong frontal emphasis, the façade displaying a much deeper columnar porch. It was deliberately designed to command a throng of people standing below and in front of it, whether for religious rites or for public secular speeches delivered from its lofty podium.

But the invention of concrete, and then the evolution of its imaginative use during

principally thought of as places to house the cult-statue of a god or goddess, and not as centres for congregational worship. But the Pantheon was a building for people to assemble in; and the unequalled cupola, which was adorned by stars to represent heaven, with its central light as the sun, was meant for them to gaze at while standing at worship.

The huge rectangular temples of Jupiter and Dionysus-Bacchus at Heliopolis (Baalbek in Lebanon) carry the tendency further, especially the latter, which dates from the late second century AD. Its lavishly ornate, flat-roofed interior is exceptionally well preserved; it terminates in flights of stairs ascending to a canopied altar platform occupying the whole of the far end of the building. This reminds us that there had been one sort of Greek shrine which, unlike the others, had envisaged the thronging of large congregations: it was the type of shrine dedicated to the secret, theatrical performance of Mysteries, in honour especially of Demeter and Dionysus-Bacchus. And it was to Dionysus that this Baalbek temple was dedicated, its platform being employed to stage his Mysteries, and to enable the god to receive his worshippers in audience.

Christian churches were to dominate the next phase of Roman social architecture. When Constantine the Great (AD 306–337), for reasons that have been endlessly discussed, converted the Empire from paganism to Christianity, he housed the new state religion with spectacular lavishness, devoting the greatest architects and engineers of the day to its needs. He had many pagan models to draw upon,

the first and second centuries AD, assisted the development of a new sort of temple that was centralized and circular. Round temples were nothing new—indeed the Temple of Vesta in the Forum was of the remotest antiquity, owing its shape to primitive reed-and-wattle huts. But concrete made it possible to erect circular temples of revolutionary size and design, exemplified above all by the Pantheon. In its present form it dates from a reconstruction by Hadrian (AD 117–138) and, despite the usual plunderings of its external surfaces throughout the ages, it still remains substantially intact today. Behind a huge colonnaded portico is a central shrine soaring up to a dome, 43.5 metres (142 feet) in height and of a similar width, which has gained the admiration of the centuries. Beneath a central opening just over 8 metres (27 feet) wide, the interior

wall, constructed of brick-faced concrete 6 metres (20 feet) thick, contains rectangular and semi-circular recesses and vaulted niches which demonstrate that the Romans were at last feeling able to lighten their concrete structures with complete confidence. This confidence is also shown by the five ranges of coffering inserted in the dome, which was so strong that it successfully survived even the removal of its gilded bronze roof tiles in AD 663.

The Pantheon has been described as perhaps the first major monument ever to be composed *as an interior*: concrete had created an architecture in which the decisive factor was no longer the solid masonry but the space it enclosed. And, in the process, this revolutionary material had helped to alter religious and social customs. The temples of the Greeks, though sometimes of great size, had been

and he borrowed from them extensively, yet always kept his own novel aims in mind. Like the Basilica of Maxentius his churches were sometimes enormous, but in contrast to that building they did not have a vaulted roof depending on a few massive piers; instead they followed the style of the older type of basilica, displaying flat roofs resting upon windowed brick walls supported by rows of columns separating the nave from the lower lateral aisles. From the windows in these upper walls, a radiant light, enhanced by the

Left above: The Roman Pantheon, temple of all the Gods, was built in 27–25 BC by Marcus Agrippa, and completely rebuilt by Hadrian.

Left below: Marble relief of a circular Temple of Vesta, possibly Augustus' temple on the Palatine Hill, which he set up in competitive imitation of her hallowed temple beside the Forum in Rome.

Above centre: View through ornate entrance-frames into the opulent interior of the Temple of Dionysus-Bacchus at Heliopolis (Baalbek in Lebanon), built c.AD 150. It was later turned into a Christian church, probably by the Emperor Theodosius I (AD 379–95).

Above right: Reconstruction of the porch of the Temple of Bacchus at Heliopolis.

rich jewel-like decoration of the buildings, descended upon the holy shadow below. The rising sun fell on the celebrant at the east end as he stood in front of the canopied altar facing the congregation, while the long row of columns formed an irresistible tide drawing the eye in the same direction. These were features reminiscent of the Temple of Bacchus at Baalbek, but Constantine's formula presented them more dramatically. There is nothing to be seen today of the great Constantinian basilicas at Rome or at his newly founded city, Constantinople, since they were too holy to escape subsequent rebuilding; and his churches of the other, centralized type at Constantinople, Jerusalem and Antioch in Syria, have likewise disappeared. But it was with these buildings that the long tradition of creating churches to accommodate great masses of people began.

HOUSING IN TOWN AND COUNTRY

From the viewpoint of the community, the famous mansions of Pompeii and Herculaneum, built round *atria* and peristyles, are of secondary importance since they housed only single families with their dependants, though in their later days, shortly before their destruction by Vesuvius (AD 79), some of the houses were divided up. In the light of recent excavations and research much more can now

be said about the poorest accommodation in these same cities, but the best place for discovering how the not-so-rich lived is Rome's harbour city, Ostia, where extensive remains of large tenements or apartment buildings can still be seen. Such multi-storeyed structures, of timber framing and plaster infill, had also been a feature of the capital since the middle Republic, and an evil reputation had been gained by some of them for their jerry-built, ugly, insanitary construction by unscrupulous speculators. Noise was terrible, collapses were frequent, and fire-risks grave. It remained for Nero, after the Great Fire of Rome (AD 64), to regularize their construction on sound lines—though poets like Juvenal and Martial still continued to complain of the squalor of the unreformed tenements. Nevertheless, by the end of the second century AD the residential blocks of Rome, outnumbering private houses by more than twenty-five to one along the 21 kilometres (13 miles) of colonnaded streets, must have been an enormous improvement over earlier times.

We can get a good idea of what these apartments were like by studying their remains at second-century Roman Ostia. It is evident that they were normally four and sometimes five storeys high, thus keeping within Trajan's limitation of the height of such buildings to 60 Roman feet—reduced from the limit of just over 70 Roman feet imposed by Augustus.

They were built of concrete-cored brick, though, in addition to the use of stone to adorn doorways and windows, details were sometimes picked out with vermilion paint. The exteriors also displayed balconies or continuous terraces, resting on projecting timber or stone corbels. Roofs were generally sloping and tiled, though occasionally flat and terraced. The apartments, sometimes shared by more than one family, often consisted of five or six rooms, with the largest room at the end, served by a corridor overlooking the street. Staircases of travertine or brick, with wooden treads, ascended to each apartment individually, either from the street (between ground-floor shops) or from interior courtyards. To our eyes these residences display a curious contrast between gracious living and discomfort. On the one hand, walls and ceilings might be elegantly painted, and floors covered with tasteful mosaics, yet although glass was known and employed in the public baths most of the windows of these private apartments were not glazed. While it is true that fragments of selenite panes have been found, they were exceptional, and elsewhere wooden shutters were the only window covers. Moreover, furniture, as usual in the ancient world, was sparse; structural heating did not exist, so that portable braziers were necessary; and

although by this time water supplies were piped to many private houses, they did not reach these apartment blocks. Sometimes, however, a group of them shared a common bath-house, as well as a garden.

About rural dwellings, we naturally have less information, at least for the vast majority of the population, since they lived in houses or hovels made of mud. But we are better informed about farming accommodation, domestic and agricultural alike, since many remains have survived of the large rural villas (*villae rusticae*) which combined residential quarters for the landowner with extensive farming operations. The Bay of Naples, in the first centuries BC and AD, was thickly clustered with such complexes. We can even detect on occasion the accommodation reserved for slaves: for example, at the villa believed to have belonged to Augustus' disgraced grandson, Agrippa Postumus, at Boscotrecase near Pompeii, excavations have revealed a slave-barracks of 18 small rooms and a prison-cell with stocks. Early in the second century AD, however, in describing his own villa at Laurentum in Latium the younger Pliny wrote more encouragingly about its rooms 'which are kept for the use of my slaves and ex-slaves, but most of them are quite presentable enough to receive guests'.

These large and partly residential farm-

complexes abounded all over the Empire, especially in the west. Llantwit-Major in South Glamorgan is an interesting example, in which the original timber buildings (*c.* AD 180) were superseded at the end of the following century by stone constructions, loosely grouped round two courtyards. Adjacent to the manor house was an aisled structure accommodating the farm-hands, animals and workshops. When the owners abandoned the main residence in about AD 350, it gradually disintegrated, but the farm-hands continued to occupy the aisled buildings for another 50 years.

Yet this was the very time when, in other parts of the Western Empire which still resisted the Germanic invasions, the *villa rustica* had attained a new and formidable apogee, owing to conditions which foreshadowed future feudal society. The late fourth and fifth centuries AD were a period when life in the Western Empire for the agricultural poor, who had always been depressed, was becoming unendurable. Ravaging raiders and immigrants were breaking down the old frontiers of Rhine and Danube for ever. The appalling oppressions of imperial tax collectors, seeking vainly and often corruptly to raise funds for armies, which nevertheless failed to hold the imperial defences, were even worse. As a result the destitute rural poor fled to the large estates, whose land-

Left: The summer dining-room of the House of the Neptune Mosaic at Herculaneum, Italy. Neptune and Salacia (Amphitrite) appear on the mosaic on the right. The niches in the grotto at the end are faced with mosaics of deer chased by hounds. Mosaics started to appear on walls as well as on floors in the first century AD.

Right: Reconstruction of middle-class housing, at Ostia, the port of Rome.

Below: The apartment 'House of Diana' at Ostia, second century AD. Brickwork was no longer concealed beneath marble or stucco façades.

owners gave them a measure of safety in return for a share of the fruits of their labours, paid in cash, or kind, or personal service, or in a combination of all three. The loss of their independence was confirmed when the landowners, in collusion with the government, forbade them or their children ever to move away again. They had become not exactly slaves (slavery still existed, though it was now economically less important), but medieval serfs. 'The poor', declared Salvian (c. AD 400—after 470), presbyter of Massilia (Marseille), 'surrender to the rich.'

Floor mosaics from rich houses in Tunisia illustrate the social emergency by depicting these heavily fortified mansions, under whose protection men and women sought refuge. At Thabraca we see a great building with a closed lower storey and towers. The Burgus Julius, shown in a mosaic at Carthage, surrounded by pictures of the tenants bringing produce to

Left above: Mosaic of late imperial times from Thabraca (Tabarka in Tunisia), showing a massive fortified residence. The arches between the two towers belong to an interior courtyard, seen in perspective.

Left below: The villa and dependencies of Llantwit-Major, south Wales, c.AD 300. At the bottom left is a basilica-barn to accommodate farm hands and animals.

Above: Relief of a walled Italian hilltown found near the Fucine Lake, east of Rome.

Below: Fourth-century mosaic from Carthage showing the great North African mansion of Julius, the sort of battlemented country palace into which destitute peasantry flocked for refuge and work. Around the buildings are scenes displaying the daily occupations of the lord and lady of the house.

their master and mistress, has a fine loggia on the first floor, a massive ground floor with an arched entrance and two high towers at the corners. The Moorish chieftain Firmus, we are informed, had a fortified villa at Zammac 'like a city', and the poet Sidonius Apollinaris (c. AD 430–480) tells us of the Burgus of Leontius, at the confluence of Dordogne and Garonne, of which the circuit of towered walls and battlements was impregnable to engines of war. The remains of another such fortified mansion exist at Thésée near Tours.

Such was the last function of the Roman architects of antiquity: to build massive castles in which refugees could survive under the lordship of their patrons. This architectural task shared one common feature with all previous feats of Roman engineering and architecture. Like Roman military organization, they all displayed a remarkable mastery in the handling of large bodies of people—a keynote in the creation of roads, fora, aqueducts, markets, basilicas, temples, apartment buildings and castles. This attention to the needs of human beings in the mass—an achievement which would earn warm approval in many socialist circles today—is paradoxical since the Romans, though community minded, were politically far from socialistic. But, in essence, their thought was concerned with humanity in large concourses, and it was in this field that the most characteristic, unequalled triumphs of their marvellous architects and engineers are to be found.

THE MIDDLE AGES

The idea of a medieval period, a Middle Age, was postulated by Renaissance historians, who saw the millennium between the death of Late Antiquity and their own classical revival as a dark, barbaric age between two periods of enlightenment. Although historical study remains in the same broad divisions, the medieval world is now recognized as the bridge between the ancient world and the emergence of modern Europe.

The architecture of this period in the West is essentially that of the Christian church. Born into the classical culture round the shores of the Mediterranean which looked to Rome as *caput mundi* (head of the world), by the end of the Middle Ages it had become the architecture of northern Europe. In the meantime, the unified late antique world had dissolved and regrouped into three power blocks: Western Europe, the Byzantine Empire of the eastern Mediterranean, and the Islamic Empire of the Middle East, North Africa and Spain.

Our knowledge of medieval architecture comes mainly from churches. There are several reasons for this. As the Middle Ages proceeded the Church became ever more powerful, a power manifest in the splendid buildings which dwarfed the hovels of the lay population. With a few exceptions, the church was the most important building in the community. Built of stone, its chances of survival were greater, and it received lavish attention as the symbol of the afterlife towards which people were being directed. Very little secular architecture has survived, and although quite a lot is known of town and village life, much of its physical setting has been destroyed, while the remaining buildings have often been restored beyond recognition of their original characteristics.

Medieval culture was aristocratic, confined to the relatively small circle of lay magnates and the higher clergy in whom real power resided. The state as understood today did not exist; there were very few hospitals and schools, and these were provided by the Church. The ruler built what he wanted, usually palaces and hunting lodges, and founded churches from various motives, to expiate sin, to express his piety and wealth, or for propaganda in the service of royalty.

Canterbury Cathedral, Bell Harry tower by John Wastell, 1493–1500. The central tower was the final addition to Canterbury Cathedral after three centuries of building. The view upwards into the lantern shows Wastell's masterly handling of the fan vault, the late medieval vault type developed in England.

Feudal society developed with varying degrees of depth and permanence until the thirteenth century when new classes of urban merchants, artisans and rural landed gentry established themselves, and peasants became more independent and socially mobile. Although the aristocracy continued to lead a peripatetic existence, travelling between their estates to administer their lands and supply themselves with food, government became more centralized. The aristocracy (lay and ecclesiastical), followed by the gentry and merchants, founded churches and chapels, and built themselves fine houses. The monasteries, presumably with faith in the permanence of their institution, built solid living quarters for the monks, and impressive barns and parish churches in the villages which they owned. Many of these churches and some of the houses and barns have survived. The dwellings of the urban poor and rural peasants, the largely unrecorded mass, have not survived. Excavation suggests that they were small, ill-built and made of timber. Architecturally, all the interest and the supply of work centred on the wealthier classes.

Although stone castles survive from the eleventh century, large, well-appointed houses were not built before the fourteenth century and architectural effort, other than that concerned with tactics of warfare, was concentrated in church buildings, the medium through which all architectural innovations were made.

The all-important element of propaganda was present in the first monumental Christian architecture, that of Constantine, who inaugurated it in the great cities of the Empire after the Peace of the Church in AD 313. Christian worship had hitherto taken place in community houses such as that of Dura-Europos in Syria, which resembled ordinary domestic dwellings. Christian architecture is largely concerned with the commemoration of Jesus Christ, martyrs and saints, and the dead in general, and in the fourth century two types of building were commonly used, both based on traditional Roman types.

For meeting halls, where large congregations buried and commemorated the dead, they chose the symbol of Roman officialdom, the aisled basilica. These large halls with apses and wooden roofs were usually built in a cemetery outside the walls; they were built all round the Mediterranean shores and north of the Alps at Trier and they survive in several places.

Holy Places connected with the story of Christ and the site of a martyrdom were marked by vaulted, centralized buildings based on Roman funerary monuments. *Martyria* were built in conjunction with basilicas, either attached by a corridor or linked more directly. The Church of the Nativity at Bethlehem, one of a series of buildings erected by Constantine in Palestine, was begun about AD 326 with an atrium, or courtyard, for assembly, a basilical nave with double aisles, and an octagon enclosing the Cave of the Nativity, visible to pilgrims from a gallery.

Rome, where saints Peter and Paul had both met their deaths, was furnished with many huge commemorative basilicas, both in cemeteries and in Constantine's palace, the Lateran. On the site of St Peter's tomb Constantine founded a basilica whose plan was to have far-reaching effects on architecture. Church buildings do not simply reflect the glories of ecclesiastical power, but seek to express, both practically and symbolically, current liturgical use and religious ideas. In St Peter's the shrine was enveloped within the basilica, the five-aisled basilical nave separated from the apse by a transept, which focused attention on the altar over the saint's tomb within a screen of columns. The functions of *martyrium* and basilica were carefully distinguished within the same building, the main altar standing in the nave; but in the sixth century Pope Gregory the Great took the logical step of moving it directly over the tomb, where it stands today. In so doing he fused the two functions of memorial and eucharist, a move which affected the planning of churches for centuries. As the head church of Western Christendom, St Peter's was exceedingly influential: other buildings were assessed by its standard.

Centralized buildings had a wider use in the eastern part of the Empire, although they are found wherever Roman cultural traditions were strong. The early-fifth-century baptisteries of Frejus and Albenga have a polygonal plan with central cupola, and the old cathedral of St Gereon at Cologne was built on the foundations of

Left: Early Christian basilica of St Peter, built by Constantine in Rome, c.333. The leading church of western Christendom, it was the first basilica to have a transept, which divided the nave from the apse, beneath which was the saint's shrine. The transept also made space for pilgrims. The five-aisled nave was designed for burials. The columns of the main arcade supported an architrave, a feature revived several centuries later in some Carolingian churches. Like all early basilicas, St Peter's had a wooden roof.

A RECONSTRUCTION OF THE CHURCH OF THE NATIVITY: AN EARLY CHRISTIAN BASILICA

For large congregations, the early Christians adopted the Roman aisled hall with an apse. They were built all over the Empire from Germany to North Africa and as time went on baptisteries and administrative buildings were attached. Constantine built a series of basilicas in Palestine to mark the Holy Places, and in Rome to mark the sites of martyrdom of Sts Peter and Paul. With these, and many others, came to be associated the centrally-planned *martyrium*, which marked the actual spot, the basilica being built to hold the congregation. The church of the Nativity in Bethlehem (right) is a combined basilica and *martyrium*. Plans varied regionally according to the needs of local ritual. They were usually preceded by an *atrium* or courtyard, and had three or more aisles. The elevation was flat and unarticulated, with columns supporting either an architrave or an arcade, a middle section of wall for decoration, and a clerestory above. The basilica has remained the basis of most church design to the present day.

Left: Church of the Nativity, Bethlehem, today. The antique columns survive from the original church. The church itself was rebuilt by Emperor Justinian in the sixth century.

Above: Church of the Nativity, reconstructed as it was in the fourth century. The atrium led to the basilica, which was connected to the octagonal martyrium, the centrally-planned structure built over the Cave of the Nativity. The atrium and five aisles allowed room for crowds of pilgrims.

an oval-shaped Roman building; but the basilica was to become the usual type for the west.

At Constantinople, the new centre of the Empire, the relationship of Church and Empire was most clearly seen. Christianity was now the official religion of the Empire, and the Church adopted the iconography and symbolism of Imperial ideas. The centralized ground-plan, associated with throne rooms, itself had specific connota-tions of empire. The patrons of the early churches were all members of the Imperial family, and heaven was invested with all the Imperial hierarchy of the secular world: God was the celestial emperor, the bishop his representative on earth, before whom the liturgy was performed in vest-ments of Imperial type and colour. Con-stantine built the church of the Holy Apostles in Constantinople as his personal mausoleum, where his body would lie amid the saints. Although the role of the Church was destined to change over the next 800 years from a reflection of Im-perial power to a force which opposed and dominated the secular (Imperial) power, great men would always wish to lie close to the saints, and the ideas behind the foundation of many medieval churches originated with Constantine.

The fourth and fifth centuries saw the division of the Empire into East and West and the adoption of Christianity as a mass religion in the Mediterranean cities. Here the power of the bishops became absolute, reflected in the conglomeration of administrative buildings and hospices round the basilicas, while the huge size of the baptistries testifies to mass baptism. The peaceful, prosperous world of late antiquity was as yet undisturbed by the migration of barbarian tribes into Italy, the Balkans and Western Europe, which occurred from the late fourth century onwards.

Most barbarians became Christians, albeit heretical Arians, preferring the easier belief in Christ as subordinate to God the Father. By the late fifth century the Western Empire, including Italy, was ruled by barbarian kings who owed theoretical allegiance to Constantinople. The Vandal chief Odoacer chose the Adriatic seaport of Ravenna as his capital after he sacked Rome in 476, thus shifting the centre of power in Italy northwards; it remained there through the conquest of Theodoric the Ostrogoth in 493, and the reconquest by Emperor Justinian in 526. Although the barbarian kings founded some of the earliest in the series of magnificent church buildings in Ravenna, their Arianism made for uneasy relations with the Catholic Church, to which they were unacceptable—a Church now increasingly abandoned by the hierarchy in Constantinople.

The barbarian leaders were excluded by their beliefs from the late classical culture they longed to share, but one small event was significant for the future: in 503 Clovis, King of the Franks, was converted to Catholicism. The Franks, adherents to the 'true' religion and placed far north of the Alps, posing no threat to the south, were left to develop their power base.

The Empire was reunited under Justinian (527–65), but the scarcity of Justinianic architecture in the West reflects Europe's position on the fringe of the real Empire. To see the embodiment of contemporary ideas of Christianity and kingship we look to Constantinople, and the great church dedicated to the 'holy wisdom', Hagia Sophia.

Hagia Sophia, rebuilt after Justinian's victory in the Nike Riot of 532, combined Greek mathematical ideas with Roman Imperial grandeur. The architects, who were engineers and mathematicians, turned the vaulted centralized type of funerary building into the accepted form for a church. The great dome, floating above a square within a rectangle, with semidomes and conches opening from the arches beneath, had profound effects on later architecture, both Christian and Moslem, in the eastern Mediterranean. The domed, centrally planned building became one of the most popular church types, and in physical terms the separation of the Eastern and Western Churches is seen most clearly in the contrast of these Eastern buildings and Western basilicas.

Like later Gothic buildings, Hagia Sophia is inward looking, sacrificing the exterior to interior effects. But in contrast to the axial viewing line of a basilica, there is deliberate concentration on the central square. Here, in the nave, occurred the processions of clergy and emperor, the public part of the Mass, witnessed by the laity crowded into the aisles and gallery. The dome, representing the vault of heaven, presided over the interaction of priest and emperor in their mission to uphold the Christian Empire.

The building, decorated sumptuously with mosaic and marble from the nearby Proconnesian islands, symbolized the heavenly kingdom, and it is easy to believe the story that when Justinian saw the finished church he exclaimed: 'Solomon, I have outdone thee!'

Left: The church of Hagia Sophia, Istanbul, built 532–7. The huge dome over the central square had great influence on the architecture of the Moslem and eastern Christian worlds. The original dome, designed with a flatter profile by Anthemius of Tralles and Isidore of Miletus, collapsed in 558 and was replaced by a steeper one. The plan of the church – a rectangle within a square – and the elevation of arched storeys and subsidiary domes and conches reveal a continuous sequence of spaces enhanced by the glittering decoration of mosaic and white marble.

Above: San Vitale, Ravenna, Italy, built c.530–48 under Imperial patronage and richly decorated with Byzantine marble and mosaics. The centrally-planned building has eight sides opening into tall niches, with a projecting choir chapel at the east. Its shape and arrangement of internal galleries probably influenced the later design of Charlemagne's chapel at Aachen.

Although the plan of Hagia Sophia, an extended octagon with an outer shell, had already appeared in Hagios Sergios and Hagios Bakhos, and most of its building techniques were familiar from Roman times, Justinian's buildings are a new departure, and the dome had a long future. St John at Ephesus used the plan of domes over a basilica from the Holy Apostles, and Hagia Irene at Constantinople has a large dome over the crossing with a smaller one over the nave.

As a result of Justinian's reconquest of Italy orthodoxy was established in Ravenna, where the new church of San Vitale (c. 530–48) was in appearance an outpost of the Imperial Court on Italian soil. Built of long, thin bricks, local imitations of the Constantinopolitan type, it has rich mosaic decoration and capitals from the Proconnesian workshops. It is a vaulted octagon on eight piers with arches opening into gigantic niches, with an ambulatory surrounding the whole.

During the century after Justinian's death, the Lombard invasion of Italy and the Arab conquest of Syria, Egypt and North Africa shattered the fragile unity of the Empire, and confined the effective power of Constantinople to the Aegean area, although it still claimed the Empire of the West. The Byzantine Empire, jolted by the sudden deprivation of wealth, population and the spiritual succour of the Holy Places, entered a disjointed period of reappraisal, visibly manifest in the Iconoclastic movement, which held sway for long periods between 726 and 842. The Arab overthrow of Visigothic Spain in 711 turned Spain towards Africa and the Arab world, and although the Moslems preserved classical learning and culture to the ultimate benefit of the Christian West, their treatment of it was so different that the classical unity of the Mediterranean was broken for ever.

In the West the Church, led by such men as Pope Gregory the Great (589–603), began to organize itself from Rome, spreading the idea of Eternal Rome, the

Holy City, into northern lands. Aided by the bishops, the Church acted through the lay rulers, who in turn infiltrated the higher ranks of the clergy, so that Church and government not only worked together but were related by ties of blood. At the defeat of Spain the kingdom of the Franks had no rivals in the West. With the emergence of this people, whose culture was entirely non-classical, on to a political scene in which the Roman hegemony was being replaced by smaller power blocks, medieval Europe began to form and crystallize.

Very little architecture of the Merovingian kingdom of the Franks has survived. The Frankish royal house is known to have founded many centres of pilgrimage and personal mausolea. Here Gallo-Roman traditions remained strong, and just as social organization was still based on the Gallo-Roman villa system, so did Merovingian basilicas follow the traditional pattern. For normal domestic purposes timber-framed buildings sufficed,

but for churches patrons turned to masons trained to build in the appropriate (i.e. 'Roman') style.

The sixth-century church of St Pierre at Vienne and possibly St Martin at Tours, the shrine of the Frankish national saint, were timber-roofed basilicas without aisles, their walls lined with a row of superimposed columns giving a suitably Roman appearance. The tradition remained strong into the seventh century: the baptistry of St Jean at Poitiers has terracotta insets and ornamental friezes typical of late Roman art.

Lesser churches were simple rectangular boxes, often abutted by covered porches—*porticus*—which contained the burials of illustrious people. They did not normally open directly to the main building, nor were they used as chapels until at a later date an altar might be placed beside an especially venerated tomb. Sometimes, as at St Martin at Autun, symbolic purpose defied available skill: here a tower over the altar, like the drum of a dome, while

giving protection against fire, was also intended to symbolize, no less powerfully than the dome of Hagia Sophia, the vault of Heaven.

Porticus appear on the seventh-century churches in Kent, founded immediately after the arrival of St Augustine's mission in 597 and possibly built by Frankish masons. The masonry of these small boxes was generally crude, but some attempt was made to introduce felicitous designs. Reculver (*c.* 669) had an apse with a polygonal exterior, and several, including Reculver and the surviving church at Bradwell, Essex, had a triple arcade between nave and sanctuary carried on properly worked columns.

Where a church could be built on Romano-British remains, the achievement was less modest; according to Bede, the cathedral church at Canterbury had aisles to the nave, and a crypt, which Eadmer, writing in the twelfth century, compared to that of St Peter's, Rome. Whatever it really looked like it was evidently on a

Left: St Pierre, Vienne, France, sixth century. For important churches, Merovingian builders took over the legacy of Roman building traditions. Here the side walls of the basilica are articulated with superimposed columns, a feature possibly used in the pilgrimage church of St Martin, Tours.

Right: All Saints, Brixworth, England, date uncertain, possibly eighth century. The largest surviving monastery church of the early Saxon period, it has an apse, choir, nave and western porch, later made into a tower. The lower arches originally led into partially walled-off aisles, neither true aisles nor true porticus. The windows and piers were arched with Roman brick. The sanctuary has an early crypt which was a passage round the apse. It was reached through doors (now blocked up) which allowed pilgrims access to the shrine.

Below: Merovingian cemetery chapel, Jouarre, France, c.630. The later groin vaults are supported on re-used antique columns, with capitals from quarries in Aquitaine. The chapel may originally have been vaulted with barrel vaults set on architraves. The tombs of the first abbesses are still in place.

different scale from the other Kentish churches, more comparable to the church at Brixworth, and perhaps to the sumptuous buildings put up in Northumbria after the Synod of Whitby in 663.

There Bishop Wilfrid of Ripon had persuaded the King of Northumbria to accept the Roman methods of calculating the date of Easter, and the established Irish rite was supplanted by that of Rome. It was followed by a spate of church building in stone. St Wilfrid seems to have deliberately used current Roman ideas in the subterranean *confessio* crypts of Hexham and Ripon, features unknown in Gaul but developed in seventh-century Rome, where the tombs of the saints in cemeteries outside the city walls were vulnerable to barbarian attack. They were brought into churches within the city, their sarcophagi inserted into small spaces dug beneath the altar. The *confessio* had a corridor allowing just enough room for the faithful to reach the tomb containing the relics.

That the churchmen of Britain and Gaul were in close touch is affirmed by Bede, who mentions journeys between Northumbria and the monasteries of the Marne valley founded by St Columbanus, of which the most famous is Jouarre, founded *c.* 630. The surviving cemetery chapel, with its original tombs, has re-used antique columns now supporting groin vaults, and capitals based on Corinthian prototypes, brought from marble quarries near the Pyrenees. The west wall is made up of *opus reticulatum*, carefully laid patterns of lozenges and hexagons in coloured stone.

Jouarre tells us something about seventh-century masons, who were evidently skilled in masonry if not engineering; and they travelled great distances, for Bede says that in the early eighth century the Pictish king asked Abbot Ceolfrid of Monkwearmouth to send him architects 'in order to build a stone church for his people in the Roman style'. The Aquitanian capitals were carved in the quarry and shipped to their destinations by sea and river, heavy commodities like stone being more easily transported by water. The art of column making had been all but lost, and columns were as far as possible reused from ancient buildings and rarely required to bear a serious load.

The finest masonry of the period is found in the churches of Spain built before the Islamic invasion. Plans are simple, vaulting is partial; but San Pedro de la Nave has beautifully worked stone combined with figured capitals and decoratively carved abaci.

CAROLINGIAN—A REVIVAL OF CHRISTIAN ROME

The eighth-century missions from Britain to the German lands by Willibrord and Boniface coincided with the increased strength of the papacy and the emergence of the Carolingian dynasty, political heirs to the Merovingian kings, and so named after the Emperor Charlemagne (768–814). Church and kingdom worked together for the extension of power and the revival of the idea of empire. The later-eighth-century Frankish rulers had conquered Italy and central Europe, and the Church assisted in government in return for the grant of land and privileges to the higher clergy, beginning a pattern which would continue for centuries. When Charle-

magne was crowned Emperor in Rome at Christmas 800 he was the first Western ruler in whom the Byzantines recognized an equal.

The *renovatio*, the revival of the idea of empire in the reign of Charlemagne, was not only a revival of the Roman Empire, but a conscious attempt to renew the Christian Empire of Constantine and the glories of fourth-century Rome, an idea whose expression was skilfully fostered by the scholar-administrators of the Court, led by Alcuin of York, Abbot of Tours, and Theodulph, Archbishop of Orleans. It was manifest equally in scholarship, the fine arts and architecture.

In Charlemagne's lifetime and beyond, patronage of all these was confined to Charlemagne himself and members of his family, many of whom had become leading abbots or bishops. In this there was direct continuity from the Merovingians, and the pattern was not destined to change in the near future.

Architecture under the Carolingians did, however, undergo a change. For the first time since late antiquity the church building, for instance St Riquier, became a monumental and imposing structure;

the two features which seem to distinguish it from its antecedents are size and a sense of organization. As far as can be judged from the scant remains, the Carolingians deliberately differentiated the parts of the building in terms of both use and appearance, especially on the exterior. In their churches they wanted both greater splendour and specific reference to the *renovatio*. We see this in the most important type of building, the monastery.

Monasticism affected most people in an Empire which now stretched from the Danube to the Pyrenees. Through it had spread much Church influence since the foundation of the first Western monastery, on the island of Lérins off the French Mediterranean coast in the early fifth century. By 585 there were 200 monastic communities south of the Loire, living to a Rule which dwelt more on the spiritual life of the individual monk than on the daily organization of the monastery. This early Western monasticism developed from the influence of Egyptian and Syrian holy men, and it spread to Ireland and thence to north Britain long before the arrival of the Roman missionaries.

After the late sixth century monasticism

ST GALL: A BENEDICTINE MONASTERY

The plan of St Gall, Switzerland, was drawn *c*.820, and is the earliest surviving architectural plan before the twelfth century. It shows a group of buildings for living, work and prayer – an idealist's plan, never built but setting a standard for others to emulate. The church is placed towards the northern edge of the site and the other buildings are set out on a grid plan round it. The conventual buildings are shut off to the south with access only to the monks' choir in the church. Farm buildings lie to west and south, accommodation for abbot, novices and guests to south and east.

changed, largely through the adoption of the Rule of St Benedict. Traditionally attributed to St Benedict of Nursia, founder of Monte Cassino (c. 529), the Rule is for communities working and praying together. The pattern of the monastic day is divided into periods of work, rest and prayer, day and night; the 'hours' vary in length according to the time of year. Far more institutional and organized than earlier Rules, its good sense, tolerance and realism commended it to Gregory the Great, whose advocacy of it hastened the decline of the older kind of monasticism practised at Lérins.

Benedictine monasticism came to Britain with Augustine and to German lands with Boniface, founder of Fulda. His missions coincided with the role monasteries were now expected to play in the community; following in the wake of forcible conversion after Charlemagne's conquests, monks remained to teach, to farm, to administer. Monasteries were efficiently run by trained Court administrators, and there is little doubt that the monastery as an institution, with groups of related buildings housing an established community, developed during this period.

Evidence suggests that by the mid-eighth century at Jumièges the church and monastic buildings were grouped round a cloister, closing off the monks' quarters from the ancillary lay dwellings within the walls of the fortified site, and the plan for St Gall (c. 820) gives a detailed picture of what was then regarded as the ideal monastery.

Benedictinism could never have spread so rapidly without Charlemagne's active

Far left: Main apse of the palace chapel of Theodulph (archbishop of Orléans, one of Charlemagne's closest advisers), Germigny-des-Prés, France. Built in 806 to a trefoil plan, the chapel was drastically restored in 1869. The mosaic, showing the Ark of the Covenant with Angels and Cherubim, survives.

Right: A capital in the church of San Pedro de la Nave, Spain, seventh century. This is a very early example of a capital sculptured with an Old Testament theme – here Daniel in the Lions' Den. The deep abacus above is carved with birds pecking grapes in a vine scroll, a traditional Christian theme. The background was hollowed out behind the figures, which are in low relief and bear traces of colour.

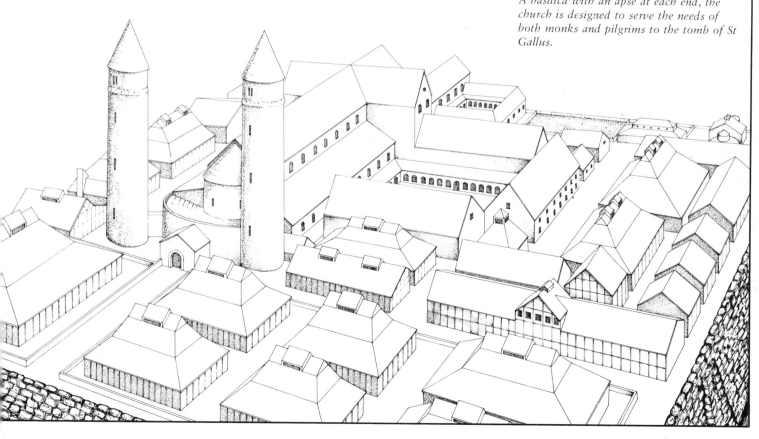

A model of St Gall, based on the plan of c.820. The rectangular site is 213 m (700 ft) long, the church the largest building on it. A basilica with an apse at each end, the church is designed to serve the needs of both monks and pilgrims to the tomb of St Gallus.

support, and that he favoured lavish ritual in a splendid setting is suggested by documents of the destroyed monastery of St Riquier. This giant monastery, more a holy city, was built in the 790s, financed by Charlemagne who spared no expense in supplying marble columns and revetments from Rome. The intended function of its 300 monks was to sing psalms in perpetual praise of God, with elaborate processions along the covered walks between the three churches on the site.

The Carolingians seem to have been trying to establish their own identity against that of the Byzantine Empire, and at the same time to reconcile their own architectural ideas with those of the *renovatio*.

In Constantinople the Iconoclastic movement, placing a ban on all religious images, had driven painters to the West; both Greek and Italian artists had come to the Court workshops at Aachen and elsewhere. There was a brief interval in Iconoclasm in the late eighth century, but the Carolingians still devoted much thought to the problem of church decoration, embodying their views in the *Libri Carolini*, a document probably compiled by Theodulph. The determination in favour of religious images resulted in large expanses of narrative painting in churches. It also asserted the West's cultural and spiritual independence.

Architecturally the Eastern and Western Empires were now quite distinct and remained so until the end of our period. The Carolingians developed certain characteristics which were peculiarly northern: they liked basilicas with choirs at each end, marked by apses, and balanced masses often flanked by towers. Cologne, on which was based the plan for St Gall, and St Riquier were of this type, which prevailed in German architecture until the twelfth century. The towers often marked altars standing over crypts, which were now being surrounded by wider passages and side rooms for lesser shrines and burials. The Torhalle, the monastery gate at Lorsch, was decorated in *opus reticulatum*.

The Torhalle also represents another vital element in Carolingian architecture. It seems to have been a deliberate attempt to re-create the arch of Constantine, the symbol of Christian victory. At first sight it scarcely resembles a Roman triumphal arch, but in the Middle Ages a copy as we understand it was seldom a close imitation of the original, more an interpretation of the idea. The Corinthian capitals at Lorsch are in fact closely based on late classical prototypes, and the inside walls of the upper room are painted with simulated classical mouldings.

The *renovatio* was expressed in other buildings: the throne rooms at the palaces of Aachen and Ingelheim were based on the *aula regia* at Trier, the most impressive surviving Roman building north of the Alps; Fulda, enlarged soon after 800, reproduced the plan of St Peter's on a slightly smaller scale, embodying in its elevation other significant details of the great basilica. The nave columns supported not arches but architraves, and the long narrow transept, in similar proportion to St Peter's, was colonnaded in the same way. The chronicler of Fulda drew attention to the atrium 'in the Roman style'. Fulda housed the tomb of St Boniface, apostle to the Germans, just as St Peter's was the resting place of the apostle to Rome; and Fulda, like St Peter's, placed the saint's tomb at the west end of the church, but where exigencies of the site demanded such departure from normal in Rome, no such conditions prevailed at Fulda.

The church at Fulda was nearly as big as St Peter's and the palace at Aachen was appreciably larger than the Lateran palace which inspired it. Both the palace chapel at Aachen and Theodulph's private chapel at Germigny-des-Prés, with its neat arrangement of apses round a central lantern, display an assured handling of the relationship of space and volume, and considerable skill with vaults. Both buildings are inspired from Italy, Aachen from San Vitale at Ravenna. Here a sixteen-

sided aisle and upper gallery surround the central octagon, whose dome contains a mosaic of Christ in Majesty. The bronze doors and other fittings are based on antique prototypes, and the throne of Charlemagne stood in the tribune gallery over the aisle whence he could witness the Mass.

This arrangement seems to have influenced the use and evolution of another characteristically Germanic feature, the westwork. These massifs, probably related to the double-ended plan, opened into the church, but stood like fortresses guarding the west end, as at Corvey, built 873–85. They could house a second choir, or a seat for the abbot; in the tenth century liturgical dramas took place there, and they were used to display relics. The westwork of the New Minster at Winchester, built on the German model, stood over the site of St Swithun's grave and probably housed his reliquary casket.

The two centuries after the death of Charlemagne saw the collapse of his Empire and its re-emergence as the Holy Roman Empire under the leadership of a Saxon noble house; and Nordic invasions devastated the coasts and river basins of France and Britain in a series of hit-and-run attacks on unfortified towns and monasteries. Some of the latter became established elsewhere: the monks of St Philibert le Grandlieu in west France fled with the relics of their saint to settle at Tournus in Burgundy. These centuries, however, also witnessed the final renunciation of Western claims by the Byzantines, the establishment of the embryo European power pattern, the spread of Christianity into central Europe, and the early development of cities based on trade.

While the cities of the Mediterranean and Italy, founded by the Greeks, Etruscans or Romans, had simply continued their existence, the less sophisticated towns of the North barely survived the departure of the Romans, and virtually ceased to exist until the ninth century. In Britain, as part of his defence against the Norsemen, Alfred established the *burhs*, primarily walled fortresses but often with a market, thus combining defence and trade. Winchester, with its palace, cathedral and mint, was also an administrative centre. *Burh* populations were small, but there is some evidence of street plans, not necessarily following the grids of their Roman predecessors; and *burhs* such as Southampton were entirely new creations. Alfred's conception of a *burh* was more sophisticated than that of the German leader, whose imitations in the Empire were fortresses without markets; but Alfred probably used his knowledge of Italy, and of the flourishing market towns of Flanders, Ghent and Bruges.

Under the Macedonian rulers of the ninth and tenth centuries the Byzantine

Empire enjoyed a degree of prosperity and civilization unattainable in the West but emulated in Moslem Spain, whose isolated Caliphate felt an affinity with Constantinople. The palaces and gardens of tenth-century Spain are thought to reflect the great palace of Constantinople; and when Caliph el-Hakim added the *mihrab* to the Great Mosque of Cordoba in the late tenth century he sent for Byzantine mosaic cubes and an artist to supervise the decoration.

Spanish prosperity may be echoed in the surviving churches of the Christian north-west, where ashlar masonry, stone vaults and articulated ground-plans are more sophisticated than any contemporary northern works. Adhering to the Visigothic rite and promulgating the cult at the supposed tomb of St James at Compostela, the Asturian people maintained their independence of Rome; and their churches belong to the local tradition established in the seventh century. Nearer the Moslem frontier Leña and Lebeña have horseshoe arches derived from Islamic buildings. Islamic decoration influenced Christian Spain throughout the Middle Ages: eleventh-century Catalan churches have details derived from the mosque at Cordoba, and the fourteenth-century stalactite vaults of the Alhambra at Granada undoubtedly influenced the delicate filigree vaulting at the cathedrals

Left: The palace chapel, Aachen, West Germany, 792–805. An octagon, with sixteen-sided ambulatory and gallery with the throne of Charlemagne. Decorated in marble and mosaics, many of the details, especially the metal-work, deliberately imitated antique or Constantinian types.

Above: Hosios Loukos monastery, Greece, mosaic of the Virgin and Child, late eleventh century. The mosaics of Christ and the saints once covered the interior.

Right: Great Mosque, Cordoba, Spain, Capella de Villaviciosa, 961–6. The double horseshoe arches are used ornamentally.

of Burgos and Segovia at the end of the period.

Renewed confidence in Constantinople after Iconoclasm developed different church plans, not all of them new. The most enduring was the cross-in-square of Our Lady of the Pharos (*c.* 860): a central dome is supported by subsidiary barrel and groin vaults, with the main cross plan contained in the square of the outside walls. There are apses at the east. The New Church (*c.* 880) was probably a cross-in-square surmounted by five domes, a type which was to enjoy immense popularity, and is seen in the West in San Marco, Venice.

The church building represented the heavenly kingdom. All over the interior were depicted, in paint or mosaic, scenes of the life of Christ, the Resurrection and representations of the saints, arranged in a scheme which varied little from one church to another. Fully developed by the twelfth century, the scheme survives in the late-eleventh-century church of Hosios Loukos in central Greece, and was used well into the seventeenth century. Churches are built on this plan in Greece today.

ROMANESQUE—CHURCH DESIGN ESTABLISHED

While Orthodox Christianity spread through Russia and the Balkans to central Europe, Catholicism spread eastward in the wake of German conquest, the line between them being finally drawn in the late tenth century when Bohemia, Poland and Hungary chose Catholicism. The German conquests enjoyed full papal support. The Saxon dynasty founded by Henry the Fowler, which was to establish the Holy Roman Empire in the late tenth century, exploited the familiar, mutually advantageous relationship with the Church.

The Holy Roman Empire was not Frankish but German, and it roughly comprised German lands and Italy. The map of Europe was beginning to settle into areas still recognizable today, although adjustments were not complete. This was the great period of German development, and it is no accident that many of the important architectural innovations were made within the Empire.

No sooner had the Empire stabilized than the balance between papacy and emperor deteriorated. Essentially a disagreement over ultimate supremacy, it was manifest in specific quarrels. The first significant victory for the papacy was the Investiture dispute of the 1070s concerning the emperor's right to appoint bishops. The Emperor was obliged publicly to yield to the brilliant reforming Pope Gregory VII, and from then on both sides were drawn ever more deeply into a feud which was to prove disastrous for each of them; but the newly won independence of the papacy was an important element in the development of the Gothic style.

houses and take them under the protection of Cluny, the movement spread very fast, reformed and new foundations together becoming independent of their secular rulers and overlords.

The Romanesque style is difficult to define and its chronological limits are vague. The so-called First Romanesque made a precocious start in north Italy and Catalonia in the ninth century, spreading through the Rhône valley and along the Rhine, both important waterways which transmitted many influences. First Romanesque buildings such as Tournus on the Rhône and the Pyrenean monastery of St Martin-du-Canigou (c. 1000) are decorated on the outside with shallow Lombard bands and hanging arches, characteristic since their first appearance at Agliate in north Italy in the ninth century. They remained in the German and Italian decorative repertory for three or four centuries. The mature style was fully developed by about 1100, becoming the accepted style for church buildings from Scandinavia and Poland to southern Italy, with marked regional variations. In the Empire it remained in current use until the thirteenth century.

Under the new Empire the tendency which had begun under Charlemagne to develop a specifically Western, Catholic architecture gathered momentum, and Western Europe was the scene of all the really profound architectural thinking. Liturgical needs and the demands of pilgrims ensured that buildings varied within an established set of conventions; and church builders were continuously pre-

Romanesque architecture developed through the reform movements which were themselves part of a renewal of hope and optimism in the tenth century. Economic recovery led to greater wealth, and while bishops such as Meinwerk of Paderborn and Bernward of Hildesheim (c. 1000) were active patrons of architecture, monasticism had, as ever, followed the conquerors eastward.

The powerful movements of Church reform began in Lotharingia and Burgundy, the two most influential monasteries being Gorze and Cluny. Cluny, founded 910, has come to symbolize all the tenth-century reform movements, many of which she absorbed. This Burgundian monastery tried anew to live the Benedictine ideal, and its strength lay in the fact that it owed allegiance only to the Pope. After Henry the Fowler had allowed Abbot Odo (926–44) to reform existing

Left above: St Martin-du-Canigou, c.1000, a typically secluded monastery in the French Pyrenees.

Left below: The interior of St Martin-du-Canigou, c.1000. It is roofed with barrel vaults, supported half-way by a transverse arch. The pressure of the tunnel-like vault precluded a clerestory.

Right: St Michael, Hildesheim, West Germany, 1001–33. In contrast to Canigou, the roof is wooden and clerestory windows are set high in the walls. Note the flat elevation and square piers regularly placed among the columns of the arcade.

Below: Sant'Abbondio, Como, Italy, c.1063–95. The window is carved in relief of vine scrolls, with spiral columns in the jamb.

occupied with the question of the appropriate form for the house of God.

Ashlar masonry was now increasingly used, protecting against fire but also symbolizing the power and confidence of a Church whose buildings now dominated the houses of the laity. The newly converted rulers of Poland and Bohemia imposed Christianity on their peoples by exploiting the cultural superiority of the new religion. In the church building itself the laity were kept separate from the priests, the former in the nave, not allowed to enter the sanctuary and choir, where the eucharist was celebrated. This was the area devoted to God and to the patron saint whose relic lay in the altar: in the northern part of the Empire only this part of the church was vaulted, the canopy-like spread of the vault setting apart as sacred the space over the altar.

The Romanesque style explored new types of plan and elevation, as well as developing such Carolingian details as towers and westworks. The arch became established as the basis of the church interior. Representing, like the vault, the grandeur of Imperial Rome, the arch was regarded as the symbol of triumph; the use of arcade and triumphal arch in the apse in Early Christian basilicas, and their subsequent acceptance by the Carolingians, provided the iconography for a church building in the tenth and eleventh centuries. To use the arch proved the continuity of Christian ideas through the centuries of dissolution after Charlemagne; and some of the earlier buildings, such as Gernrode (*c.* 961), seem to be deliberately recalling early churches. Gernrode and St Michael's, Hildesheim (*c.* 1001), are aisled basilicas with wooden ceilings over a flat elevation of three storeys: arcades of alternately round and square piers, tribune galleries over the aisles with arched openings to the nave, and clerestory windows high under the ceiling. This elevation most closely recalls such fifth-century basilicas as St Demetrios at Salonica, and may have been used to establish legitimate descent from earlier times.

Regions nearer the Mediterranean were interested in vaulting the whole church, not at first combining vaults with arched elevations. Although the increased skills of masons, which are an important element in Romanesque, may have come from study of Near Eastern buildings, vaulting techniques were inherited from the visible Roman remains.

Several First Romanesque churches in north-east Spain have barrel-vaulted naves and aisles. One such is St Martin-du-Canigou, where the three dark tunnels have no clerestory (upper windows) and demonstrate the disadvantage of the barrel: it

Above: Ste Foy, Conques, France, a late eleventh-century pilgrimage church. The choir has an ambulatory with radiating chapels, and extra chapels on the transepts to accommodate more altars. The separate elements are assembled in a carefully balanced composition.

Left: The cathedral complex at Pisa, late eleventh century onwards. Built to celebrate a famous victory, the cathedral, separate bell-tower, round baptistry and cemetery (Campo Santo), were planned as a coherent group. The arcaded style of the tower, church and baptistry is typical of Romanesque architecture in that part of northern Italy. The cathedral has apses on the transept ends and a dome over the crossing.

Far right: Ely Cathedral, England, nave, early twelfth century. The Anglo-Norman elevation, with a steady rhythm of carefully defined bays, big tribune gallery and clerestory passage, was influential in the formation of the earliest Gothic style.

exerts even pressure outwards and downwards for its whole length, needing regular and frequent buttressing. At Chapaize (*c.* 1050), a Burgundian follower of the second church of Cluny, transverse arches under the vault and supported on wall shafts allow a clerestory in the upper wall. This result was achieved at Tournus by vaulting the nave in a series of barrels set at right angles to the nave on diaphragm arches; with little weight on the side walls, windows may safely be cut.

Aisles were often vaulted in groin vaults, in essence two intersecting barrels, making diagonally crossed arches with webs of stone or rubble between them. Here the arches carry the thrust of the vault to the four corners, relieving pressure on the walls and allowing greater spaces to be cut beneath.

The mature Romanesque of the late eleventh century arose from the interdependence of many ideas and forces. The Church was, naturally, the leader, but it was backed by greatly increased wealth and the patronage of individual laymen. The organization of the parish system, whereby every community had its own church and priest, was well under way by now, and had indeed been part of the method by which Christianity was imposed on central Europe.

If Church propaganda was a vital element, so was the role of the laity, whether as patrons or pilgrims. All patronage depends on wealth, and it is no coincidence that the most fertile source of ideas and art objects in the Middle Ages was the region of the Meuse, the Low Countries and Lotharingia, where the cloth towns of Arras, Ghent and Bruges were already flourishing in the late eleventh century. The prosperity of England was more fully exploited in the huge cathedrals, castles and myriad parish churches built after the Conquest undertaken with papal blessing on the pretext of Church reform, but already, before 1066, Edward the Confessor had built Westminster Abbey on the grand scale typical of the late-eleventh-century great church.

As town life became established the wealthier citizens joined the greater nobility in founding churches: York had eighty parish churches, Lucca twenty in Romanesque times. Surplus wealth was turned to building: the defeat of the Arab navy in 1062 enabled Pisa to build a new group made up of cathedral, baptistry and the famous leaning tower. The largest urban complex of the Slav world was Prague, with the two castles Hradčany

and Vyšehrad, a stone bridge over the Vltava and thirty churches, followed by Cracow with fifteen churches and the collegiate church of St Andrew, a miniature Rhineland church with two towers.

Church building could, then, be seen as a thank-offering to God, but it also ensured salvation. Monasteries were founded as personal mausolea by the greater nobility, where Masses would be sung for their souls. William the Conqueror and his wife Matilda founded twin monas-

teries at Caen to expiate the sin of their marriage within the forbidden degrees of kinship. Monasteries could also be founded for political reasons, to establish rival powers, as at Monreale in twelfth-century Sicily. In eleventh-century Germany, however, the magnificent Imperial foundations were for church reform and Imperial propaganda.

The new buildings embodied new ideas; at Limburg an der Haardt and Hersfeld (*c.* 1030) we find the beginning of the

mulgated as a form of penance and the way to salvation, the proximity of the relics purifying the sinner. Lesser shrines proliferated on the routes to Jerusalem, Rome and Compostela, and church coffers filled.

The Cluniac liturgy, involving the perpetual praise of God, was especially elaborate and the need of the monks to sing the services undisturbed had to be reconciled with the access of pilgrims to the main shrine, which was now usually not displayed in the crypt, but behind the high altar in the main church. Solutions varied: the First Romanesque plan of three apses in echelon (a main apse flanked by shorter ones) remained in favour until about 1100; Germany still preferred double-ended churches. The choir plan with the most significant future was that of the ambulatory with radiating chapels, which was adopted with full elaboration soon after 1050 in the great pilgrimage churches of France, and at Compostela. Cluny had the addition of a second transept.

Here the walkway, giving access to the main shrine, and lesser ones in the chapels, was a practical solution, and symbolically this circular pattern may have represented the *martyrium*, the centralized building over the saint's shrine; it implies acceptance of the arrangement made in St Peter's by Gregory the Great, where *martyrium* and basilica became one, and this is perhaps why, of all Romanesque ground-plans, this one endured to be adapted in the early Gothic cathedrals.

With this plan was developed the arched interior elevation leading to a barrel vault, with big tribune galleries at St Sernin, Toulouse, a clerestory but no gallery at Cluny, and, in the smaller contemporary church of St Etienne, Nevers, an elevation including both clerestory and gallery.

Romanesque churches tend to have massive walls and round-arched openings, but the enormous regional differences demonstrate the absence of any shared belief in what a church should look like. The Church had no official policy or rule. Practical demands affected planning, and the liturgies of different monastic movements seem to have influenced the placing of chapels and altars in the major churches. Beyond this, style remained regional. Even the third church at Cluny, centre of the Cluniac movement and cynosure of all eyes, had no *stylistic* influence outside Burgundy and Auvergne, where a series of octagonal lantern towers reflects the great abbey.

notion that a wall may be articulated with mouldings, pilasters at Limburg, and blind arcading at Hersfeld. By the mid-eleventh century the practice of dividing the elevation visually into bays was well-established. In the greatest Imperial foundation of all, the cathedral of Speyer, we find fully coherent interior planning.

Begun in 1030 as the Imperial mausoleum, Speyer was reconditioned for Henry IV in the late eleventh century, perhaps as a statement of Imperial power after his humiliating defeat at the hands of Gregory VII. The nave elevation already included enormous containing arches recalling the *aula regia* at Trier, and to these were added shafts with meticulously cut Corinthian capitals, supporting a groin vault, the earliest surviving groin vault over a main span. In its use of the grandest type of Roman vault, Speyer stresses the Roman legitimacy of the Imperial house.

Reminders of Rome were apparent everywhere, as Italian influence in the form of bronze doors and decorative schemes travelled north. Abbot Suger of St Denis would later try to obtain Roman columns for his new church. The late-eleventh-century church at Cluny made deliberate use of Roman motifs in its decoration to emphasize its dedication to St Peter and its sole responsibility to Rome. There is no doubt that the Rome of St Peter was still a powerful influence on people's ideas, but different circumstances led to new developments, particularly in planning.

Pilgrimage had been an important aspect of Church life since the fourth century, but in the tenth and eleventh centuries it seems to have been deliberately exploited by the Church to derive revenue from those people not rich enough to endow monasteries. Pilgrimage was pro-

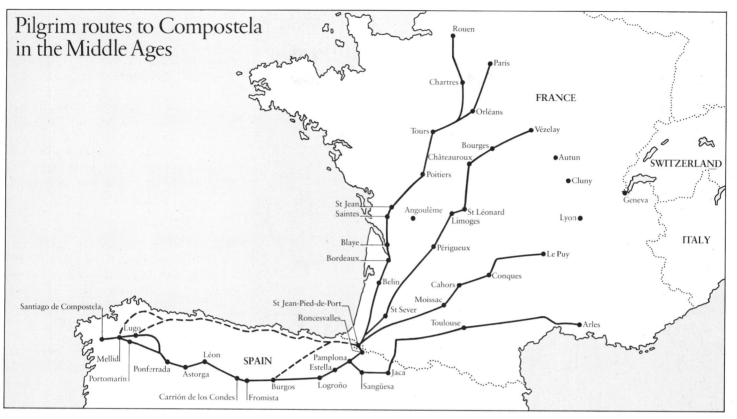

Pilgrim routes to Compostela in the Middle Ages

Far left: Santo Domingo de Silos, Spain, cloister, late eleventh century. The capitals and reliefs on the piers at the corners are among the earliest to be carved in strong relief. The pier illustrated shows a pilgrim to Compostela, with the shell of St James on his satchel. There is Mozarabic influence on the sculpture of the capitals.

Above: The pilgrim routes to Santiago de Compostela ran through the main pilgrimage centres of western, central and southern France to converge beyond the Pyrenees. Architectural and sculptural ideas were transmitted along them: the great churches at Tours, Limoges, Toulouse, Conques and Compostela had similar designs transcending local styles.

Left: Speyer Cathedral, West Germany, c.1030 and late eleventh century. The burial church of the German emperors has containing arches around the arcade and clerestory derived from the Roman basilica at Trier. The Roman connotation was further emphasized by the addition of groin vaults over the main span, making Speyer the earliest surviving fully groin-vaulted church. The short choir is raised over a groin-vaulted 'hall'-crypt, which extends beneath the choir and transepts. Behind it, to the west, is the original burial vault of the German emperors.

Left: San Miniato, Florence, finished 1062. The basilica with open rafter roof, simple two-storey elevation and diaphragm arches across the nave is a typical Italian Romanesque design. Italy also favoured choirs raised over crypts at ground level. The coloured marble decoration was popular in Tuscan Romanesque.

Below left: Autun Cathedral, France, capital, c.1130. Burgundy was particularly rich in high quality Romanesque sculpture, and the main sculptor at Autun signed his name, Gislebertus, on the west door. This capital, depicting the Flight into Egypt, shows the characteristics of his style: deep undercutting, high relief, much use of the drill for decoration, texture created by surface lines. The vigorous narrative style is found in many Burgundian churches.

Below right: St Mary, Iffley, England, west door, c.1175. This door illustrates two of the commonest motifs in English Romanesque sculpture: the zig-zag chevron ornament, and the beak-head monsters. The abstract and the grotesque were prominent features of Romanesque decoration.

Far right: San Marco, Venice, late eleventh century. Venice was in close touch with the Byzantine Empire, and the five-dome plan imitates Byzantine church design, a connection emphasized by the twelfth-century mosaics in Byzantine style which decorate the interior.

The English monastic cathedrals such as Ely and Norwich had long, squat profiles, with naves of superimposed arches under wooden roofs. Although at this stage not very competent at figure sculpture, the English indulged the new fashion for sculptured doors and arcade capitals with patterns of chevrons, and blind arcading on wall surfaces. The steady flow of Scandinavian influence into England brought with it the twisted monsters of Nordic imagination.

North Italy and the German part of the Empire had a certain amount in common: both regions used towers flanking the apse, and decorated their exteriors with open arcaded galleries, a motif found as late as the thirteenth century at Ják, Hungary. Brick was a material common to Lombardy and Holland, and Italian sculptors worked at Speyer, Lund and Esztergom.

Italy, however, had preoccupations of its own, which would ultimately remove it from the main stream of development: its churches remained barnlike basilicas of

Early Christian type, with vast expanses of plain wall for narrative paintings. Walls were also lined with coloured marbles, as at San Miniato in Florence, columns were reused from antiquity, and Italian Romanesque sculpture is, like that of Provence, indebted to its classical past, in style if not in subject matter. San Nicola at Bari has delicate curling vine scrolls carved in its door jambs, Modena has variations on the classical acanthus leaf, and everywhere copious use was made of the drill for undercutting relief sculpture.

Italy was also at this time part of the Byzantine cultural hegemony, with Byzantine mosaicists working at Venice and Sicily. On the mainland Greek artists worked at Monte Cassino and Salerno in the late eleventh century, powerfully stimulating artistic ideas, which were used both there and in twelfth-century Sicily to convey complicated Byzantine notions of kingship in the battle for supremacy between the papacy and the kings of Sicily.

The development away from the Early Christian past was a phenomenon of transalpine regions which had little or no classical tradition. In France the Romanesque churches of the twelfth century explored the achievements of their predecessors with increasingly masterful variations on the theme. All buildings, as far as possible, were highly coloured with paint and stained glass, and sculptured

decoration was mostly concentrated on doors and capitals. Always subordinate to the architectural member it adorns, the twisting ingenuity of Romanesque sculpture is matched by its wide diversity of subject matter, from mythical beasts to Bible stories.

At Vézelay the figures were flattened and twisted to keep within the shallow depth of the flat, semi-circular tympanum over the main door. Capitals were either block-shaped, as at Speyer or Canterbury, or loosely based on a Corinthian prototype, as at St Benoît-sur-Loire, with stylized acanthus leaves and volutes often transformed into animal heads. The culturally unified area of southern France and Christian Spain had cloister arcades with twin columns supporting double capitals portraying Bible stories, deeply

undercut foliage patterns and, at Santo Domingo de Silos, twinned animals caught in plant tendrils. Rarely was the sculpture systematically arranged in logical sequences: the enormous programme of sculptured capitals by Gislebertus at Autun in Burgundy mixes the Old and New Testaments and lives of the saints quite indiscriminately. Although events in the Old Testament were selected to provide parallels for those in the New Testament, the arrangement at Autun does not emphasize them.

The great carved tympana over the main doors of the pilgrimage churches, showing Christ in Majesty, the Last Judgment, or the Apocalyptic Vision, were a perpetual and awe-inspiring reminder of the afterlife, and as such bridged the gap between the everyday world and the kingdom of heaven represented by the church interior. The tympana of Moissac,

Vézelay and Autun, each a unique vision of Christ's mission on earth, followed that of Cluny, whose western tympanum of Christ in Majesty celebrated, like theirs, the triumph of the faith.

GOTHIC—FRAMEWORK FOR GLASS AND SCULPTURE

The Gothic style emerged not from a dying Romanesque, but from a vigorous tradition at its zenith—one which was not supplanted for many years. The term 'Gothic' is a Renaissance term of abuse, descriptive of a style the humanists found barbaric and anti-classical. Their contemptuous word embraces several important changes in architectural thought, and between the twelfth and sixteenth centuries there were highly significant developments.

The change of style in France from the mid-twelfth century was born in an atmosphere of intense intellectual excitement,

Above: St Pierre, Moissac, France, tympanum of south door, c.1120. Carvings of the Apocalyptic vision reminded worshippers of the next world as they entered the church building, which symbolized the Heavenly Jerusalem. This famous southern French example, based on Spanish manuscript painting, shows God the Father with the Evangelist symbols, angels and the Elders of the Apocalypse, carved in a stylized anti-classical manner.

Right: Capella Palatina, Palermo, c.1140–60. In Roger II's private chapel the Latin, Greek and Arabic cultures of Sicily were perfectly combined in the western plan, Byzantine mosaics and Siculo-Arabic wooden ceiling. The mosaics depict scenes of the life of Christ and the ceiling has decorative and figured motifs.

political development and the vastly increased dominance of the secular church. If Romanesque is monastic, to be sought in remote valleys, Early Gothic is an essentially urban style, developed in wealthy cities by the secular clergy conscious of the Church's power. Although monks such as Bernard of Clairvaux could still dominate the scene, a new era, that of the great canon lawyers, was launched, to culminate in the triumphant pontificate of Innocent III in the early thirteenth century, when the power of the papacy and the unity of the Church were at their peak.

The so-called twelfth-century Renaissance was manifest in the theology and learning of the cathedral schools of northern France, learning reflected in the great cathedrals of the early thirteenth century. The new learning owed part of its existence to the Arab cultures of Spain and Sicily. Despite the Crusades against the Infidel in the Holy Land, twelfth-century Sicily was a land in which Moslem, Orthodox and Catholic lived peaceably according to their own laws, contributing the best of their cultures to make the unique civilization which is represented in the castles and churches of Norman Sicily. The mixture is perhaps embodied in the Latin ground-plan, Greek mosaics and Siculo-Arabic stalactite ceiling of the Palatine Chapel at Palermo.

While Holy War was being preached against the Moslems, scholars such as Adelard of Bath were in Spain translating the works of Euclid, and Archbishop Raymond of Toledo presided over a school translating the Greek philosophers from Arabic to Latin. These pagan works were of course turned to Christian purposes; the problem this posed for theologians is no detailed concern of ours, but the great statements of faith to which it led and the arguments it provoked have some bearing on the appearance of developed Gothic buildings.

The new style began in the Ile de France, the small domain of the French kings round Paris. From the early twelfth century they had begun to strengthen their position against their more powerful vassals, among whom were the kings of England, who ruled over more French soil than their feudal overlords until the defeat of King John by Philip Augustus in the early thirteenth century.

The emergence of France on to the European political stage is an essential element in the history of Gothic architecture. The papacy, now free of Imperial domination, found in the French kings

valuable allies against the Empire and Sicily, and such was the power of the Church that the backing of the papacy pushed the French kings into the limelight. From now on the Empire, ungovernable and entangled in intrigues against the pope and the Byzantines, began to fade. England, though powerful enough in her way, was peripheral. As France became politically dominant, so too did she establish cultural hegemony.

It is not surprising, therefore, that all serious architectural experiment and achievement should take place in France. For all but a period in the fourteenth century, France was now the centre of developments, and other countries designed buildings with France perpetually in mind. In the later twelfth and early thirteenth centuries this was part of France's relationship with the papacy and with learning: if the early Gothic cathedrals represent a

triumph of engineering techniques, these techniques were evolved in the service of new ideas about the appearance of a church, and new assertions about the Church's role.

The Gothic style is generally held to begin with the rebuilding of St Denis in the 1140s, and while the same ideas were explored in one or two contemporary buildings, there is good reason to acknowledge the importance of the royal abbey. Suger (1081–1151), Abbot of St Denis, who left an account of the building, was one of the few medieval patrons to have given an idea of what he wanted in a building. Thus we know what the building represented in Suger's mind, and the problems the designer was asked to tackle.

Suger believed in the transcendental power of light and colour, following the ideas of the third-century pagan, Dionysus the Areopagite, whose identity was happily fused with that of the patron saint of Paris. This belief led him to require large windows for stained glass. At the same time adequate circulation was needed on feast days for pilgrims to the shrine, as the old Carolingian building was too small.

The solution to these problems involved the use of devices known to Romanesque builders but hitherto unexploited: the pointed arch and the rib vault. The rib vault, a groin vault with the crossed arches exposed on the under surface, had been used since the late eleventh century in north Italy, Durham and Picardy. At St Denis, where the smooth, rippling plan of the choir chapels allowed floods of colour to pour into the church through much bigger windows, and the double ambulatory allowed more room for circulation, the bays are very irregular in shape. The architect built all the arches first, for both arcade and vault, making some of them pointed so that arches of different spans had keystones of the same height. He then built the masonry infill, the webs, of irregular shape between the ribs, demonstrating that the function of the web can be separated from that of the rib, to ease the construction of vaulting. What had been a decorative device to give visual cohesion to the interior had now become a structural aid.

The pointed arch and rib vault, which

are commonly said to distinguish the Gothic style, were both part of the Romanesque tradition in which Suger's architect received his training; but he used them in a new combination to solve a practical problem, and they were later adapted to express ideas about the ideal appearance of a great church.

From the experiments in the Ile de France and Low Countries over the next half century it seems clear that the organic changes to which these discoveries led were part of a growing and conscious desire to devise a style of architecture specifically for the Church: it was establishing a distinct style of its own. The towering arched structures now being built were quite impractical for domestic life. As we shall see, secular buildings imitated vault mouldings and decoration, and occasionally contributed ideas such as horizontal transoms across windows; but from now until the late fourteenth century there was a wide divergence between styles for churches and styles for houses.

In church style the arch was paramount, and by the early thirteenth century the structure had undergone a complete

Above: The west front of Laon Cathedral, France, c.1190. Early Gothic façades were divided into three with two towers above. Here the sculptured doorways are under deep gabled porches. The upper parts of the towers are polygonal with added turrets from which peer figures of oxen said to represent those which hauled the carts of stone to the cathedral site.

Left: St Denis abbey, France, ambulatory of choir, 1140–44. The use of rib vaults and pointed arches allowed more versatile bay shapes, to give greater space. The chapels were fused in a continuous shallow ripple, with large windows for stained glass.

Right: Laon Cathedral, interior. The marked division of bays, the use of galleries and passages may show Norman influence, but the linkage of ribbed vault to piers via the vault shafts related parts to the whole in a manner characteristic of early Gothic. The capitals are carved with crockets, stylized leaves which supplanted the monsters and figured scenes of the Romanesque period. Both round and pointed arches are used.

change. A Romanesque church is essentially inert and thick walled, with small windows and doors reluctantly allowed in massive walls. The cathedral of Laon, started about 1165, demonstrates that the visual and structural implications of a rib vault were being explored to produce what was effectively the opposite to this.

At Laon the vault ribs are connected to shafts running up from the piers, visually connecting the piers to the vault. As the thrust of a rib vault is towards the corners of the bay, with little pressure on the walls, the masons emphasized the non-supporting function of the wall by linking the vault to its corner supports and cutting passages and windows in the wall itself. Laon has, like several others, a clerestory, a squat triforium passage cut below the clerestory in the thickness of the wall and a big vaulted tribune gallery above the aisles, which helps to buttress the vault and give more light. The elevation is a series of superimposed arches, with elements taken from Anglo-Norman and Flemish Romanesque buildings. No Romanesque building, however, could achieve the linkage of vault to piers: the pilgrimage churches had a bay system, but a wall is essential to a barrel vault; the Anglo-Norman cathedrals had wooden ceilings unrelated to the bay system; and the crossed vaults of Durham and Speyer are unrelated both structurally and visually to the piers.

In the later twelfth century, then, there slowly developed structures dependent not on inert masses of wall, but on the opposite: a skeletal framework of vault and piers, which, buttressed at the corners, stood independent of the walls. At the same time the arches of the elevation were visually related to the arches of the vault.

This was not achieved overnight, nor did they begin with a complete set of preconceived ideas. The key to it lay in buttressing, and various unsatisfactory experiments were made before finding the answer. St Etienne, Caen, is one of several Romanesque churches whose upper storey is partly supported by arches built under the lean-to roof of the gallery: in effect, concealed flying buttresses. In the late twelfth century these were brought into the open and applied at the most efficacious point, the lowest part of the vault, where maximum outward pressure was exerted. The arched buttresses carried the weight out over the aisles to the aisle buttresses, making superfluous the buttressing effect of the gallery. This was not realized at once, but an important advance was made at Notre Dame, Paris, in 1160, the first of the giant cathedrals of which Chartres, Reims and Beauvais are notable examples. Here, exposed flying buttresses took the weight of the vault, allowing the immense and very thin upper wall between the vault and the tribune to be occupied by windows. The way was now clear for the solution so triumphantly realized at Chartres.

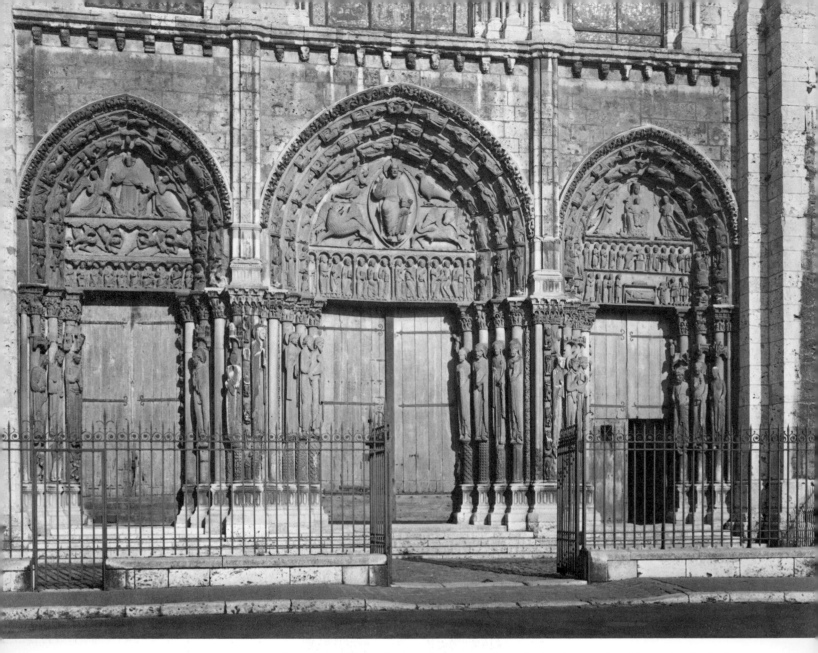

The designers of Chartres after the fire of 1194, and of Bourges slightly earlier, both realized the implication of the flying buttress and promptly suppressed the tribune gallery. Bourges Cathedral, planned like Paris with five aisles and no transept, is a vast hall of glass interrupted by triforium passages. The main elevation is repeated on the inner aisle, so that twice over the columns soar upwards, pushing the triforia and clerestories high under the floating canopy of the vault.

Chartres is effectively a stone framework for glass and sculpture. The architect, the master mason, doubled the height of the clerestory, and brought it down to the slender triforium passage which in the absence of the tribune was now just above the arcade. The weight of the vault is taken on fliers, and the wall is almost nonexistent. Looking across the nave the spectator sees the aisle window framed in the arcade, the low, elegant triforium arches, and the gigantic clerestory leading

into the vault over 30 metres (100 feet) above his head. The stained glass at Chartres enables the visitor to appreciate, as in no other church, the effect of the glowing coloured darkness that Suger had desired.

Coloured windows were not the only decorative element: figure sculpture now played a vital role. Although suppressed on the interior, where capitals were carved with dreary, stylized leaves called crockets, it achieved a new order on the outside. The western block of St Denis, with two towers and three doorways, was to become the basis of every important west façade in France for at least a century. The iconographical programme of the sculptured portals was almost immediately developed on the west front of Chartres, which has the earliest surviving column statues, the silent guardians of every Gothic doorway. The Royal Portal of Chartres is lavishly decorated with sculpture, but the three horizontal zones have

been ordered into a theological programme of some complexity. The illogicalities and fantasies of Romanesque have been tidied away in favour of a serene, hieratic style. The familiar Majesties and Judgments were still present on twelfth-century doors, but were now set amid minor sculptures of theological and symbolic importance. These parallels and references were almost certainly devised by the scholars at the cathedral schools, and can only have been understood by the highly educated. We may assume that the churches and windows were adorned not to educate the illiterate, but to glorify the House of God.

In this ordered sobriety may be detected the influence of the Cistercian Abbot Bernard of Clairvaux (1080–1153). The Cistercian movement, founded in Burgundy in 1098, was dedicated to the revival of the monastic austerities which the liturgical elaborations of the Cluniacs had rather obscured. The Order, far more ascetic than anything envisaged in the

Left: Chartres Cathedral, France, Royal portal, c.1150. This is the earliest surviving doorway with column statues and a coherent programme of narrative and symbolic biblical representations. The column figures are probably Old Testament ancestors of Christ, whose Life and Passion are shown on the frieze of capitals above them. The subjects on the tympana are related to the Second Coming of the Saviour. As all the sculpture substitutes for architecture, it is subordinate to it: the tympanum sculptures are spread on the surface in low relief, while the figures on the capitals are more squat and block-like, and the stiff, columnar pose of the statues emphasizes their function as door jambs.

Right: Chartres Cathedral, nave c.1200. The invention of flying buttresses to take the weight of the vault allowed the nave wall to be reduced in mass. The tribune was suppressed, and the clerestory lengthened below the spring of the vault. The vaults and piers were now visually related to each other by thin supporting columns, and the effect is that of a skeletal framework for stained glass.

Below: Bourges Cathedral, France, nave buttresses, designed c.1190. The arched flying buttresses took the main thrust of the high vault over the aisles and away from the main elevation, allowing the interior wall to be reduced in mass.

Benedictine Rule, was beginning to attract thousands of followers, inspired by Bernard's strong personality and oratorical gifts. The strength of the Cistercian view in its early years is reflected in the astonishing uniformity of its buildings, which transcended regional differences. From Fossanova near Naples to Fountains in Yorkshire we find Cistercian churches built not in the local style but in the solid, plain accents of the movement's native Burgundy.

Bernard roundly condemned the elaborate decoration of churches, believing that a bare liturgy should be performed in a plain, unadorned church, without the distractions of inappropriate, irrelevant sculptures. Suger's belief that colour and jewels could assist to mystical union with God was the opposite of this, and in the ensuing arguments a change came over the decoration of churches, beginning a period of classic restraint and bringing order to the doorways in the manner we have seen.

The highly intricate iconography of the sculptured transept façades at Chartres celebrates, together with the stained glass, the heavenly universe at the height of the Church's power. This sculpture coincides with the pontificate of Innocent III and the absolute power of Church and papacy. It is no accident that the transept sculptures contain clear references to this power and its implications for laymen from kings to peasants. The early Gothic cathedrals breathe the physical and spiritual victories of the Church.

The only country outside France to respond to the new approach in the late twelfth century was England, influenced more by Flanders than the Ile de France. Trade connections encouraged the passage of ideas, some of which were grafted on to a native taste for surface ornament. When the choir of Canterbury was rebuilt after the fire of 1174 as a glorious setting for the shrine of Thomas Becket, the architect

William of Sens introduced coloured marble shafting from the Valenciennes area and a logical cross-ribbed vault. The late-twelfth-century buildings in the north adopted the arches and shafts of France, but applied them as surface decoration on a solid wall; only Roche Abbey in Yorkshire betrays true appreciation of French ideas, relating shafts and vaults with some visual logic.

In France itself reactions to the new moves varied. The Chartres elevation, followed at Soissons and Amiens, was further developed at Reims after 1210 with the introduction of window tracery, thin bars of stone dividing the window spaces into patterns, which replaced the much thicker masonry of former times.

From about 1190 onwards, however, those who did not follow the standards set by the major cathedrals began to produce solutions of their own. Although most buildings followed Chartres and

Below left: Reims Cathedral, France, choir, c.1220. The elevation with a tall clerestory and no tribune follows the type established at Chartres, but here the windows have the earliest known patterns of bar tracery. The radiating chapels are visible beyond the piers.

Below: A page from the notebook of Villehard de Honnecourt, a contemporary mason, showing a Reims choir chapel, inside and out.

Right: Bourges Cathedral, France, ambulatory, c.1190. There are two aisles either side of the main vessel continuing round the choir to make a double ambulatory. The surviving thirteenth-century stained glass gives an idea of the jewelled effects of colour in great church interiors. Colour and light were believed to represent the presence of God and to help in the creation and confirmation of faith. The Old Testament, the Life of Christ and the saints were the subjects depicted in the windows.

Bourges in eliminating the tribune, in general their expense was hard to bear by all but the richest sees, for although masonry had been pared away to give flat, skeletal interiors, the exteriors were now bristling with buttresses and supportive masonry, as well as a large number of towers, a feature enthusiastically adopted from the Empire.

Much of north-east France and Burgundy explored the theme of the hollow wall, an idea taken over from Anglo-Norman buildings of 'thick-wall' construction, in which a continuous passage was hollowed out of the thickness of the wall at clerestory level. Passages on superimposed levels appear in Geneva Cathedral and several churches in Burgundy. At St Remi at Reims wall passages in the aisles were used in conjunction with screens of columns across the entrance to each choir chapel, adumbrating the fusion of walls and spaces by appearing to barricade the spaces and open out the walls.

The colossal height of the major cathe-

drals is often emphasized, but love of height was a passing phase. When the 48 metre (157 foot) high vaults of Beauvais Cathedral collapsed on their insecure foundations in 1284, interest had long since turned towards smaller buildings.

The Church reached the height of its power in the early thirteenth century and thereafter suffered a period of decline, with the papacy eventually banished to Avignon and subject to unedifying political manoeuvres. It is often assumed that architecture declined with it. This is far from the truth. Church building is not dependent for its survival on statements of religious or even political belief, of the kind seen at Chartres, but upon the wish of patrons to build churches and the supply of masons able to realize those wishes. The types of church building were destined to change as religious attitudes altered, but architects adapted themselves to new conditions and remained supremely creative.

The mobility of masons as a group at

this time is demonstrated by the rapid spread of ideas, and, specifically, by the notebook of Villehard de Honnecourt, a unique survival of a mason's commonplace book. Villehard recorded details that interested him on buildings he visited during the 1220s, most notably the new window tracery of Reims, the plan of Cambrai, and the delightful oxen on the towers at Laon.

The notebook does not, however, tell us anything useful about masonic method. The sheer size of the early Gothic cathedrals demanded precise engineering techniques and knowledge of the behaviour of stone under certain stresses. There had always been considerable trial and error; towers especially were prone to subsidence, usually from inadequate foundations. But buildings tended to be overbuttressed, and vaults were often thicker than modern engineers know to be necessary, which has led some commentators to say that medieval masons knew little of structural engineering. This is belied by the exactness with which buttresses were applied to the points of greatest stress. The fall of a building was an event so rare that it was almost invariably recorded as newsworthy, and an enormous number remain standing, if restored, after 800 years.

Masonic theory was not written down in the early Gothic period, so we must infer it from the buildings themselves, a hazardous exercise which has provoked many treatises on the use of magic numbers and expression of celestial harmonies in the measurements of medieval buildings. While such things remain elusive, recent study suggests that skills were enhanced by the introduction of Euclidian mathematics, and that mathematics were used in a practical way to overcome problems in construction. Difficulties in calculating, say, the height of an arch were solved by applying a fixed mathematical proportion, which related the parts of the building by a simple ratio. The commonest, used for example at Laon and Norwich, was a proportion based on the ratio of $1:\sqrt{2}$ $(1:1.414)$, which could be obtained by taking the diagonal of a square. It was more usually expressed in the traditional number sequence $12:17:24:34:48$ etc. ($\sqrt{2} \times 12 = 17$), which was familiar from use in late Roman field survey systems. The height of a pier, the proportions of the storeys, the width of the nave, even the thickness of a buttress could be related by such a system: for example an arch of radius 17 feet might stand on piers 24 feet high. Proportions were related to the ground-plan, which was usually set out in full; the building was often put up a few bays at a time, nearly always begun from the choir, and the use of such ratios eased constructional difficulties in an age without elaborate techniques for making measured drawings.

Building proceeded as money allowed, and speed depended on many things. The eight-year campaign at Canterbury was interrupted for a season when funds ran out; at Reims rioting in the town prevented building for three years; Chartres, with its miraculous relic of the Virgin's robe, could derive large revenues from pilgrims and 'voluntary' contributions, and the building was finished within about forty years. The famous contribution of the citizens in personally hauling the carts of stone to the building site tells us more about religious hysteria than the logistics of a building campaign.

The rise in the status of masons is difficult to assess: that Abbot Suger of St

WELLS: A GOTHIC CATHEDRAL

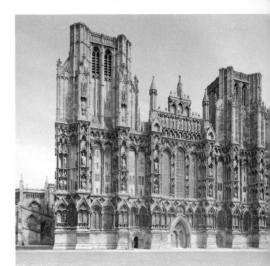

Like nearly every English cathedral, Wells has buildings of different periods. All are of the highest quality, and harmonize well through a shared characteristic: each exhibits English stylistic traits in a slightly exaggerated form. The nave is lower and more tunnel-like than in most English cathedrals, while the retro-choir and polygonal Lady chapel to the east show experiments in the fusion of architectural spaces practised by many fourteenth-century architects but rarely with such finesse. The screen façade demonstrates the English dislike of big sculptured doorways: the sculptures, representing the Last Judgement, are spread across the whole west front, and comprise the greatest surviving collection in England of thirteenth-century figure sculptures. The south-west tower, by William Wynford c.1390, influenced the design of many Somerset church towers. The cathedral was administered by the Dean and Chapter, secular clergy, represented in their absence by Vicars, for whom the Vicars' Close (*below far right*) was built. The Dean presided at meetings in the Chapter House (*far right*). Although Wells was not, like many English cathedrals, a monastic foundation, it had a cloister which was rebuilt in the fourteenth century.

The cutaway of the drawing shows the nave and lantern. Built in the late 1180s, the nave has a typically English clerestory passage. Although it has a rib vault there are no bay divisions and the continuous row of triforium arches emphasizes the horizontal line. The four strainer arches were added in the fourteenth century, as the final part of a successful programme to stabilize the central tower.

Left: Bishop Burnell's Hall, c.1280, part of the bishop's palace. 34 × 18 m (111 × 59 ft), the hall had a screens passage and kitchens. It is noteworthy for its unfortified appearance and huge traceried windows with delicate transoms.

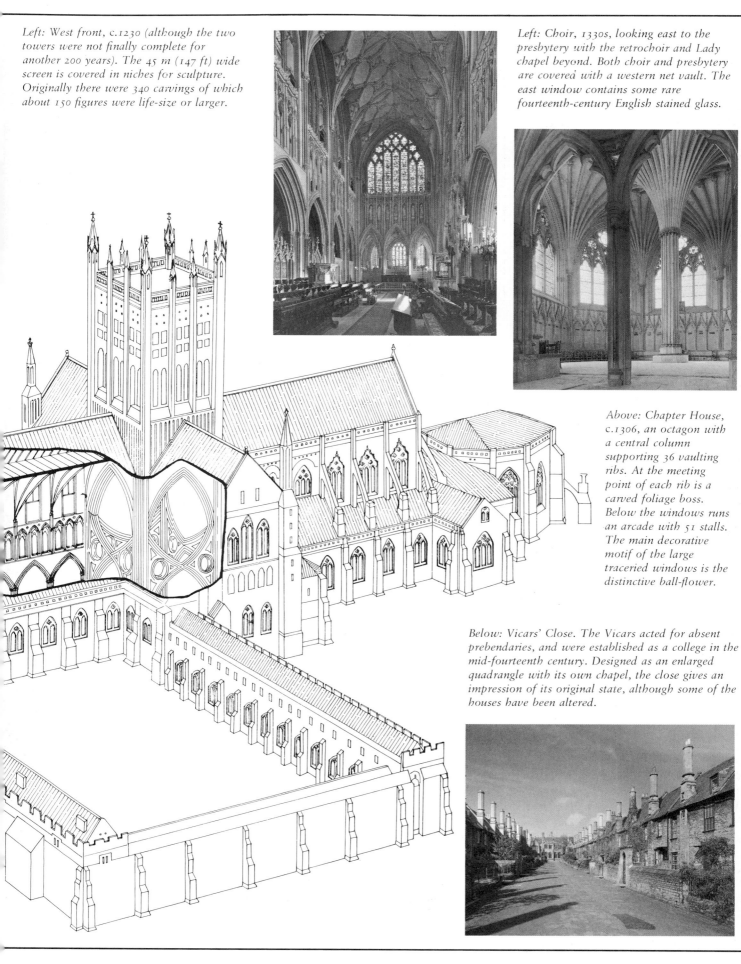

Left: West front, c.1230 (although the two towers were not finally complete for another 200 years). The 45 m (147 ft) wide screen is covered in niches for sculpture. Originally there were 340 carvings of which about 150 figures were life-size or larger.

Left: Choir, 1330s, looking east to the presbytery with the retrochoir and Lady chapel beyond. Both choir and presbytery are covered with a western net vault. The east window contains some rare fourteenth-century English stained glass.

Above: Chapter House, c.1306, an octagon with a central column supporting 36 vaulting ribs. At the meeting point of each rib is a carved foliage boss. Below the windows runs an arcade with 51 stalls. The main decorative motif of the large traceried windows is the distinctive ball-flower.

Below: Vicars' Close. The Vicars acted for absent prebendaries, and were established as a college in the mid-fourteenth century. Designed as an enlarged quadrangle with its own chapel, the close gives an impression of its original state, although some of the houses have been altered.

Denis never mentions his master masons perhaps reveals more about Suger's character, for fifty years later the monk Gervase mentions both Canterbury masters with admiration. By the mid-thirteenth century the masters of the great French cathedrals were recording their names in the building, and the fine tomb slab of Hugh Libergier, architect of St Nicaise at Reims, depicts the instruments of his profession beside the effigy.

By this time the architecture of other countries was becoming conditioned by their response to developments in France. Italy, however, was not yet ready to absorb French ideas and at, for example, Assisi continued to build in her own Romanesque style. The outer fringes of the Empire produced a hybrid of the two styles for some time, but nearer the Rhineland those buildings whose patrons had travelled to France were at first wholly imitative, as at Limburg-an-der-Lahn, which is a German version of Laon, dating from about 1220. But not so much later, St Elisabeth at Marburg combined a trefoil-plan choir, derived from Romanesque buildings in Cologne, with a hall-nave, and, like the centralized Liebfrauenkirche at Trier, it has tall, slender piers and huge traceried windows.

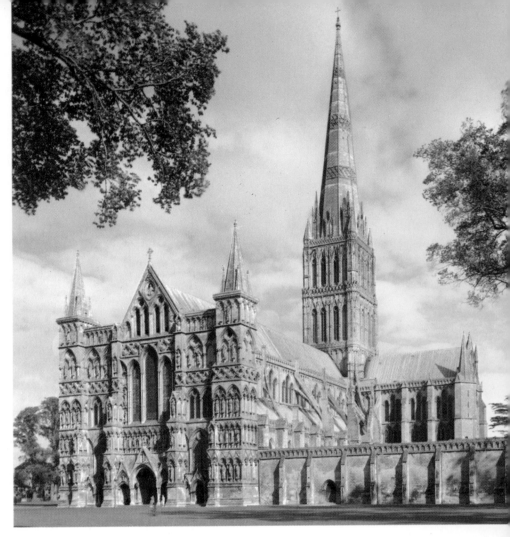

Germany, too, used French sculptural ideas more expressively, adapting at Bamberg the classicizing style of Reims, but with a new naturalism. The retrospective figures of benefactors in the west choir of Naumburg, and the mounted knight at Bamberg, represent the secular side of life, which as yet had no official existence in French churches. But in France itself the austere phase of the last hundred years was ending, and the crevices of Reims have many small grotesque heads, heirs to the Romanesque monsters, and ancestors of the fantastic creatures of late medieval English sculpture.

England absorbed the lessons of France with the least shock, largely by continuing to misinterpret them. The tendency to build squat, thick churches with strong horizontal emphasis and copious surface ornament continued, with French ideas adapted or neglected at will. Wells (1180s) has a rib vault corbelled into the upper wall; there are no vertical bay divisions and no attempt is made to relate the vaults to the piers. The three continuous storeys resemble an elongated sandwich. At Lincoln (1190s) the Canterbury elevation was exploited with greater depth of shaftwork; the famous Crazy Vault, which denies all the organic upward growth implied in a

Gothic vault, and the double layer of blind arcading in the aisles, demonstrate the English love of mobile ornament on a static wall. Even the restraint of Salisbury (1220s) is enlivened by rich accumulations of Purbeck marble. The screen façades of Salisbury and Wells, extending beyond the width of the building and with tiny, insignificant doors, are part of an English tradition which ignores the French.

Churches were built against a background of flourishing wealth. That of the Low Countries, so central to the north European economy and therefore to its art, was well established by the mid-eleventh century, and by 1100 Arras was among the richest cloth towns, its trade with England having made that country a desirable prize for the Normans.

Italian towns had never ceased to flourish, and although city government developed all over Europe in the later twelfth century, Italian towns enjoyed increasing independence. The vastly increased wealth and power of the greater cities halted the growth of smaller ones, such as San Gimignano, in the thirteenth century; but the cessation of growth there has preserved the high towers inhabited by a population continually ready for war.

Above left: Salisbury Cathedral, begun 1220. Built on a new site, it gives a complete idea of how an early Gothic English cathedral was expected to look. With two pairs of transepts, and a Lady chapel (now the Trinity chapel) projecting at the east, its angular severity is enhanced by the groups of lancet windows. The wide screen façade originally contained statues in niches. The tower and spire were added in the fourteenth century, after the rest of the building was finished.

Left: Reims Cathedral, France, west front, central portal, c.1245. The column figures have taken on a life of their own. They now enact scenes, here the Annunciation of Gabriel to Mary, and the Visitation of Mary to Elizabeth. The two figures in the latter scene show the influence of late Roman sculpture.

Right: Lincoln Cathedral, Angel choir, 1256–80. The thick wall, squat proportions and surface decoration are typical of English architecture in the late thirteenth century. This building is particularly noted for its patterned vaults, use of coloured marble, and the huge traceried window in the flat east wall. The angels which gave the choir its name flank the vault springers.

Independence was manifest in such early town halls as that of Volterra. Verona and other cities grew on the grid plan of their Roman streets; in the North, Roman plans were lost and English towns developed on the looser grids of Alfred's day; but Rome survives in the line of walls and gates at Trier and York, and in the gates themselves of Autun, whose fluted pilaster decoration was imitated in the Romanesque cathedral. The modern town of Split in Dalmatia grew within the walls of Diocletian's palace.

The earliest surviving town houses date from the twelfth century at Cluny and Lincoln. Much restored and built of stone, their decorative details are borrowed from the local Romanesque church style. Houses continued to reflect developments in church decoration, although mouldings were always coarser until the late Middle Ages. Masons moved from churches to houses and castles, taking with them styles in foliage carving and window tracery. Houses were always strictly functional, often with a vaulted undercroft for animals and storage, and living rooms above. The brick houses at Torún, Poland, and the stone Hôtel de Vauluisant at Provins have contemporary window tracery for the upper living quarters.

Stone castles survive from the late eleventh century, solid, square structures in the current style of round arches and massive walls, designed for defence and to dominate the surrounding country. The early type of square keep on a mound ('motte') within a bailey or courtyard was gradually superseded during the twelfth century by a plan in which the bailey itself was fortified with defensive towers and gates and the keep became less of a stronghold. Changes in castle design were dictated by experience and fresh thinking in war. Medieval castle builders, while paying attention to the good looks of the final result, were nothing if not pragmatists: when Edward I built his castles in mountainous Wales, he employed an architect from mountainous Savoy. There is little evidence that Crusader castles influenced Western design: the Syrian castles such as Saone and Krak des Chevaliers were designed to meet local conditions, which were not those of Europe.

There was by no means a castle to every village, nor was there a manor house. There were almost as many types of village as there were villages, and there architectural effort was confined to the church, the barn and the mill, if such things were even provided. Early stone houses such as Boothby Pagnell, Lincolnshire (c. 1200) are already divided into separate rooms, and from now on there was a tendency towards smaller rooms and greater privacy. Standards of comfort rose as conditions become more settled. Orford Castle is noted for its high standards of hygiene. The best use of running water was made in monasteries: the Cistercians made very effective drainage systems by channelling streams, and on the twelfth-century plan of the precinct at Canterbury, the sewers are carefully marked.

DECORATIVE UNITY IN LATE GOTHIC

The development of window tracery coincided with the reign of Louis IX (1215–70), a central figure in European politics. The contest between Empire and papacy, which ultimately diminished them both, had entered its final phase, and the King of France, whose piety was equalled by his shrewdness, became an international symbol of power and wisdom, as

well as of Christian kingship. He expressed this in, among other things, active patronage of art and architecture in the service of the Church. If France was the centre of European cultural life, Paris was the centre of French culture, with a personality so strong that one may accurately speak of a Parisian style in architecture.

The preoccupation of Louis IX and his cousin Henry III of England with defining the sacerdotal nature of kingship, was part of a trend in the thirteenth century towards a more personal and, in some ways, more compassionate religion. Where the early twelfth century emphasized judgement, the early thirteenth spoke of forgiveness, placing the figures of the Virgin and St John beside Christ on the sculptured tympana, interceding on behalf of mortal men. The deeply felt personal response of St Francis of Assisi (1181–1226), founder of the Franciscan Order of wandering preachers, which spread his message across Europe, pointed towards the mysticism of the later Middle Ages; but to balance the emotions was the cool intellect of St Thomas Aquinas (1225–74) and of the Dominican Friars, an Order founded to combat the dualist Cathar or Albigensian heresy through reasoned argument.

Not surprisingly, the idea of a church underwent another important change, best seen in the Sainte-Chapelle in Paris. This two-storey chapel was built in 1240s to house the relic of the True Cross which Louis had recently acquired. The relics

LAXTON: A MEDIEVAL VILLAGE

Right: The plan of Laxton, England, a village with a surviving medieval plan. Most medieval people lived in rural communities, isolated by stretches of forest or marsh, and greatly varying in size and character. There were almost as many types of village as there were villages, some being clusters of houses, others scattered or, as at Laxton, strung out along a road with the church in the centre. Feudal society was defined by the castle, and was reflected in its development from a wooden defensive structure to a stone architectural complex with room for many houses within its walls; but few villages were near a castle, and not every village had a manor house or even a church. Peasants lived in small houses built side by side; at Laxton there was a plot of land round each one. The arable fields held in common surrounded the village, with meadow grazing and forest beyond. The so-called three field system survives intact at Laxton. Houses varied from region to region, and were built with

Below: Krak des Chevaliers, Syria, late twelfth century and after. The central garrison of the Knights Hospitallers, it lay off the main fighting routes and acted as a supply base. In plan it combines a roughly concentric plan of inner and outer circuits of walls and towers, with provision inside for peaceful domestic life. It fell to the Arabs in 1271.

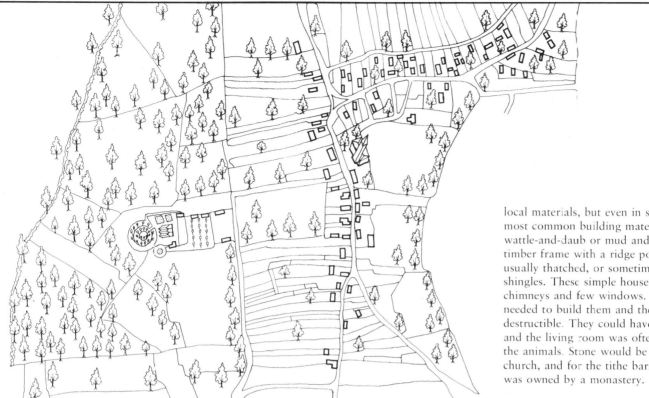

local materials, but even in stone areas the most common building material was wattle-and-daub or mud and straw, on a timber frame with a ridge pole. Roofs were usually thatched, or sometimes had wooden shingles. These simple houses had no chimneys and few windows. Little skill was needed to build them and they were easily destructible. They could have two rooms, and the living room was often shared with the animals. Stone would be used for the church, and for the tithe barn if the village was owned by a monastery.

Right: Boothby Pagnell, England, 1200. A small stone manor house with living rooms above a vaulted store room.

Below: Hôtel de Vauluisant, Provins, France. A typical thirteenth-century town house, on a narrow site at right angles to the street. The arrangement is the same as Boothby, but here the upper floor has fashionable tracery.

were placed in the upper chapel, a single cell in which the masonry has largely been replaced by enormous stained-glass windows. On the vaulting shafts stand figures of the apostles, witnesses to the events of the Passion symbolized by the relics. Statues now witnessed the rite inside the building rather than guarding the entrance. It is as if a metal reliquary has been turned inside out, and records tell us that contemporaries saw it in the same way. A small, highly decorated building has itself become the reliquary.

This idea had widespread effects. Two buildings in particular, the cathedrals of Amiens and Cologne, with important relics of their own, have an interesting stylistic relationship to the Sainte-Chapelle: Cologne, the only wholly French-looking church on German soil, was rebuilt for the relics of the Three Kings in 1248, its close stylistic affinity to Amiens and the Sainte-Chapelle suggesting that the style itself had come to symbolize the reliquary, a view strengthened by a version of it found in Henry III's great reliquary-cum-coronation church at Westminster.

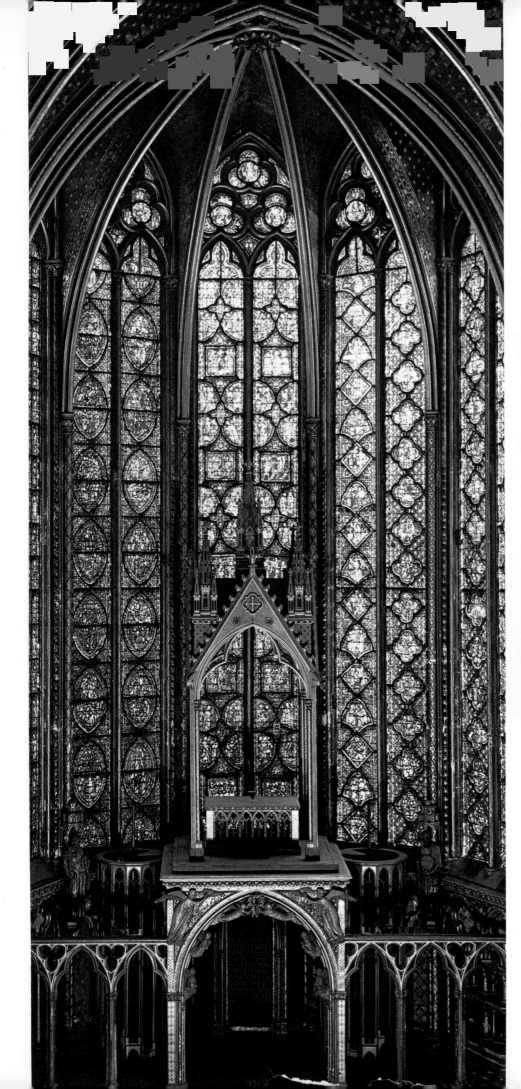

Although the idea of the church as reliquary began a move towards smaller buildings, most of the earliest manifestations of the Parisian style were in large ones, and engineering skills were still learned in the workshops attached to the new buildings at Strasbourg and Cologne. The style, called Rayonnant from the radiating patterns in its huge rose windows, deploys tracery for purely decorative purposes over all surfaces, both inside and out, with a tendency towards moulded piers and the apparent dissolution of solid walls.

The expanses of glass in the new nave of

Left: The Sainte-Chapelle, Paris, 1241–8. A reliquary chapel with huge windows and every wall surface decorated in paint and gesso, it expressed new ideas in fusing structure, glass and decoration into a cohesive unity.

Above: Barcelona Cathedral, Spain, begun 1298. The high arcades perhaps show the influence of Bourges, but southern taste is reflected in the dark nave with flanking chapels which keep out strong sunlight.

Right: Strasbourg Cathedral, France, façade c.1300. Layers of delicate free-standing tracery act as a curtain to conceal the wall surface.

St Denis (1230s) are suspended between tall, moulded piers on which the capitals are all but invisible, and light seems to flicker and shape the forms. In the Sainte-Chapelle the supports are concealed beneath copious carved and painted decoration, and the rebuilt transepts of Notre Dame form walls of coloured glass held in place by panels of tracery.

The style can be followed into the provinces as far south as Carcassonne, through Parisian tracery patterns. Towards Burgundy, two buildings in particular emphasize the symbolism of the reliquary: St Urbain at Troyes, a family memorial church of 1260s and St Thibault, a reliquary church of about 1300. Here the supports have all but dissolved into the surrounding tracery. The walls consist of huge windows and hollow passages, glazed and unglazed, with a net of tracery thrown across them. The wall covering of St Thibault is a trellis of rectilinear panels.

No country was able to ignore Rayonnant, although in its purely French form it was not wholeheartedly adopted. Even Spain and Italy took some account of its tracery forms, while retaining their characteristic styles.

The cathedral at Carcassonne had a pure Rayonnant choir, and French masons also found their way to Leon, Burgos and Toledo; but Albi, begun in 1281, is a single cell with a line of side chapels, its heavily fortified exterior following Romanesque precedents in the area, such as Agde. Together with the high, craggy castles of the Roussillon, it testifies to the Albigensian wars in Languedoc.

Catalonia produced its own style of high-aisled basilicas with side chapels, as at Barcelona and Palma de Mallorca. Across the Tyrrhenian sea, French tastes were adopted enthusiastically in the Angevin kingdom of Naples, and indeed

spread as far east as the cathedral of Famagusta in Cyprus; but in the main part of Italy they were associated mostly with the Friars, who did much of the building in the thirteenth and fourteenth centuries.

Friars' churches, big and barnlike in the Italian tradition, tend to be light and roomy with slender supports, to enable large congregations to hear the preacher. Their tastes may have influenced the adoption of hall churches in Germany, and certainly influenced the style of the late medieval parish church in England.

Displays of structural logic did not interest them, and the Franciscan Santa Croce in Florence, begun in 1295, has a wooden-roofed nave with a two-storey elevation and no shafting. Most churches did, however, use simple forms of Rayonnant tracery, and a type of rather domed vaulting was used in the mother church of the Franciscans at Assisi (c. 1220s), Siena Cathedral (c. 1270s), and in the Dominican church of Santa Maria Novella, Florence. The elevation of two storeys with round clerestory windows was used again in the

enormous late-fourteenth-century church of San Petronio, Bologna.

The octagonal crossings of Florence and Siena cathedrals show that the engineering skills were there, although plans were made amid raucous debate. That the Italians were not theorists is shown in the discussions in late-fourteenth-century Milan, when northern masons were summoned to help the Milanese build a cathedral in the northern style, which they fully saw was different from their own. Northern architectural theory, rooted in established tradition, was rejected by the pragmatic Milanese, who finally provoked the French master Jean into exclaiming: '*Ars sine scientia nihil est!*' (Skill is nothing without knowledge [theory]).

In the North Rayonnant was adapted in fashioning the style of the late Middle Ages. For a time, architectural initiative passed to Germany and England, which created their own styles and exchanged ideas.

Architects were now preoccupied with two main themes, both hinted in the Sainte-Chapelle: surface decoration and spatial unity. These ideas are present in most late medieval churches. They developed the notion of a church as a stage set, a small, highly decorated world-within-a-world. It was a period in which art and life were to be inextricably fused: the whole of life, from a celebratory feast in which the food was presented as a series

Above left: Siena Cathedral, Italy, begun 1269, modified in the fourteenth century. This aisled basilica has the striped marble decoration of Tuscan architecture, and the nave leads to a hexagonal crossing supporting a dome. This is an early instance of the interest in polygonal shapes in architecture, which was widespread in the early fourteenth century. The vault and clerestory were added later.

Left: San Francesco, Assisi, begun 1228. A pilgrimage church which was designed to display frescoes of the Bible and the life of St Francis. Italian Gothic was a style of simple forms, not much structural daring, and clear spaces to allow for preaching. However, French influence can be seen here in the choir tracery, the vault, the pier forms and the passage at the windows.

Right: Santa Maria Novella, Florence, begun 1278. A Dominican church with a flat east end. The two-storey elevation and domical vaulting are found in many Italian Gothic churches.

of sculptures, to the decoration of a chapel, was regarded as in some senses a work of art, and they moved smoothly between illusion and reality. The Arena chapel at Padua and St Stephen's, Westminster, both used *grisaille* monochrome paintwork to give the illusion of figure sculpture. At Westminster it was used together with real sculpture, and living people were portrayed kneeling to the altar, so that hardly a distinction was drawn between sculpture, paint, and flesh and blood.

The unity, or lack of distinction between art and the everyday world, was emphasized by the use of some tracery patterns and, above all, the niche as decorative motifs. The niche, defining as sacred the space which it enclosed, appeared on buildings, paintings, tapestries, metalwork and ivory reliefs; tracery was used on all these and at the same time on mundane objects such as shoe buckles. Both church and secular living was conducted within a mantle of unifying ornament.

It was also a period of intense personal awareness, seen in literature as well as in the visual arts, and while this is traceable at least to the twelfth century, its architectural manifestations are more apparent later on. Private chapels were founded by the score, chantries built inside existing churches, exquisitely adorned, tiny build-

ings in which priests prayed for the souls of the founders, now buried amid increased personal splendour. The fifteenth century in particular was a period of enhanced morbidity and preoccupation with the corruption of death.

In architecture these themes inevitably gave added importance to individual detail. Masons were turning their knowledge of geometry to the design of tracery patterns and pinnacles, and although engineering talent was displayed in the high towers of churches such as Ulm Minster, it is perhaps significant that the fifteenth-century design books of Matthaus Roriczer deal with the design of small details.

The love of artifice and illusionism led to ambiguity, seen in the uncertain depths and spatial limits of the polygonal structures and encrusted surface ornament of the English Decorated style at Wells and Ely. It was eventually resolved in the trellis of slender rectilinear tracery panelling applied to the choir of Gloucester (c. 1335). This, the beginning of the so-called Perpendicular style of late medieval England, restated the aims of Troyes and St Thibault, blending surface ornament in spatial unity and harmony.

The attempt to resolve these ideas did not cease there, and it is best seen in those buildings whose design theoretically works against it. The mid-fourteenth-century choir of Aachen, a Sainte-Chapelle with enormous windows and no capitals to interrupt the smooth flow of its vaulting shafts, is unified by definition; but in the late-fourteenth-century basilical nave of Canterbury Cathedral the clerestory and triforium are pushed up above aisles lofty enough to suggest a hall church. The emerging parish church style of late medieval England had huge windows and wide-spaced, slender piers, a solution adopted in Germany.

The hall churches of Germany exploited surface ornament, and developed structural illogicality and unified space to the utmost. A church with aisles of equal height and no clerestory can more easily suggest a single space; and patterned windows and vaults derived from England were developed with great originality.

In England the fan vault, Perpendicular tracery over a conoid core, was not risked over large spans until the late fifteenth

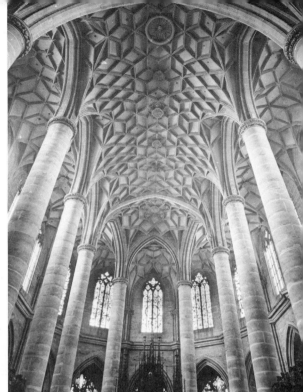

Left: Prague Cathedral, choir, 1353. The second architect, Peter Parler, introduced a net vault, with niches and passages in the clerestory, possibly derived from England.

Above: Ely Cathedral, England, stalls of the Lady chapel, 1320s. The undulating wall of niches with nodding ogee arches and thick encrustation of sculpture contrasts with the flat elevation of Gloucester.

Above right: Holy Cross, Schwäbisch Gmund, West Germany, 1351. Designed by Peter Parler's father Heinrich, it is a hall church with an elaborate net vault unifying the interior.

Right: Gloucester Cathedral, choir, c.1337. The flat network of thin rectilinear panels applied to the piers of the Norman choir was the first complete essay in the English Perpendicular style.

century. Lierne vaults were arranged in rectilinear patterns to suit the recti-linearity of the elevations with four-centred arches and panelling. In Germany net vaults were expanded into intricate patterns like carpets, as at Schwäbisch Gmund (c. 1351). Vienna Cathedral and the brick Sandkirche at Wroclaw have quite thick, heavy ribs, but St Martin at Landshut has a pattern of the greatest delicacy.

The tall windows of hall churches were possibly inspired by Cologne, whose dis-continued workshop dispatched many skilled masons to other towns. An early hall church, the Wiesenkirche at Soest, was begun by a Cologne master in 1331. In the late fourteenth century St Sebaldus, Nuremberg, and the choir of Landshut continued the hall theme, and the early-fifteenth-century Spitalkirche at Landshut arrested the longitudinal plod of paired columns with an axial column at the east, while in the Franciscan church at Salzburg the vault pattern of the choir pays no regard to the bay divisions beneath.

The different technical problems in brick produced churches in the Hansa towns of the Baltic coast which, while imitating their stone cousins, have a richer, denser feel. Brick spread to Poland, where the pinnacles of St James at Torún are an essay in pure virtuosity; but al-though the fashion for brick spread south-wards a little, when Charles IV brought the centre of Imperial culture to Prague in the mid-fourteenth century, he built the cathedral in stone, in a style manifestly indebted to the depth and mobility of English architecture, which his second architect, Peter Parler, had probably seen while training as a mason.

The last phase of Gothic architecture is in some ways the most exciting and inventive of all. It developed at a time of greatly decentralized patronage in the years around 1400, when the Courts of London,

Left: St James, Torún, Poland, early fourteenth century. A brick church, typical of the region, it was elaborately embellished to achieve the same effects as a stonebuilt church.

Above: Spitalkirche, Landshut, after 1407. A South German hall church, with a delicate net vault springing directly from the tall columnar piers. The high altar is marked by a pier placed on the axis of the building.

Far right: St Mary Redcliffe, Bristol, thirteenth to fifteenth centuries. A town church in the Perpendicular style, it is one of the largest parish churches in England. It has a box-like profile with flat roof, huge clerestory windows with a pattern of rectilinear tracery, and a square porch. Late medieval parish churches were built by local merchants and gentry who often used their coats of arms or heraldic devices to decorate the church both inside and out.

Prague, north Italy and the royal dukes of France were as artistically active as Paris. The effects, such as they were, of war and the Black Death, were now largely over; the fifteenth century was a time of renewed growth and redistributed wealth, which resulted in very few enormously grand buildings, and many rich lesser ones. Cities, merchants and the minor gentry were now important patrons. The religious reform movements of the late Middle Ages, those of Wycliffe and Hus, had little effect on architecture, although the churches of the Hussite town of Tabor have more austere vault patterns than their more ebullient neighbours.

The style of architecture in these years shows no sign of decline or lack of inspiration. Contemporaries outside Italy were unaware that their traditions were to be superseded by the classical revival whose effects were beginning to spread across the Alps. The penetration northwards of Renaissance forms was at first slow and unobtrusive, outside a tiny circle. Architects, living in the present, developed the Gothic while embracing the new motifs: in many fifteenth- and early-sixteenth-century churches of northern France Renaissance details are cheerfully incorporated into the traditional style, with no thought to their implications. French architects in fact treated them as French motifs had been treated in England in the early thirteenth century, as amusing decorative devices to be absorbed without comprehension of their structural significance. Whatever the reason for the eclipse of Gothic, it was not that architects had reached their limit.

Individual and civic wealth was manifest in new parish churches and chantry chapels: the city of Nuremberg built St Lorenz, the cardinals of Amboise St Maclou at Rouen. The great parish churches of East Anglia were the result of wealth from the cloth trade and political rivalry.

Although national styles remain instantly recognizable, certain features are common to all. Space is still unified, but now moulded by shaped walls and deep encrustations of surface ornament. Sculpture, paint, gilded gesso and stained glass were still being pressed into service to create a complete, jewelled world-within-a-world.

France adopted curvilinear tracery in the late fourteenth century, its flame-like patterns giving the style its name: Flamboyant. Traditional pier shapes were abandoned, and mouldings were more

Below left: Divinity Schools, Oxford, England, late fifteenth century. The flattened four-centred arches support pendant vaults, a variation of the fan vault, in which the centres of the fan cones hang in space. Here they end in sculptured tabernacles.

Right: Batalha, Portugal, cloister, 1387–1415. The elaborately encrusted tracery represents the latest style of Gothic in Portugal, sometimes using marine motifs.

Far right above: Notre Dame, Alençon, France, detail of west porch, 1477. The late Gothic Flamboyant style exploited curvilinear tracery, polygonal structure and sculpture, to achieve movement and depth.

Far right below: St Barbara, Kutna Hora, Czechoslovakia, vault, early sixteenth century, by Benedikt Rejt. Very late Gothic vaults swooped and curved through three dimensions, and were often cut off in mid-air as if to emphasize their divorce from structural function.

than ever designed to catch light and deep shadows. Façades such as La Trinité, Vendôme, and the transept of Beauvais, are a swirling mass of Flamboyant tracery, and at Notre Dame d'Alençon it thrust forward on the bowed out shape of the porch. France and the Empire alike denied structural logic: the vaults at Kutna Hora in Bohemia bend through three dimensions, spirals are applied to the piers of Brunswick Cathedral and St Severin in Paris. Vaults with intersecting mouldings grew like palm branches out of the piers. The brick façade of St Anne at Wilno has a huge ogee arch growing to the top through the other mouldings.

The crustiness appealed to the Spanish peninsula. At Tomar, Portugal, the carved ropes and barnacles speak of the growing maritime Empire of the Portuguese; in Spain the elegant starred vault of the lantern at Burgos Cathedral recalls Islam; but the ornament, covering the surface like a growth, has the layered quality of the sculpture in Henry VII's chapel at Westminster Abbey.

Late Gothic has its cool side: the delicate piers and vaults of Solesmes abbey have the same austere calm as the contemporary Frauenkirche at Munich (1470s). The two aspects perhaps meet in that monument to royal piety and patronage, the chapel of King's College, Cambridge. Here the absolute balance of walls and roof is realized in the fluid grace with

which the enormous Perpendicular windows merge with the fan vaulting. Everything is calm, static and austere, but in the later ante-chapel, the walls are encrusted with the sculptured badges of Tudor majesty.

Among the greatest non-royal patrons were now the merchants, who had come to control city government, and whose civic pride and wealth led to the building not only of parish churches but of town halls. The fortress-like Bargello in Florence reflects the turbulent local conditions of the thirteenth century, but the Palazzo dei Priori at Perugia had open *loggie* on the ground floor. As time went on the decoration of town halls was barely distinguishable from that of churches, except that builders usually preferred straight-headed windows with transoms and avoided the most complicated tracery patterns. Even so Nuremberg town hall has a patterned vault, while those of Brunswick and Wroclaw have fine late Gothic detailing.

By the later Middle Ages conditions in towns were so crowded that houses were built end-on to the street, in several storeys. The majority were timber-framed, in plain or crossed patterns. Although much ecclesiastical timber work has survived from the Middle Ages, in ceilings, vaulting and roof beams, losses in secular architecture have been very great, and magnificent survivors such as the late-fourteenth-century hammer-beam roof of Westminster Hall indicate the quality of what has gone. There is some evidence that ideas in carpentry even influenced stone masons, which makes the loss more tantalizing.

The Italians, with a long tradition of urban life, were pioneers in the art of city planning. They introduced the idea of a planned city centre to give a town a focal point. The many new towns established in northern Europe in the thirteenth century, Winchelsea for instance or the Crusading port of Aigues Mortes, were unimaginatively planned on a grid system, although the Gascon *bastides* of Edward I, such as Libourne, were designed round a central market-place, with a fortified church and solid town walls. But in Italy cathedral and administrative buildings were brought together: a group of three civic palaces and a cathedral was designed for the main square of Todi in the early thirteenth century, and when the Palazzo Pubblico was built in

Above: Conway, Wales, late thirteenth century. The walled town and castle were designed together as a fortified settlement on a triangular site. The castle is in the top corner.

Right: Todi, a thirteenth-century planned town centre in Italy. The cathedral and three civic palaces were designed to complement each other.

Far right above: Sirmione Castle, Italy, late thirteenth century. Built by the Scaligeri on an isthmus on Lake Garda, the carefully related gates and towers form a series of defensive barriers to the keep.

Far right below: Hôtel Jacques Coeur, Bourges, France, c.1450. The house of a rich merchant financier, built round a courtyard, its living rooms were on the first floor, a sequence of state apartments reached by spiral staircases from the courtyard. The sculptured decoration of shells and hearts by the entrance is a pun on the name of Jacques Coeur. The large windows and open aspect contrast strongly with the well protected doorway, watched by two carved figures in mock windows.

Siena in 1298 a regulation was made that in future all the houses in the square must have windows similar to those of the Palazzo.

Castles continued to become more elegant and less martial, the last important strategic development being the concentric plan seen in Edward I's castles such as Harlech: here a low curtain wall with towers and fortified gate is the first line of defence with a high, heavily fortified inner curtain giving the main strength. But Edward's castles were administrative centres as well as fighting machines, and Conway is a fully walled town, with the castle in the eastern corner dominating the two rivers, Gyffin and Conway.

Peaceable conditions in the late Middle Ages led to the abandonment of strongholds, and the gentry used their increased wealth to build fine country houses with only a hint of martial purpose, as can be seen by comparison of the late-fourteenth-century hall at Kenilworth Castle, with its large oriel window, to the strong earlier keep next to it. When the walls of Paris were extended in the late fourteenth century to accommodate the expanding population, Charles V built an hôtel for himself outside the walls, to be followed by his brother the Duc de Berry and half the newly rich professional classes of Paris, who aped their social superiors by building fine suburban houses around courtyards with strutting peacocks. The chapel in every house, from the largest to the most modest, was always more highly decorated with sculpture and paint than the other rooms, and the window tracery was apt to be more ornate.

The wit and ebullience of the late Middle Ages is best summed up in the sculptured figures leaning from windows in the courtyard of the house of Jacques Coeur in Bourges. But we will leave the medieval period where we began it, with royal mausolea: here the vibrant, twisting forms of late Gothic were preferred to calm serenity. In Henry VII's chapel at Westminster and the burial church of Margaret of Austria at Brou, the rich inventiveness of architects at the height of their powers is readily apparent. The complete fusion of architecture and sculpture makes buildings appear unified in their constantly changing visual effects. The northern countries indulged this mobility of style to the utmost, and they continued it unabated until well into the sixteenth century, alongside the newly emerging Renaissance forms.

THE RENAISSANCE

The Renaissance was one of those rare periods in history that gave itself a name. The word derives from the Italian *rinascità*, rebirth, a term used by artists and humanists to express the dramatic changes ushered in by the turn of the fifteenth century. Europe was just emerging from a century of holocaust: the Hundred Years' War had devastated France and England, while the Black Death and economic regression disrupted patterns of life throughout the Continent. Trade, farming, and industry only recovered gradually, but by the end of the fourteenth century, a new confidence, as well as a revival of international trade, was discernible. The revival of trade brought wealth, and navigation gained new empires —a widening of the western world. The invention of movable type printing also enhanced the communication of ideas as well as establishing standards of language and literacy. 'Now, indeed,' wrote the Florentine humanist Matteo Palmieri in 1435, 'may every thoughtful spirit thank God that it has been permitted to him to be born in this new age, so full of hope and promise, which now rejoices in a greater army of noble souls than the world has seen in the thousand years that preceded it.'

New wealth, new stability, and a new civic pride fostered, during the Renaissance, an expansion of religious and secular building on a scale unknown since ancient times; yet the Renaissance did not create a uniform social fabric like feudalism, or an international style of architecture in the sense that Romanesque or Gothic were. The fifteenth and sixteenth centuries were a period of great transition, reshaping the contours of the West. The optimism of men like Matteo Palmieri was countered by a deep vein of pessimism in the writings of Aeneas Sylvius Piccolomini, the future Pope Pius II (1405–64): 'Christianity has no head whom all will obey . . . There is no reverence and no obedience; we look on pope and emperor as figureheads and empty titles. Every city state has its king and there are as many princes as there are households.' Piccolomini was responding to the news of the fall of Constantinople in 1453, but his vision was prophetic of the shape of the modern world and the role of the Renaissance within it. The old idea of Christendom was crumbling before the new fact of Europe, politically and religiously divided into national states.

The Old Sacristy of San Lorenzo, Florence, designed by Brunelleschi in the 1420s. It embodies one of his most important contributions to Renaissance architecture: the domed cube. The combination of dome and pendentives goes back to Byzantine architecture, but the idea was probably suggested by the medieval baptistry of Padua.

In much the same way, when looking at Renaissance architecture, one is aware of national styles which are more than variations on international themes. New developments in art and architecture took a long time to spread through the Italian peninsula, and even longer to reach the rest of Europe. Moreover, the first stages of the Renaissance coincided with the last flourish of Gothic during the fifteenth century. From Milan to London, and from Seville to Rouen, Gothic remained the preferred style in ecclesiastical architecture, while in France and England, it continued into the eighteenth century as an acceptable alternative to Renaissance. Yet, there were factors that slowly tipped the balance in favour of the new style of building associated with Italy. During the first phase of the Renaissance, which reached its peak at the beginning of the sixteenth century, the Italians enjoyed a political and cultural sophistication envied by much of Europe. As the first states to enter the modern period, their art and architecture seemed the embodiment of antique grandeur. Then, with the political balance shifting away from Italy in the sixteenth century, a new phase of the Renaissance began. The richer northern states now achieved their Renaissance by domesticating the new Italian style or, in some cases, by rejecting it in preference for building types more recognizably their own.

Renaissance architecture was not an Italian monopoly but many of its most distinctive features originated in Italy. These features include the creative study of ancient, chiefly Roman, architecture; the use of private and public buildings as an expression of civic or lordly power; the communication of architecture as a system of standardized components through books and prints; the adaptation of theories like perspective to the creation of architectural ensembles, whether squares, streets, or whole towns; and, in the end, an ability to flout these conventions through a kind of architectural licence that developed in the last stage of the Renaissance, retrospectively termed Mannerism. By looking in turn at innovations in ecclesiastical and domestic architecture, in town planning and finally in Mannerism, we can begin to appreciate what the Italian contribution was to the Renaissance and what other Europeans chose to make of it.

ECCLESIASTICAL ARCHITECTURE

Innovations in architecture, like all changes in man's attitude to his environment, are the result of challenges which defy a conventional response. The construction of the dome of Florence Cathedral, one of the germinal events of Renaissance architecture, exemplifies this process. The problem had been posed in the middle of the fourteenth century when the definitive plan for the octagonal crossing had been laid down. The diameter of the dome at 39.5 metres (130 feet) precluded the traditional use of wooden structuring to support the construction of the vault, while the use of buttresses as in northern Gothic cathedrals was ruled out by the building's design. Eventually, in 1418, a competition was held to find a solution; it was won by a goldsmith named Filippo Brunelleschi (1377–1446). His proposals for the dome were radical, so radical that he had to battle against the misgivings of those in charge of the cathedral fabric.

The novelty of Brunelleschi's solution lay in the fusion of two types of domes: the domical vault, which he knew from the early medieval Florentine baptistry, and the hemispheric domes of Roman architecture. The dual nature of this invention reduced the weight of the dome and dispensed with the need for external buttressing. Major ribs stood on each corner of the octagon with two minor ribs between each pair of major ones. These ribs were further buttressed by a series of lateral ribs that equalized the thrust of the dome as well as supporting the lighter, internal cone of brick. His first biographer reports that Brunelleschi spent years in Rome, studying the remains of classical buildings and the achievements of Roman engineering. Temples like the Minerva Medica may have suggested the application of horizontal and vertical ribs to the cathedral dome, but Brunelleschi also borrowed from Byzantine vault construction the technique of using each level of masonry in the dome as a support for the next.

Below: A bird's eye view of Florence, c.1480, reflects contemporary pride in the city's dominance over the surrounding countryside, 'like a guardian and master' of a regional state. The view also underscores a second aspect of Renaissance cities: the symbolic importance of architecture as part of a city's identity.

The boldness and novelty of Brunelleschi's design struck contemporaries, both in Florence and beyond, as miraculous. In a letter to Brunelleschi, the humanist and architectural theorist Leon Battista Alberti (1404–72) described the Florentine dome as 'a feat of engineering . . . that people did not believe possible . . . and was probably equally unknown and unimaginable among the ancients'. Alberti wrote these words in 1436 as construction had reached the level of the lantern. At that moment the only comparable building project in Italy was Milan Cathedral, which pursued a late Gothic format throughout the fifteenth and sixteenth centuries. The difference between the two works emphasizes the singularity of Brunelleschi's achievement.

The dome of Florence Cathedral, Gothic in silhouette yet classical and paleo-Christian in decoration, reflects the hybrid nature of Renaissance architecture's sources. More importantly, it symbolizes the way in which architectural monuments begin to dominate the city. This can be grasped by comparing a late fourteenth-century with a late fifteenth-century view of Florence. In the latter, the identity of Florence is bound up as much with its major architectural features—the cathedral dome, the Medici and Pitti palaces among others—as it is with the topographic and symbolic elements (such as defensive walls) that constituted the late medieval image of a city. Thus Brunelleschi not only accomplished a minor revolution in construction, but he also set in motion a

change in the relationship between buildings and cities, by a powerful exploitation of scale and of the scenic set piece.

Brunelleschi's contemporaries were aware that he had established the foundations for a new style in architecture comparable to the revival of letters and the other arts in the fourteenth century. Significantly, too, his contemporaries recognized the merit of Brunelleschi's work as it created the *appearance* of classical architecture without simply imitating it. This distinction goes some way to explaining the manner in which the best of Renaissance architecture strove to capture the spirit of ancient buildings without necessarily copying them too literally. It is also one of the striking features of Renaissance architecture throughout Eu-

RENAISSANCE DOMES

To men of the Renaissance, the dome was hallowed by ancient and Christian associations, for it represented the technical achievements of Hadrian's Pantheon as well as the ecclesiastical tradition of martyria. Typically, the greatest domes of the Renaissance were not slavish imitations of antiquity but reflected a compromise between the antique and the more familiar Gothic vaulting.

Left: The dome of Florence Cathedral (Santa Maria del Fiore), designed by Brunelleschi, 1420–34. Generations of architects would be indebted to this dome for a synthesis of antique style and experimental discovery that resulted in a two-tiered structure, relatively light and self-supporting. It could be built in successive layers without the necessity of centring (as in Gothic vaulting), and the major and minor ribs functioned as buttresses.

Right: The dome of St Peter's, Rome, completed 1588–93. When Michelangelo designed it in the years before his death in 1564, he used Brunelleschi's dome as a structural reference and point of departure. Both domes share a double shell and rib construction, surmounted by a lantern, but St Peter's differs in the suggestion of a hemispheric form that recalls the Pantheon and also the original intention of Bramante.

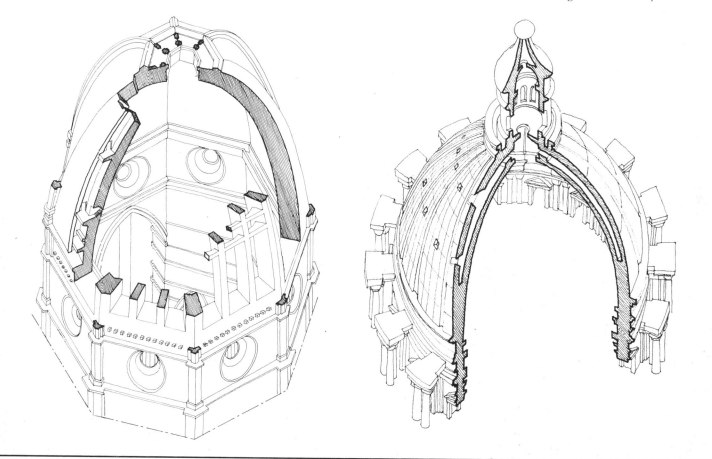

rope that the new style made its impact more easily in religious architecture than in secular buildings. The innate conservatism of domestic arrangements contributed to the slower adaptation of Renaissance forms in palaces, but ecclesiastical architecture lent itself more easily to the application of Renaissance theories.

There is, perhaps, no better example of the Renaissance synthesis of pagan and Christian than in the modelling of sacred buildings in the form of Roman temples. This was especially the case in Italy, which had not witnessed a period of Gothic architecture comparable to that of northern Europe. Italian architects and their patrons considered the architecture of their immediate predecessors inferior to the tangible achievements of classical Rome, and they attempted to reconcile the functions of Christian architecture with the proportions and plans admired in classical temples. Two names, above all, can be associated with the main innova-

tions in Italian religious architecture: Brunelleschi, again, and Leon Battista Alberti. Both came of Florentine families, and both had received a humanist training, Alberti, having spent much of his life in the papal civil service. More importantly, they were among the first to recognize the value of Roman ruins as an instrument for improving contemporary architecture. Brunelleschi, the older man, had studied Roman architecture for its techniques of construction, while Alberti sought to extract the principles of Roman architecture from what he saw in Rome and throughout Italy.

Alberti's unrivalled knowledge of classical literature and ancient architecture led him to produce the first and most fundamental architectural treatise since Roman times: the *De Re Aedificatoria* of 1452. He saw his object as presenting to his contemporaries the work of Vitruvius, whom Alberti described as writing in a language half Latin and half Greek. While Alberti

treats many of the same topics as Vitruvius, he presents his ideas in a clearer, more logical manner, beginning with drawings and building materials and then proceeding to houses and cities. Where Vitruvius is obscure, Alberti appeals to the evidence of classical ruins in order to understand the basis of Roman architecture. Like Vitruvius, and indeed like architects up to the nineteenth century, Alberti held that architecture imitated nature, and he derived his criteria of judging buildings—harmony, proportion, and symmetry—from what he conceived to be the underlying principles of the natural world. At the same time, Alberti's treatise is imbued with a strong sense of the social function of architecture in creating a happy and well-ordered state. Alberti's influence on later architecture was more long lasting than Brunelleschi's, but together they contributed to the popularity of two types of church synonymous with the achievements of Renaissance architec-

ture: the centralized plan, and the barrel-vaulted nave with lateral chapels.

The central plan lent itself to the size of a small chapel or votive church, where the liturgical need for processions and the pressures to have several private altars were absent. Its earliest application in Italian Renaissance architecture can be traced to Brunelleschi's sacristy for the Medici in San Lorenzo and to his Pazzi Chapel in Santa Croce, both designed in the 1420s. As well as being chapels for rival families, both buildings had to serve ecclesiastical functions (the Pazzi Chapel was also chapterhouse and meeting place for the Pazzi clan), which may explain some of the similarities in their design. The basic structure from which they began, however, is remarkable and without precedent in Tuscan architecture. In both cases, Brunelleschi established a domed cube as the focal point of the building with subordinate elements carefully proportioned to it. The domed cube was a Byzantine motif adapted by Brunelleschi from examples like the medieval baptistry in Padua. Consonant with the use of the domed cube is the re-introduction of the pendentive into the vocabulary of European architecture. These are the three-dimensional triangles of masonry that allow a circular dome to be raised over a square crossing, and in this case, again, Brunelleschi appears to have adapted them from examples of late antique or Byzantine architecture. Details of capitals for the pilasters look classical from a distance, but they are, in fact, close to the capitals in Romanesque Florentine churches. The Pazzi Chapel, even more than the Old Sacristy, represents the purest expression of Brunelleschian architecture. The grey sandstone membering against the whitewashed walls derives as much from Tuscan Gothic as from ancient architecture, but it emphasizes the logic of the building's structure. In addition, the use of colour is restrained to the majolica frieze and the roundels of the evangelists, an early and striking example of the subservience of detail to a unifying design.

Above: The presbytery and choir of Santa Maria delle Grazie, Milan, Italy, begun in 1492, by Bramante. The idea for a domed crossing flanked by semi-circular niches may have been taken from the church of San Bernardino in Bramante's native Urbino; both churches were intended as mausolea for ruling families: the Sforza in Milan, the Montefeltro in Urbino. Here, the build-up of masses and the decoration is in the native Milanese tradition of San Lorenzo Maggiore. The extension to Santa Maria delle Grazie marks a stage in Bramante's development before his arrival in Rome in 1500.

The adoption of the central plan gained currency in late fifteenth- and early sixteenth-century Italy. It was sanctioned by the writings of Alberti and by the evidence of Roman architecture; in a revival of Platonic arguments, the circle was seen as the most perfect form, mirroring the divine order of the universe. Often the central plan was employed for churches of a special character—votive churches dedicated to the Virgin, like Giuliano da Sangallo's Santa Maria delle Carceri in Prato. Further north, in Venice, the central plan was also employed in parish churches like San Giovanni Crisostomo by Mauro Codussi. Both of these churches adopted a Greek cross for their ground plan; this enabled them to reconcile clerical preferences for cruciform churches with the focal point of a central domed crossing. The Greek cross was especially suitable to Venetian architecture since it represented a continuation of a building type frequently employed in the earliest Venetian churches.

The high point in the fortunes of the central-plan church in Italy came with its selection as the form in which the new St Peter's in Rome would be built. The first architect of the new St Peter's was Donato Bramante (1444–1514), whose famous project for the premier church in Christendom marked a revival of Brunelleschi's concepts of space, volume, and architectural mass. The influence of Brunelleschi upon Bramante was probably mediated by Leonardo da Vinci (1452–1519). Both artists were active at the Milanese court of Ludovico Sforza in the late 1480s and may have collaborated on the remarkable east end of the church of Santa Maria delle Grazie. The intention was to rebuild the entire building in a composite form reminiscent of Brunelleschian churches with domed crossing, nave, and aisles. In the event only the centrally planned tribune and choir were built, forming the sharpest of contrasts with the early fifteenth-century nave. Bramante's solution of two domed cubes in sequence returns to the plan of Brunelleschi's Old Sacristy in Florence; yet the serenity of the earlier composition becomes, in Bramante's hands, more dramatic through the vastly increased scale and through the introduction of large semicircular apses. The crossing of Santa Maria delle Grazie marks a watershed between fifteenth- and sixteenth-century architecture, for as one enters it from the nave of the church, one leaves the modular, static architecture of the Late Gothic for the dynamic, three-dimensional structures of the High Renaissance.

The beginning of the sixteenth century saw Bramante in the service of Pope Julius II (1443–1513) in Rome. Both the impact of ancient Roman architecture and the imperial dreams of Julius inspired Bramante to refine and expand his conception of architecture, and together the pope and his architect embarked upon a series of building projects to rival those of the Roman emperors. None of these was more grandiose than the decision to rebuild the ancient basilica of St Peter's as a centrally planned *martyrium*. Work started on the new church in 1506 and for much of the century centred upon the domed crossing, the nucleus that absorbed the attention of Bramante and his patron. We know that Bramante wanted, metaphorically, to place the hemispheric dome of the Pantheon on the enormous piers of the Basilica of Maxentius. Something of the architect's intention can be gathered from the famous parchment plan in the Uffizi and the foundation medal, where the first hemispheric dome since antiquity rises above a welter of smaller domes and towers. The plan of a Greek cross inside a square, and the clustering of small domed spaces around a larger central one, may be indebted to Leonardo's projects, but the relationship of solid to void as well as the diagonal placing of the crossing piers that support the arches of the dome were Bramante's invention. Although the final form of St Peter's is markedly different from Bramante's first conception, the language of ecclesiastical architecture from

THE GESU: A CHURCH FOR THE CATHOLIC REFORMATION

Among Renaissance churches the Gesù in Rome brought to perfection a type of building first associated with Alberti (Sant' Andrea in Mantua). The single nave with side chapels and a suppressed transept was popular in Rome at the beginning of the sixteenth century, especially for smaller churches like Santa Maria di Monserrato. The Gesù was important as much for the influence of the Jesuits within the Catholic Church as for the scale of the church itself. Since the main function of the church was for preaching, the greater part of the structure was given over to a large nave almost 18 metres (nearly 60 feet) wide, with a handsome barrel vault. On either side of the nave are four interconnecting chapels. The nave is followed by a domed crossing and then the presbytery with a broad shallow apse. The abbreviated transept arms were necessary as the church was hemmed in by a street on one side and monastic buildings on the other. Work on the new church only began through the financial support of Cardinal Alessandro Farnese, who brought in his own architect, Vignola, and stipulated the broad features of the design. His power over the Gesù is reflected in a contemporary saying that Farnese owned the three most beautiful things in Rome: his daughter, the Palazzo Farnese and the Gesù. When Vignola's façade design failed to suit the Cardinal, another architect, Giacomo della Porta, was commissioned and provided a vigorous imitation of Michelangelo.

Right: The cutaway shows how the thrust of the barrel vault is absorbed by buttresses resting on the chapel walls.

the sixteenth to the eighteenth century remained largely indebted to his vision.

The later history of St Peter's, like Wren's St Paul's in the seventeenth century, shows how strong clerical opposition was to the central plan. The Italian Renaissance did, however, provide a second form of temple-church that gained wide popularity by virtue of its adoption in one of the most important churches of the sixteenth century, the Gesù in Rome. The Gesù was begun in 1568 for the Society of Jesus, one of the new preaching orders called into being to meet the challenge of the Protestant Reformation. Between the laying of the first stone of the new St Peter's and that of the Gesù, two catastrophes had befallen the Catholic world. One was the threat of total disintegration of the Roman Church through

the successful spread of Protestant revolt in much of Europe, even within Italy itself. Then, too, Rome had been sacked in 1527 by the troops of the Catholic emperor Charles V. In a letter to Henry VIII, Charles defended the pillage and looting of the Eternal City as the will of God in revenge for the sins and worldly ambitions of the popes. Many, both Protestant and Catholic, agreed with him, and the sack of Rome forced what was left of Catholic Europe to consider the necessity of a Catholic Reformation.

The Society of Jesus arose in response to this crisis as the Franciscans and Dominicans had done in an earlier period of Christian revival. One of the chief tasks of the Jesuits was preaching, and for their churches they needed a large hall in the manner of the medieval preaching orders.

The architect of their 'mother' church in Rome was Giacomo Vignola (1507–63), who received the commission and detailed instructions on the design from the patron, rather than from the Jesuits themselves. Cardinal Farnese, the man who paid for the building, wanted a large and magnificent church, apparently against the wishes of the Jesuits themselves. In a famous letter to Vignola, he dictated the requirements of the new church: 'The church is not to have a nave and two aisles, but is to have a nave with chapels down either side ... The nave is to be vaulted, and not to be roofed in any other fashion, despite objections they, the Jesuits, may raise, saying the voice of the preacher may be lost because of the echo.'

Following his patron's brief, Vignola designed what was to become one of the

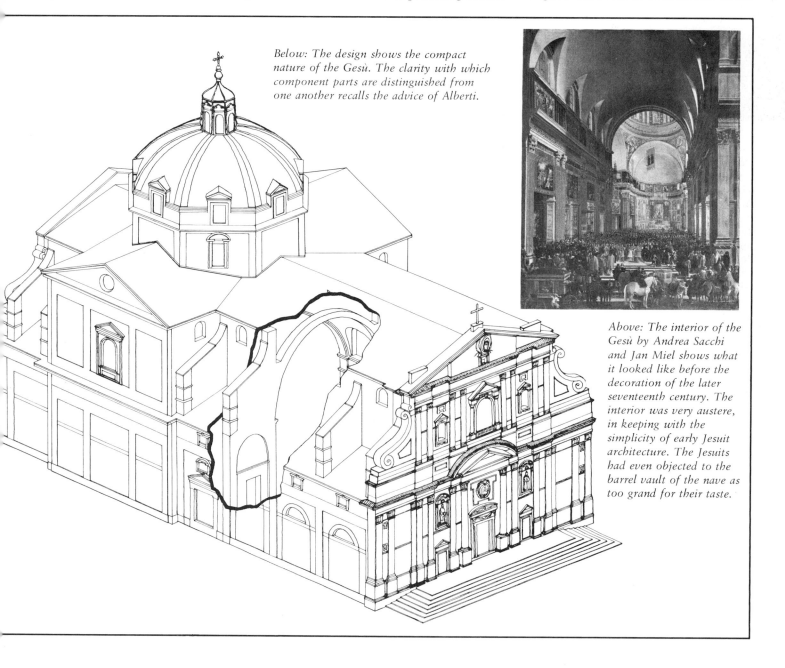

Below: The design shows the compact nature of the Gesù. The clarity with which component parts are distinguished from one another recalls the advice of Alberti.

Above: The interior of the Gesù by Andrea Sacchi and Jan Miel shows what it looked like before the decoration of the later seventeenth century. The interior was very austere, in keeping with the simplicity of early Jesuit architecture. The Jesuits had even objected to the barrel vault of the nave as too grand for their taste.

most influential churches of modern times. He took as his point of departure the church of Sant' Andrea in Mantua, begun in 1470 by Alberti. This earlier church had been inspired by Vitruvius' description of an Etruscan temple and consisted of a single barrel-vaulted nave with lateral chapels. The compactness of Alberti's design recommended it for the density of urban sites, and there are a number of examples built in Rome before Vignola's Gesù. These earlier churches were, however, small with simple beam roofs while the Gesù immediately commanded attention by virtue of its size—particularly its magnificent vaulted nave—and the inherent importance of the Jesuits within the Catholic world. With its adoption by the Jesuits and other new preaching congregations like the Theatines and Oratorians, the Albertian Etruscan temple became the established form of preaching church. With the spread of the religious orders of the Catholic Reformation across Europe and the New World, the plan of the Gesù was widely diffused in the seventeenth and eighteenth centuries.

The success of the new Italian church types outside Italy was highly varied and points to a significant difference between eastern and northern Europe. Small centrally planned chapels proved enormously popular in eastern Europe; Poland alone still has over 200 while western Europe saw very few central-plan churches built. The differences go beyond the question of the Reformation, which obviously limited the development of religious architecture

in the north, to suggest that eastern countries like Poland and Hungary wished to establish their 'European' identity in the face of a continual Turkish threat. The eastern courts adopted Italian styles of building and pursued humanist studies shortly after they had become diffused throughout Italy. By the end of the fifteenth century, Cardinal Bakócz had built a splendid chapel in the style of Brunelleschi and Giuliano da Sangallo at the cathedral of Esztergom, and by 1517 Sigismund I of Poland could contemplate a funerary chapel which in its use of sculpture and architecture ceded little to contemporary Roman structures and can be compared with the Chigi Chapel by Raphael (1483–1520) in Santa Maria del Popolo.

Raphael's chapel, begun in 1513, was an early and influential example of the 'total work of art' that became exceptionally popular in the next century; painting, sculpture, mosaics, and architecture were employed to effect an allegory of the soul's ascent to heaven. Sigismund's chapel achieves a similar goal, but the Italianate forms are used with a freedom that renders the chapel a highly individual work of art.

Western Europe, as a whole, proved far less receptive to the new Italian tendencies in ecclesiastical architecture. There, the survival of late Gothic indicates a deep aesthetic divide between Italian architects and their transalpine colleagues. In a famous letter to Pope Leo X, Raphael observed that the Gothic pointed arch was structurally weaker than the Roman round arch, something which was not actually correct but became a familiar theme in Italian discussions of architecture. In the north the attitude was more ambiguous and is best typified by the treatise of the Frenchman Philibert de l'Orme (1510–70), who had spent several years in Italy and knew Renaissance Italian architecture better than most of his contemporaries. Despite his bias towards Renaissance forms, de l'Orme conceded that Gothic vaulting had a proven technical capacity for ecclesiastical building.

The mixed reception of Italianate forms outside Italy is reflected in the rarity of uncompromisingly Renaissance works like the church of the Escorial or the chapel of the château at Anet. Much more common was the attempt to marry Gothic structure with Renaissance decoration that one finds in churches like St Eustache in Paris, Granada Cathedral in Spain, or St Michael's in Munich. In St Eustache and

in the cathedral at Granada, the only element that tells us the church is not pure Gothic is the presence of Renaissance Orders applied uncomfortably to the pier shafts. St Michael's is more interesting because it represents the first wave of church building in Catholic Bavaria after the disruptions of the Reformation. It served the dual functions of a court church for the duke of Bavaria, William V, and was part of the Jesuit college in Munich. Consequently, its splendid interior proclaims a dependence upon the Gesù in Rome, but the proportions of the nave are rooted in the tradition of late German Gothic churches. Likewise, the façade was

conceived in the local style with a high stepped gable. Moreover, the façade is conceived as an almost secular celebration of the patron and his family, overshadowing reference to the patron saint.

It is not surprising to find the most perfectly Renaissance of non-Italian churches being built by French and Spanish court architects. Unlike England, where Protestantism drove a wedge between the court and Italian art, France and Spain were locked in a struggle for the Italian peninsula during the early sixteenth century, and the importation of Italian artists and ideas became a status symbol. One is not surprised to learn that the architect of the Escorial, Juan Bautista de Toledo (*d.* 1567), had been employed on St Peter's in Rome, from which he derived the monumental Greek cross inscribed within a square. By comparison with the exuberant decorative quality of most contemporary Spanish architecture, the Doric simplicity of the Escorial assumes a polemical character, as its patron, Philip II, doubtless intended. A few years earlier, Philibert de l'Orme furnished a comparable example of the new Italian style with the chapel for the château of Henri II's mistress. The chapel of Anet is a tho-

roughly Renaissance work, inspired by the Pantheon. Like the Pantheon, the dome is hemispheric, but its coffering marks an inventive departure from earlier practice by adapting a pattern of intersecting circles echoed in the stone pavement beneath. The articulation of the ground floor of the chapel is indebted to Italian Renaissance churches, but the pilasters are not of a recognizably classical Order. Their capitals with two rows of laurel leaves crowned by berries are a creation of the architect, called by him a French Ionic Order. De l'Orme's departure from the ancient Orders would have been unthinkable to an Italian architect, but it is indicative of the freshness of approach to foreign styles that swayed even the most learned of non-Italian architects.

DOMESTIC ARCHITECTURE

From the Middle Ages, Italy had been a highly urbanized society with a power base for both nobles and the emergent bourgeoisie deriving from their standing in the city, not from landed estates. Thus the importance of the city in Italian life, buttressed by new wealth and humanist defences of it, gave birth to a revolution in domestic living during the fifteenth century that found expression in the Renaissance palace. Medieval palaces with their towers and loggia had been a focal point of family clans; they were designed for defensive and commercial rather than aesthetic purposes. Branches of the same family would live, work and gather there in times of crisis. All of this changed, however, during the course of little more

than a century, and Florence was one of the first cities in which a new type of dwelling, exclusively residential and for one family unit, became common. Over the previous centuries both Franciscan preaching and conventional wisdom had counselled against ostentation as sinful and potentially dangerous, but by the beginning of the fifteenth century humanists, following Aristotle, argued that wealth offered the great man a means of enhancing his reputation, that of his family, and that of his city or country. One means of accomplishing this was to build, or, as Alberti phrased it: 'since all agree that we should endeavour to leave a reputation behind us, not only for our wisdom but our power too, for this reason . . . we erect great structures, that our posterity may suppose us to have been great persons'. That Alberti's words were not wasted can be seen by the explosion of private palace building that occurred in Florence during the fifteenth and sixteenth centuries.

The Medici palace exemplifies the changes that took place in many Renaissance palaces. In the 1440s the Medici moved away from their banking concerns and built a new palace on what was the outskirts of medieval Florence. Much of the design derives from earlier Florentine palaces and the number of rooms is not appreciably more than in earlier buildings. Yet a greater attention has been given to the aesthetic effect of the palace. The façade is composed of three floors of masonry blocks with a gradation from large, roughly cut (or rusticated) stone on the ground floor to smooth, progressively

Above: The façade of the Palazzo Medici, Florence, designed by Michelozzo in the 1440s. Florentine palaces had already established a severe style of stone façade; size and stone cladding were more important in central Italian palaces than ornamental decoration.

Right: The Palazzo Farnese by Antonio da Sangallo was the most important Roman palace of the sixteenth century. The courtyard's use of an applied Order with arches recreates the effect of antique theatres.

Far right above: A distant view of the ducal palace of Urbino, Italy, built by Federico da Montefeltro in the mid-fifteenth century, shows the triple loggia, later copied by French châteaux and Tudor houses.

Far right below: The studiolo of the ducal palace at Urbino is an early example of a room designed for only one person.

smaller stones on the upper floors. The façade is further distinguished by the rhythmic distribution of windows; this is something that was to become a standard feature of Renaissance architecture, although here the arrangement of windows and rooms is not always well co-ordinated. Originally, the ground floor also contained shops which were entered from the large arches still visible. These were intended to bring in some revenue for the owner but fell out of fashion as the palace became more of an aristocratic dwelling. The large windows on the ground floor were designed by Michelangelo (1475–1564) in the early sixteenth century and were widely imitated on other Florentine palaces where the same transition from middle-class to noble palace was occurring.

The type of the Florentine palace was carried to other parts of Italy in the second half of the fifteenth century, but it flourished particularly in Rome. The restoration of Rome—after centuries of decline and even the absence of the papacy —stimulated the imagination of popes like Martin V, Paul II, and Sixtus IV. They were aided in their grand designs by humanist architects like Alberti and the Veronese Fra Giocondo (1433–1515). Loans were given to facilitate the construction of new palaces, and new roads and bridges were planned to improve communications between the Vatican and the rest of the city. Construction became a boom industry, and Tuscan builders largely dominated it. Comparison of a late Renaissance palace like the Palazzo Farnese with the Palazzo Medici of a hundred

years before show how little change there had been. The Palazzo Farnese was largely designed by one Tuscan architect, Antonio da Sangallo the younger, and completed by another, Michelangelo. Sheer scale is its most conspicuous feature,

as it was designed for a cardinal (the future Paul III) with a family and retinue of 300. The façade is only saved from monotony by the late intervention of Michelangelo, who added the gigantic papal coat-of-arms and the imposing

cornice. As with Tuscan palaces, the *cortile* is the focal point of the plan of the Palazzo Farnese, but its massive bay units with attached Doric, Ionic, and Corinthian Orders, reflect a closer study of Roman architecture, chiefly the Orders of the Colosseum, typical of High Renaissance correctness.

The difference between medieval and Renaissance domestic architecture in Italy can best be appreciated, not in central Italy, but rather in a small town situated in the mountainous terrain of the Marches in the north-east: Urbino. The palace of Urbino was built by Federico da Montefeltro (1422–82), who combined brilliance as a soldier with an equally brilliant patronage of the arts. 'On the harsh site of Urbino, he built a palace that many think the finest in Italy, and in every aspect he furnished it so well that it appears not so much a palace but more like a city in the

form of a palace.' So wrote the diplomat and friend of Raphael, Baldassare Castiglione, who knew Urbino in its greatest days around the turn of the sixteenth century. The comparison between house and city strikes a particular resonance with Urbino, for the Montefeltro palace was one of the first to demonstrate a new rational planning of every aspect as advo-

cated by Alberti in his *De Re Aedificatoria*. Federico's palace lies on the slope of one of the hills that comprise Urbino and consists of a sequence of wings that link a number of pre-existing structures. The wings divide the palace into a series of suites around two large courts with spectacular views over the surrounding countryside. The scale of the main court-

yard is much ampler though less functional than its prototypes in Florence. The same spaciousness and grandeur invest the suite of public rooms, reached by an unusually wide staircase, the first example of the monumental stairway in Renaissance Italian palaces. The rooms of the duke's private apartment are justly famous for the quality of their decoration, but their size, too, is novel as they were designed to accommodate only one person. The decision of the Duke of Urbino to build on such a scale marks the beginning of a new force in domestic architecture: the concept of privacy. The idea may have been suggested by an attentive reading of the Roman Pliny's description of his villa at Laurentium, where there was a similar retreat with small chambers. For the Renaissance, the palace of Urbino was novel for its exploitation of its 'harsh' site as well as its attention to the public and private, the twin ideals of the *vita activa* and *contemplativa*, so successfully reconciled in the life of its patron.

Mention of Pliny introduces a second type of Italian Renaissance domestic architecture that would exercise a great influence on European architecture for centuries—the villa. The appeal of retirement to a country house, like privacy, was born of a keener awareness of one's surroundings and stimulated in Renaissance patrons the desire to emulate their Roman forebears. Villas represented more than a simple return to the countryside, for they also reflect the increased investment in land and farming by city-dwelling Italians from the close of the fifteenth century. The appeal of villas for Renaissance architects was twofold: it enabled

Left: The garden loggia of the Villa Madama, Rome, built by Raphael for the future Pope Clement VII de' Medici. Its decoration imitates Roman stucco and wall paintings discovered by Renaissance artists in buildings like Nero's Golden House. Begun about 1518, the villa was never finished.

Right above: Sangallo's Poggio a Caiano is a late fifteenth-century Medici villa, one of several built around Florence. It is rigorously Albertian in layout and in its alignment of solids and voids. The façade is embellished by an applied temple portico, more than two generations before Palladio popularized the motif.

Right: Palladio's Villa Rotonda at Vicenza, Italy, of the late 1560s, is one of the most admired of Renaissance buildings. Its novel features are the four porticos, to enjoy the views, and the stepped dome.

them to recreate an ancient building type of which many written accounts were known, and it allowed them to build on an open plot of land, untrammelled by the confining sites of urban buildings. When Lorenzo de' Medici wished to build a villa on his farm at Poggio a Caiano, he held a competition which Giuliano da Sangallo won. Sangallo, the future architect of Santa Maria delle Carceri, had the scope to realize a monumental work, dignified by its simple Roman arcades on the ground floor and a novel application of a Roman temple portico to the façade.

The villa in the sixteenth century became a commonplace feature in Italy, the Italian equivalent of the French château or the English country house. One of the most impressive of these later villas was the Villa Madama by Raphael. Inspired by the scale and techniques of ancient building, the Villa Madama stands on the slopes of Monte Mario to the north of the Vatican. It was conceived as a show-piece of Medici patronage under the reigning Pope Leo X and would have included a theatre, stables for 200 horses,

and a large circular court if it had not been abandoned in the early 1520s. Fortunately, part of the villa was built, and the surviving garden loggia, with its combination of painted and stucco decorations remains one of the most imaginative re-creations of ancient architecture produced during the Renaissance.

Raphael's contribution to villa architecture was fragmentary, and the most influential type of villa arose in the north of Italy with Andrea Palladio as its architect. While most Renaissance architects had begun their careers as painters or sculptors, Palladio's training more nearly approximates to the modern idea of the architect as a trained professional. Born in Padua in 1508, Palladio worked his way up the artistic and social hierarchy to become, by his death in 1580, the unofficial first

Above: The Villa Badoer, Italy, 1556, has a classic Palladian solution: a central portico with the owner's crest in its pediment.

architect of Venice. His working life coincided with a change in the economy of the Venetian provinces with capital being invested more heavily in land than in mercantile activities. The Venetian nobles were following the example of Benedictine monasteries, which had made large profits from land reclamation and efficient farming in the fifteenth century. Palladio received numerous commissions to build country houses which were intended, partly, to reflect the new importance of estates in the life of Venetian gentlemen.

In Venice, palaces had evolved along lines peculiar to the site of the lagoon, with raft-like foundations to provide a flexible base for the sandy subsoil. The upper floors were designed to provide an equalization of stress, and windows were given prominence in the façades of the tightly packed houses in order to maximize the major source of light. Houses were also divided by a corridor that ran their length, and provided a central reception room and passageway. This pattern spread to the neighbouring territories and pre-Palladian villas often had the look of a fortified Cà

d'Oro. Palladio's achievement lay in rationalizing the basic elements of the Veneto house and grafting onto them principles drawn from earlier Renaissance architects and from Roman architecture.

Mature versions of the Palladian villa, like the Villa Cornaro at Piombino or the Villa Badoer at Fratta Polesine, show how effectively Palladio could combine traditional building types with a classical-Renaissance vocabulary. The traditional villa portico becomes a temple portico with the arms of the owner inscribed in the pediment; the division of the interior allows for a symmetrical placing of small, medium, and large rooms on either side of the central hall or *salone*. Thus the villa's suite of rooms demonstrates a pleasing sequence of spaces, while door frames, window mouldings, ceilings, and the portico are given a distinctly classical appearance. If Giuliano da Sangallo had been the first to secularize the temple portico, Palladio went further and made domes as well as porticoes part of the vocabulary of domestic architecture.

Palladio seems to have made little distinction between palaces and villas as building types, and often the characteristics that seem quintessential to the latter can be found in the former. Nonetheless,

when Palladio published *The Four Books of Architecture* (1570), he allocated the country houses (*case di villa*) a section to themselves, recognizing that they formed a conspicuous part of his achievement as an architect. Palladio became an influential architect through his villas, but equally through the medium of his treatise. There, he conveyed the particulars of building, from the ground up, writing in the vernacular and illustrating his ideas and his works with woodcuts of a high quality. Architectural treatises were not a novelty by the time that Palladio's appeared, but none were as systematic nor as well illustrated as was *The Four Books*. Palladio presented to his readers a complete architectural system that covered all aspects of building and presented them in a modular relationship to one another. It was his comprehensiveness and unrivalled culling of the best models in ancient architecture that made Palladio the most influential architect in the modern period.

While villas remained largely an Italian phenomenon, the new principles of domestic architecture spread across Europe through the late fifteenth and sixteenth centuries. By the 1490s, Vladislav II of the Jagellonian dynasty ruling in Hungary, Bohemia, and Poland, planned a magnificent extension to the royal castle in Prague that invites comparison with Federico da Montefeltro's earlier achievements at Urbino. Vladislav sent his court-architect, Benedikt Rejt, to Budapest in order to study the new Italian style in the now vanished palace of Matthias Corvinus. Rejt had been an accomplished Gothic architect, and his subsequent work in Prague castle demonstrates his personal response to the innovations he had seen in Budapest. This can be clearly seen in the most important addition to the castle, the great hall. The great hall rivals the courtyard of Urbino in size and impact, and, being designed to accommodate indoor tournaments of more than 100 horsemen, comparison of the great hall's dimensions with those of a courtyard are apposite. The amplitude of the Gothic vaulting almost eclipses the rhythmic effect of the Renaissance windows.

More often, however, interiors in eastern and central Europe proved intractable to an easy assimilation of the internal arrangements of Italian villas and palaces. Renaissance influences, when they came, were often confined to a new treatment of the external façade. This led to the introduction of such Italian motifs as the arcaded courtyard in palaces like the royal castle on Wawel Hill in Cracow, or the Stallburg in the Hofburg complex in Vienna. Hitherto, outside of monastic or collegiate cloisters, arcades had been rare in eastern and central Europe, while in Italy arcading was generally conceived as a functional shelter in palaces as in cloisters.

In the 1550s, Maximilian II began extensive building around the medieval castle of Vienna in the new style. His architect was an Italian, Pietro Ferrabosco, and in addition to the triumphal arch leading to the Schweizerhof, Ferrabosco probably designed the structure now known as the Stallburg. The exterior is as

reticent as that of the Schweizerhof, but the interior consists of a large courtyard with three floors of arcading with elongated bays between robust piers. Each floor division is marked by a projecting entablature countering the verticality of the arcades.

In Germany, the Gothic style remained

FONTAINEBLEAU: A RENAISSANCE PALACE OF THE NORTH

What was to become one of the most celebrated complexes in Renaissance architecture began as a series of small additions to a medieval hunting lodge. In 1528 François I entrusted the enlargement of the old castle at Fontainebleau to a French mason named Gilles Le Breton, who worked together with a number of Italian artists drawn into the French king's service. The new features included an imposing entrance called the Porte Dorée, a gallery that connected the old Cour de l'Ovale with the keep and new wings that formed the basis of the Cour du Cheval Blanc. In keeping with the accretive nature of Fontainebleau, the variety of style is pronounced, ranging from the majestic sweep of the east wing of the Cour du Cheval Blanc to its humble neighbour to the north of white plaster and brick. François I sought the best Italian craftsmen to work on Fontainebleau. Guilio Romano, student of Raphael and court artist in Mantua, contributed advice and perhaps designs. He also sent his pupil Primaticcio, who, together with the Florentine artist Rosso, made Fontainebleau, in the words of Giorgio Vasari, 'a second Rome'.

Below: A bird's eye view of Fontainebleau during the mid-sixteenth century, looking north, based on a drawing by Jacques Androuet du Cerceau the Elder.

Right: The decoration of the Galerie François I was a collaborative effort of Primaticcio and Rosso. Begun in the 1530s and finished after Rosso's death in 1540, it proved to be a successful adaptation of Italian decoration to the traditional French gallery. Above the wainscoting, frescoes with painted or stuccoed frames alternate with window bays. Between the windows there were casts, by Primaticcio, after antique statues. The idea of a decorated gallery was later introduced into Italian palaces, such as the Palazzo Spada and Palazzo Farnese in Rome.

Left: The most important of Primaticcio's designs for Fontainebleau was the massive Aile de la Belle Cheminée of 1568. The monumental stairs may echo Michelangelo's Palazzo dei Senatori in Rome, but the pilasters and rustication are typical of French architecture of the mid-sixteenth century.

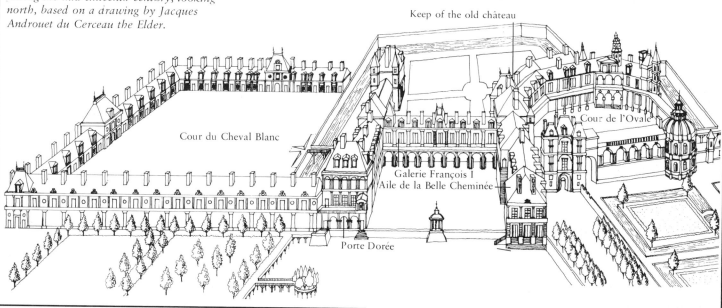

Keep of the old château

Cour du Cheval Blanc

Cour de l'Ovale

Galerie François I
Aile de la Belle Cheminée

Porte Dorée

very active during the sixteenth century, and Renaissance motifs did not really begin to supplant it until the turn of the seventeenth. The additions to Heidelberg Castle by the elector Ottheinrich in his four-year reign (1556–9) were a notable exception to contemporary building styles, just as the elector was a greater devotee of humanism and all things southern than most of his German peers. The Ottheinrichsbau was underway at the same time as the Stallburg in Vienna, but its impact is more sculptural than architectural. In spite of classical motifs and the alignment of windows and niches, the whole façade remains little more than a mask over a late medieval building, like the arcades of Wawel Castle. Even the later addition to the castle at Heidelberg by the elector Friedrich (1601–7) represents only a slight advance upon the Ottheinrichsbau in terms of sophistication. It is worth noting that Flemish sculptors worked on both buildings, and the popularity of sculptural elements in northern architecture may explain the prominence given to caryatids and other figures here. The gables on the Friedrichsbau, moreover, show a direct importation from the Renaissance in the

Low Countries, an example of Renaissance influences beginning to come from other areas besides Italy.

RENAISSANCE STYLES IN FRANCE, ENGLAND AND SPAIN

The examples of domestic architecture outside Italy that we have considered thus far have each been the product of a court. The appearance of the Renaissance style in French architecture conforms to this pattern. Throughout the sixteenth century the châteaux of the Loire and Ile-de-France occupied the attention of the French kings and their subjects, as Paris remained relatively stagnant until the end of the century. The earliest manifestation of the new style came, typically, with decorative motifs like pilasters and window mouldings embedded in medieval piles. Soon, regularity of plan, symmetry, and an Italianate bay system became widely employed. In the château of Chambord, begun in 1519, the old and new coalesced. The plan shows a large square keep with corner towers set against one side of a large rectangular court, which also has four corner towers. Its unusualness lies in the division of the keep into four parts by two corridors that form a Greek cross around the central staircase.

Each part follows the same sequence of three rooms and a closet, known as the *appartement*, which was to become the standard domestic arrangement of French living quarters for the next two centuries. But the values stressed in the ground plan of the château, probably the work of an Italian architect, are hardly visible in elevation. The towers, chimneys, and dormers of Chambord are more suggestive of the Middle Ages, albeit the

Left above: A Frenchman visiting northern Italy in the early sixteenth century described the Certosa of Pavia as 'the finest church I ever saw, and all of fine marble'. Conceived as a monument to the Sforza rule in Milan, the profuse decoration of the façade has greater affinities with northern Renaissance architecture than with the work of Alberti or Bramante.

Left below: The Vladislav Hall of Hradčany castle, Prague, designed by Benedikt Rejt in the 1490s, combines late Gothic vaulting with Renaissance proportions.

Below: Although Italianate in plan, the appearance of Chambord in France, begun in 1519, adheres to the traditional château style.

individual motifs of pilasters and dormer surrounds are close copies of Italian models. The discrepancy between sources and their application is a recurrent theme in Renaissance architecture, and with the château as a Renaissance building, one quickly appreciates how defensive attributes like moats and turrets continued as aesthetic prerequisites throughout the century, whether in a royal residence like Chambord or in a more modest country residence like Chenonceau.

By the middle of the sixteenth century, new attitudes towards architecture crystallized around François I's project to rebuild the medieval Louvre. The task was given to Pierre Lescot (1510–78), a contemporary of Philibert de l'Orme, but unlike him, a well-to-do man who was an amateur architect. Lescot was well educated and steeped in classical learning; like the poetry of the *Pléiade* his façade for the west wing of the Louvre was classical in inspiration, yet unmistakably French. The most directly classical element is his use of Orders, applied with a rigorous attention to detail that would have pleased the most pedantic of scholars. They are matched in their severity by the sculpture

of Jean Goujon. The overall effect suggests a refined but direct derivation from the style of the châteaux. The triple pavilion is reminiscent of those on medieval French castles, and the horizontal sweep of the block, the criss-cross of the horizontal and vertical members, can be paralleled in earlier châteaux of the sixteenth century. Moreover, the pronounced flatness of the design marks it as French in contrast with an Italian façade's reliance upon a greater plasticity of treatment.

When considering Lescot's work, it is important to remember that he had not been to Rome before he began the Louvre. Hence, his knowledge of the Renaissance was at second hand, gained from books, woodcuts, and Roman ruins in France. The result is different from the distant original model and marks the beginning of a reaching-back to antiquity that does not necessarily go through Italian architecture. This is a feature that becomes very common by the end of the century, especially with the town architecture of the Low Countries. In France, this phenomenon is also prophetic of the eventual rejection of Italian influence that became such a distinctive feature of all aspects of French

culture during the seventeenth and eighteenth centuries.

In England, too, the appearance of the new style in domestic architecture occurred within the orbit of the court, notably in Cardinal Wolsey's magnificent undertaking at Hampton Court. There, as with early French châteaux, Wolsey commissioned roundels of the Roman emperors from an Italian sculptor, and the roundels were placed in the façade of a building that differed only slightly from a late medieval castle. Application of the new style was fitful in the early years of the century. An antique ceiling like that of Wolsey's closet could be followed by the massive hammer beam roof of the hall, which was built by Henry VIII after Wolsey's fall. Such a coexistence of old and new can be seen in other examples, like Pietro Torrigiano's splendid bronze tomb of Henry VII in his flamboyant Gothic chapel at Westminster Abbey, or the Flemish screen with a Renaissance bay system of classical Orders in King's College, Cambridge. The Reformation soon drove a wedge between Italy and England while trade and political ties with the Low Countries meant that the Renaissance in England was largely imported *via* Antwerp. In contrast with France, the Crown exerted little influence in creating a Renaissance architecture, for during the second half of the sixteenth century, Elizabeth chose to encourage her courtiers, the new men who rose with the Tudor monarchy, to build for her. This led to Britain's most conspicuous contribution to Renaissance architecture, the 'prodigy' houses, such as Burghley.

A veritable mania for building broke out during the latter part of the century; its leaders were for the most part courtiers, seeking to create a power base for themselves in their native counties or in the home counties. Burghley, the creation of Elizabeth's secretary William Cecil, sprawls over two courtyards and has a massive gatehouse with engaged columns suggested by Philibert de l'Orme's entrance to the château of Anet or one of its many imitations. While many of the decorative details at Burghley have a Franco-Flemish pedigree, the overall impression of the house from a distance is more suggestive of native creations like Henry VII's palace at Richmond.

The greatest monument to the new Elizabethan style is, without question, Longleat in Wiltshire. Its builder was Sir John Thynne, a courtier who first came to building through his work for the Duke of Somerset. On first sight, Longleat shows remarkable affinities with the French style: the horizontal sweep, the flatness of decorative effect, and the obvious concern for symmetry evident in the deployment of the bay window units. The absence of a pitched roof and a sober skyline may be

Below: Hampton Court, near London, was begun by Cardinal Wolsey in 1515 and later enlarged by Henry VIII. Busts of the Roman emperors adorn an otherwise traditional façade, and although built 1531–6, the Hall is resolutely Gothic with a magnificent hammer beam roof.

Right above: The High Great Chamber of Hardwick Hall, Derbyshire, England. Such rooms were of major importance in great houses during the reigns of Elizabeth and James I. Entertainments, dinners and lyings-in-state, all took place in the great chamber.

Right below: Kirby Hall, Northamptonshire, England, dates from sixty years after Hampton Court, and its courtyard reflects an awareness of contemporary French and Italian architecture. The buttress-pilasters are the earliest example of the use of a giant Order in English architecture.

the first non-French elements to strike the eye, and these observations are reinforced by the movement of the bay windows away from the corners and in confining the slender pilasters to them. Any attempt to reconcile the external symmetry with the inner disposition of courts and rooms would have been thwarted by the traditional living arrangements which required the hall, where eating and all communal activities took place, to be on one side of the entrance, with the kitchen and buttery on the other. The hall led to a parlour where the chief members of the family could retire and the rest of the house was given over to lodgings and a long gallery, the latter being an importation from France.

The supreme achievement of the Elizabethan age, and one of the greatest buildings produced anywhere in Europe during the Renaissance, was Hardwick Hall in Derbyshire. It was the most notable of a clutch of houses built by the Countess of Shrewsbury, better known as Bess of Hardwick. She began work on Hardwick in 1590 at the age of 70 and ceremoniously moved into it seven years later. By the time she began Hardwick, Bess had a considerable knowledge of building, and the result of her experience is telling in its combination of continental and native elements. The problem of symmetry, which had never been solved satisfactorily in earlier Elizabethan houses, was here dealt with by turning the hall into an internal courtyard. To the left and right of the hall, the rooms were distributed uniformly. Large staircases led from either side of the hall to the main living rooms, everyday rooms on the first floor and the impressive state chambers placed as a dramatic culmination on the top floor. The exterior is equally masterful in its projection and recession of mass, an aspect later architects as disparate as Hawksmoor and Adam were to admire.

Nothing could be further removed from

the sober exteriors of Elizabethan or French houses than the Plateresque architecture of Spain. Spain's experience of the Renaissance style was much the same as that of France; she inherited the control of Genoa and Lombardy from France, and Spanish nobles and prelates brought in Italianate motifs through tombs and chapels. The Crown at first continued to patronize the Gothic, and only later, under Charles V and Philip II, turned to an extremely restrained version of Italian Renaissance. In general, however, the understanding of the Renaissance remained as a decorative equivalent of late Gothic. The term 'Plateresque' originated with the ornamental work of silversmiths and later came to be applied to the architecture of the first phase of the Spanish Renaissance, from 1500 to 1570. In comparison with the achievements of central Italy, the Spanish Plateresque seems little different from Spanish Gothic; indeed, both occur on many buildings. Nonetheless, to contemporary architects and aestheticians, the new 'Roman' style (*a lo romano*) seemed a revival of the principles of ancient Roman architecture, for al-

though the Spanish appreciated contemporary Italian architecture as a guide to interpreting classical buildings, they also relied upon visual evidence of the ruins in the Iberian peninsula and in France. Thus Diego Sagredo, in his influential treatise on Vitruvius, wrote of an architectural Order not mentioned by the Roman architect, but frequently seen in Roman buildings. This 'baluster' column was employed by Diego de Siloes, the architect of Granada Cathedral, shortly after Sagredo's publication, in the cloister of the Colegio de los Irlandeses at Salamanca; other architects with even less understanding of the principles of Italian architecture adopted it too. Buildings like the Medinaceli Palace of Cogollado, or the façade of Salamanca University, were greeted by Spanish theorists as pure examples of the 'Roman' style but with these and with many others, the new style remained a screen applied to traditional castellar building types.

Some explanation for this phenomenon comes from a comparison of Spanish treatises with their Italian counterparts. Basically, the difference stems from a lack

of concern on the part of Spaniards for the proportional relationships that governed so much of the Italian approach to Renaissance architecture. To most non-Italians, Rome was a magical name and little more; hence, the essential qualities of the Spanish 'Roman' style lay, in addition to the presence of some kind of order, in a decorative richness. The fantastic blend of Renaissance and Gothic ornamentation on the gate of the Condestable Chapel in the cathedral of Burgos, for example, was accepted as a model of the style of ancient architecture. In a building like the town hall of Seville, the profusion of north Italian ornament also represented the embodiment of the new wealth and opulence which gold and silver from the New World brought to that city.

A closer approximation to the Italian Renaissance was at length introduced by the Crown. From the late 1520s, Charles V employed Pedro Machuca to build a palace on the Alhambra in Granada. Only the outer walls and central court were built, but the scale of the building, the consistency of its design, and the novelty of its layout proclaim that the designer was not chosen at random. Consequently, it is not surprising to learn that Machuca was referred to by a later writer as a follower of Raphael or Michelangelo. Both the 30 metre (100 foot) diameter of the circular courtyard and the triangular stairs suggest that Machuca knew the Villa Madama; the exterior rustication and the Doric and Ionic Orders indicate inspiration from Giulio Romano's Palazzo del Té in Mantua.

Charles V's lack of finance never allowed him to complete the palace at Granada, but later versions of the Italian style had a more lasting impact upon contemporary buildings. His son, the future Philip II, is supposed to have intervened in the construction of the new royal palace of the Alcázar in Toledo, dismissing one architect and bringing in another. The new architect, Villalpando, contributed the majestic courtyard and staircase, which Charles V said made him *feel* an emperor while he ascended it. Here there was a Genoese source of inspiration; in particular, Philip had copied the new mid-century palaces of Galeazzo Alessi, almost as they were being built.

The most significant example of the anti-Plateresque, or *estilo desornamentado*, was Philip II's Escorial, begun in 1563. The Escorial started as the fulfilment of a vow to St Lawrence, to which was added the concept of a Habsburg memorial, Jeronomite monastery, and a retreat for the king. It stands with grey granite walls among the mountains above Madrid, remote and austere as was its patron. This formidable undertaking was the successive responsibility of two main architects, Juan Bautista de Toledo and Juan Herrera (1530–97). In spite of a lengthy period of construction and its formidable scale—204 by 162 metres (670 by 530 feet)—the Escorial is not only coherent but a masterpiece of planning. The large rectangular block contains seventeen major courtyards and in some portions rises to five storeys; yet it

manages to give the impression of building up to the towers and dome of the church, which becomes the central, dominant element. The total absence of decoration (not even the windows have frames) and a selective use of the Doric Order must have been intended as a polemic against the waning Plateresque style, which had specifically avoided both austerity and the Doric column. The influence of the Escorial led to a brief vogue for buildings in the simpler 'Herreran' style, notably the Exchange in Seville. In 1585, a Spanish writer praised the Escorial for following

'the rules of ancient architecture . . . the laws and Orders of Vitruvius, abandoning as vanities the petty projectionism, reversed pyramids, brackets, and other foolish things usually seen in Flemish and French plans and prints with which artists decorate (or rather mar) their work without preserving either proportion or significance'. But the *estilo desornamentado* was doomed to be swept away by the stronger current of the Baroque, which, like the Plateresque, was more congenial to the traditional exuberance of Spanish architecture.

Left: The portal of the university in Salamanca, Spain, of the late 1520s, is conceived as a decoration applied to the building. Although it looks back to Spanish Gothic, the main features are based upon Italian motifs.

Right: Charles V's unfinished palace at Granada, Spain, begun in 1526. Charles' architect had studied in Rome, and the palace's great feature, a circular court for tournaments, implies a knowledge of Raphael's Villa Madama.

Below: The Escorial, begun in 1563 was a major project of Philip II. It combined a royal palace and monastery on the scale of a small town, to the north of Madrid. Its first architect, Juan Bautista de Toledo, had worked on St Peter's under Michelangelo and had designed a new street, the Via Toledo, for the Spanish viceroy in Naples. The sober exterior and sparing use of ornament in the Escorial gave vogue to a severe style of architecture in late sixteenth-century Spain, which came as a reaction to the exuberance of the Plateresque.

cultivating an almost theatrical sense of a city as a series of *prospettive* or perspective views. Pienza, near Siena, is one of the most renowned examples of fifteenth-century town planning, as well as being one of the most perfect expressions of Albertian architectural principles. It was the creation of the humanist Pope Pius II Piccolomini and his architect Bernardo Rossellino (1409–64). Its centre was the piazza in front of the cathedral, flanked on either side by the episcopal palace and that of the Piccolomini family. These three buildings and the civic palace opposite

Left: A bird's eye view of Vitry-le-François, France. This was a new town laid out in the 1540s to strengthen the borders between France and Germany. Its design follows the Roman grid plan with a large central square and Italianate triangular bastions.

TOWN PLANNING

The Escorial came closer than any other Renaissance building to the concept of a house as a small city, and a city as a large house. Although it was rare for Renaissance architects to build new cities, as Bautista and Herrera effectively did, town planning exerted an attraction for Renaissance architects unmatched since ancient times. New towns and cities in the Renaissance were born of one or more factors: warfare, trade, or colonization. It is, perhaps, significant that the greatest achievements in this field of architecture occurred in Spanish America where the ancient Roman gridiron was revived for the scores of new towns that quickly underpinned colonial rule in the New World. By the middle of the sixteenth century, Mexico City could lay claim to being one of the most advanced examples of Renaissance planning anywhere in the Western world. About the central *plaza major* were placed the cathedral, government offices, and the houses of the wealthiest colonists. Streets were laid out at right angles to one another, and house fronts had to be aligned with the street as well as having an obligatory portico. The clarity of the plan ended, however, beyond the centre, where poorer sections were allowed to grow haphazardly. The overall effect was impressive, nevertheless, and with the adaptation of contemporary European views of planning, the transformation of the New World into an extension of the Old was accomplished.

The planning of city streets along orthogonal lines had its roots in Hellenistic and Near Eastern culture. Its popularity in Europe and, as we have seen, Latin America derived from its diffusion throughout northern Italy and northern Europe by the Romans with their colonial towns. The French new towns of the fourteenth century were also patterned along the same rational lines. To Renaissance architects the gridiron lent itself to the application of the aesthetic canons of harmony, proportion, and symmetry popularized by Alberti and later theoreticians. Alberti had introduced the new conception of a city as a balanced ensemble of impressive buildings, each related to its site and to the whole. His famous comparison of cities with houses established a common set of principles to govern both and, more importantly, refocused men's attitudes towards the city as a work of art, like painting or sculpture. Significantly, Alberti knew and admired Brunelleschi and Donatello, two artists who were pre-eminent in the rediscovery of pictorial perspective. Perspective in painting sought to render the relationship of three-dimensional objects within two dimensions; it was used not only by artists to give a more realistic sense of depth and foreshortening to their works, but also by architects to give an appearance of a building in elevation. Alberti himself was to write the first theoretical explanation of perspective, and from the second quarter of the fifteenth century buildings assumed a new importance as protagonists in the paintings of Masaccio or in the sculpture of Ghiberti.

This sensitivity to an ensemble was reflected in some of the earliest examples of town planning in Renaissance Italy,

STRADA NUOVA: URBAN GRANDEUR

Genoa's Strada Nuova was one of the most impressive urban projects of the sixteenth century. It began as an extension of the city with a wide street of ten palaces, five on each side. The idea originated with a nobleman-turned-architect, Galeazzo Alessi, who may have planned some of the first houses. They had common features of a wide façade, imposing courtyards and staircases. The street so impressed Rubens that he published a book on it in 1622, hoping to introduce similar ideas to northern Europe.

Above: The balanced ensemble of palaces reflects Renaissance love of symmetry.

establish a trapezoidal square that gives emphasis to the cathedral's façade. The appearance of each building carefully relates to Alberti's doctrine of decorum, or the suitability of a structure to the status of its owner and to its function. Thus, the bishop's palace is small and has a simple façade without an architectural Order, while the Piccolomini palace is much larger and is articulated by pilasters on each floor. The cathedral towers over the other buildings and has the most elaborate façade, with a double order of columns. Both the cathedral and the garden of the Piccolomini palace required extensive substructures in order to be built where they are. This enabled the principal buildings around the main square to be set back, thus creating a 'view', and it also gave a splendid view from the garden over the Val d'Orcia below. In Pienza, buildings and nature itself are treated as stage properties in the creation of a Renaissance city.

Princes like Pius II could will new cities into being, but the majority of men in the Renaissance had to content themselves with making additions to their cities correspond to contemporary theory. We saw that when the Medici wished to build a new palace in the 1440s, they chose a site on the outskirts of medieval Florence. New building in most cities followed the same pattern and was typified by the cutting of new rectilinear streets like the Via Giulia in Rome, laid out during the pontificacy of Julius II by Bramante. The Via Giulia began symbolically at the Ponte Sisto, the first modern bridge in Rome built by Julius's uncle Sixtus IV, and it continued in a straight line towards the city port at Ripa. There it was to be joined with the Vatican by a new bridge, the Ponte Giulio. With new palaces, a central plan church, and a large palace for the papal tribunal, the Via Giulia was conceived as a consciously manipulated piece of urban scenery, not unlike contemporary theatrical scenery that relied upon a long vista of balanced buildings. It also anticipated the way in which later popes, notably Sixtus V, would continue to add new, rectilinear streets to the fabric of Rome and achieve, almost by accident, the enchanting vistas that now form such an integral part of the city's appearance.

Projects like the Via Giulia were conducted in other parts of Italy, but none were as striking or as successful as the Strada Nuova of Genoa. Medieval Genoa had grown up against the rocky Ligurian coast with the slopes of the Appenines at her back. The city was densely crowded

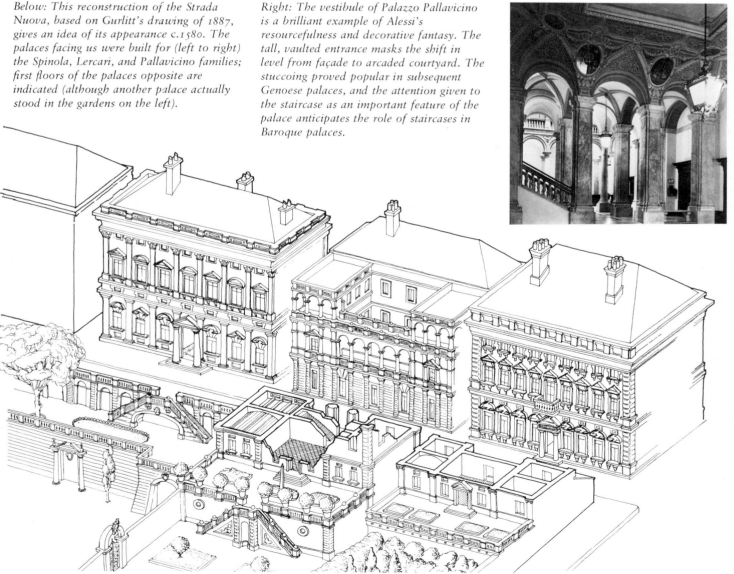

Below: This reconstruction of the Strada Nuova, based on Gurlitt's drawing of 1887, gives an idea of its appearance c.1580. The palaces facing us were built for (left to right) the Spinola, Lercari, and Pallavicino families; first floors of the palaces opposite are indicated (although another palace actually stood in the gardens on the left).

Right: The vestibule of Palazzo Pallavicino is a brilliant example of Alessi's resourcefulness and decorative fantasy. The tall, vaulted entrance masks the shift in level from façade to arcaded courtyard. The stuccoing proved popular in subsequent Genoese palaces, and the attention given to the staircase as an important feature of the palace anticipates the role of staircases in Baroque palaces.

entrance vestibule leads to a large court-yard with the main staircase on the left. The rooms on the interior are evenly distributed around the courtyard, which now becomes the centre of the palace. To a later generation, such palaces may seem little more than a Renaissance form of conspicuous consumption, but to their creators and to contemporaries the Strada Nuova became a monument of civic esteem, and it still draws visitors to Genoa long after the power of the city has disappeared.

Streets were not the only subjects of attention in Italian Renaissance cities. The squares to which they led also reflected new tendencies in Renaissance planning. Not surprisingly, Florence furnishes one of the earliest examples of this in the sixteenth century, with the completion of the Piazza Annunziata. The square was already defined by two monuments of the early Renaissance, the Foundling Hospital, Brunelleschi's first public building, and Michelozzo's SS. Annunziata. The presence of these buildings may have conditioned the completion of the square in 1517 with a loggia opposite the Foundlings'

and saw no expansion of palaces on the scale of Florence or Venice in the fifteenth century. Genoese palaces were typically tall and narrow, with courtyards that were little more than a shaft for staircases. In 1550, the Genoese Senate approved a site to the north of the city for a building project along contemporary lines. The purpose was twofold: on the one hand, there was a need to extend the habitable limits of the city, and on the other hand, to rehabilitate a disreputable portion of the city's perimeter. In 1558 a lottery was held to determine which of the patricians could buy the limited number of sites (ten on each side of the street). As planned, each house was to be detached from its neighbours and had to border the street uniformly. The Strada Nuova was the creation of a Perugian nobleman named Galeazzo Alessi (1512–72), who had begun a distinguished architectural career in Rome before going to northern Italy. The Palazzo Pallavicino was the first of the palaces begun and set the tone for the others. Alessi designed it as a large rectangular block without an architectural Order but with a surface of smooth rusticated stone, punctuated by large window frames in a central Italian manner. The layout of the interior is also patterned on palaces in Rome, rather than on the traditional Genoese plans. The

Left above: Michelangelo's Capitoline Hill, Rome, begun in 1537, demonstrates Renaissance preoccupations with uniformity and bilateral symmetry: older buildings were given new façades (centre and right) and a new structure created to disguise the irregular alignment of the older palaces.

Left below: Piazza Annunziata, Florence, where arcading begun by Brunelleschi for the Foundlings' Hospital was copied in 1516 for the building opposite, and again in 1600 for the portico of the church.

Above: Place des Voges (Place Royale), Paris, 1605, the first Italianate square in France.

Hospital as an exact replica of Brunelleschi's façade. Thus, the idea of a balanced composition, rather than the new building itself, determined the completion of the square. Just twenty years later, the same process was at work in Rome when Michelangelo was charged by Pope Paul III to design a new square for the Capitoline Hill. The problems facing Michelangelo were awkward: his square had to accommodate five entrances, the recently transported equestrian statue of Marcus Aurelius, and two pre-existing buildings which described an angle of eighty degrees one to the other. Michelangelo's solution resembles that of the main square of Pienza; he adopted a trapezoidal plan for the Capitoline by constructing a third palace aligned with the other two. Between the lateral buildings, Michelangelo placed an oval piazza, an unusual form in Renaissance architecture, but one that

combines the twin virtues of axiality and centrality. The Capitoline Hill is one of the most notable urban projects of sixteenth-century Italy, comparable to Sansovino's work in the piazza of San Marco in Venice. In both cases, a distinctive feature of Italian squares can be seen in the attempt to treat an outside space as if it were the *salone* of a palace. The piazza-*salone* is a frequently encountered element in Italian life, one that could not be translated to countries with less mild climates. As such, it demonstrates both the traditional importance of public places in Italian life and one of the major successes of Italian town planning.

The impact of town planning in the north of Europe was generally limited, but on occasion it could prove remarkably advanced. During the sixteenth century a variety of factors, primarily economic, allowed most northern cities to grow without preordained plans or even obedience to existing building regulations. In France, the most forceful examples of town planning were not to be seen in its capital, but rather in new towns like Vitry-le-François and Le Havre. Of the two, commercial interests dictated the creation of the latter, and preoccupation with the defences of the French border led to the former. The port of Le Havre and Vitry-le-François reflect popular ideas on the building of new cities: the laying-out and intersecting of streets along straight lines, triangular bastions for defence, and a central square. Although Italian treatise writers, especially the Sienese Francesco di

Giorgio, had already established a theoretical approach to the laying-out of new defensive towns, the French—albeit with the help of Italian architects—actually put these ideas into practice long before Palma Nova was created to defend Venice's eastern border with the Turks.

Aside from the new towns in France, little of architectural note was accomplished there during the sixteenth century. The great projects devised by the Valois dynasty for Paris were pre-empted by the turbulent political struggles of the second half of the century. It is significant that Catherine de' Medici, widow of Henri II, introduced the concept of squares with uniform houses in her plans for a Place de Valois in 1563. Likewise, her son Henri III laid the foundation stone for the first modern bridge and began the building of quays and streets set in line. These projects were finally completed by Henri IV as the Place Royale and the Pont-Neuf, two of the earliest ingredients in the grand rebuilding of the city during the next century.

The concept of uniformly built streets was probably introduced into the vocabulary of French architecture before Catherine de' Medici by another Italian, the Bolognese architect Sebastiano Serlio (1475–1554). Although Serlio built little himself, his position at the court of François I made his ideas influential upon other architects. None were of more significance than the unpublished sixth book of his survey on architecture. This book was remarkably advanced for its

time as it sets out a comprehensive model for urban housing, from the poorest worker to the prince. Serlio's projects, especially the simplest ones, conform to the traditional type of French city dwelling: one room with an alcove for a bed, followed by a court with a shared well, then a garden and lavatory. Serlio takes this as a module and then adds more rooms and floors to it as he goes up the social scale to the homes of craftsmen and merchants.

The conception of the uniform street façade also spread to Germany at an early date through the rebuilding of the Fugger houses on the Weinmarkt in Augsburg. Augsburg had strong commercial links with Venice, and was one of the first cities in which the southern style of building was adopted. The chief protagonists of this introduction of Renaissance architecture were the family of merchant princes named Fugger. Jacob II Fugger had spent his youth in Venice, and it was probably his knowledge of Italian squares that led him to turn several houses on a square in Augsburg into one large, uniform palace. They were under construction from 1511 and finished by 1525. The exterior may seem remote from contemporary Italian practice, but the three storeys and their windows form a continuous motif across what were originally disparate buildings. The inner courts offer a prospect more in keeping with Italian models; that in the so-called 'Damenhof' again suggests Venetian prototypes for the elegant Doric columns and arches of the arcades.

The Fuggers were also connected with a more ambitious version of Renaissance planning, parallel to Serlio's urban projects. This was the Fuggerei, a series of cottages for the poor on the outskirts of Augsburg. The houses were built in long rows or blocks with a common roof and shared chimneys; they created a community in miniature with the addition of a clinic, artisans' shops, and a nearby church. By 1560 there were almost 100 individual dwellings within the complex, forming a discernible addition to contemporary maps of the city. The inspiration for the Fuggerei may have been the layout of religious communities like the Carthusians or the Flemish Begijnhofs, and arguments for buildings like the Fuggerei go back to Aristotle's *Politics*. Yet the novelty of the Fuggerei is that the houses are not built around a cloister but rather along several streets and for a specific class of person. This makes the Fuggerei strangely prophetic, in part a creation of the Renaissance, in part a foreshadowing of the industrial communities of the turn of the nineteenth century. The urban activity in Augsburg remained largely without peer in Germany even though Dürer published a much-read treatise on fortification and planning, which helped to circulate Italian theories on cities. But Dürer's treatise and others like it were only to bear fruit at the end of the next century with the enlightened planning of cities like Mannheim.

In the second decade of the sixteenth century, an Englishman named Thomas More wrote a book of fiction and political satire that seized the imagination of Europe. It concerned an imaginary country and the government of its inhabitants. One of its most memorable passages concerns the cities, specifically Amaurotum. Its description reads like a handlist of learned opinion from ancient times to More's day, conforming to the specifications of ideal cities as designed by architects. As Vitruvius had recommended, Amaurotum was laid out on a slope with ample water for drinking and sanitation. It stood foursquare and was well fortified; the streets were large enough for traffic while the houses, of fire-proof stone or brick, were built in rectangular blocks with a garden behind each one. One other remarkable feature was that the windows were commonly of glass or at the least had linen treated with a translucent oil. The country described by More was, of course, Utopia, and part of his intent in writing about its cities lay in stimulating a greater interest in planning and design in London.

In More's day, London was far from Utopian: no large squares existed, and streets were narrow and winding, with dangerously inflammable timber structures. Most houses were built on narrow, deep plots, one room to a floor and several storeys in height. Upper floors often extended over streets, thus increasing the sense of congestion and restriction. Much of London would have looked like the row of half-timber houses still to be seen in Holborn now called Staple Inn. During the Renaissance the form of houses in northern Europe, whether in town or country, was very much the same, as a comparison between a typical yeoman's house and those of Staple Inn shows. In both cases the ground floor held a combination of hall and kitchen, the upper floor was for chambers, and the garret held a servants' room and storage space. While some adventurous town houses were built in the early seventeenth century, the pattern of London's development was set by the Elizabethan terraces with their economical use of land. As for public buildings, the most distinguished attempt to create a work of Renaissance scale and style came with the opening of the Royal Exchange in 1571. Its chief patron, Sir Thomas Gresham, had spent a number of years in Antwerp and returned to England with the intention of beginning an exchange to siphon away some of the international trade enjoyed by the Low Countries. He brought with him a Flemish architect and a large quantity of ready-made building material from Antwerp. The result was one of the first Renaissance buildings in England, a Renaissance, however, that drew its inspiration not from the south but from another northern country. Its most notable feature was a large courtyard with Doric arcading that supported an upper storey with Ionic pilasters and niches containing statues of English kings. The Royal Exchange not only supplied London with a grand square in the European manner, but it also stood as a manifesto of a new style that would effect a revolution in English architecture in the next century.

Throughout the late Middle Ages and the Renaissance, the Low Countries held a key position in trade between southern and northern Europe. This also meant that the Renaissance tended to travel across northern and central Europe *via* great entrepots like Bruges and Antwerp. The arrival of the Renaissance style in architecture coincided with the great period of Antwerp's dominance in the Low Countries. Its importance was confirmed by the attention given to Antwerp by its Spanish rulers, notably Charles V, during the middle of the century. The city was enlarged in a series of grid-like extensions, and its medieval walls were replaced by modern bastions, in both cases guided by Italian military architects who brought new concepts of rational planning to the north. The focal point of civic attention centred upon the Grote Markt, the main square with the largest houses, the guild halls, and the town hall. It was with these buildings, chiefly the town hall designed by Cornelis Floris (1514–75), that northern Europe achieved a monumental indigenous style of architecture, capable of comparison with urban planning in Italy. The town hall in Antwerp was under construction in the 1560s. Typologically, it is very close to its late Gothic predecessor, the town hall on the Grand' Place in Brussels. As in England, Flemish urban houses were tall and narrow with maximized window space, but through the influence of Floris's town hall and a flood of Flemish architectural treatises the gables began to receive a fanciful application of Renaissance columns and scrolls as can still be seen in the guild houses around Antwerp's Grote Markt.

The building activity which took place in Antwerp marked a new phase, not only in Renaissance architecture, but also in terms of urban building in general. The economic strength of the Low Countries enabled their version of Renaissance architecture to spread across northern Europe from London to Danzig. In the north civic pride expressed itself more in the attention which public buildings,

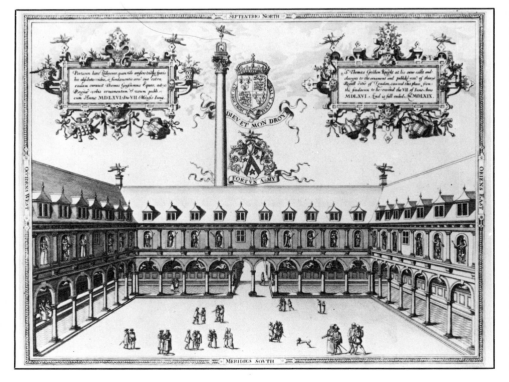

whether exchange or arsenal, began to receive as opposed to private palaces. The rise of the modern city, which had had no place in the medieval stratification of society, now attained a new significance in the life of Europe; town planning and the attention to the growing diversity of public buildings reflected the Renaissance's attempt to deal with an urgent problem.

MANNERISM

By the beginning of the sixteenth century Renaissance architecture in Italy attained a level of perfection and a universality of language that seemed the equivalent of ancient Roman architecture. In the work of Bramante architects and patrons found a standard against which subsequent work could be measured. The spread of High Renaissance architecture to other parts of Italy and to Europe as a whole took place during the second half of the sixteenth century. This did not, however, mark the conclusion of the growth of Renaissance architecture. Instead, the architecture of the Renaissance enjoyed a late flowering in northern and southern Europe alike. This later development, which has been retrospectively called Mannerism, sought a greater elaboration of decoration and a pursuit of novelty which often compromised the clarity and restraint of High Renaissance architecture. Although Mannerism occurred first in central Italy, it reached the rest of Europe quickly, and in some cases Mannerism and Renaissance are hardly distinguishable.

Bramante had been the first modern architect to use the vocabulary of Roman buildings correctly. This was a landmark in the history of modern architecture, and it was recognized as such by his contemporaries. But Bramante's achievement was not seen as a goal; rather it became a turning point in the development of architecture, something which later architects felt they had to surpass. Thus Raphael, who followed Bramante as architect of St Peter's, found fault with Bramante's architecture for its lack of the brilliant decorative quality of ancient architecture. By this Raphael meant the combination of painting and stucco which he had observed in buildings like Nero's Golden House and the Baths of Titus. The garden loggia of the Villa Madama was intended by Raphael as a critique of Bramante's sparer style, and the façade of the Palazzo Branconio dell' Aquila shows the same aesthetic criticism in operation. It stood on a street near the papal palace, and the façade could have been viewed by Pope

Leo X from his balcony. In it, Raphael blended the novelty of effect often associated with temporary architecture erected for festivals and special occasions with a reading of ancient architecture far removed from the spirit of Bramante's. Where Bramante had taken pains in his façades to establish a coherent structural pattern through the ancient Orders, Raphael merely adopted them as an elaborate series of motifs on a level with other decorative elements. The façade of the Palazzo dell' Aquila established a vogue for stucco decoration that bore fruit in the splendid plasterwork on Genoese palaces in the late sixteenth century, and even in northern buildings like the Maison Milsand in Dijon.

Raphael's alternative reading of the spirit of ancient architecture characterizes a dilemma that confronted Renaissance architects after Bramante, namely, how to reconcile obedience to the rules (as represented by Vitruvius and Bramante himself) with the necessity to express an individual artistic personality. Benvenuto Cellini, the goldsmith and Mannerist

artist *par excellence*, told the story of an architect named Baldassare Peruzzi (1481–1536) who studied all the examples of Roman architecture that he could find in order to discover the finest styles and elements. Peruzzi's conclusion from his study of the Roman ruins was that Vitruvius had not selected the best of Roman architecture when writing his treatise. Cellini viewed Peruzzi's critical approach to ancient architecture with approval and held up to ridicule Antonio da Sangallo, the architect of the Farnese Palace, for his unimaginative approach to architecture and his fidelity to an early sixteenth-century style which seemed timid by the middle of that century. Mannerism in architecture, then, arose as a new initiative to find other expressions of an antique style.

New motifs from ancient sources were not the only elements which architects began to introduce into Italian architecture during the sixteenth century. Under the influence of Michelangelo, an injection of the artist's personality into a building's design also became permissible. Much of

Michelangelo's architecture was, like the planning of the Capitoline Hill, dictated by specific problems or pre-existing structures; yet he managed to impart to each of his commissions a strong impression of his highly individual conception of art. The vestibule of the Laurentian Library in Florence was an equally dramatic work that contained the seeds of a revolutionary approach to antiquity. Michelangelo was commissioned to design an entrance for the Library (which he had also designed) that would bridge the difference in levels between the ground and the library one storey above. The area for the vestibule was narrow and high, ruling out the possibility of a simple and conventional solution. In the event, Michelangelo treated the interior wall as if it were an external one and gave it an ostensibly classical articulation of paired columns and tabernacles for the main floor with windows and pilasters above. The revolutionary aspect, however, lies in the fact that the conventional roles of these elements are turned around so that the columns are recessed while the walls project, and in the upper floor the pilasters project while the window bays are recessed. The other ingredient in this extraordinary composition of the vestibule is the staircase which fills the greater part of the floor space and seems to pour like lava from the library above. Michelangelo's licence in the face of the accepted Roman canon, both in the Laurentiana and a late work like the Porta Pia, was greeted by

Far left above: The façade of the Maison Milsand in Dijon, France, c.1561, is one of the most inventive examples of contemporary French domestic architecture. The builder was Hugues Samblin.

Above: The Casino of Pius IV in the gardens of the Vatican by the antiquarian and architect, Pirro Ligorio, was begun in 1559 for Pope Paul IV. Like Raphael, Ligorio studied the remains of Roman architecture in order to recreate its decorative effects. The façade is deliberately conceived without the customary Renaissance succession of applied Orders, favouring instead a combination of stuccoing and statues.

Left: Michelangelo's famous vestibule for the Laurentian Library in Florence was completed at the end of the 1550s, more than two decades after it had been begun. The imposing staircase takes up half the floor of the vestibule and has the effect of a free-standing sculptural monument. Its unconventional scale heightens the effect.

is no balance in the application of decoration, especially to the elevation of the courtyard. The niches placed above the columns of the ground floor, like those of Raphael's Palazzo dell' Aquila, defy normal expectations of the alignment of solids and voids while the sculpture has a restless energy absent from Goujon's figures on the Louvre. The elevation of the exterior of the château also contains an insistence upon decoration and a syncopated use of rhythm in its projection and recession of mass that points away from the Renaissance and towards the Baroque.

Mannerist architecture, as a purely decorative phenomenon, had entered France even before Lescot had begun to practise architecture. It came with the entry of the talented Mannerist painter Rosso Fiorentino into the service of the French king, François I, in 1530. Rosso, together with the painter Francesco Primaticcio brought to the decoration of the famous gallery at Fontainebleau a combination of stuccoed figures, scrolls, and paintings that derived from Raphael's Villa Madama through later versions like Giulio Romano's Palazzo del Té. Their work in the gallery at Fontainebleau was disseminated throughout Europe by woodcuts and had enormous influence in creating a vogue for highly decorated surfaces, both interior and exterior, and for the spread of one motif that became particularly identified with the architecture of the northern Renaissance—strapwork, the simulation in stone or stucco of interlacing bands which resemble strips of leather.

Strapwork is largely associated with the architecture of the Low Countries and symbolized the linguistic contamination suffered by Renaissance forms during the last stages of the Renaissance. Philibert de l'Orme, as was noted earlier, could engage in Renaissance and Mannerist styles simultaneously, and the same phenomenon can be seen in a work like Cornelis Floris's town hall in Antwerp. There the body of the building conforms almost rigidly to a simple Renaissance articulation of the bays of the façade, but in the gable the architect allowed himself greater freedom in drawing upon a mixture of motifs often found in temporary architecture built for special events such as masques and royal receptions. What began as a rather fanciful decorative style soon established itself as the predominant form of the Renaissance in the north. In a slightly later version of Floris's town hall, that by Lieven de Key (1560–1627) in Leyden, the restraint of the Antwerp façade has been jettisoned for the

other architects as a notable achievement.

In the north the consequences of Mannerism were in many respects more far-reaching and pronounced. We noted earlier that proportions held little interest for most non-Italian architects and architectural theorists. Sumptuousness and a profusion of embellishments often passed for Renaissance architecture. While the Renaissance in Spain began that way, it became increasingly pure and more restrained. In the Low Countries and France, the development of the Renaissance followed the lines of the Italian experience, that is, a period of classic statement was succeeded by one of greater licence.

In France the contrast can be seen as early as Philibert de l'Orme, whose chapel at Anet already contained elements of a dynamic type, far removed from the calm of his Italian models. To de l'Orme, the two styles that we would label Renaissance and Mannerist were simply different modes of a single style. Likewise, his introduction of a 'French' Order of columns reflects a Mannerist appeal to the genius of the architect as final arbiter of what is and is not permissible. The judgement of the architect played a prominent role in the domestication of the Renaissance in northern Europe, and it was this factor that inevitably prepared the ground for an early flight into Mannerism. The contrast between the work of a mid-century French architect like Pierre Lescot and a younger contemporary like Jacques Androuet du Cerceau illuminates the difference between the Renaissance ideal and its later rejection. With the west wing of the Louvre, Lescot had achieved a balance of Italian and native French elements in a restrained and eloquent composition. Du Cerceau's designs for the Château at Verneuil, which post-dates it by a generation, achieves a totally different effect with much the same elements. There

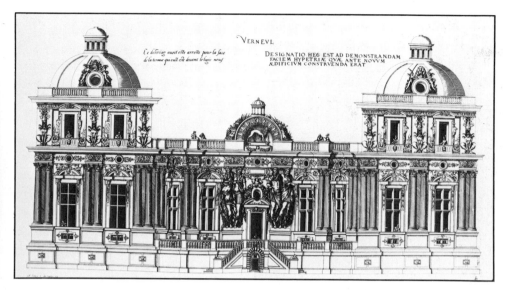

VERNEVL

Ce dessein auoit este arreste pour la face de la terrasse qui eult este devant le logis neuf

DESIGNATIO HEC EST AD DEMONSTRANDAM
FACIEM HYPETRIÆ QVÆ ANTE NOVVM
ÆDIFICIVM CONSTRVENDA ERAT

reduce the architectural members to recognizably naturalistic and even animal forms. These fantastic creations—architecture invested with a human personality—led in the seventeenth and eighteenth centuries to the exploitation of sculptural forms, especially herms, in architecture and to the integration of sculpture and architecture in the 'total work of art'. It is, perhaps, in the triumph of decorative motifs over rational structure that the Mannerism of northern architecture differs from that of Italy. In both cases, however, Mannerism demonstrated a need to go beyond the established Vitruvian canon and to assert the personality of the architect himself. The way that led from Renaissance to Baroque had been opened.

Left: On the palace of the electors in Heidelberg, West Germany, c.1601–07, the Orders are made to fit the proportions of the building.

Above: Du Cerceau's design for Verneuil, France (begun 1565), has a restless energy that is lacking in Lescot's Louvre façade of the previous generation.

Right: Dietterlin's fantastic portal, c.1590, dissolves architecture into animalistic forms appropriate to a hunting lodge or villa.

caprice of its gable; in effect, the solution that Floris reserved for the gable has been applied by de Key to the whole of the façade. Even the rusticated order used on the stairs and ground floor are not Italian, but rather an 'invented' type, analogous to de l'Orme's creation of a French Order. The gable of the Leyden town hall, like that of the arsenal at Danzig, shows the distinctive Flemish contribution to Mannerist architecture, with the blending of Orders, strapwork, and obelisks that proclaims the northern architect's *horror vacui*.

Underlying Renaissance architecture was a series of implicit, often explicit, comparisons between the Orders and the natural world. Vitruvius had likened the Orders to human beings—Doric was manly, Ionic matronly, Corinthian maidenly. Such comparisons were taken into account when considering the kind of structure to be built. Thus Serlio would design a portal for a country residence as a mixture of the robust Doric Order and the equally robust blocks of rough stone called rustication. In northern architecture, the sense of architectural personality was pushed even farther by Mannerist architects like the German Wendel Dietterlin, who published a series of designs for rustic portals that

24

BAROQUE, ROCOCO AND CLASSICISM

Two churches, well under a hundred miles distant from each other, define the state of Europe in the early seventeenth century: the church of the Jesuits in Antwerp, and the Nieuwe Kerk in Haarlem. The two buildings have exactly the same function—that of a preaching church—but are very different. The Antwerp church, richly decorated inside and out under the supervision of Rubens, has a façade articulated with classical elements, which is modelled very closely on the Gesù in Rome, mother church of the Jesuit Order throughout the world. It is a totally Italian façade quite unrelated to the architecture of the Low Countries, into which it has strayed. The Nieuwe Kerk, on the other hand, whose spire is exactly contemporary and whose bulk is only slightly later, remains within its local traditions. The spire is simply a development of the northern Gothic steeples of the preceding three centuries. Like the spire, the hall behind is scarcely articulated at all and has only restrained, rather severe, decoration. Why are there these enormous differences? Why has the Antwerp church abandoned the North and chosen to look to Rome? And why has the Haarlem one eschewed the ornament in which the Jesuit church delights?

A glance at a contemporary map of Europe quickly answers these questions. As the melancholic Sir Thomas Browne sadly observed, there was now 'a Geography of Religions as well as Lands, and every Clime distinguished not onely by their lawes and limits, but circumscribed by their doctrines and rules of Faith'. The split between Protestant and Catholic in northern Europe ran from the mouth of the River Scheldt and it is this divide which our two churches straddle: it is this divide which explains their differences.

Both buildings, by their choice of style, are making a statement about their function and, more important, about their ideological assumptions. Whereas the sixteenth century, and especially Mannerism, had insisted on the aesthetic significance of style, the seventeenth and eighteenth centuries are preoccupied with the *meaning* of style: it is a phenomenon which dominated the architecture of the period, and to which we shall have to return again and again until the outbreak of the French Revolution.

The library of the great south German abbey of Wiblingen, built and decorated in the mid-eighteenth century. Elements of classical architecture are dynamically disposed to give an impression of movement – the characteristic of the Baroque, developed in Rome around 1600. In central Europe it combined with white and gilt plaster, coloured marbles and illusionistic painting to produce one of the most striking decorative styles ever.

lands, after their successful revolt against the Spanish Crown, had through trade, merchant venture and the manipulation of the financial market, set up what may be called the first modern capitalist system. Trade flourished in an atmosphere of free association, where investment was not controlled by the state and where there was no centralized court or bureaucracy to support through taxation. And so, the merchant classes in the Northern Netherlands and in England persistently supported the liberal, Parliamentary movement against the attempted encroachments of kings, whether of the House of Stuart or the House of Orange.

In the Catholic South, the source of wealth was not, as in the North, trade, but either took the form of land or was the product of service to the Crown, which

The Dutch church, local and vernacular in style just as the liturgy was vernacular in language, has rejected everything Roman which the Antwerp church has adopted: it is simply what it appears to be, a local, national church, based on a Puritan mistrust of sensual enjoyment, in which God is worshipped in spirit only. The Antwerp church proclaims itself at once Roman and part of a world-wide grouping in exactly the same way as its equally alien contemporary sister, the Jesuit church in Cracow. Its decoration accords with the value attached by Saint Ignatius, the founder of the Order, to every physical and sensual experience, as possibly leading to communion with God.

The Europe of 1600, however, is not divided just by religion. The two different styles also reflect two political approaches. The Haarlem church, built by a Dutch architect, fits a national view of politics based on the liberty of the individual conscience and opposed to extreme central control. It is the system of libertarian oligarchy which was to be followed by England and most of north Germany as well.

The Antwerp church, partly designed by Italians, was completed under Rubens, who insisted on his status as a subject of the King of Spain—at that time the ruler of the Southern Netherlands. And the Spanish —one could almost say the Catholic— view of government was supra-national (Spain possessed large dominions in Italy as well as in Flanders), depending on loyalty to an autocratic sovereign.

These closely interconnected political and religious divisions were paralleled by an economic one. The Northern Nether-

recruited an ever-larger number of officials to centralize power in the person of the king. In the South, also, the Church remained an extremely important secular, land-owning body, often more influential than the local nobility.

These differences in social organization were central to the architecture which was produced; for they explain why the buildings typical of Catholic Europe are palaces and monasteries, whereas the Protestant North built meeting-halls for commerce and recreation and houses for merchants and squires.

To come back to our two churches (both sides went on building churches vigorously) another important point arises. To the eye of any North American the Haarlem building will look somehow familiar; to any Latin American the Antwerp model will seem closer to the norm. The reasons for this are obvious: the seventeenth century was a period of sustained colonial expansion and the European powers took their architecture with them; the English adopted a Dutch style modified by Wren, the Spaniards and the Portuguese a Roman style, heavily influenced by the Jesuits. Indeed, one of the most fascinating aspects of the architecture of this period lies in the adaptability of European styles to non-European cultures and building traditions.

Yet although the seventeenth century may appear to us as a time of heady expansion and development, determining the relationship between the individual and the state in political thought, laying the foundations of modern physics with Galileo and Newton and revolutionizing

Far left above: The Royal Palace, Madrid, designed by Giovanni Battista Sacchetti c.1740.

Far left below: The Jesuit church in Antwerp, Belgium, designed by Huyssens with advice from Rubens, begun in 1613. Antwerp was on the frontier of Catholic Europe and as eager to show her loyalty to Rome in architecture as in religion. This church and the Royal Palace in Madrid are buildings typical of Catholic absolutist Europe throughout the period; by contrast, the Protestant North favoured an indigenous church style and its powerful merchant class encouraged buildings useful for commerce – exemplified by the two buildings on the right.

Above: The Meat Hall in Haarlem, Netherlands, by Lieven de Key, built c.1603.

Left: The Nieuwe Kerk in Haarlem, whose tower was also by Lieven de Key, c.1613, but whose hall was built by Jacob van Campen, c.1645.

economic structures, this was not how men of the time saw their experience.

Sir Thomas Browne was speaking for most of his contemporaries when he observed that more than half of the history of the world had already been played out: 'generations are ordained in this setting part of time'. The noontide, there was no doubt about it, was behind and referred, of course, to the world of classical antiquity. It is essential to remember that until the nineteenth century the classical repertory was not just the best there was; it was the best that could be, from which point standards had slowly and irreversibly declined. Hence, throughout the period, there is a constant reference to the forms of antiquity—references which were easily

began—where the Dutch held out, irreducible behind their dykes.

Finally, it must not be forgotten that in Europe this was the last heroic age of faith. In both Protestant and Catholic countries many died for their religious convictions; the preparation for martyrdom was fundamental to early Jesuit training; the Catholic Church's almost obsessive concern in architecture and art with physical suffering in the name of God was quite simply a reflection of what had been, and was still to be, the experience of many.

BAROQUE— AN AGE OF RHETORIC

An age of faith, the seventeenth century was also an age of rhetoric. For both Protestant and Catholic, preaching had become one of the principal elements of religion and the sermon a literary form in its own right. Indeed, listening to sermons constituted probably the major form of entertainment publicly allowed to women in both North and South.

It is perhaps because of this habit of making grand public statements that architects of the period were so concerned with the problem of the façade. Curiously, this had always been a secondary consideration for architects of the High Renaissance, more concerned with the balancing of harmonious spaces in a building's interior. Clearly, however, any architecture aiming at propaganda—and that means most architecture at this period —must pay particular attention to the exterior visible to the public.

Sometimes, this self-advertisement is blatant in the extreme, as on the façade of

legible even to the semi-literate—and a constant endeavour to do everything possible to arrest the decline, to return, in so far as was possible, to the perfection of the ancients.

We have conjured with the image of a divided Europe, living out the end of allotted time. Which way were the divisions heading? At the time that the two churches were being built, it was a question of fine balance. The political power of Spain was declining, but France was in the ascendant and the battles between France and the Protestant powers of the North were to continue till the middle of the eighteenth century.

In religious terms, the balance seemed to lie with the Catholics. In the East, they had won a series of victories over the Turks, beginning with the Battle of Lepanto in 1571, commemorated by the spectacular building programme of Lecce,

and continuing until the advantageous treaty of 1718, celebrated by the church of Santa Maria Victoria in Ingolstadt.

In western Europe, also, the reforms of the Council of Trent seemed to be winning people back to the Catholic Church. France had emerged from the Wars of Religion as a Catholic country, if a rather idiosyncratic one; central Europe was being successfully re-evangelized, and cartloads of martyrs' relics were being sent across the Alps to help with the process; England's Charles I was certainly not anti-Roman and had an openly Catholic consort. The whole of Germany was about to become a vast battlefield, as Catholics and Protestants attacked each other with unimaginable savagery, reducing the Holy Roman Empire to desolation and, at times, cannibalism. In short, none of the boundaries seemed unalterable, except perhaps that with which we

Far left: To the church of Santa Susanna, Rome, Carlo Maderno added a new façade in 1602. Its freer, more plastic handling of mass and its exploitation of light and shadow set the Roman fashion for much of the seventeenth century and was to be copied across most of western Europe.

Left: The entire front of the church of Madonna delle Grazie at Gravina in southern Italy is given over to advertising the heraldic emblem of Vincenzo Giustaniani, bishop between 1598 and 1612.

Below: The Prayer Hall of Santa Maria Victoria at Ingolstadt in south Germany, designed and decorated by the Asam brothers c.1735, celebrated Catholic victories over the Turks. Throughout the period, central Europe remained very conscious of the threat to Christendom from the East.

the church at Gravina in southern Italy, where the heraldic emblem of the bishop dominates entirely. Normally, however, the aim is to make the façade interesting, puzzling and inviting.

Here, the new movement really does begin with the century, in Maderno's façade for the church of Santa Susanna in Rome. Significantly, as a façade added to an already existing church, it is for the first time conceived of as an entity in its own right: an entity which takes up space, with its projecting columns and its sections stepping forward to the central door; an entity in which the play of light and shade over the columns makes a clear boundary difficult to discern. This façade is part of the church behind it, but it also has a presence in the spectator's space. The classical elements are no longer disposed

in static equilibrium, but are massed to give dominance to one central element, the doorway, through which the spectator is thus encouraged to enter.

This manipulation of the classical language of architecture to create an impression of movement and climax, while leaving great uncertainty about the precise limits of a building's space, is the characteristic of the Baroque. Initially a term of abuse applied to malformed pearls, it was soon used to describe that style of building which, beginning in Rome in the early seventeenth century, rapidly swept Europe. Although the use of colour to heighten and dramatize this new treatment of Renaissance forms later became widespread, Baroque remains fundamentally a structural rather than a decorative style.

The capricious, dynamic use of classical

Above: In the entrance to his church of Sant' Andrea al Quirinale, Rome, built between 1658 and 1679, Bernini develops to the full the implications of Maderno's Santa Susanna façade. The façade now projects into the surrounding space, to attract the attention of the passer-by and encourage him to enter. The church, a few hundred yards from Borromini's San Carlino, shows how much more theatrical is Bernini's approach. Built for the Jesuit Novitiate, the whole church celebrates the martyrdom of Saint Andrew, whose statue rises as if miraculously above the principal altar to meet his reward in heaven. Bernini does not attempt the structural virtuosity of Borromini, but aims instead at striking, dramatic organization of space and imagery.

elements we shall find in England in the works of Hawksmoor and in the chapel at Smirice in Bohemia; the dominance of the central feature will recur at Vaux-le-Vicomte and at the Zwinger in Dresden; and the textural intricacies and ambiguities of the Santa Susanna façade will pale beside the *tour de force* of the Liechtensteins' palace at Plumlov in Moravia seventy years later.

It was, however, in Rome that this new architectural syntax was forged and it is there that we must follow its early development. Pietro da Cortona (1596–1669) exploits the spatial possibilities of Maderno's façade in the interior of his church of SS. Luca e Martina, where he splits the wall into a bewildering arrangement of columns, pilasters and curtain wall; this, combined with the diffuse and partly hidden sources of light, makes it quite impossible to establish where the church's space comes to an end.

Similarly, Gianlorenzo Bernini (1598–1680) in the church of Sant' Andrea al Quirinale abandons the idea of the façade as such, replacing it with a triumphal doorway and quadrant wings which move forward towards us, while the portico and steps curve boldly into the world outside; they invite us in, persuading us that the distinctions between the world in and out of the church are not as sharp as we imagine.

This architecture is interested, above all, in the idea of limits—or, more exactly, in the idea that there can be no precise limits. Where the architecture of the Renaissance aims at definition and clarity, there is now an attempt to produce a controlled confusion in the mind of the onlooker. Why? It seems that this remarkable development in the architect's purpose is explicable largely in terms of his philosophical assumptions.

Central to the teaching of the Roman Catholic Church in the seventeenth century is the idea that knowledge of God cannot be attained by reason alone but demands the use of the senses and, above all, of faith—faith which begins at the point where the senses and the intellect leave off in bafflement. Hence to bewilder the eyes and the mind of the worshipper is to prepare him for the exercise of the higher faculty through which he may attain salvation. This is profoundly different from the Protestant approach and that of certain branches of deviant Catholic thought, who held a much greater brief for the light of reason. Their views will, as we shall see, be reflected in their buildings.

What one can broadly say, then, is that in the seventeenth and eighteenth centuries the structural clarity or mystification of a church will bear a direct relationship to the views of the creed for which it was built, on the power of reason to bring the worshipper into sight of the divine.

Nowhere is the Catholic delight in puzzlement and ingenuity more apparent than in the Roman churches of Francesco Borromini (1599–1667), and it is not accidental that most of his patrons were of the Spanish faction, and therefore the most committed to a mystic, supra-rational view of religion.

It was just such a Spaniard who commissioned Borromini's perhaps most appealing work, the tiny church of San Carlo alle Quattro Fontane. This was built for

SAN CARLO: BAROQUE STRUCTURE AND SPACE

The Discalced, or Unshod, Trinitarians were typical of the revival of Catholic spirituality after the Council of Trent. A poor order, recently reformed in Spain, they devoted themselves to nursing and pastoral work. Their church in Rome was thus dedicated to the Trinity and Saint Charles Borromeo, the reforming Archbishop of Milan. The site is tiny – the whole church could fit into one of the pillars supporting the dome of Saint Peter's – and Borromini was commissioned in the late 1630s to design a church using the cheapest materials. He worked on it for some thirty years, the inside being his first major work, while the façade was still unfinished at the time of his death. This challenge of constricted space and extreme economy produced one of his greatest works.

Far left: The view of the high altar showing almost half the church. Borromini curved elements normally left flat, such as the triangular pediment above the altar, thus wrapping the wall and columns round the central space. This space is ambiguously perceived as oval, two triangles, or a compressed cross.

Above: Looking up to the cupola, these ambiguities of plan are restated, first by the strong cornice, which resumes all three shapes, then in the dome, where Borromini characteristically adapted an antique Roman pavement design to echo the shapes once again before dissolving them in the light from above.

the poor Order of the Discalced Trinitarians, and it is because of the role of the Trinity as focus of the Order's devotions that the ground-plan is composed of two equilateral triangles, traditional symbols of the Trinity.

Yet it is not as such that we perceive the church. The two triangles have been indissolubly fused by the introduction of curves in the wall, setting up a continuous, running motion. The impression of perpetual undulation is heightened by the fact that every unit of the architectural composition can be read in different groupings of threes. For example, the high altar is flanked by two supporting bays. These, however, do not give the effect of stable balance one might expect, for they also act as flanking elements for the small doorways in the next bay. They

are, therefore, simultaneously the end of one aspect and the lead-in to another. As we might expect by now in a Baroque church, the boundaries between the elements have been dissolved, the divisions have become connections, and the church demands that we regard it not as an assemblage of parts but as an indivisible whole.

As we look upwards, the same thing happens. The two triangles of the ground-plan are transformed into a cross, which becomes an oval. Far above, in a light which seems to come from nowhere, and at a distance which we could not possibly assess, hovers once more the symbolic triangle. The mystery of the Trinity is thus around us, about us and above us, and at every stage it eludes comprehension or analysis.

In a comparable way, at his other great church of Sant' Ivo, the six-pointed star, symbol of the Divine Wisdom to which this university church is dedicated, appears in the ground-plan and reappears in the roof, before being dissolved into the perfect circle of the lantern, in the middle of which, floating above us, is another star. This breathtaking structural virtuosity is possible only because of Borromini's thorough training as a stone mason, acquired during his work on the still unfinished Milan Cathedral before he became an architect.

It could be imitated in Italy by only one man, similarly trained in the Gothic stone-cutting tradition, similarly expert in the calculation of the thrust of these vertiginous buildings: Guarino Guarini (1624–83). The only buildings in Italy which

stand comparison with Borromini's are the two Guarini built in Turin, and especially the chapel he constructed to house the most sacred relic of the city—the Holy Shroud. The contemplation of so holy an object is intended to arouse in the faithful a soaring exaltation which transcends any rationalistic quibbles on authenticity, and it is just such a state which is induced by Guarini's dome.

Such brilliant mastery of complicated structural theory was, however, exceptional among architects. Bernini, indeed, was so far from possessing it that the simple bell tower which he erected on the façade of Saint Peter's actually began to collapse and had to be demolished—to the delight of his many enemies, not least of them Borromini, who offered to suggest improvements to help it stand up.

Bernini, however, had other gifts. The desire to create a unified space in which the worshipper could experience a heightened state of emotional intensity was not one he could realize through sheer structure, like Borromini or Guarini. Yet he achieved it no less successfully, as the interior of the church of Sant'Andrea al Quirinale shows.

Opposite the door of the church, compelling attention on the high altar, is a

painting of the martyrdom of Saint Andrew, contemplation of which was part of the Jesuit training, for the church was used by the Jesuit novices who had to be ready to face such a death. Yet the saint's suffering is not the whole story, as above the altar his figure rises heavenwards on a cloud of glory, while all around cherubs prepare to lift off the roof with garland-chains to enable him to continue his ascent. The whole church has become a stage for the drama of his death and glorification.

What Bernini has done is to exploit the area of expertise in which he truly was supreme—that of the stage. He was a prolific scene-designer and even wrote his own plays, as well as staging them with sumptuous effects. More than anyone else, he created the theatrical religious architecture of the High Baroque.

The supreme example of this is to be found in the Cornaro Chapel of Santa Maria della Vittoria, where he was responsible for the architecture, the painting and the sculpture. Again, the building is conceived as a theatre, this time for the miraculous vision of Saint Teresa of Avila, the Spanish mystic, whose ecstatic communion with angels had been much discussed since her canonization earlier in the century. The huge marble group represents her most celebrated encounter. It hovers, unsupported, before us, lit apparently from the splendour of the heavens opening in the ceiling above, although in fact by a concealed window. The drama, however, is not limited to the

Italian seventeenth-century churches exploit directed light, illusionistic sculpture, colour and constructional complexity to induce an attitude of worship and reverence.

Left above: The dome of the chapel of the Holy Shroud, Turin Cathedral, designed by Guarini and built between 1667 and 1690, appears miraculously suspended overhead.

Left below: Carlo Rainaldi develops Bernini's methods in the church of Gesù e Maria, Rome, c.1670, where, in the nave, sculptured figures summon us to prayer.

Right above: Bernini's Cornaro Chapel in Santa Maria della Vittoria, Rome, built c.1646. The marble group represents Saint Teresa's mystic vision of a smiling angel, who pierced her several times with the arrow of divine love. Her ecstasy is witnessed not only by the spectator but also by the flanking statues of members of the Cornaro family.

altar. On either side of us members of the Cornaro family lean out from behind their prie-dieu and involve us in the spectacle, urge us to share the vision with them and, indeed, with Saint Teresa.

This represents total architecture of a new kind. The architect is directly concerned with all details of the building, and he endeavours to create an emotionally charged zone which will completely surround and—it is hoped—transport the spectator. The architect now has two tasks: he must make the spectator feel immediately involved in the unified space which he has created, as Rainaldi does brilliantly in the church of Gesù e Maria, where the whole nave is lined by members

of the Bolognetti family who lean out of their theatre-boxes and beckon us to the altar; he must also, through the organization of light and the arrangement often of a great deal of specific detail, try to make a visionary experience real, to make the sporadic illuminations of the mystic accessible to the ordinary man. Thus, as we stand in the chapel of Santa Cecilia in the church of San Carlo ai Catinari, we gaze up into a dazzling, light-filled world, in which the dove of the Holy Ghost hovers with an assured disregard for the laws of physics, while cherubs, leaning over the ledge, smile down at us.

If, until now, we have been talking of the riotous assault on the senses and the

In South America, as in the Far East, the efforts above all of the Jesuits had succeeded in making the Church Militant, locally at least, the Church Triumphant, and churches recognizably deriving from the great monuments of Baroque Rome were erected in celebration from Cuzco in Peru to Macao in southern China.

The mystic, Spanish Catholicism of the Jesuits was not, however, the only brand of Catholicism available. The military power of His Most Catholic Majesty, the King of Spain, was declining in favour of the neighbouring power, His Most Christian Majesty, the King of France, and in France the Jesuits were attacked with greatest venom. This was partly because they were perceived as the instruments of Spanish diplomacy, partly because many French, under the impact of the rationalistic teachings of Descartes, were profoundly antipathetic to the Jesuit approach to faith.

The major anti-Jesuit group were the Jansenists—finally condemned as heretical, but only after they had put up a long and a very good fight. In spite of the acres of written controversy, it is, curiously, easier to grasp the essential differences between the two points of view by looking at their architecture. The final condemnation of the Jansenists by the Pope in 1713 led to the creation of one of the most extreme Churrigueresque fantasies in Spain, the gloating exultation which we know as the Transparente in Toledo Cathedral. In its simultaneous manipulation of architecture, sculpture, painting and directed light, it is a lineal descendant of Bernini's Cornaro Chapel and all that it stood for.

In the seventeenth century, however, the French Jansenists had already built their reply. The tiny chapel of Port-Royal en Ville is an exercise in the building of lucid geometrical shapes. This was appropriate because, for the Jansenists, geometry was the model of belief in God—the shapes in geometry need have no physical existence (lines indeed *can* have no physical existence) and yet we can build our physical lives on the rules derived from their contemplation. Nothing could be further from the physicality of Jesuit religious art than this austere, light-filled space.

THE NORTHERN CHURCH

The even illumination, the anti-mystical, unemotional quality of this architecture is close to that of the Protestant North. Protestant architects, however, had the added —and greater—problem that they had to

intellect in terms of Rome, that is because Rome was so very much the centre of this development, from which other towns took their direction. Yet the remoter centres carried many of these elements further. The delight in profuse decoration was joyously exploited in the south of Italy, especially in Lecce and in Naples, where Cosimo Fanzago (1591–1678) added the infinite possibilities of polychrome marble to the Roman repertoire.

Naples was, of course, a Spanish town and it is in Spain itself that this decorative

tendency reached its highest development. There had always been an Iberian predisposition to heavy ornament, and one feels that local craftsmen must have been delighted to discover that their taste now had the sanction of the high Roman fashion behind it. Spanish decorative Baroque reaches its apogee in the works of the Churriguera family, and it is this florid style—Churrigueresque—primarily, which was exported to the New World, where it miraculously married with a native carving tradition of no less sophistication.

build for a new set of liturgical requirements. With the Reformation had come a totally different relationship between the priest, or celebrant, and the people: no longer called on to perform the mystery of transubstantiation, the priest was now simply the leader of his people, not set apart in any more mystical way. His task was now to preach and expound the reformed doctrines as much as to administer the sacraments.

This meant that Protestant churches normally had to be smaller. 'The Romanists', argued Wren when talking about these problems, 'indeed may build larger churches, it is enough if they hear the murmur of the Mass and see the Elevation of the Host, but ours are to be fitted for auditories.' And so the small, English church had galleries so that all could see and hear, and gave almost equal importance to altar, pulpit and reading desk.

When Christopher Wren (1632–1723) began his career, there was in fact only one church in England which had been built for Protestant worship—Inigo Jones's Saint Paul's, Covent Garden, which the architect himself had rather harshly described as 'the finest barn in the Kingdom'. This had been necessitated by the new urban development around Covent Garden but, in general, there were so many churches in England surviving from the late Middle Ages that there was no possibility of needing to build any more.

No possibility, that is, until 2 September 1666. 'This fatal night', wrote John Evelyn in his diary, 'about ten, began that deplorable fire neere Fish Streete in London. . . . Oh, the miserable and calamitous spectacle! . . . the fall of Towers, Houses and Churches was like an hideous

Far left: The Pilgrimage Church, Ocotlán, Mexico, built c.1745. The divisions which had emerged in Europe between a decorative, Southern, Catholic style and an austere Northern Protestant one were transported to the Americas. Here Spanish predilection for rich surface ornament combines with a local Indian tradition to produce a façade of remarkable interest and opulence.

Below: Within the Catholic Church, the different currents of thought produced their own architectural styles. In the chapel of Port-Royal-en-Ville, Paris, by Antoine le Pautre, c.1646, simple geometric forms express the austere, intellectual religious ideals of the Jansenists. After a long campaign led by the Jesuits, this movement was ultimately condemned as heretical.

Right: The Jesuits in Spain celebrated their victory over the Jansenists with the Transparente, a highly Berninian monument in Toledo Cathedral designed by Narciso Tomé in 1721.

storme . . . the ruines resembling the picture of Troy. London was, but is no more.'

This was Wren's chance. The vast majority of the City churches had burned down. With tremendous speed a tax was levied on coal to raise the money to rebuild them, the Government finding the money for the fabric, while the decoration and any extra embellishments were to be met by local bodies. Wren was put in charge of the building of fifty-two churches simultaneously; in the process, he created the typical Protestant English church.

With an extraordinary mixture of simplicity and ingenuity, he fitted airy, well-lit, commodious churches on to plots which were frequently irregular and cramped. In spite of the number, he contrived the greatest variety in plan and organization. It is obvious, looking at these churches, how much they owe to Dutch churches, like the Nieuwe Kerk in Haarlem. The borrowing is not accidental, for the Dutch were the strongest Protestant power, the natural source of inspiration for such a theme, and indeed, the natural source for a Protestant king when one was required in 1688.

The ancestry of these churches, however, is less startling than their descendants, which immediately included the great London churches of the eighteenth century, such as Gibbs's grandiloquent Saint Martin-in-the-Fields. That was only the beginning.

When in the 1720s the Anglican colonists of Philadelphia wished to demonstrate their growing social importance in the Quaker city, and their loyalty to the English Church and Crown, they built, in Christ Church, one of the key colonial churches. With its galleries, its Venetian window and its clear, even light, it would look perfectly in place in the Home Counties. The unknown architect of Saint Michael's, Charleston, was, in the 1760s, making a precisely similar reference to London fashion and to the achievement of Wren and James Gibbs (1682–1754), as did Saint Paul's Chapel, New York, and

ST PAUL'S CATHEDRAL: BAROQUE DOMING

The foundation stone of the new Saint Paul's was laid in June 1675: Wren lived to see his cathedral completed in 1711. Everywhere he courted comparison with Saint Peter's in Rome and throughout he sought to surpass it, especially in the balance between dome and façade. The great towers at the west end have the stature Bernini intended for the similar towers at Saint Peter's (which fell down) while beyond appears the almost hemispherical dome, more sedate, more majestically at rest than the elongated Roman prototype.

Right: The west front and principal façade, showing how Wren tackled the problematic relationship between towers and dome.

Below: The cutaway shows Saint Paul's large outer dome, designed to be the dominant landmark on the London skyline; the shallower saucer-dome to be seen from inside the cathedral; and the concealed brick cone, running between the two to carry the weight of the lantern and the cross.

the Baptist Church at Providence, Rhode Island. Whenever English speakers had to confront the problem of church-building, the first, the instinctive, solution was recourse to Wren.

These City churches of the 1670s and 1680s were, above all, the expression of a communal pride, of a partnership between government and local organizations, especially the City companies, in the creation of a new environment. Suitably, the lower part, the halls, tended to be simple and practical. Above, the fantasies of Wren's steeples formed the delicate setting for the mass of Saint Paul's.

Saint Paul's demonstrates a very curious phenomenon. As long as Wren was operating on the scale of a small church, he was content to remain largely in the northern tradition. But when confronted with the task of a cathedral for London, he could not resist the challenge of the Roman heritage. Although a convinced Protestant, he determined to take on Saint Peter's.

Predictably, the clergy were hostile.

Far left: Saint Stephen Walbrook, London, the most splendid and perhaps most ingenious interior of Wren's parish churches, built between 1672 and 1679. The site of the church was a simple near-rectangle, but within that rather boring space, Wren has played architectural games with the spectator. By careful disposition of sixteen elegant Corinthian columns, he has been able to imply a plan in the shape of a cross, with nave, chancel and transepts. A central space is defined by eight arches carried on the columns and, in spite of the small scale of the church, this space is covered with a dome coffered in the same way as the Pantheon in Rome. In its use of the dome and its ambiguities between a central and a longitudinal building this church is in many ways a trial run for Saint Paul's.

Right: The church of Saint Bride, Fleet Street, London, was designed by Wren between 1671 and 1678. The church sits low, near the old Fleet River, and its spire, added in 1701 as an important vertical accent beside the dome of Saint Paul's, is the tallest that Wren built.

They wanted a cathedral as close as possible to the Gothic character of the old one which they had lost. Wren, however, wanted a high dome, which would act as the focal point in the sky-scape of the city; he also wanted to avoid the appearance of the Gothic high nave and lower side aisles favoured by the clergy. By the simple device of getting the clergy to agree to one plan and fundamentally altering it into another as building proceeded, Wren was eventually able to get most of what he wanted. The building is a masterpiece of sophisticated deception.

It can be seen that the clergy were granted their high nave and lower aisles. It can also be seen that Wren got his uniform two-storey building—by running a blank second-storey wall all round the church, thus concealing the differences in height as well as the very un-Roman Gothic buttresses which he was obliged to use to support the nave roof and the dome. But the dome itself is the greatest deception.

Wren wanted, as we have said, to build a landmark and so he placed the dome on a large drum and a high attic. However, such an ovoid drum, placed so high, would produce a very unpleasant effect from inside the church, where it would be like standing at the bottom of a tunnel. His solution was to build a second dome, saucer-shaped, inside the larger one. It had been decided, however, to put a stone steeple-lantern on the top of the dome, and since the outer dome is not made of stone

—that would have required huge buttresses to support it—but of wood, it could not carry the stone lantern. Wren's solution to this was a third dome, built in brick, running between the existing two and hidden by them. It is this which supports the lantern and the huge gold orb and cross which dominate the East of London.

It was this eastern end of the city which was to cause the church-building problems of the future. The population of London was growing very fast and, after the expulsion of the Huguenots from France in the persecution of 1685, it was swollen by large numbers of refugees. These settled, for the most part, in the East End, working mainly in the textile trade. They were, of course, not members of the Church of England, and the Government became increasingly alarmed about this large centre of non-conformist thought and perhaps doubtful political allegiance.

So, in 1711, the newly elected Tory Government passed an Act for the Building of Fifty New Churches, to reassert the primacy of the Established Church and, through it, the supremacy of the established government. In the East End, there was little of the pressure of cramped sites which had exercised Wren in the City; besides, it was always intended that these should be demonstrations of authority, and it was therefore appropriate that they should be large. They are immense. But they do include, especially in the churches designed by Nicholas Hawksmoor (1661–1736), some of the most exciting buildings ever put up in England.

A church like Saint George in the East has none of the intimate charm of one of Wren's City churches, although it was designed for a parish of similar numbers. In these churches, nothing is dainty, nothing is gentle. They are massive, overwhelming, almost terrifying statements of power, using elements of Roman Baroque architecture and of Wren's vernacular vocabulary, but with a strong accent of the castellated fortress. In the spires and

Above: Saint George in the East, Stepney, by Hawksmoor, 1714–17.

Left: Christ Church, Spitalfields, also by Hawksmoor, begun in 1714, but not completed before 1729. Both these Hawksmoor churches in the East End of London were built under the 1711 Act. Although the Act provided for the construction of fifty churches, only twelve were actually completed. All were to be built in stone and fitted with towers or steeples. These two churches show the idiosyncratic quality of Hawksmoor's genius. The tower in each case has lost all the Gothic delicacy of Wren's spires, and exploits echoes of Roman triumphal arches and areas of heavy shade to acquire a powerful severity. Hawksmoor's ability to draw on a wide range of architectural vocabulary to create his effects is evident in the Gothic towers he added to Westminster Abbey, and the classical mausoleum at Castle Howard.

Right below: Gibbs designed the interior of Saint Martin-in-the-Fields, London, between 1722 and 1726. While still clearly in the tradition of the Wren parish churches, the scale is grander, the nave wider and the effect richer.

Right above: Saint Paul's Chapel, the oldest public building on Manhattan Island, New York. The church was designed by Thomas McBean in the 1760s, the portico and spire being added in the 1790s. Even after the War of Independence, London churches remained valuable models for American architects. Here the influence of Saint Martin-in-the-Fields is very apparent.

turrets there is the same fantastic element as in the City churches, but it is fantasy of a sombre, brooding kind.

It would seem that, as propaganda, they were not very successful. One of the most striking contrasts in London architecture is in the juxtaposition of Hawksmoor's Christ Church, Spitalfields, the hulking official church, and the little Huguenot chapel beside it. Christ Church, spectacular though it is, has always been underused, and is now derelict, having only recently escaped from the threat of demolition.

The Huguenot chapel, on the other hand, has continued to serve its function as a place of worship for those who did not fit into the Established Church. Once the Huguenots had prospered and moved on to more fashionable areas, their chapel was taken over by the next batch of poor immigrants. It became a synagogue in the nineteenth century and now that the Jews have also largely moved West, it has been taken over by the latest overseas workers in the still flourishing rag-trade, and is being used as a mosque by Asians.

But if the great breakthroughs of Roman Baroque church architecture were always to remain alien to England, even in the hands of Wren and Hawksmoor, there was one northern country eager to absorb them, and brilliantly able to do so: Germany.

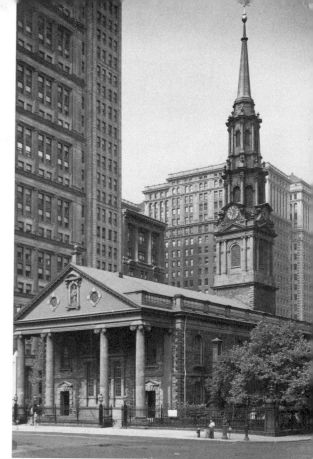

South Germany and the Habsburg lands had been the great success story of the Counter-Reformation. The Jesuits were extremely active throughout Bavaria, Austria and Bohemia and by the end of the seventeenth century these had been saved for the Roman Catholic church. The reconversion had been of the greatest intensity, frequently accompanied by miraculous healings and by visions of the saints. As the economy of the region began to recover from the destruction of the Thirty Years' War, church building was resumed on a titanic scale.

Unlike the churches in Rome and London, these were built predominantly for

paintings and sculptures which direct our attention upwards from that particular person of the Trinity to the dome, where, in fresco, all three are combined in glory. What has happened in this church is what characterizes the greatest monuments of central European Baroque: the two poles of Roman Baroque have been synthesized. Structural complexity and dramatic conceit are fused and to them has been added the sharper, almost dazzling daylight of the North.

Indeed, it could be argued that each of the main Roman strands is carried further in Germany than it ever was in Rome. Because the Church in Bavaria had had to fight so hard against Protestantism, it was natural that the main focus of veneration should be precisely those elements of belief which the Protestants rejected. Thus the cult of the Virgin and the Saints becomes the dominant theme of church building and decoration, and the churches themselves become theatres in which these great mysteries can be revealed to the faithful and celebrated as victories over unbelief.

The Assumption of the Virgin, one of the doctrines most vigorously disputed by the Lutherans, is therefore taken as the main theme of the whole church at Rohr. All attention is focused on the high altar, where even Bernini is surpassed. In front of a billowing stucco curtain, the huge figure of the Virgin is borne aloft by angels, entirely supported by concealed metal struts, while below, the apostles, larger than life, strike attitudes of astonishment; and beyond, in the illusionistic space

peasants; above all they were built as a focus for pilgrimage, the favourite manifestation of peasant piety. Just such a church is the tiny pilgrimage sanctuary of Stadl Paura, near Linz in upper Austria.

In the terrible plague of 1713, the Abbot of Lambach vowed to build a church in honour of the Trinity should his town be spared. Miraculously, the plague stopped at the gates. His thank-offering church is triangular, with a door in each side and three high altars, one for every person of the Trinity. In its combination of the

triangular and circular elements it is clearly indebted to that other church representing the Trinity, Borromini's San Carlo alle Quattro Fontane. There is the same indivisible, fluid space, the same delight in spatial transformations, the same coherent symbolism of the Trinity from the ground-plan to the lantern of the cupola.

But there is much more: to the Borrominian repertoire the architect has added the colour and the theatricality of Bernini. The walls are articulated in rich greens and pinks and on each of the altars are

behind the apostles, can be seen some wondering eighteenth-century heads.

The same artists, the Asam brothers, Cosmas Damian (1686–1739) and Egid Quirin (1692–1750), created a yet more powerful image at the monastery of Weltenburg on the Danube. The oval church sweeps round to the climax of the High Altar, which is in shadow. Behind is very intense, yellow light from a concealed source. And through the flames riding into the observer's space comes the figure of Saint George, the symbol of the ultimate victory of Christian light over the powers of darkness.

In an atmosphere of such fervid, mystical Catholicism, one would expect that architecture would tend towards the pursuit of spatial bewilderment, as in Rome. Again, one might claim that the German developments are even more remarkable —and nowhere more so than in the work of Balthasar Neumann (1687–1753).

An early work, such as the chapel of the Bishop of Bamberg's Palace in Würzburg, has many echoes of Borromini, in the curving entablatures and the puzzling relationship of column to wall. The spectator finds his view obstructed by free-standing coloured columns, which make it impossible to grasp the shape of the chapel; this appears to change as the spectator moves forward, while above him is an extremely complex net of interlocking oval domes. Structurally, it is as hard to grasp as San Carlo alle Quattro Fontane, and like Borromini, Neumann had begun life as a practical builder—in fact as a military engineer—and had also studied local Gothic traditions with great care.

These elements appear in fully developed form in his great church of Vierzehnheiligen. Even by the standards of Counter-Reformation Bavaria, the simultaneous appearance in a vision of fourteen saints on this spot was exceptional, and by the beginning of the eighteenth century the site was one of the most popular pilgrimage centres of south Germany.

The church which Neumann designed in the 1740s takes account of the huge numbers of pilgrims who came to pray at the shrine by placing the principal altar in the middle of the nave. This acts as a focus, around which he gives his structural virtuosity full range. Developing the late-Gothic nodding ogee, Neumann makes every arch around this central space bend three-dimensionally, so that it moves and changes axis with the spectator. The columns supporting the vaults are set well forward from the walls, creating a profound uncertainty about the limits of the church and about its stability. The lighting, reflected from the white and gilt, streams from hidden sources and dazzles the eye.

Amidst the brilliant colour of the false marble and the frescoes, nothing is static, nothing can be fixed. In a remarkable development beyond the Roman prototypes, the church has now become not just the stage for a visionary experience, like the Cornaro Chapel, but an apparition in itself—an apparently ephemeral glimpse of celestial beauty.

The down-grading of the supporting elements at Vierzehnheiligen in the interests of a much less tectonic structure indicates that Neumann was moving away from the manipulation of mass, which we

Left: The pilgrimage church of Vierzehnheiligen, near Bamberg, West Germany, designed by Neumann in 1742 and completed after his death in 1772. The centrally placed altar, focus of the pilgrims' devotions and site of the miraculous vision, was designed by J.J.M. Küchel. Here Neumann has developed even more fully the possibilities of architectural mass in movement which he had explored earlier at the nearby Residenz chapel in Würzburg.

Above: One of the chief delights of Bavarian Rococo architecture is the quality of its stucco decorative detail, which frequently brings a humorous note to serious surroundings. The prancing putto with the outsize biretta is from the monastery of Oberzell, West Germany.

Right below: The simple white-washed exterior of the Wieskirche, a church near Munich, West Germany, built for peasant pilgrimage by Dominikus Zimmermann between 1746 and 1754.

Right above: The interior of the Wieskirche, frescoed by Johann Baptist Zimmermann. Architectonic elements have been reduced to a minimum to create an effect of airy impermanence.

throne. For this church, although filled with worldly elegance, is in fact already an image of heaven—a vision, suspended in time, as the architecture appears to be suspended in space, until it is made complete by the arrival of its ruler at the Second Coming. It is a fantastical French drawing-room, in which Bavarian peasants can await, with happy expectation, the end of the world.

IMAGES OF ABSOLUTISM

If it is true to say that the seventeenth century saw the final settling of Europe's religious boundaries, it saw only the beginning of the great political upheavals. The debate about the relationship between individual and state was to continue throughout the period, across the civil wars in Holland and England, to the continental dislocation of the French Revolutionary wars.

With the decline of the feudal structure of society, it became increasingly a matter for controversy whether power should be unitary, centralized in the hands of an absolute monarch, or wielded more diffusely by an oligarchy. Just as in the religious debate, architecture clearly had a very significant role to play, and it is not accidental that the characteristic Baroque building type, other than the church, is the palace.

associate with the Baroque, towards a more Rococo pursuit of shimmering transparency. This less structural style, which we shall see evolving at Versailles in secular architecture, was transformed in Germany into a vehicle for the most intense religious feeling.

It is one of the greatest achievements of German architecture that this style, elsewhere almost exclusively regarded as decorative, or even frivolous, could be a mode capable of expressing the greatest piety. All the worldly refinement of a Parisian salon is present in the pilgrimage church of Die Wies, not far from Munich. Erected to honour a miracle-working image, the church carries the anti-structural elements of Vierzehnheiligen even further. The roof is of wood, so that the supporting walls and columns can be as light as possible, and surfaces are painted white and gilt, decorated with elegantly attenuated figures in pastel colours.

Yet there is nothing secular about its intention or its effect. The entire shimmering confection—one might almost say confectionery—is dominated by the presence in the ceiling fresco of an empty

At the beginning of the century the debate about the relationship between subject and monarch was nowhere more acrimonious than in England. The Stuarts, recently arrived from Scotland, were anxious to project themselves as God-sent authoritarian rulers, cultured men of letters, rather than the Northern barbarians for whom they might have been taken. The architecture of Elizabeth had to be surpassed.

It was. In Inigo Jones (1573–1662) James I and Charles I found exactly the architect they required, and in the Banqueting House in Whitehall their aspirations found their highest expression. Building in stone, Jones's interpretation of Italian Renaissance, and especially of Palladian models, at a stroke made the great prodigy houses of the Elizabethans look outdated and provincial. The restrained, correct use of the classical Orders indicated at once that comparison was being sought with the greatest buildings of Europe.

The hall was to be used for masques and Court receptions. Jones selected the shape of the classical basilica, with a huge niche behind the throne end, which was subsequently filled in.

The basilical ground-plan has exactly those associations in antiquity which his patrons welcomed: it was used for royal courts of justice and for divine worship.

Nothing could have been more suitable for a king eager to argue his Divine Right. On to this classical base Jones had grafted Palladio, who, it was thought, of all Renaissance architects most nearly approximated to the purity and the grandeur of the Romans.

Palladio's dependence on ratio and balance for his architectural effects gave to James's aspirations the cachet of inevitable rightness which he so wanted. England could now bear comparison not only with ancient Rome, but also with the most splendid courts of Renaissance Italy, still regarded as the arbiter of all manners and fashion.

The huge double cube of the Banqueting House was from the beginning intended to carry ceiling decorations by Rubens, already celebrated as a great propagandist for absolute monarchy. Jones divided the ceiling into large sections, which would allow clearly legible canvases to be inserted and so spell out in painting the message already carried by the building itself.

Still one of the most majestic interiors in England, the room at the time was incomparably grander than anything else visible. The associations of the architecture are reiterated by the allegory of the ceiling. In the central panel, the fusion of royal and religious elements is completed in the Apotheosis of James I, rising heavenwards for all the world as though he were some martyred saint of the new religion of Absolute Kingship.

That role, of course, was in fact to be filled by his son, Charles I, who walked from the north window of the room to his death on the scaffold outside. As was to be the case with the Hawksmoor churches, the architectural propaganda of the Crown had proved singularly unsuccessful. By one of the most remarkable of historical

Left above: An aerial view of the Palace of Versailles, France, after its enlargement in the 1680s, with the King's bedroom at the centre. Le Nôtre's grand formal park continues the axes of the house.

Left below: The Hall of Mirrors, Versailles, designed by Jules Hardouin Mansart and decorated by Charles Le Brun in the 1680s.

Right above: The Banqueting House in Whitehall, London, designed by Inigo Jones for James I, c.1620. The room was probably intended to be used for masques and court celebrations. On the ceiling are painted allegories by Rubens, celebrating the virtues and achievements of James I.

ironies, when the Palladian style—transformed into the architectural hallmark of the liberal aristocrat—returned to England at the beginning of the eighteenth century, it was to be as the style perfectl adapted to those most opposed to the ideas of absolutism.

There was, then, no true sequel to the Banqueting House in England. If we wish to look for its successor, we must seek for it in France. There, the Crown was making claims very similar to those of the Stuarts, also employing Rubens for its purposes, and also encountering serious opposition. In the year of Charles I's execution his nephew, Louis XIV of France, had to flee from the Paris mob storming the Louvre.

The Crown in France, however, won the battles which the Stuarts lost and went on to build the great monument of absolute monarchy, Versailles. Even more than the Banqueting House, Versailles is the expression of political intent and, indeed, of political necessity.

The major threat to centralized power in France came from the recently dispossessed feudal aristocracy. As late as

the 1640s the nobles had shown that, by making common cause with malcontent elements in Paris society, they could almost topple the authoritarian structure which Richelieu had created. It was therefore essential that they be neutralized. By removing them from Paris and their potential allies, and by occupying them with a minutely detailed round of etiquette, their political wings were clipped almost without being noticed.

Versailles is a brilliant confidence trick: it focuses all power on the king ruling through a middle-class bureaucracy, while in appearance it is dominated by the ritual of a hereditary military nobility. It is thus both a hotel and a prison for the aristocracy, and a temple to the glory of the king around whom it revolved.

The word 'revolved' is not accidental. The old courtly image of the king as the sun was given a totally new twist by the scientific discoveries of the late Renaissance. Now the sun was known to be not just the source of light and favour but the central controlling force from which all power emanated—and indeed was to correspond uncannily with the new concept of kingship.

Everything in the planning and decoration of Versailles reinforces this view: everything in its ritual expresses it. The king's bedroom is placed right at the centre of the palace on the axis which determines not only the line of the buildings, but also the lay-out of the gardens. His rising and setting—the French *lever* and *coucher* are appropriate to both planets and monarchs—were conducted in a blaze of public attention. The greatest nobles took it in turn to witness the event, pass the royal shirt, remove the royal stockings. The daily motions of the king— motions in every bodily sense—were elevated to match the divinely ordained rhythms of the universe.

This was essential, for the king was not just the king, he was the state. That state had the widest military ambitions and the palace was built to stun the visitor into submissive admiration.

Arriving at the main entrance, to the right of the central courtyard on the plan, the visitor was confronted by the Ambassadors' Staircase. Behind the double marble flight painted figures represented the rulers of the world coming to pay tribute. There followed a long sequence of planetary rooms, each illustrating one aspect of the

Left below: The great double-return staircase of the Bishop's Residenz at Würzburg, West Germany, designed by Neumann between 1737 and 1742, and frescoed by Giambattista Tiepolo, for Carl Friedrich von Schönborn.

Right above: Schönbrunn Palace, Vienna, designed by Fischer von Erlach and Nicolas Pacassi between 1696 and 1746. Like the Bourbons, the Habsburgs wanted a palace outside the city, where living quarters had come to seem cramped. Like the Bourbons, they chose a long façade of repeated blocks.

Right below: The hall and staircase designed by Johann Lucas von Hildebrandt in 1721 at the Upper Belvedere, Vienna.

reflected magnificence of the central sun.

Then, at the change of axis, came the Salon de la Guerre: marble reliefs indicated the military might of France, reminding the visitor of what lay in store for those who thwarted Louis's designs. Suitably chastened, he proceeded to the climax of the Galerie des Glaces, from which lay access to the Royal Bedroom and Council Chamber. At the far end the Salon de la Paix demonstrated what could be gained by respectful co-operation.

The absurd prodigality of this ensemble, with its marbles, painted ceilings of French triumphs, silver furniture and huge expanses of mirror to give the effect of a gallery open on both sides, all conspired to produce one emotion in the beholder—awe.

The exterior of the building had the same aim and the same effect. On arrival from Paris, the visitor was led through a series of dwindling courtyards, past stables, chapel, servants' buildings, in towards the central point, that of the royal presence, situated on the axis of the road to the capital. On the garden side this funnelling was abandoned for the impact of sheer size. On the top of its hill stretched the apparently endless façade, treated very flatly, with only the rare punctuation of forward-breaking, free-standing columns.

Meanwhile, all around, the fountains running with water pumped up at immense cost, the regimented plants and alleys, and the symbolic sculpture—all related to the glorification of Louis. Nature had been reduced by art, as continental Europe had been by Louis's armies, to a state of disciplined admiration.

The architectural resonance of Versailles was enormous. Wherever monarchs sought the absolute status of the French Crown, the obvious model for their residence was Louis's palace. The Habsburgs at Schönbrunn and the Romanovs at the

Würzburg shows clearly the great potential of staircases in the hands of a Baroque architect. To anyone interested in the effect of movement in architecture, or the possibilities of using directed light to create spatial excitement, the staircase is the natural climax of a building. More and more space is devoted to staircases and to their approach, whether inside as at the Upper Belvedere in Vienna, or as external motifs, as at the Troja Palace in Prague. Finally, in a schloss such as Brühl, the stairhall becomes such a spatial *tour de force* in its own right that the visitor is almost reluctant to pass on into the rooms to which it leads.

The function of these stair-chambers, of course, is not primarily one of passage. They are there to impress the visitor, and any reader of *Candide* will remember how much status of this sort meant to the eighteenth-century German aristocrat. His highest claim to consideration ultimately lay not in his staircase, but in whether he held his lands direct from the emperor himself. Only such a ruler was entitled to receive the emperor, should he pass through. This led to the quite remarkable phenomenon of eligible landowners building a special room, a Kaisersaal, for the unlikely event of an imperial visit. Usually the most splendid room in the schloss, probably rarely used for its true function in generations, it formed the architectural highlight of the building and vindicated, beyond challenge, the highest privilege of caste.

The impact of Versailles was not limited to the buildings erected by Louis during the heady years of the sixties and seventies. As old age overtook him, Louis, like the rest of the court, fell increasingly under the spell of the beautiful Duchesse de Bourgogne, married to his eldest grandson. It is said that it was to honour her that he asked

Hermitage, in spite of their anti-French policies, paid the sincerest form of flattery in their buildings.

By a curious inversion, it is almost true to say that this kind of glorification of an individual sovereign through his architecture becomes more lavish and more visually appealing as the monarch declines in importance. Nowhere is this truer than in Germany, where a multitude of tiny courts vied with each other in their attempts to equal the magnificence of the King of France.

This is carried to the stage of parody at Ansbach, a well-connected though otherwise secondary margraviate in Franconia. Casting around for a design for his orangery, the margrave hit upon the idea of copying the most prestigious building in Paris, the ceremonial east front of the Louvre. The original, so splendidly imposing as an entrance to the Bourbons' city residence, cuts an odd figure as a monument to pretension in provincial Germany.

Some of the aping was more successful. The exterior of the Bishop's Residenz at Würzburg is heavily dependent on Versailles, but the interior is one of Neumann's greatest creations, and especially the entrance hall and staircase.

The entrance is wide enough to allow a carriage to be driven right inside the palace, to the foot of the huge double-return staircase. Overhead, still in the tradition of the Escalier des Ambassadeurs, but much grander and more spirited, Tiepolo's frescoes show the four corners of the world bringing gifts to the ruler of this pocket state.

took firm hold in England, in face of the austere competition of the Palladian revival. In Germany, however, we have already seen how it was taken up in religious architecture, and its secular application was no less widespread and no less remarkable.

After the Bavarian Court at Munich had evolved its own variant of Rococo in the work of François Cuvilliés (1695–1768), the style spread rapidly through south Germany and central Europe, where a delight in applied decoration extended very far down the social scale. Essentially, however, it is a palace idiom. Like the French aristocracy for whom it was created, the German noble houses had lost much of their real power, and it is hard not to see the Rococo as a deliberate attempt to create an artificial world. Walls are dissolved by the application of tiles or mirrors; ornament starts looking like one thing, ends by being completely transformed; balance is avoided; reason is not considered. In a peculiar way, the 'message' of this kind of architecture is not to the outside world, but rather to those who live within it. It is designed to offer a factitious world in which the inhabitants may enjoy every fantasy of luxury and ease.

for the creation of a lighter, less bombastic style—'*de la jeunesse semée partout*' (youth scattered everywhere).

However that may be, it is certain that the latter years of Louis' long reign and those immediately following his death in 1715 did witness a major architectural change.

The beginnings can be seen in the Salon de l'Oeil de Boeuf at Versailles, transformed, with neat historical timing, in the first year of the eighteenth century. There is no attempt to articulate the wall surface with classical members; the key structural points in the room—corners and cornice—are understated or curved and their tectonic function is denied by the application of light-hearted surface decoration.

These are the essential characteristics of the style known as Rococo, which we see far more fully developed in the Hôtel de Rohan-Soubise in Paris of twenty years later. Here, the structural function of the walls is further undermined by the cutting of panels and mirrors; and the decoration draws more freely on asymmetrical, natural forms such as ferns, shells and rocks. Indeed the style acquired its originally pejorative title from the fashion for collecting such objects, *rocaille*.

A consciously luxurious style, it never

THE NEW REFINEMENT: POLITE, PALLADIAN, PICTURESQUE

Until now we have been concerned with the houses of heads of state, even if very minor ones. The passing of the old feudal order and its replacement by royal absolutism had, however, obvious repercussions on the living quarters of subjects as well.

The feudal household community, organized for the defence and exploitation of agricultural land, gives way to the household of the man who is rich because he is in the service of the king. The quasi-military bond of master and servant, with its considerable personal contact, is replaced by one much closer to that of employer and employee. Land and servants, in short, become no longer the source of wealth and power, but their result and manifestation. The new lord will seek a new division between the polite and the menial aspects of his household. Two castles near Paris make this point.

Coulommiers, built in 1613 by Salomon de Brosse, is still a castle conceived for defence, running round a courtyard and looking inwards. Yet it is closely linked to the land on which it is set, accommodating servants, horses, and store-rooms, at close quarters with the family who own it. The castle is what it appears—a little world housing a microcosm of society.

The castle of Maisons, built thirty years later by François Mansart (1598–1666), is different. The house is a free-standing block, looking outward into the park set around it. All the visible house above ground level is reserved for polite living, while the domestic offices have been removed from contact with the family. The stables are set well away from the house and arranged to form an impressive approach, their function subordinated to their aesthetic impact on the visitor. The servants' quarters and kitchens are in the basement below the level of the dry moat, from which they draw light and air without being seen.

As the owner's income derives from his official position, all the land can be organized for promenade and riding, rather than farming. Indeed, every appearance of physical dependence on the real world is suppressed. Supplies of food and fuel, which in Coulommiers would be stored in the courtyard, in Maisons are brought in by an underground passage large enough for a horse and cart from the neighbouring village. Everything bodily, necessary, vulgar, has gone underground.

MAISONS: A SEVENTEENTH-CENTURY CHÂTEAU

Maisons is perhaps the epitome of domestic architecture in seventeenth-century France. Commissioned from François Mansart by René de Longueil in 1642, the château demonstrates the preoccupations and ambitions of the new rich professional middle class. All round the extensive grounds are impressive gateways, placed to entice a visit from the king and other notables who might be hunting in the forests between the royal châteaux of Saint Germain and Versailles. Avenues of trees lead to the huge stables – status symbols par excellence – which might almost be taken for the house, and then on to the château itself. On the edge of a hill running down to the Seine stands the house, articulated with very correct classical Orders: Doric for the entrance floor; Ionic for the first floor, or 'bel étage', where polite living was concentrated in the reception rooms and bedrooms; and Corinthian for the top storey of the central elements. The servants' quarters are placed out of sight in the basement, which is linked by a tunnel to the neighbouring village – perhaps the supreme example of French culture's endeavour to suppress the physical aspects of life in favour of the intellectual and social. The main building itself is constructed with the analytic clarity characteristic of Cartesian thought. The mass of the house is divided into several blocks, all of which retain a separate and clearly legible identity, expressed in the roofing and in the plasticity of the Orders. The decoration, although very limited in extent, is a model of austere opulence, and of the highest quality. Magnificent white eagles, for example, whose far sight – 'long oeil'—is a punning reference to Longueil the patron, crown the severe Doric pilasters of the otherwise chillingly sober entrance hall.

From beginning to end, the effect aimed at, and achieved, is of great wealth, expressed through restrained, rational and exquisite good taste. In spite of Mansart's being a notoriously slow architect, the main house was completed in only four years. Although the château remains virtually intact, the park was destroyed by speculators in the last century.

Left: The majestic stables are not just a device to indicate status and wealth: they are part of the build-up to the château itself. Even for Longueil's horses, Mansart used classical Orders and stone, but eliminated the Ionic Order, to show the absence of 'polite' life.

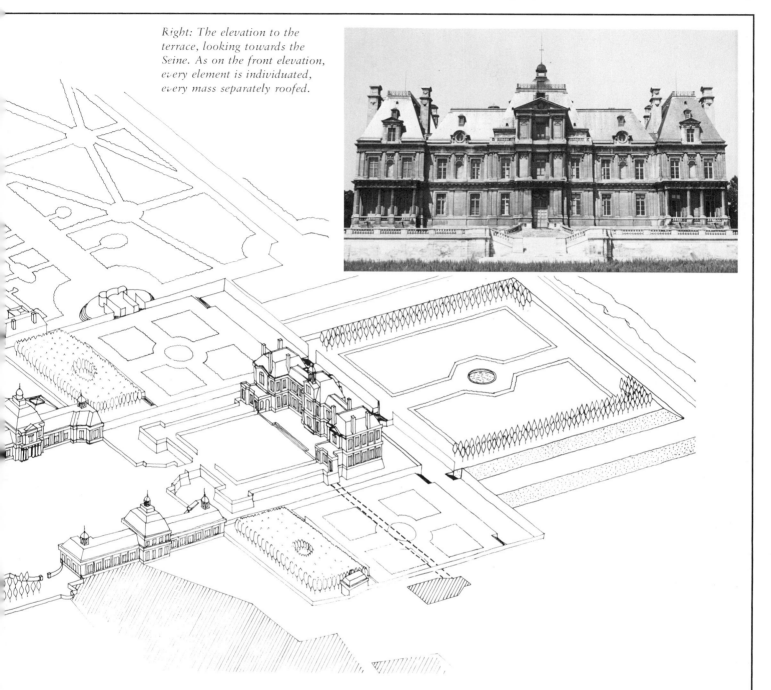

Right: The elevation to the terrace, looking towards the Seine. As on the front elevation, every element is individuated, every mass separately roofed.

Right: The Salle des Fêtes, or ceremonial reception room, on the first floor, used for dances or banqueting.

Far right: The austerely elegant entrance-hall, decorated almost exclusively in white stucco, looking towards the grand staircase. As in the staircase, the walls have been kept plain, and sculptural incident concentrated above the cornice.

This division of the elegant from the coarse, a dominant theme in contemporary literature, is easy enough to achieve in the country, where space is plentiful. In Paris, however, where the patrons were perhaps less rich and therefore all the keener to achieve refinement, the problems were greater, and frequently compounded by irregularities of site. In solving these problems the French architects of the day produced some of their most ingenious and compelling works.

Supreme among these 'Hôtels', as town-houses were called, was that built by Antoine Le Pautre (c.1621–82) for Madame de Beauvais, who had allegedly furnished the young Louis XIV with his first heterosexual experience. She was not rich. The site was irregular, with two entrances. She needed to let out some of the ground floor as shops to provide income. Yet she wanted a grand hôtel—room for three carriages and their horses, an imposing staircase, a garden, a chapel, a terrace—and she wanted a symmetrical design.

Le Pautre gave her everything that she wanted and a little bit more. Taking advantage of the problematic double entrance, he banished stables and staff to the lesser street door, and in the centre of the plot created a triangular courtyard with a semi-circular end. As the rooms at this end, close up to the neighbouring plot, had no light, they were used as carriage sheds. Passing between the shops, a carriage brought the visitor to the im-

pressive circular porch, where he would alight at the foot of the ceremonial staircase. The carriage, which had no room to turn round, drove through and out the secondary door, while the visitor, after climbing the staircase, passed through the vestibule, into the gallery and on, either to the chapel, over the carriage sheds, or to the garden-walk laid out over the servants' quarters. And here Le Pautre had even been able to fit in the last word in garden

smartness, a small grotto.

These transformations in social architecture are perhaps most apparent in France, but they are in fact a European phenomenon. There were similar developments in Vienna and in England, where the word 'hall', for instance, at this date ceases to mean the central room in which the old, unitary, household gathers, and becomes the name for nothing more than an entrance vestibule.

In England, however, it is fair to say that the main concern at this period was not so much with the town house as the country house. England had not become a Court society in the same way as France, the aristocracy and gentry preferring to remain on their estates and come to town largely when Parliament was sitting. The typical English house, therefore, is the sober, substantial country seat, such as Coleshill in Berkshire. This kind of architecture had an obvious appeal to the squirearchy of the English colonies in the New World and became one of the types of the colonial mansion, as at Westover, Virginia.

The architectural developments which we have been looking at posited a peaceful, stable society, and it is salutary to remember that in the north of Britain, as the century began, such conditions did not prevail. A castle like Fyvie, in Aberdeenshire, is still conceived entirely in terms of recurrent local warfare.

In the latter part of the century, however, the main military concern of England was the wars with France, and it was in celebration of her ultimate victory over the ambitions of Louis XIV that the most spectacular house of the period was built. Blenheim was the nation's grateful gift to Marlborough and was the joint creation of the dilettante architect Sir John Vanbrugh (1664–1726), and Nicholas Hawksmoor. Like the Hawksmoor churches, it was promoted by an assertive central government, and, like them, it represents one of the high-water marks of Baroque in England.

It is in fact somewhere between a house and a monument. High over the portico on the south front stands the bust of Louis, captured at Tournai, while on the clock tower in the kitchen court, the British lion mauls the puny and pretentious cock of France. The scale of the house is colossal. The progression of forecourts and towers and curving, quadrant wings leads up to the grand central portico with a combination of mass and movement very similar to that we have seen in the East End churches. The note of fantasy presented there is matched by the weirdly grenaded, square towers, repeated at the corners of the main blocks.

The interior aims at the grand manner in a similar key. Grinling Gibbons, who had collaborated with Wren in Saint Paul's, supervised the carvings, while, in the saloon, Laguerre's murals show the world admiring the military prowess of Marlborough. Ironically, it is the English building which most nearly approximates to the mood of Versailles. The decoration took years to complete, and was marred by the most savage brawls between Vanbrugh and the Duchess. By the time it was finished, architectural taste had moved dramatically in a new direction.

The arrival of George I from Hanover had meant the end of the High Tory supremacy, which, as we have seen, favoured rhetorical public buildings to glorify national achievements or to house the High Church. The day was now to the Whigs—liberal oligarchs who were opposed to strong central government and whose outlook on the world was Protestant, mercantile and, above all, rational. To men like this, Blenheim, and all it represented, was 'a false and counterfeit Piece of Magnificence, as can be justly arraigned for its Deformity'.

Shaftesbury was not alone in his rejection of a Baroque style as bombastic and, above all, as carrying associations of a foreign tyranny. His lead was soon followed by Colen Campbell (1673–1729), in his book *Vitruvius Britannicus*. Campbell argues for a national architectural style, fundamentally different from the Baroque of the absolutist powers: and he argues that it has already been created once, in the simple, noble architecture of Inigo Jones—the British Vitruvius of the title.

The return to the works of Jones and Palladio hinges on a fundamental reinterpretation of their style. No longer is it viewed as a vehicle of Stuart pretensions. Instead, Palladio is esteemed for adapting the buildings of Roman antiquity to suit a governing class closely linked to the land. The English country gentleman felt strong affinities with the Venetian landowner of the *terra firma*, and, beyond him, with the Roman patrician commuting from his estates in the country to the Senate.

The movement, articulate by the time

that George I arrived, needed only a rich and powerful patron. This it found in Richard Boyle (1694–1753), Earl of Burlington. After travelling in Italy, Burlington returned to England to devote his life and his fortune to the perfection of the national taste, assisted by his close friend, the painter and architect William Kent (1685–1748). Between them, they dominated domestic architecture in England and North America for the rest of the century.

In a very real sense, this is backward-looking architecture. Palladio is valued above all as a guide to the true creations of the ancients, in the hope that a regenerated architecture might be accompanied by a morally renewed society.

The antiquarian element in the movement is very apparent in the Assembly Rooms at York, designed by Burlington himself. These were to be the social focus of the county town. Burlington turned to Palladio's interpretation of Vitruvius' Egyptian Hall, for that was held to be the kind of building in which the Romans had gathered for light-hearted enjoyment.

Antique correctness takes absolute precedence over common sense or practical considerations. The hall is a faithful reconstruction of Palladio's Vitruvius—but it was useless for eighteenth-century dancing. The orthodox gap of two columns width between columns and wall, however aesthetically pleasing, was too narrow to allow the passage of a hooped petticoat, and the hall had to be altered in such a way as to wreck Burlington's proportions.

With the buildings of Palladio himself,

the same degree of deference was not necessary, and both the great Palladian houses in the south of England deviate substantially from their Veneto model. At Chiswick, the villa designed by Burlington has shed three of the porticoes, and is smaller than the Rotonda which inspired it, while at Mereworth, Campbell enlarged the prototype in order to increase the accommodation available.

English Palladianism, then, is a mood rather than an archaeological exercise, as can be seen in perhaps its most important creation away from London. Kent's Holkham was the Norfolk home of the Whig magnate, notably liberal in arts and politics, the Earl of Leicester. The main façade of Holkham employs many elements taken from Palladio—the portico and the Venetian windows are the most obvious, but they are deployed in a totally un-Palladian way, to give a very elongated, rather staccato rhythm, in which no unit is like the unit next to it. In contradistinction to Blenheim, which depends on the repetition and climaxing of similar elements with considerable fantasy, Holkham is rather an exercise in static symmetry, the rational, austere house of a man of taste.

The wealth of Leicester, however, makes its appearance in the famous hall. This combines the York Assembly Rooms with a Roman basilical apse (as Jones had in the Banqueting House), adding more than a touch of Palladio's Redentore. Through this you pass into the saloon and the collection of antiquities. It is the house of the ideal Palladian man, familiar with the best of the classical past, living modestly on the land.

These ideals naturally appealed strongly to the liberal landowners in America, where men of very similar aspirations took up the style. In Philadelphia, for example, the complex of State House, Supreme Court and Congress Hall has, in its massing and balancing, an uncanny affinity with the staccato grouping of Holkham.

The Library Hall of 1790 in the same city is almost indistinguishable from an English Palladian mansion. The reason for this striking similarity can be seen at once if we look at Abraham Swan's *Collection of Designs in Architecture* published in London in 1757. Palladianism is easily reducible to the two-dimensional form of engravings and is therefore much more exportable than a dynamic, three-dimensional style such as the High Baroque.

By the late eighteenth century many copies of Palladio and of works inspired by him had reached America. The associations with moral integrity and regeneration made the style the natural choice for Thomas Jefferson (1743–1826) in his designs for Monticello and for the state Capitol at Richmond, Virginia—just as Wren had been the obvious model for the Protestant church. It is perhaps a similar taste for the uplifting implications of English Palladianism which accounts for the spread of the style to Poland. Zawadzki's mansion at Lubostrom in the 1790s is as appealing a reinterpretation of the master as anything in England or North America.

The main development of Palladianism in Britain came through the work of the Scottish architect Robert Adam (1728–92). Bringing to the style a new concern for variety and surface decoration, he frequently achieves a kind of delicate elegance very different from the chunky simplicity of the earlier Palladians.

In his use of curving colonnades, as, for example, at Hopetoun, Adam brings to the Burlington repertoire some of the fluency and movement which is so signally lacking in a building like Holkham. But it is essentially in his interiors that he is important, indeed revolutionary. The Palladians in general had opted for straightforward room-shapes—rectangles relating to each other in developing ratios, but always instantly legible. Adam constantly rings the changes on oblongs, apse ends, circular rooms, deploying the greatest ingenuity to keep the visitor surprised and enchanted. The Music Room at Kenwood is typical, with its curved end, its bold colouring and its abundant surface decoration. Eager to create a total environment, he insisted on controlling every element of decoration, woodwork and furnishing.

Left: The Library of Kenwood House, London, designed by Robert Adam in 1767. Although Adam uses massive elements of classical architecture, the final effect remains highly decorative. His use of charming colour and widespread surface ornament gives a Rococo character to much of his work.

Above: An excellent example of Robert Adam's intimate monumentality is the staircase at 20 Portman Square, London, built for the Countess of Home in the 1770s.

Right above: The Chinese Pavilion, Sans-Souci, Potsdam, near Berlin, built by Georg Wenzeslaus von Knobelsdorff for Frederick the Great in 1745. 'Chinese' architecture was very popular in France, but is also found in England and Spain.

Right below: Among the most charming of Chinese decorations are the 'grandes singeries' at Chantilly, near Paris, designed by Christophe Huet c.1736.

At the same time, when building in a different tradition, as at Culzean in Scotland, he is able to adapt to a rugged, embattled style reminiscent of Fyvie, and to exploit to the full the magnificent site, high on a cliff overlooking the Firth of Clyde.

Perhaps his most appealing work is Home House in London, built in the 1770s for the ageing and immensely rich Countess of Home. The purpose of the house was, above all, social, and into the narrow plot available he has fitted an astonishing number and variety of reception rooms. Mounting the double-return horseshoe staircase, the visitor passes from one room into the next—they all interconnect—and at every turn a surprise in shape or arrangement awaits him. The variety of plan is matched by the range of decoration, from the slender classical pilasters of the Music Room to the bold Etruscan treatment of the Countess's bedroom.

Like Palladianism, the Adam style also had considerable impact in North America. New York's City Hall makes its bold public statement of liberalism with a façade closely derived from French models.

But inside, and especially in its staircase, it was designed for men still fundamentally English in their taste and ideals.

The work of Robert Adam is a convenient point at which to try to resume the main currents of late-eighteenth-century building. The 'Rococo classicism' of some of his interiors is matched by the more rigorous Etruscan decoration, derived from models excavated at Pompeii and Herculaneum. The variety of room-shapes, however, owes a great deal to Adam's investigations of antique sites. This growing concern with archaeology in the application of classical models was to be of the greatest importance. No less so is his ability, which we saw at Culzean, to work in an alien stylistic tradition, where it had associations on which he wished to play.

One such alien tradition had connotations almost as elevated as those of ancient Rome—the Chinese. China's stock stood remarkably high in eighteenth-century liberal thought. Without the benefit—or the hindrance, depending on one's liberality of outlook—of the Christian tradition, the Chinese had established an unparalleled reputation for efficient administration and, more important, for peaceful relations with their neighbours. So it is not surprising that, while south German potentates were indulging in high Rococo, the serious Frederick the Great,

dreaming of reforming his state on the most modern lines, should turn to the East. The Chinese tea-house at Sans-Souci is the perfect retreat for a progressive administrator, complete with statues of Chinese figures relaxing under palm trees —who, after all, knew for certain what trees actually grew in China?

The taste for chinoiserie swept Europe, providing decorative motifs for furniture and porcelain, as well as inspiring some of the most beautiful carving in England, in the Chinese Room at Claydon in Buckinghamshire. In its wake came a fashion for exotica of all kinds, often verging on the ridiculous. The Countess of Home, Adam's patron, eagerly 'acquired' two feathered African minstrels; while at Drottningholm in Sweden Adelcrantz carefully designed a replica of a Turkish pleasure-tent.

The other exotic style was, of course, Gothic or 'Gothick' as it is usually called in reference to the eighteenth century. Here, however, we hit a major problem of terminology and distinction. Gothic was also, in a very serious sense, an indigenous and contemporary style, never having been totally abandoned since the sixteenth century. Right across Europe Gothic had survived, not just in the transformations of Borromini, Guarini and Neumann. In buildings as diverse as Tom Tower at Christ Church, Oxford, the cathedral at

was built to inspire similar thoughts in his
visitors. Most of them must have been
awe-struck by the huge spire and the great
octagon.

Curiously, this building has something
in common with the elegant interiors of
Robert Adam. Adam's room-shapes in
part derive from study of the remains of
the Palace of Diocletian at Split; similarly,
the secret of the compelling power of the
octagon is careful investigation of the
prototype at Ely Cathedral. Fonthill is not
only a great deal more moving than Batty
Langley's Gothick: it is also a great deal
more correct.

Architecture as a whole was becoming
more and more closely linked with
archaeology. And archaeology was concerned increasingly with the more primitive forms of classical building. Temples
such as those at Paestum were studied
closely by young architects, and their more
simple, rugged grandeur is reflected in
many buildings—the icy austerity of
Soufflot's Panthéon in Paris, the Greek
simplicity of Harrison's Chester Castle,
and the refined purity of Aigner's Saint
Alexander Church in Warsaw.

The new concern with stylistic purity
and correctness is part of a European
reaction against the Rococo. A decorated
style becomes equated with luxury and a
concern with outdated social distinctions.
And just as Palladianism had appealed to
the political orientation of the English
squire, so now Neo-classical simplicity is
taken up by those eager to reorganize
society on rational, moral lines. It becomes,
in fact, the style of the political avant-
garde, of those who seek a return to

Orléans, and the brilliant works of Giovanni Santini (1667–1723) at Kladruby
and Sedlec in Bohemia, Gothic had remained alive as the natural mode in which
to complete a building already begun in
that style.

During the early eighteenth century,
largely under literary stimulus, Gothic
came to be seen not as an old-fashioned
style which allowed certain kinds of structural virtuosity, but as *the* style containing
sublime elements of wildness and savagery.
This developed slowly, from dinky
Gothick follies like Batty Langley's Garden Umbrello, to Walpole's Strawberry
Hill. The latter marked a new departure

not just because of its Gothicism, but
rather because of the startling irregularity
of its off-centre tower. It is quite clear from
the disequilibrium of the garden front that
the ideals of Palladian reason and balance
have been discarded for something much
less secure and potentially much more
sinister.

The darker implications of Gothic,
lovingly itemized in novels like *The Castle
of Otranto*, came to full flower at Fonthill
in Wiltshire, built by James Wyatt (1747–
1813) for the young William Beckford.
Beckford, author of the exotic tale *Vathek*,
was given to fantasies of the most
mysterious and macabre kind; his house

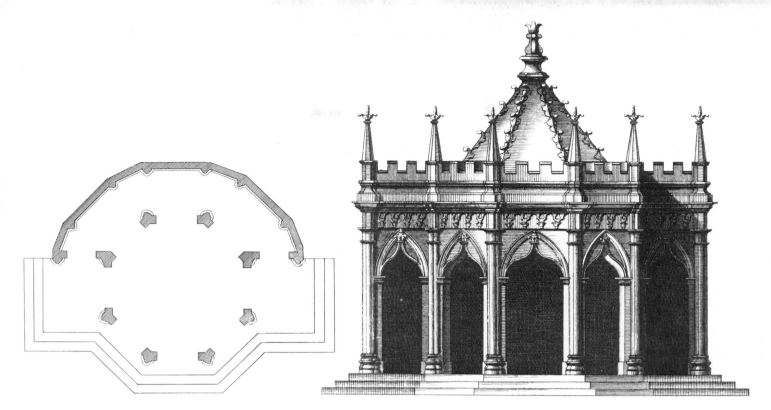

antique purity in public life as well as in architecture. The identification with a certain kind of early Greek or Roman was to be part of the mythology of the French and the American Revolutions, and it is not surprising that it is in those countries that Neo-classicism produced some of its finest works.

Architecture is inherently a public art, and rarely more so than in the seventeenth and eighteenth centuries. The desire to impress or to make a public statement is closely connected with the tendency of Baroque architecture to dominate and move into the space surrounding it. Predictably, it led during the period to a growing concern with the organization of the setting for a building. In domestic architecture, this tended to mean the arrangement of the garden: and here, as in state buildings, the pattern is set initially by France and later by England.

The French garden, like the French château, culminates in Versailles. Everything in the park is subordinate to the palace. The axes of the building continue in the garden as does the inhuman, dwarfing scale. Between the miniature box-hedges of the parterres and the giant vases, the spectator feels uneasy, deprived of a valid yard-stick to measure his own importance. This, of course, is precisely what is intended. The crushing effect of the interior cannot be side-stepped simply by moving into the garden.

But Le Nôtre's park is not French solely by virtue of its implicit absolutism. It epitomizes that reticence about sensual enjoyment, that preference for lucid, geometric forms, which we noticed as characteristic at Port-Royal. Versailles is a *'jardin de l'intelligence'*, to be grasped above all with the mind. Flowers' colour, scent and charm are minor considerations in this garden, which is about order. Geometric shapes recede decorously from the house, balancing each other in perfect and patent symmetry as far as the eye can see. There is nothing irregular. The spectator is immediately in control of a garden like this, or rather, both spectator and garden are controlled by the same organizing will, that of Louis XIV.

Le Nôtre's garden was recorded in engraving, his method expounded in books, and both were quickly copied. Wherever the French taste for clarity and rules prevailed, wherever a local monarch hankered after absolutism, there one was likely to find a *'jardin à la française'*. In the classicizing, Tory England of Queen Anne, Hampton Court, like Blenheim, was equipped with a French garden; in Vienna, the

Emperor paid reluctant homage in the layout of the park at Schönbrunn; and in Germany and the Netherlands, much smaller land-owners gave free range to their grandiloquent fantasy, in the parks at Karlsruhe and Heemstede. By 1710, the French garden was everywhere.

The reaction, as to French architecture, was most forcefully articulated in England. The poet James Thomson echoes Shaftesbury's strictures of Baroque architecture in his apostrophe to the ordered French garden:

'Detested forms! that, on the mind
    impressed,
  Corrupt, confound and barbarise an
    age.'

Like architecture, gardens are held to reflect the whole political system, tyrannical in France, free in England. The English garden, at least that belonging to a liberal thinker, eschews the strong central

control of the house, leaving the walker to make his own discoveries at his own pace:

'Let not each beauty everywhere be
    spied.
  When half the skill is decently to hide
  He gains all point who pleasingly
    confounds,
  Surprises, varies and conceals the
    bounds.'

Pope's advice is for a garden which will not make propaganda for the owner, like the French model, but allow the individual his private progress. At Rousham, perhaps the perfect English garden, a series of winding walks reveals to the visitor classical scenes, punctuated by Gothic seats and the odd pyramid. The concealing of the elements gives the continuing and deeply satisfying sense of personal discovery—it is your own journey, a kind of Grand Tour in miniature.

The scenes at Rousham are composed like paintings: they are, in a literal sense, picturesque. The impact of the works of Gaspard Poussin and Salvator Rosa on English gardens was strong throughout the century, and to them was added the taste for the surprising and the irregular which we noted at Strawberry Hill. The uneven massing and the clumping of trees in open park became part of the stock-in-trade of the greatest garden designer of the eighteenth century, Lancelot 'Capability' Brown (1716–83). In the 1760s the grand formal park which Vanbrugh had designed for Blenheim, with its intersecting avenues and French parterres, was removed. In its place, Brown designed the wilder, apparently more random, open park which sweeps right up to the house. The taste for freedom and naturalness in art had reached even to the most authoritarian Baroque house in England, while abroad

Left: The formal linear garden at Vaux-le-Vicomte near Paris, designed c.1660 by Le Nôtre, who later worked at Versailles. Much copied, it is the prototype garden 'à la française'. This sort of garden came increasingly to be seen as symbolizing the oppressive absolutism of the French state, in its denial to the individual of elements of choice or surprise, and in its curbing of natural profusion.

Right: The picturesque 'natural' garden at Stourhead, in the south of England, which was designed by the owner, Henry Hoare, between 1741 and 1772: typical of the progressive, 'liberal' garden, which became extremely popular in mid-eighteenth-century Europe.

the 'Englischer Garten' was soon to enjoy the same measure of popularity as Versailles fifty years before.

THE CITY:
PLANNING FOR MOVEMENT

In a period of rapidly rising population, the major problems concerning the relation between house and surroundings were bound to arise in the expanding towns. It can be said that the seventeenth century invented—or reinvented—the square. The commercial development of Paris under Henry IV necessitated the building of shops, ateliers and accommodation on the largest scale: the result was the first true modern square, the Place Royale, now the Place des Vosges. The large open space was to be used as a promenoir by the people; arcades provided shelter; and above were uniform, modest but spacious houses. The use of cheap material—plaster rather than stone—for most of the structure made the project economical and popular. It was soon imitated by Inigo Jones, in his piazza design for Covent Garden in London, and has since proliferated, more or less modified, throughout the world.

The simple, geometric town plan is, in fact, the norm where it is possible to start a whole town, or suburb, from the beginning, and it is found in Roman camps, in German thirteenth-century settlements in Eastern Europe and Spanish new towns in South America. The fact that we perceive such plans as largely seventeenth-century is eloquent of the expansion of population and of European power during the period.

Certainly, when William Penn in the 1680s drew up the plan for the state capital, destined soon to become the second city of the English-speaking world, the obvious model was the rectangular grid. Thomas Holme's map of Philadelphia in 1683 shows the area between the Scoll Kill and the Delaware rivers entirely divided by streets which cross each other at right angles, with one public square set at the heart. The advantages of such a scheme are many, not least those of military convenience. In coping with invasion from without or riot within, it is very useful to have the defined sections and easy sightlines of a rectangular plan—as Haussmann knew when he redesigned the Paris boulevards in the nineteenth century.

In a sense, though, the freshly con-

ceived square for living and shopping is easier to realize than the organization of space to set off an existing building. In this latter aspect of town planning the great breakthroughs were made not in Paris but in Rome.

The supreme example, of course, is the piazza of Saint Peter's, designed by Bernini to stun the visitor as he approached the basilica along the constricted artery of the Borgo. As he suddenly burst into the huge open space, he was surrounded by the colonnades, emblems of the arms of the enfolding church, forming a world complete in itself, yet still open to the world beyond.

Mussolini's opening up of the Borgo into the massive approach avenue has largely destroyed the effect which Bernini sought. There is, however, one seventeenth-century Roman square which survives almost intact, and which demonstrates that town planning, then as now, was motivated as much by practical as by aesthetic considerations.

The little church of Santa Maria della Pace had a long connection with the Chigi family. When, in 1655, one of their members became Pope Alexander VII, the

SANTA MARIA DELLA PACE: A BAROQUE PIAZZA

Santa Maria della Pace had long been a fashionable Roman church – both Raphael and Bramante had worked in it – when Pope Alexander VII commissioned Pietro da Cortona to modernize the exterior in 1656. Cortona here tackled the characteristically Baroque problems of relating the building to its surroundings, equipping it with a façade and adapting it to the new requirements of heavy carriage traffic. As there was not enough money to re-align the main access symmetrically, Cortona built the church porch forward so that its central bay is on the main sight-line of the approach, ingeniously using the semi-circular form to conceal the shift of axis. The porch not only provides shelter, it also exemplifies the Baroque erosion of boundaries. Open to the air, it is part of the piazza, yet it is integrally related to the façade, and this façade spills on to the neighbouring houses, uniting the piazza under the dominance of the church.

Far right: The plan shows quite clearly one of the greatest difficulties that Cortona had to surmount—the extreme proximity of the German church of Santa Maria dell' Anima, now totally invisible behind the new screening wall of the square.

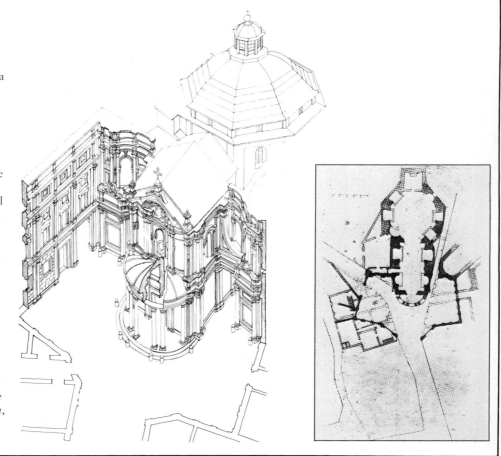

Pietro da Cortona (1596–1669) was called in by the Pope. His solution was to create a square just big enough to allow a carriage to turn in front of the church—and very grand ones would have to do a three-point turn. He built out a semi-circular porch where visitors could be put down dry, and which forms the focal point of the view along the approach road. The road to the left of the church was made a one-way street. The making of the piazza required the compulsory purchase and demolition of several houses and the paving of the space cleared. The whole square was then covered by Cortona with a homogeneous façade, which continues right over the apse of the rival German church, totally concealing its existence. Finally, by a clever manipulation of planning law, Cortona argued that the owners of the houses on the square had had their property greatly improved in quality and increased in value, and should therefore pay the costs. And so the Pope and the church got their smart new piazza almost for nothing.

What is important about these two piazzas is that they cater for a moving spectator, and show great concern with

church at once became fashionable. Its popularity was enhanced by the convenient fact that it was possible to hear Mass there in the afternoon—an obvious attraction to late risers. This would have posed no difficulties had it not been that by the middle of the century people no longer travelled in town on horseback or by litter: the carriage was a social necessity, and a public menace. There were traffic jams across Europe; Pepys complained of them in London; Henry IV of France was assassinated while his carriage was held up in one in Paris. A glance at the ground-plan of the streets around Santa Maria will show what chaos must have resulted at the beginning of every afternoon Mass. Only the street to the left of the church could accommodate a carriage —and then only one, which led to dramatic scenes when two met head-on; for to reverse your carriage was to lose face quite considerably, while there was no room to turn at the end of the main approach. Furthermore, on the immediate right was another church, that of the German congregation, blocking any through passage and competing for the spectator's attention.

vista. These two elements determine the large square organized by Bernini and Rainaldi at the northern entrance to Rome, the Piazza del Popolo. This is the gate at which almost all pilgrims enter the city, and the transverse sweep of the square is balanced by the two churches, on either side of whose domes the roads divide, leading on to the holy places.

This open, moving concept of town planning produced spectacular results when applied to hillsides, such as the Bom Jesus in Portugal or the swirling cascade of the Spanish Steps in Rome. Even on the flat, it informed some of the most exciting townscapes in Europe—the sweeping prospects along the river in Saint Petersburg, the succession of squares in Nancy, and the extraordinary, one-sided square of the Place de la Concorde in Paris, with one row of buildings and three vistas.

The Place de la Concorde typifies the eighteenth-century desire to bring the country into the town, and to blend street with landscape. The most impressive example of this fusion was achieved at Bath spa where, by taking the town into the country, all the pleasures of the city were combined with the healthy air and waters of the countryside. The fashion for these invalid idylls endured well into this century and produced some of the most charming towns in Europe. It is doubtful, however, if any of them approaches Bath.

The splendid hillside site allows an apparently regular architecture of circus and terrace to combine with the new dynamic town planning and the delight in surprise which characterizes the English garden. As the visitor walks, he finds that axes are not directly aligned, that everything is—just—not what he might expect. Scale changes, vistas open—to walk in a town like this is to discover (as at Rousham), to be amazed, and to admire.

In spite of the vertiginous diversity of European architecture in these two centuries, one factor remains constant: the leadership of Rome. Whether ancient or modern, she was seen by Protestant and Catholic throughout the period as the authority and the clearing house of architectural ideas. A building like Borromini's Sant Agnese in Piazza Navona is studied by visitors, and reappears, recognizable in spite of foreign accents, in almost every country of Europe.

Of the architectural modes which we have considered, only the Rococo bears no reference to Rome. It is symptomatic. For although Rococo was in decline by the 1780s the dominance of French taste, which it represented, was not. The attention of Europe now fell on Paris; and political developments there were to shape the ideas, and hence the buildings, of the next century.

Right: The swirling, spilling stone mass of the Spanish Steps leading down from the church of Santa Trinità dei Monti in Rome – designed by Francesco de Sanctis c.1723. While owing more than a little to the staircase in Michelangelo's Laurentian Library in Florence, the steps demonstrate that the Baroque principles of curving movement can apply just as much to town planning as to architecture properly so called.

Below: The links between garden-design and urban development can be seen clearly in this aerial view of Bath, England. On the right is the Circus designed by John Wood the Elder c.1754, on the left Royal Crescent, by his son, c.1767.

THE FIRST INDUSTRIAL AGE

The new age of reason germinating in eighteenth-century France had not long to wait for its expression in built form. Both America and France, struggling for political democracy and independence, were inevitably attracted to the forms of classical architecture with all their associations with civic virtue, and noble and republican antiquity. But more profound than any stylistic shift or consolidation of taste were the changes occurring in the way the age looked at its objects—including, centrally, its architecture—changes in the social and technical roles it expected these objects to perform.

It is this new relationship, based on a radical viewpoint and compounded by subsequent technical possibilities rather than any new form, that so clearly links this era with our own. The criteria of previous centuries no longer apply. This is the first era of our own time, and inevitably it sticks to us as part of our culture.

The first construction of this new age is not a temple nor a palace, but a machine. With Dr Guillotin's contraption—'A machine', as the Todd edition of Johnson's dictionary puts it, 'for separating at one stroke the head of a person from the body'—utilitarian, scientific functionalism in design had arrived. And at that time the view of buildings as functioning machines was born.

The growth of rationalism and of materialism, the explosion in scientific enquiry and the first flowering of the long passion for novelty, all belong to the eighteenth century. These forces crystallized in the nineteenth-century faith in uninhibited technological progress, the spirit of free enterprise and open-minded desire for new results—a belief in the power of calculation and rational thought.

The very modern notion of functionalism in architecture originating in mid-eighteenth-century France, was in part the legacy of Neo-classicism's great theorist, Marc-Antoine Laugier (1713–69). He abhorred the ambiguity of Baroque space, or any rhetoric in architecture, preferring clean surfaces, comprehensible forms and 'real' columns instead of 'fake' pilasters.

Galleria Vittorio Emanuele II, Milan, Italy 1865–77, designed by Giuseppe Mengoni and built with English finance, epitomizes the outstanding contribution of the first industrial age to urban architecture. 'The Bourgeoisie . . . has accomplished wonders far surpassing Egyptian pyramids, Roman aqueducts and Gothic cathedrals. In a word, it creates a world after its own image.' ('The Communist Manifesto', 1847.) That image is clearest in the great covered space, typified by the Gallerias, where parade and commerce could mingle. The bourgeois agora – market, exhibition, or concourse – went under glass and its urban space was appropriated by architecture.

Later, as the nineteenth century progressed, this 'honest' expression of materials, structure and plan form was bound up even tighter with a system of 'morality'. The moral argument was used on behalf both of Neo-classic and Neo-gothic forms; it was then taken over by the Modern Movement in the 1920s and is still so strong that even today it is difficult for architects to escape its fallacies.

In his *L'Ancien Régime et la Révolution* (1856), De Tocqueville describes how the French Revolution inspired many abstract books on government, each with 'the same attraction for general theories, complete systems of legislation and exact symmetry in the laws; the same contempt for existing facts; the same confidence in theory, the same taste for the original, the ingenious, the novel . . .'. This was the new age, and that description could equally fit the megalomaniac architectural projects of Etienne-Louis Boullée (1728–99), who, defining architecture as a 'production of the mind', was the first architect to be known for his fantastical drawings rather than for his buildings. The abstract and pure nature of late-eighteenth-century designs is clear from the many architectural projects based on simple forms (often impracticable and terrifying in scale) such as the cube, pyramid, cone and, above all, that image of majestic science—of the Newton-god—the sphere.

This form of abstraction even reached daily life as revolutionary France adopted a system of measure unrelated to human proportions (the metre, it was said, is a forty-millionth of the earth's meridian). In America, a system every bit as abstract and of even more consequence for its architecture took hold in Thomas Jefferson's Land Ordinance which geometrically divided land with a Cartesian grid, planting seeds of a new view of town planning far from the Baroque concept of total design. Its implications were to be realized over the country as it became the commercial speculator's ground-plan.

This intellectual development was accompanied by a growing inquisitiveness such that the late eighteenth century seemed to be a laboratory where exciting experiments, both social and material, bubbled. In 1776 Adam Smith published his *Inquiry into the Nature and Causes of the Wealth of Nations*; in 1798 Thomas Malthus published his *Essay on the Principle of Population*; in his writings two decades later, the French socialist Saint-Simon was urging government by experts. Buildings could now be instruments for the new thinkers. Although the optimistic belief in an enlightened technocracy and in man's perfectibility was to be short-lived, by 1800 it had generated a strong social purpose in architecture. With education and health as a route to salvation,

hospitals, elementary schools, prisons and technical schools multiplied, as did plans for enlightened model industrial communities.

The practical Welshman Robert Owen (1771–1858), for example, held to the implicit Enlightenment doctrine that men only have to be shown the way to moral conduct in order to adopt it, and that rationality, science and technique would solve environmental and social problems. This socially minded mill-owner moved to New Lanark near Glasgow where David Dale had started a settlement with Richard Arkwright in 1783. In 1799 Owen bought out Dale and built up the township towards his model of a new society based on principles of understanding and co-operation. While only one further mill was built in Owen's time at New Lanark, he instigated immediate reforms offering better pay, shorter working hours and the abolition of child labour. He built better housing, organized the retailing of household necessities at cost, and in 1816 set up his Institute for the Formation of Character. This was the first time permanent education had related to and complemented factory work.

In 1817 Owen published a *Universal Remedy for the Problem of Poverty and Unemployment*, proposing villages of co-operation where a parallelogram of continuous terraces would house 500 to 1,500

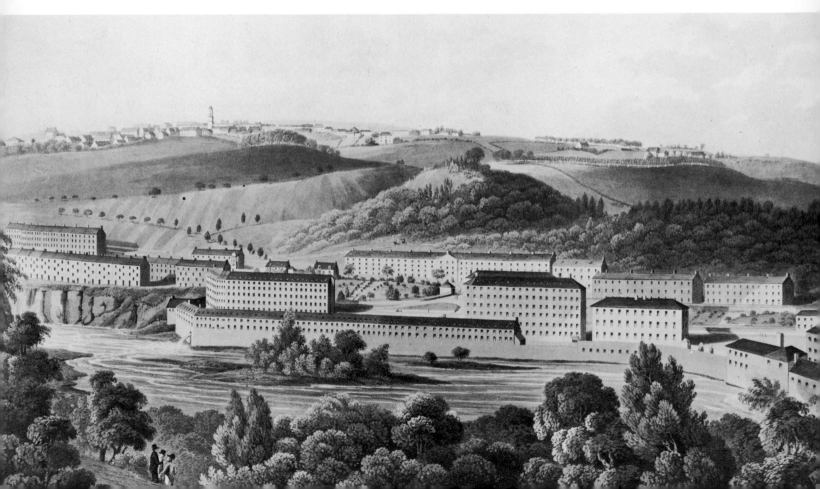

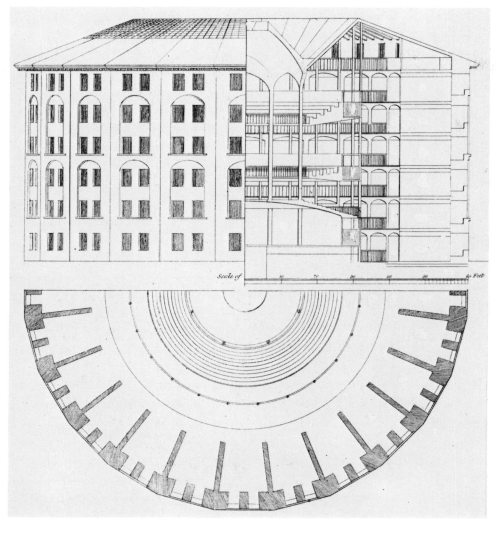

people; this was to be surrounded by vegetable gardens and set in 10–15,000 acres of countryside. A few years later he sold New Lanark and sailed for America hoping to establish similar communities there (like New Harmony, Indiana, for instance), starting from scratch.

Early attempts such as these to solve social problems through architecture had been taken to the utilitarian extreme by Jeremy Bentham (1748–1832) some years earlier. His architectural enthusiasm was as strong as Owen's, but he went even further: a building's form, he argued, could, and indeed should, actually influence and improve behaviour. The Panopticon, or Inspection House, was first devised by him in 1787, but never built, and for decades the notion haunted him as he developed it and canvassed for its support. From the start he saw it as a machine for living in, a model for all possible types of institution where the control of people was important; a home for the destitute, the orphaned, deserted young women or the blind; a house of correction or lunatic asylum, prison or hospital, lazaretto or school, factory or nursery.

The form was to be a well-lit cylinder lined with four or six storeys of small rooms; these cells all faced a large, covered, central space within which sat a smaller cylindrical kiosk. From here a

Left: The stern, formal elegance of New Lanark, near Glasgow, Scotland, remains today substantially as engraved in 1825, never having become Arkwright's 'Manchester of the North'. A gap in the mills lining the Clyde river (filled shortly after the view was engraved) reveals a garden in front of New Buildings which date from 1799.

Right: The sturdy counting house on the end of Caithness Row in New Lanark, which was built to house displaced highlanders in 1785. When Owen took over, he shifted concern to his 'living machines', feeding and clothing a better workforce, instituting work study in the mills and building an environment for 'the formation of character'.

Above: Elsewhere architecture was being proposed as a device for controlling more closely the order of the social engine. Embodiment of this utilitarianism is seen in Bentham's penitentiary panopticon of 1791. Bentham, with amazing grasp of the new technology, elaborated fold-away beds, WC and cold water services, bugging devices and convected warm air to every cell. Unlike Owen, however, he never got beyond paper speculation.

perfect view of every portion of each cell was afforded to the governor or manager in the centre.

A very different use of centralized geometry is seen in the greatest achievement of Claude-Nicolas Ledoux (1736–1806), the 'Ideal City of Chaux', a project which grew from his having been made *Inspecteur* of the saltworks there in 1771. Little was built of what would have been a centralized community, its circular form 'as pure as that described by the sun on its daily round'.

Bentham's geometry, of course, had nothing to do with such mirrors of the order of the universe; rather, it was concerned with efficiency and an abhorrence of waste (such as emotion). Ledoux's forms were reminiscent of Bentham's although his heart was elsewhere. Chaux is crisp and geometrical. At its centre is the Director's house and over it, typically, Ledoux designed a sanctuary dedicated to the Supreme Being. A projected outer circle of public buildings, including bourse, market and hospital, a *Temple de Mémoire* dedicated to women, a *Maison d'union* dedicated to the cultivation of moral values, and buildings for education and recreation, all remained unbuilt. Deeply

involved with symbolism, Ledoux aimed for expressive forms, for what was called *une architecture parlante*, which would make the meaning obvious. The plan of the Oikema, or House of Sexual Education, was in the form of a phallus; the coopery, or wheelwright's house, had a circular, wheel-like façade; the cemetery —a huge unbuildable semi-underground sphere—symbolized eternity.

Such projects illustrate the new ideals

of the age, whether built, as New Lanark, begun, as at Chaux, or remaining on paper, as did Bentham's designs. While everyday building work remained untouched by this instrumentalism another talker rather than builder was to become the strongest influence behind architectural design right through the century, and even up to today. Jean-Nicolas-Louis Durand (1760–1834), a pupil of Boullée and teacher at the new *Ecole Polytechnique*

Left above and below: Work began c.1775 on Ledoux's scheme for the salt-works at Chaux, France. At the centre is the director's house flanked by the works themselves. The project developed on paper long after building stopped and, as published in 1804, it was transformed into a Utopian city.

Above: Nothing could be further from Ledoux's plans than the light-hearted transformations of a pleasant country farmhouse at Brighton which in 1786 was leased to the Prince of Wales. Becoming a classical pavilion in 1787, its interior was transformed to Chinese fantasy in 1797. An Indian restyling was proposed by Repton in 1807, and finally, in 1815–18 Nash reformed the 'turban domes and lofty pinnacles' which, in 1830, became one of Britain's Royal Palaces.

in Paris, put forward a utilitarian goal in his lectures which, if banal in comparison with the radicals of his age, was easy to accept and straightforwardly practical.

He argued that the aim of architecture was suitability and economy. Architecture should be stripped of pointless decoration; aesthetic pleasure is a myth, while what people appreciate is convenience and value for money. Such rational boorishness was powerful stuff. 'The architect's

skill lies in his ability to resolve two problems: one, given a sum of money, to produce the most decent building possible, as in a private building; two, given the decencies required of a building, to produce the building for the smallest expense possible, as in a public building.'

In Neo-classical France, this 'decency', inevitably, was a taste which preferred regular geometric shapes, built up and aggregated into symmetrical masses. Durand's method for the 'suitable and economical' arrangement of the various elements of building—columns, arches and walls; cubes, vaults, domes and pitched roofs— is only too clearly shown in his primer, *Précis des leçons*, where the use of the grid plan, a crutch which still underpins most architectural design, first appeared.

There were others for whom architecture was more than a mechanism and for whom its central appeal was emotional. By the early nineteenth century they had all the evidence of history before them. Art and architectural history had been developing fast in the late eighteenth century; exotic delight combined with serious instruction in ancient Egypt, distant India, and Europe's own barbarian Gothic past.

New ways of looking at the world were

introduced—new categories of judgment appeared, new points of view rather than styles: the picturesque and the sublime. If the picturesque can be characterized by saying that it aimed at pretty and less serious effects, developing the importance of charming romantic associations, whether of medievalized rusticity or Indian exoticism, it might be contrasted with the sublime, that fearful thrill of 'awful' sublimity, which became the key viewpoint of the first industrial age. This can be seen in the romantic vision of dark tunnels and huge cuttings, in the looming gasworks and the huge prisons, the infinite viaducts, the hot and powerful, dark satanic mills. All styles of building became acceptable, with classical but one possibility; new perceptions—picturesque and sublime—shaped men's minds, with beauty but one criterion. The century of historicism had begun.

Playing with history, the fancy-dress party of architecture, found its first monument in Versailles park where in 1781 Marie-Antoinette built an English-inspired *hameau* in mock medieval charm, complete with milk-maid dress and silver milk-pail. At the same time 'the classical Stuart and the indefatigable Revett', as

mining the foundations of what architecture was about.

The picturesque did not raise these problems. Its virtuoso, Nash, treated classicism as an easy convention every bit as much as his French counterparts, Percier and Fontaine. In fact, Nash designed in any style, and although he was conventional he was also light-handed, and although careless he could be impressive. The form of Regent Street, a cut through London from the new Regent's Park to St James's Park, is a brilliant piece of picturesque town design; Nash's own town house was acceptably Neo-classical but his country mansion was Gothic. The effect is theatrical, and it somehow all feels paper-thin (indeed Nash's streets were often very inadequately built).

Thus, Neo-classicism became a modern approach to the antique—not just a continuation of the tradition, but a romantic application of classical language. At the turn of the century it was just one of the exotic styles available, but within a decade it had become the hallmark of distinction, and by 1820 the great classical cities of Petersburg, Edinburgh, Berlin and Copenhagen had a powerful stylistic coherence in their streets. This language had, naturally, a lot of arguments to support its use. Rationalists stressed its logical expression of structure. The new engineers were attracted by its symmetry and constructional economy. Its indication of civic virtue and historical association with the noble republics of Greece and Rome attracted it to both American and French Revolutions, and then to the aggressively nationalist European states.

Ornament became a corrupt luxury, and simple geometry noble. The cathedral designed by Benjamin Latrobe (1764–1820) in Baltimore was typically spare in ornament and strong on geometric space. With unconscious precision, the revolutionary French took Soufflot's Ste Geneviève, the clearest eighteenth-century expression of Laugier's principles and Neo-classical functional clarity, and declared it their Panthéon.

This neo-Greek ideology, based on revolutionary and liberal humanism, is most aptly reflected in the social buildings it produced. Its key building types were the temple-like monument, the school (or, as they so often said, academy) and the museum, a temple to art pantheism but essentially a house of instruction, of education. Mercier, in his *The Year 2440*, had in his utopian future a museum where 'all the different sorts of animals, vege-

John Soane called them, began publishing *The Antiquities of Athens*, becoming arbiters of the new Doric taste which swept Europe. The literary Gothic of Beckford and Walpole showed another face of this romantic mood, as did the chinoiserie craze and then the 'Hindoo taste', which Thomas Daniell and his nephew William introduced by the end of the eighteenth century. They influenced Humphry Repton (1752–1818) and the Prince of Wales, who then commissioned Repton to produce a pavilion in the 'Indian style' at Brighton. Although Repton's design was not accepted, the one that was, by John Nash (1752–1835), was every bit as exotic as the setting for Mozart's *Il Seraglio* and just as gay, charming, historically naïve and theatrical. This was the picturesque—a stage-set for romantic action, as was the sublime, the other side of the same coin. For only in theatre, with that suspension of disbelief, does one really thrill to terror,

obscurity, power, privation, infinity and all Burke's other adjectives for that sublime terror which he called 'the strongest emotion of which the mind is capable'.

The massive, aggressive forms of Dance's Newgate Prison, or Ledoux's Paris Tollhouses, were early attempts to generate this emotion of awe. But the sublime sensibility is perhaps better illustrated by one of the early nineteenth century's greatest architects, Karl Friedrich von Schinkel (1781–1841), who toured Britain in the 1820s; he neglected what was traditionally regarded as architecture but, rather, was inspired by the industrially sublime. He thrilled to Telford's viaducts, sketched the chimneys and the mills, and at Dudley noted that 'the thousands of smoking obelisks are a grandoise sight'. Such contemporary praise for these new, intrusive but non-'designed' parts of the environment was a fundamental step into the modern world's frame of reference, under-

tables and minerals were placed under the four wings and were visible by one glance of the eye'. On its façade was inscribed AN ABRIDGEMENT OF THE UNIVERSE. Nothing sums it up better than that image written in 1770, even down to the panopticon viewpoint.

In this mood those architects not content to copy archaeological models were producing rare buildings of great force and vigour. Smirke's British Museum (begun in 1823) is vast but simply framed by forty-eight Ionic columns on its main façade; the Berlin Museum (1823–8) by Schinkel is even more majestic with its purist, superbly detailed and powerful Ionic colonnade. The Bourse (1804–16) in St Petersburg by Thomas de Thomon (1754–1813), pre-dating those buildings, displays a strength approaching Ledoux's; and the 1798 project for a national theatre in Berlin by Friedrich Gilly (1771–1800), yet more stripped in its classicism, had a semi-circular drum auditorium attached to a cube, while semi-circular windows were all that pierced its surface other than a restrained Doric portico.

Europe's most brilliant and inventive architect at the turn of the century was John Soane (1753–1837). This uncomfortable Englishman was far from either a conventional classicist or dedicated Greek; strangely, in many ways, he even retained much of the Baroque. By the 1790s his interiors at the Bank of England (now destroyed)—soaring spaces with the barest of ornament—had left classicism far behind, adding his individual touch of cleanly articulated forms to the heritage of Ledoux and Dance. Simple masses and flat surfaces articulated with virtuosity are seen in the Dulwich Art Gallery (1811–14).

Soane's own house (1812–13), in a typical classical London terrace at Lincoln's Inn Fields, gives no scope for the boldly architectonic; but here is a minor masterpiece of romantic classicism. It is, as when he left it to the nation, a museum, a warren of small and surprising spaces full of fragments, classic, Gothic and even Neo-gothic, and centred on a genuine Egyptian sarcophagus. The play of light—

were overtaken by Edinburgh where the 'Athens of the North' formed a powerful image and neo-Greek had its most lingering success. Here, where classical buildings gain immeasurably from a setting as picturesque as the Athens Acropolis, the romantic classical language is seen at its finest. Perhaps this is epitomized in the Scottish national monument. Like William Strickland's Bank in Philadelphia (1819–24) or Leo von Klenze's Bavarian Walhalla near Regensburg (1821–42), this was to be a facsimile of the Parthenon but unlike them it ran out of cash with little more built than an end row of columns to give the huge scale and suggest a form. In 1825

The range of architectural response to the classical taste in the early eighteenth century is seen in these three buildings – from John Soane's highly personal and rhetorical excitement, via the polite associations of the neo-Greek by Strickland for his merchant bankers, to the necrophilia of historicist imitation in the monument of Walhalla.

Left: The tiny, enchanting and jewel-like breakfast room in Soane's house, London, 1813.

Below: The Greek revival, freely interpreted, in Strickland's Merchants' Exchange, Philadelphia, Pennsylvania, USA, 1834.

Right: The Greek revival – more archaeologically rigid – in Klenze's Walhalla, near Regensburg, West Germany. Ludwig of Bavaria invited designs for this national shrine and, although some argued that Gothic was more naturally German (Schinkel entered in the Gothic style), he stipulated Athenian purity. Klenze was commissioned in 1816, and in 1842 this marble-clad – but cast-iron-roofed – Parthenon was completed on its picturesque hillside.

reflected in glass or hidden by lowered ceilings—is a virtuoso display, a highly romantic and personal vision far from the classic calm of his powerful bank rotundas.

Buildings such as these, far from both the utilitarian machine and the historical pastiche, offer glimpses of a new contemporary architecture. But Soane's non-historical path was very personal; Gilly died before he was thirty; and somehow the potential of a clean, spacious and exciting new architecture became, with the new bourgeois client, submerged for a century under the power of conventional associationism.

After Thomas de Thomon and A.D. Zakharov (1767–1811) died, St Petersburg stagnated, and the great new classical cities, Copenhagen, Berlin and Munich,

Thomas Hamilton (1784–1858) built the High School. Here he showed that the lesson of Athens's Propylaea—the classical and picturesque blended—had been superbly learned.

The obsession with archaeological accuracy was dead-end but some architects brought Greek alive in applied detail as in Strickland's fine Merchants' Exchange in Philadelphia (1832–4), or the Inwoods' St Pancras Church, London (1819), but this was now a stylistic cloak. Indeed, a few decades into the nineteenth century all the new generation of clients wanted from their architects was a conventional association. These new men were not trained to appreciate visual criteria. The designers obliged, and engineers set the pace.

THE INDUSTRIAL ENVIRONMENT

The first constructional efforts of the industrial era were channelled into communications which were revolutionizing the ease and speed of movement, of people and of goods. This created roads, canals, bridges and tunnels, and it located the new buildings which industry demanded—the mills and warehouses, factories and railway halts, docks and termini and, in the city, the hotels, exchanges and banks.

In the second half of the eighteenth century McAdam's and Metcalf's properly compacted roads, with their water-resistant top layer of consolidated limestone dust, reached a standard forgotten since the Romans. With England no longer virtually impassable by land, Brindley's

and Telford's canals opened up the new manufacturing centres to easy freight movement beyond even the dreams of these new trunk routes. The first great canal, Brindley's Grand Trunk Navigation (1766–77), rose 120 metres (395 feet) to a 2,635 metre (8,640 feet) long tunnel at its summit. The 225 kilometre (140 mile) artery linked England's industrial heart from Mersey to Trent.

To leap the newly demanded spans new heights and lengths of structure were necessary. Masonry was stretched to its limit by Telford; the theories of timber-trussed bridges, neglected since Palladio in the seventeenth century, were looked at again and iron came quickly into its own.

Eighteenth-century industry was located close to timber for its furnaces, and

and mills. The transport needed dockyards and engine sheds. Later, the railways demanded halts and termini, and the passengers their hotels. The new goods needed larger factories, warehouses, wharves and dock buildings, entrepreneurs their markets and their exchanges for coal and corn, iron or cotton. The growth of breweries and maltings followed closely; the rising bourgeoisie developed urbane terraces, and their urban workers lived in acres of unrelieved squalidly built homes.

These early factories for spinning and weaving wool, cotton, flax or silk, were usually fine-looking, solid, simple stone and brick buildings which never saw an architect nor needed dressing up with decoration. They were near water and to their source of raw materials—such as the Cotswold sheep farms—and a rural remoteness gave added advantage to employers trying to avoid anti-machine riots. And so today one finds these stranded piles, like Cressbrook (1779) deep in remote Derbyshire and the great Calver Mill (1785) not far away, near Middleton. This was nineteen bays long and six storeys high, with a grand stone face (about a metre or a yard thick at the base) round a cast iron column grid, and held on timber beams.

The early solutions to this new design problem—such as Arkwright, Strutt and Need's mill on the Cromford Canal (1771), Arkwright and Strutt's mill at nearby Belper (1776), and Arkwright and Dale's mill at New Lanark (1788)—were traditionally comprised of timber floor and roof within a stone skin. Disasters, particularly fire, multiplied, and when the most up-to-date mill in Europe burned down in 1791, insurance premiums shot up, forcing attention on the development of fireproof constructions. The wooden floors of Boulton and Watt's mill (built 1783, destroyed 1786) at Blackfriars proved fatal, and immediately afterwards brick-on-iron construction made its appearance.

Typically, the new mill had brick arch floors spanning between iron beams on cruciform iron columns. This is seen in what is thought to be probably the first multi-storey iron building, an English flax mill at Shrewsbury begun by Charles Bage in 1796.

After 1800, iron frames spread rapidly, although façades usually remained massive, well-proportioned piles of local stone. As the century moved on metal-frame buildings began to come out from behind their old-fashioned overcoats, particularly in the towns. In warehouses and

then moved close to the coal pits and iron ore. As hydraulic energy developed, used for spinning by Arkwright (1768–75), and weaving by Cartwright (1784–5), the essentially home-based textile industry was transformed. The factory (called 'mill', a name derived from its water power and the form which had been developed to mill or grind corn but one which stuck whatever the use, and then long after water was superseded) was invented. Like New Lanark, early industrial communities had grown up round their water power; but, from 1790 with Watt's steam engine for power and the canal system for transportation, the locational ties were loosened, and the new industrial towns germinated.

The first third of the nineteenth century saw the onset of the modern world; by 1830 the real problems of the steam age had been solved and all today's main types

of machine tools had been evolved by a brilliant generation of mechanical engineers. When in 1835 electoral reform in England gave local administrations powers—however little used—to intervene in the construction of roads, public housing, sewers and drainage, the industrial town had finally arrived and 'planning' in this modern sense had begun.

In the first half of the nineteenth century the population in Britain increased by 111 per cent, but in the same period its coal output rose by 470 per cent, pig iron by 946 per cent and raw cotton imports for British manufacture by 1,400 per cent. As Britain became the workshop of the world, it inevitably became the centre of interest for new commercial and industrial architecture.

The new buildings which accompanied this development began with the forges commercial buildings, the cast-iron frames became increasingly light and delicate. Light panels, often of glass, filled more and more of the space between.

But a series of fires in London, when the cast-iron frames melted and collapsed, raised doubts; then a London Building Act in 1843 regulated internal spaces and

Left: Oriel Chambers, Liverpool, England, by Ellis, 1864, had metal and glass oriels hung in front of the frame. Two years later, round the corner at 16 Cork Street, Ellis further simplified his glazed façade so that it resembles modern curtain walling.

Right: A. Gardner and Son's warehouse, Glasgow, Scotland, 1855–6, by Baird, showed an unmatched architectural refinement and restraint in iron and glass. In this appealing and graceful building, the fenestration subtly changes from floor to floor – for example, the arch shapes flatten as they get lower, while the storeys become deeper. On the side elevation (left) four arch bays alter the perspective, increasing the effect of the building's depth. With its clarity of expressions and subtlety of form, this very early iron-clad building is unique.

Below: Stanley Mill, Stroud, England, 1813. Masonry-clad, yet it is one of the earliest cast iron frame mills.

the openings in external walls. Thus, once again, exposed frames began to retreat behind an increasingly self-conscious variety of historicist masonry styles.

Jumping ahead, away from London's restrictions, by the mid-nineteenth century in New York James Bogardus, developing the tradition, was glazing directly into iron, and this was quickly taken up in Glasgow by Alexander Thomson and others. In Liverpool Peter Ellis produced the scintillating Oriel Chambers (1864–5), but perhaps the finest of all these glass and iron structures was John Baird's warehouse for A. Gardner and Son, built in Jamaica Street, Glasgow (1855–6).

The vast increase in Britain's maritime trade led to the building of four great London docks at the start of the century. Two were designed by engineer John Rennie—Surrey Docks (1804) and East India Dock (1805). The West India Dock and London Dock, both begun in 1802, were designed by William Jessop and the Gwilts, and Daniel Alexander respectively. All four were grand and monumental. With huge, sheer, occasionally curving brick screen walls, the massive rhythm of these powerful structures with dark slits for hoists was of almost Piranesian impact.

The sublime's terrifying associations, aroused by London Dock, perhaps the finest, were to be expected from Alexander, for he also designed Maidstone and Dartmoor gaols.

A generation later London also saw Hardwick and Telford's yellow stock brick St Katherine's Dock at the Tower, on its massive iron Tuscan columns; and, yet a generation on, in 1845, Jesse Hartley built in Liverpool what remains the best surviving range of dock buildings anywhere (although now empty and decaying). Here the cast iron Doric columns are unevenly spaced, bridging wide elliptical arches which stand right at the quayside to save space (as do Telford's at St Katherine's).

Very different cast iron waterside architecture was going up in the large dockyards, and this is best seen in Britain's naval dockyards at Sheerness and at Chatham where, in the 1850s and 1860s, remarkable boathouses, designed by the Admiralty's Director of Engineering and Architectural Works, appeared. The multistorey, iron-framed structure at Sheerness, with its straightforward glass and clapboard cladding, and the tall Chatham iron frame with its huge, vertical glazing units up the side, are obvious icons of the

Left above: Coal Exchange, London, 1844–9, by J.B. Bunning. Its balconies and elegant, slender ribs covered an interior all of glass, tile and iron.

Left below: Stanley Dock, Liverpool, England, 1844–8, by Hartley. Its sheer walls hang at the water's edge on superbly confident Venetian arches and Doric columns.

Above: Sheerness, England, a cast iron framed boathouse, 1856–60, with an elegance and ordinariness which could let one mistake its date by a century.

Modern Movement, with their expression seeming to derive so directly from function and material, yet remaining able to excite the heart.

The commercial markets for primary products took on a new and modern force in the industrial age, with the national and international commodity market opening up. Exchanges for all products, from the organic and cyclic—hops or corn—to the inorganic and non-returnable—coal or copper—proliferated developing their own, new form of building, based on internal centralized space, usually circular, often galleried and top-lit. Bunning's Coal Exchange (1844–9) in London, now de-

molished, was a fine early example. Edinburgh Corn Exchange was one of the first to be top-lit, said to be for the purpose of examining the seed corn better. Cuthbert Brodrick's magnificent Leeds Corn Exchange, an 1860 competition winner, conveys these qualities very well. Its great dome is huge and vertiginous, yet it is completely hidden behind an ordinary street façade; its deep brown space is at once not only womb-like and protecting, but soaring and weightless.

But the railways—the greatest visible growth among the mid-century bourgeois nations—took this roof fascination further, from the sinuous glazed tunnels—as at York station—to the vast sheds at the termini—as at Glasgow's St Enoch's (now wantonly destroyed)—and from Paris's second Gare du Nord to London's St Pancras or Frankfurt's Hauptbanhof.

The first public railway line had opened in England in 1825; within the next decade France, the United States, Belgium, Germany, Russia, Italy and Holland (in that order) followed suit, and new industrial development came in its wake. By 1854 there were 15,000 kilometres (9,000 miles) of rail in Britain and 5,000 kilometres (3,000 miles) a year were being built in Europe.

As trains could climb very little more than the barges (a slope of over 1:50 was nearly impossible), they tended to help concentrate settlements in valleys, and industrial plains developed—the Lille area of France, Merseburg and Ruhr in Germany, the Eastern Coastal Plain and the Great Lakes in the United States of America—but they also produced viaducts, cuts and tunnels of ever more extraordinary size.

New communications encouraged new towns; Middlesbrough, Crewe and Swindon, for example, all became huge English railway towns by 1870; in 1830 each was a single farmhouse. But, equally, planners had no compunction when driving the rail through an existing town—or at least the poorer areas of it—to reach a centrally convenient terminus.

The plan adopted for any of these termini shows clearly how the 'architecture' was tacked on to hide the naked structure and show a decent dress to the street. It is also a pointer to the changing role of the architect. A shed to house trains and interchanging passengers and freight, while not stifling them in smoke and steam, was needed. It must be bright and high, but what should it look like? King's

Cross (1851–2) in London, designed by Lewis Cubitt who practised as both engineer and architect, was one solution—a large double barrel vault, clearly expressed, where the lack of traditional styling caused a mixed but strong reaction. The next year Brunel called in an architect, Matthew Digby Wyatt (1820–77), to help him at Paddington with the architectural content; the result was an embarrassing mishmash. From then on the professional divorce between architect and engineer in Britain was complete.

The problem was solved from the client's point of view by commissioning train sheds from engineers to be hidden by a huge, ornate and profitable hotel designed by an architect. This is epitomized at St Pancras (by engineer Barlow and architect Scott), also in London.

The flash gap between the two buildings does more than avoid the nasty question of how to join the two styles, and it is more than an essential flue for the release of fumes from the steam engines: it is a neat symbol of the final professional split. This antipathy, though it looks nice in these examples, and though it does reflect a basic truth, was usually more subtly obscured in reality by the engineers' own taste. Rarely were they as keen on the clean lines and functionalism as their Modern Movement apologists would have us believe. Where these did result, it was more likely to be where the appearance did not matter; and where they differed from leading architects was primarily in their more easy-going acceptance of visual contradiction and loose associationism.

In Europe the engineer/architect division had been pronounced much earlier. Rigorously scientific teaching of civil engineering began in Paris in the mid-eighteenth century at the *Ecole des Ingénieurs de Mézières*, and after the revolution the *Ecole Polytechnique*, set up in 1794, again firmly grounded its courses in maths and physics. This model for advanced technical education was adopted in Prague (1806), Vienna (1815) and Karlsruhe (1825).

The science of statics, particularly in the refinement of masonry design, was revitalized by Jean Perronet who was concerned with the optimal use of materials, and became the key principle of competitive civil and structural engineering as it remains to this day. In the late eighteenth century Perronet pushed traditional techniques and materials to their limits, carefully designing foundations and inventing the four-centred arch still used today in bridges. With the new materials, basically wrought iron and cast iron, and the new possibilities opened by mass-produced glass, this desire to use material economically and aptly, and to calculate their strength and in consequence the minimum sizes required, was taken further; and, of course, out of the diminishing province of the architect.

It was the age of engineers, of whom I.K. Brunel (1806–59) was the most lauded in Europe. He built his Thames tunnel at the age of twenty, the Great Western Railway, the first ocean-going steamship, and then the first metal one, while still in his thirties. When not building his twenty-

ST PANCRAS STATION: ARCHITECT/ENGINEER SPLIT

St Pancras hotel and station in London were designed by architect G.G. Scott, while the train-shed behind was designed by engineers W.H. Barlow and R.M. Ordish; and there was an actual as well as ideological gap between them. In limited competition with Lockwood and Mawson, E.M. Barry, Owen Jones and others, Scott's design won the day in 1865. While it ingeniously solves the problem of the tracks having to arrive considerably above road level, it was, he admitted, 'in the same style which I had originated several years earlier for the government offices . . .' (the Foreign and India offices, whose Gothic cloak had been rejected by Palmerston). That scheme having been thwarted, Scott now produced one of the largest High Victorian Gothic structures in the world, and surely the genre's most emphatic application to a secular purpose. Despite the most picturesque skyline, the towers and flèches of a cathedral choir or Flemish town hall, it seemed scarcely appropriate for 'bagmen's bedrooms'. Scott himself suggested 'it is possibly *too good* for its purpose'. It was left to a later wit to add 'c'est magnifique, mais ce n'est pas la gare'.

Right: When Scott won the commission for the frontage building, as he said, 'the great shed-like roof had already been designed by Mr Barlow and, as if by anticipation, its section was a pointed arch.' Despite this apparent harmony which contemporary critics also read into the two buildings, the shed, in contrast to the hotel and station, is clean, neat, logical and impressively huge. The first such structure to be just arch – without division between 'wall' and 'roof' – at 75 m (243 ft) it remained the widest clear span in the world for many years.

Left: York Central station, England, built in 1870–77, designed by Prosser, Burley and Peachey. Like Newcastle station by John Dobson (1846–55), it is an elegant curving double canopy, forming a pair of sinuous glazed tunnels, in each case hidden behind a stylistically separate masonry façade. The magnificent railways, which covered the country at breakneck speeds of up to 50 kph (30 mph), had to be reflected in suitably magnificent architectural expression on the station front. The actual umbrella over tracks and platforms, which today's taste admires, was architecturally invisible. Being so unimportant, it attracted less funding, and therefore strove towards both economy and physical invisibility in minimal, light designs.

five railways, eight piers and dry docks, five suspension bridges and 125 railway bridges, he found time to invent the compartmented freight car, and argue for a canal at Panama. For the Crimean War he designed both a gunboat and a 1,500 bed military hospital; the latter was pre-fabricated in units handlable by two men, and was shipped out and erected by eighteen men in ten weeks at Renkioi. It had excellent plumbing and circulated 37 cubic metres of air (1,300 cubic feet) per minute around each bed.

Beside this, where then did the architect stand? The engineer—that empirically minded genius who would design any-thing afresh, from an exhibition hall to a contraption for removing a fish bone from his own throat—was the man of the age; Smiles's *Lives of the Engineers* clearly matched Vasari's *Lives of the Artists*; the splendour of Michelangelo's Rome was to be upstaged by Brunel's London. With barely an exception, the architects were at a remove from this company.

A NEW MORALITY

While engineering feats and even industrial landscapes could be marvelled at in the eighteenth century, the criteria by which traditional architectural values were judged became outworn as the nineteenth century grew closer. Lightly adopted styles were used with abandon, and order came only from weak association: classic for learning, Gothic for religion, palazzo for pomp and Egyptian for exotic.

The early eclecticism of the 1820s and 1830s did have more subtle associational nuances—the spirit of nationalism (then the rising force all over Europe) and a linking medievalism produced a surge of Gothic forms—or at least of Gothic details, for only too often the same build-ing plan could be Gothic, Greek or Renaissance. The Whigs favoured Cinque-cento for their banks and clubs, associat-ing themselves with Renaissance merchant

point Gothic turned from the delightful and playful to the sincere and 'genuine'. But it is Pugin's *Contrasts* rather than the Palace which marked the turning point. What has become the moral virtuousness of 'functionalism' began when Pugin subtly and insidiously muddled pleasant architecture and honest behaviour, then was confirmed when John Ruskin confused beauty with morality. This potent mixture, which turned the subject of architecture from a style into a religion, almost defies brief explanation.

Pugin's most influential lectures, *The True Principles of Pointed or Christian Architecture*, open thus: 'The two great rules for design are these: that there should be no features about a building which are not necessary for convenience,

---

princes; High Tories held hard to their reinterpreted Gothic heritage; the educational establishment built Grecian temples of learning, and so on.

The same building could be clothed in countless masks. It was far from either rational building or coherent style, and one troubled voice spoke up: 'Will the architecture of our times, even supposing it solid enough to last, hand down to posterity any certain clue or guide to the system under which it was erected? Surely not; it is not the expression of existing opinions and circumstances, but a confused jumble of styles and symbols borrowed from all nations and periods.'

The author, Augustus Welby Pugin (1812–52), was perhaps no better as an architect than Durand, but as a writer he

firmly established the critical foundations of modern architecture. The importance of Pugin is not that he was a Goth—and he was an unsurpassed designer of Gothic detail—but that he was a moralist.

He is well known as the 'ghost' who detailed the design that won Charles Barry (1795–1860) the competition for a new parliament building; but it is really despite this that he became the greatest single influence for Gothic in the mid-century. The Palace of Westminster (built 1840–65), that fine but, beneath the surface, far from Gothic building, stands at the hinge of Gothic revival; at the break between its picturesque ancestry, which stretched back through the eighteenth century, and the ethical phase which was to dominate the next half century. At that

crib-sheets in their influential *Recueil de décorations*, could be transformed by machine into equally impersonal forms on any scale, in any material, to any quantity. The reaction that took place was against the machine's potential for the economic production of complex designs.

Pugin, Ruskin and Morris not only hated the town: they hated the machine. They were all medievalists. Although their argument inevitably led to social criticism —Ruskin's to his remarkable writing on social and economic topics, and Morris to direct socialist action—and led architectural ideas up to the twentieth century, their aim was never less than aesthetic.

GOTHIC—OLD AND NEW

Contemporary with Pugin's work, a High Anglican revival was already gathering strength, and a revival of Gothic architecture was called for to frame its revival of old forms of worship. Thus, Puginian Gothic (from the 'purest' period only) quickly became the accepted religious architecture and the new designs were discussed critically in their journal *The Ecclesiologist*.

By mid-century this force dominated religious architecture in England, in the British Empire and then in the United States, where Richard Upjohn (1802–78) was the leading ecclesiologist, Gothic became the accepted form for church buildings; Scotland, led by Alexander Thomson (1817–75) in Glasgow, nearly fought it off, and continental Europe, despite some good Gothic churches and later public buildings in Germany, never let it become a major force. Only in England did it produce architects of really great quality: notably, George Edmund Street (1824–81) and William Butterfield (1814–1900).

Inevitably, much emphasis was on the original monuments. J.B.S. Lassus restored the Sainte-Chapelle and, with that greatest of the non-English Goths, Eugène-Emmanuel Viollet-le-Duc (1814–79), he began restoring—if this is a fair term— Notre Dame de Paris itself in 1845.

In the following year, the French Academy, while approving the restoration of historic monuments, attacked the building of new Gothic, for 'is it really possible to go back four centuries and impose the style of buildings born of the needs, customs and habits of the twelfth century upon a society which has its own needs, customs and habits?'

However, what the restorers themselves did was just as bizarre as building Gothic

construction or propriety; second, that all ornament should consist of enrichment of the essential construction of the building.' As the argument builds up, we are told that 'the smallest details should have a meaning or serve a purpose . . . construction should vary with the materials employed . . . the appearance should be illustrative of, and in accordance with, the purpose for which it is designed.'

The appeal of such argument, with its functionalist overtones, is almost irresistible today although it was startlingly novel then. But what is he really arguing? There is no mention of Gothic architecture, or of its revival; does all this result from an analysis of past styles, or is it not a justification for his *a priori* attachment to the Gothic? 'Strange as it may appear at first sight,' he wrote, disingenuously playing his trump card, 'it is in pointed architecture [i.e. Gothic] alone that these great principles have been carried.'

Pugin's replacement of a question of taste by moral principle was insidious and profound. *Contrasts or a Parallel between the Noble Edifices of the Middle Ages and the Corresponding Buildings of the Present Day, showing the Present Decay of Taste*, published privately when he was twenty-four, with its bitter sarcasm aimed at his society and its leading architects, shows the argument at its sharpest, and its point is made most effectively in the plates.

Pugin hated the contemporary industrial town and its ethos, but his venom extended to cover the current taste of his father's generation. He admired fifteenth-century buildings and so argued that today we should emulate fifteenth-century behaviour, and by being honest workmen and good Catholics emulate, of course, fifteenth-century buildings.

Pugin's emphasis on particular fitness for specific function, and on the role of the individual designer and craftsman, is clearly antithetical to the Neo-classical architects of the previous generation such as Nash, Percier and Fontaine. The French architects' interiors, repeated as abstract anew. Egged on by the religious enthusiasts, the aim became not to preserve the building as it was, nor to halt decay; often it was not even enough to restore it to its former glory. Rather their aim was to make it as it should have been, to censor it, rewriting it to remove any idiom considered anachronistic, any expression—however beautiful—more modern than their notionally 'pure' style.

Viollet-le-Duc, in his writings as important as Ruskin, is best known for his 'restorations' of Carcassonne, Vézelay or St Denis, but his contribution to contemporary building was less memorable.

In Britain it was different, for the chief vandal was also the country's most respected and prolific architect, George Gilbert Scott (1811–78), architect of over 700 buildings. He desecrated, ripped out

and destroyed fine late medieval architecture wherever he could find it. Usually this was to make the existing 'Early English' more complete, but at Oxford, for example, he removed the whole east end of the cathedral and rebuilt it in the Norman style, because, as he rationally surmised, it must once have been Norman.

If Scott was not among England's greatest architects, what he lacked in quality he made up in quantity. His work was almost exclusively ecclesiastical although his most noted designs—the Albert Memorial, St Pancras Station Hotel, the Foreign Office—were secular; noted, perhaps, not so much for their brilliance as for typifying a problem. Despite his overwhelmingly religious clientele, Scott more than anyone, with one exception, converted England in the mid-century to the use of Gothic for its secular buildings.

That exception was John Ruskin (1819–1900). Despite his slighting references to Pugin, Ruskin took on his mantle, rid Gothic of its Catholic and ecclesiological association, and argued for its more widespread secular use in his *Seven Lamps of Architecture* (1849), however much he was later to recant when he saw the results of his propaganda. In the intoxicating prose of *The Stones of Venice* (1851–3) he demonstrated that Venetian Gothic had been the style adopted by the greatest commercial aristocracy in the world before Manchester. No wonder it was now so eagerly taken up by the new English merchant princes and subsequently in the United States, where both books were a phenomenal success.

Ruskin's direct intervention in architecture was very rare, and only notable at the

Above far left and left: The French walled town of Carcassonne, before and after the wholesale restoration by Viollet-le-Duc during the mid-century.

Below far left: The court of Deane and Woodward's University Museum of Oxford, England, begun in 1855. Ruskin was in constant touch during building, encouraging the masons, and designing at least one window himself.

Below: All Saints, Margaret Street, London, 1851, by Butterfield, was the model of the Ecclesiological Society. Both All Saints and Oxford University Museum are masterpieces of English high Gothic; the buildings, both with fine strong exteriors, come alive in their tactile, sharp interiors – the church in a blaze of richly varied materials, the museum in the metallic vegetation of its glazed court.

University Museum of Oxford where his influence caused the Irish architect Benjamin Woodward (1815–61) to be commissioned in 1855. The fantastic thing about the Museum is the iron and glass structure over its court. How different it was from contemporary engineering feats for here *architects* were trying to build in iron as the medieval builders would have done had that been possible. The result was a highly articulated structure with elaborate but very metallic ornament; an amazing and wonderful space.

So it was that to architects like Street— in his magnificent St James the Less (1858), or Butterfield—in his equally amazing All Saints, Margaret Street (designed 1850)— Gothic was an obvious idiom to use, first of all for liturgical correctness; then as an exhibition of the honest, proper use of materials; and finally, of course, it was a style of which each had an idiomatic and unique command.

All Saints, an object lesson in urban planning, explodes in space and colour on entering. It is difficult to find, sitting tightly and awkwardly on a back street site in central London, but once found it could never be ignored. This was to be the model church of the Ecclesiological Society which funded it. Externally of bright red brick with black patterns and stripes, the polychromy inside is even richer, hitting the spectator with a profusion of colour and variety of material.

Street's St James, also in London, must have been delightfully bizarre, hard, gay and bright, amid the shabby Pimlico stucco housing, now replaced by the tastefully sympathetic brick housing estate which encircles it. Here again the brick is pat-

terned red and black; the sculptural shapes are hard and forceful, the tall square tower has a strange spiky roof, and the interior is rich with naturalistic carving and polychromy.

However, it was in secular buildings that architects produced something that really was new, something which even a Gothic skin—as in the Royal Courts of Justice (1870s)—could not hide: a new concept of covered space, neither outside nor inside, which was a meeting place, a social umbrella. At last an architecture appeared which was defined not by its façades, its styling or external form, but by its enclosure of space—an architecture that could be as Gothic as Street's Royal Courts of Justice in London, or as bland as the Crystal Palace.

THE URBAN UMBRELLA

The great congregating space covered in glass and iron, which is neither outside nor really inside, was the most important built contribution to urban culture in the nineteenth century. The arcades and ex-

changes, conservatories and exhibitions, markets and halls, department stores and concourses, which began early in the century, flourished in its third quarter and petered out into the present times, threw glass and iron veils over streets and squares. As the façade dwindled into irrelevance, an architecture of the inside emerged; for the first time we find the enclosure of people *en masse*, not for a specific ritual as in cathedral or theatre, but on the contrary to give the greatest freedom 'under one roof'—a phrase which links socio-economic ideas of fraternity in the free market, with the engineering brilliance in the literal accomplishment of this shelter.

The nineteenth-century search for quality in pomp and show, in bombast and sheer size, inevitably produced other breathtaking spaces, not covered with glass and iron but made up in classical, Gothic or an elaborate cosmetic style called Deuxième Empire. These exuberant halls for congregation and parade stretch over half a century, from the vast Euston

Booking Hall to the foyers and magnificent staircase of Charles Garnier's Paris Opéra, from hotel interiors which dwarfed their clients to the gross 'coffee room' in the Great Western Hotel at Paddington (1850–2) by P.C. Hardwick, or the curved promenade at St Pancras (1866–7) which G.G. Scott labelled 'coffee-room'. But the significance of these is far less than the glass/iron phenomenon, which had a

Left: The Royal Courts of Justice, London, built 1866–82. Despite this fine façade, symmetrical in general but not in detail, the building is in fact a poverty-stricken version of Street's competition-winning design of 1865. While every competitor was asked to design 1304 specific rooms, Street produced, in addition, a vast, lofty central hall. Another competitor, Alfred Waterhouse, included an internal street, flanked by three-storey buildings, the whole covered in iron and glass.

Below right: Burton and Turner's Palm House at Kew Gardens, England, 1844.

Below left: The 'urban umbrella' ranged from the pure conservatory epitomized by the Palm House to this 'immense metal cage' of Bon Marché, the famous Paris store, 1876, as the designer, Louis-Auguste Boileau, described it.

hypnotic effect on the nineteenth-century mind.

The possibilities of glazed arcades developed fast in the second quarter of the century so that by 1850 there were covered streets in every commercial city from Naples and Genoa to Glasgow and Brussels. Glazed retail markets and trading stores (typified eventually in Moscow's famous GUM (1888–93) by A.N. Pomeranzev, a market subsumed into one multiple store) easily led the transition to the great department stores like the cast iron ZCMI in Salt Lake City (1868) or Bon Marché in Paris, where under one roof (at Bon Marché engineered by Gustave Eiffel (1832–1923) and, typically, behind an undistinguished façade) the goods of all nations were exhibited for admiration and consumption. Amongst the largest were the three great Italian arcades in Genoa (1875), Naples (1887–91) and, earlier and finer than either, the majestic Galleria Vittorio Emanuele II (1865–77) in Milan. This vast cruciform space designed by Giuseppe Mengoni (1829–77) provided a centre for urbane living, both comfortable and magnificent, that has not been surpassed. A slightly different tradition, the galleried arcade, produced the

three-tier Barton Arcade in Manchester (1871) and the finest American example, the late (1889–90) Cleveland Arcade in Cleveland, Ohio.

Meanwhile, wholesale markets were developing a pattern of their own. Because of the inevitably more bulky and unrefined state of their merchandise, the indoor/outdoor ambiguity was retained more strongly—animals and trucks penetrating deep underneath the glass umbrellas. From Fowler's Covent Garden, London (1831–3) the new tradition led to the complex by Victor Baltard (1805–74) for Paris's equivalent market, Les Halles Centrales (1850), recently wantonly destroyed; meat and fruit, fish and flower markets, built on a pattern of aisle stalls off glazed nave and transepts, proliferated, while the smaller market towns all adopted this pattern for their markets.

The other tradition that merged so successfully in the mid-century with the market came from the conservatory. The 1833 Jardin des Plantes in Paris by Charles Rouhalt de Fleury (1801–75) led the field (although J.C. Loudon had proposed curvilinear glass-and-iron greenhouses in 1817–18). The pure, logical structures of Paxton's first furrowed masterpiece, the

Great Stove at Chatsworth (1836–40), and the magnificent Palm House at Kew (1844–7), by Decimus Burton and Richard Turner, followed. With Horeau's Jardin d'Hiver (1847) on the Champs Elysées in Paris—the winter garden or hot house where an artificial climate allows exotic plants and their tasteful patrons to flourish together—we have the first whiff of that potent mixture, exotic conservatory and public promenade. This new combination was to reach its apogee in the Crystal Palace, in 1851, when Britain, fearless of rivalry, invited all to take part in her coming-of-age party, in the spirit of free trade.

A site was chosen in Hyde Park and a competition held for a building for which 245 schemes were submitted. None was acceptable to the committee, which included the engineers Robert Stephenson and I.K. Brunel.

At this point Stephenson was approached by Joseph Paxton (1801–65), who felt he could improve on the committee design, a nasty, lumpish scheme already in the hands of contractors. Paxton, the ideal self-made Victorian, ingenious, industrious and life-long gardener to the Duke of Devonshire, had by 1850 become director of a railway company. At one of their meetings, he scribbled his famous doodle on a blotting pad, and within a week the 1,851 foot building was detailed (expressed as 564 metres, it loses the crude symbolism).

A tender, prepared within a further week, was accepted from Fox and Henderson of Smethwick and the Crystal Palace was built within both the budgeted money and time, a feat for which much of the credit must go to engineer Charles Fox (1810–74).

For the first time, a major building was being designed as a system to be prefabricated from millions of identical units; designed for a very limited life, for easy demolition and possible reuse. With the structural aim allowing for neither finality nor individuality, it was built up from small, simple components.

More than with any other building, all descriptions of the Crystal Palace (the apposite name was given by the satirical magazine *Punch*) are, from the very first, thick with catalogues of quantity and celerity. The structure was built in three months: there were three standard truss sizes, 23,000 in cast iron, 358 smaller ones in wrought iron (in all, 4,500 tons of iron), and a timber one. There were 83,613 square metres (900,000 square feet) of glazing (all based on a standard size sheet) and 16,990 cubic metres (600,000 cubic feet) of timber; it was 32.9 metres (108 feet) high in the transept . . . and so the figures which we find impossible to comprehend roll on. They simply mean it was impossibly big and went up unbelievably fast.

All the structure was erected without scaffolding, being raised by block and tackle, man and horse power. Trolleys for glazing, with their wheels in the grooves of Paxton's patent structural guttering, let eighty men glaze 18,000 panels in a week. While the main structural members were prefabricated, the 'Paxton gutters' were made up on site, with planing machines, multiple groove-cutters, and end-finishing machines to hand. Glazing bars were cut and drilled by machine on site and there were also mechanical adzers, metal punchers and shearers, power drills, handrail cutting machines and even a glazing-bar painting machine.

With cast iron columns, the material is only structurally effective round the edge, hence Paxton used hollow columns of minimum cross section, allowing for rigidity to be provided by diagonal bracing. Technological ingenuity was evident at all levels, from the basic strategy of complete standardization and co-ordination of dimensions, through the dual use of these structural columns and beams as a rainwater drainage system, to the suspended timber floor which kept down dust and saved on-site levelling. With 2,000 workers on site virtually all the time, considerable organizational ingenuity and programming was involved.

But the real importance of this building is not in its structural originality or in the social and contract organization, nor in the constructional ingenuity, the prefabrication and other techniques. It is the new relationship *between* all these techniques and the expressive aims and images. For here was the first great official building to omit all references to past styles. And it was wildly successful. Here was the first in a line of halls (and unbuilt schemes) which were experienced as visionary images, of infinite—or more

precisely indefinite—shape and size. Here, quite unwittingly, was a new sort of architectural space.

Where the formal order depends on the small 2.4 metre (8 foot) module, the impression of an endless building was not altered by lengthening or shortening the huge tunnel; rather than being seen as a single finite object, its coherence was gained through repetition. At last, Alberti's classical rule of architectural form, that 'nothing might be added or taken away' is finally obsolete.

Though itself an exciting experience, as an architectural statement the Crystal Palace was remarkably vacuous and banal. Its daring, direct and simple character has been related to Paxton's own, that of a pure free-thinking home-made engineer who lacked training as an architect. Hence he was neither persuaded to express pompous over-enthusiasm (for structurally it was nothing sensational) nor worried about an 'immoral' dressing up of the façade with traditional ornamentation. But that is far too easy an explanation. The paradox is that not only when Paxton was let loose on a more traditional commission—a Rothschild country house at

CRYSTAL PALACE: BUILDING IN IRON AND GLASS

Paxton said of his Crystal Palace: 'From the simplicity of all its parts, together with the simplicity of the detail, the structure does not offer a subject of long description: it is only by the multiplication of these parts that the stupendous structure now in progress is extended.' This clarity grew from re-thinking the whole structure and the building process from first principles. Hollow columns were erected at nodes of a network of pipes which stabilized the whole as well as carrying the rain. With no wet trades above ground – no messy piles of sand or lime, no waiting for mortar to dry or cement to set – columns and girders were each erected in minutes, even though everything was moved by man or horse. The 'Paxton gutters' – 38.6 kilometres (24 miles) of them – were solid timbers grooved by a special machine to carry both rainwater off the outside and condensation off the inside of the glazed roof. During construction they also carried trolleys spanning the 2.44 metres (8 feet) between them, which crept about in the London November sky of 1850, and from which every day an area the size of a railway station was glazed. The building was perfectly water-tight, a feat we would have difficulty equalling today.

The glazing trolley (right), the open-web beams fixed to the head of a hollow column (below right), and one of the central aisle girders (diagram below) raised in fact by a large gang and two teams of three horses.

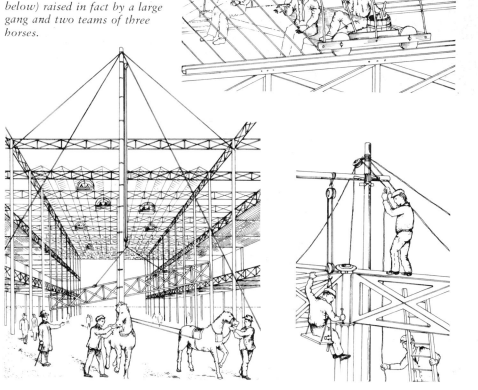

Left: The Galerie des Machines, by Contamin, Pierron and Charton. Like the Eiffel Tower, it was a metal structure of breathtaking size, built for the Paris exhibition of 1889.

Below: The Eiffel Tower, widely vilified as a 'disgrace to Paris' when it was new in 1889, now symbolizes the city.

Right: When the French decided to build a reading room in Paris for the Bibliothèque Nationale, the architect Labrouste, who had previously designed the brilliant Ste Geneviève library, was the obvious choice. Like the British Museum reading room (a fine cast iron rotunda), it has no proper exterior, but inside it is superb. Lighter and more elegant than its British counterpart, sixteen slender iron pillars support its nine terracotta and glass domes. It was built in 1862–8.

Mentmore Towers (1852)—did he produce the most tasteless mishmash of grandiose masonry styles, but that when he was offered a free hand at the Crystal Palace itself it too was transformed, losing much of its earlier cool elegance.

Paxton's taste, and that of his friends, became clearer when, despite much protest, the building was closed and demolished after the six months' exhibition. Paxton bought the bits and obtained a site in south London. With Charles Barry's help, the nave was vaulted, transept doubled, and in the end the original tunnel —a direct, three-storey 'infinite' building, ended in a Durandesque composition (in iron and glass), a huge but more comprehensible building; one half again as big, but now tamed. In this transformation, also, the Crystal Palace is illustrative of its age.

Following the success of the Great Exhibition, a rage began for universal exhibitions all over Europe and in the United States. The most important was the Paris Exhibition of 1889. Here two structures were of outstanding note: best known is the huge iron tower by engineers Eiffel, Nougier and Koechlin, which today has become the symbol of Paris, but as significant was the Galerie des Machines by engineers Contamin, Pierron and Charton. Here was dynamic lightness manifest with a new brilliance. A huge, limitless, luminous space was supported on twenty-three massive winged arches with a clear span nearly as wide as the Crystal Palace (which had been divided up with columns), each landing on tiny points. It was the first great pin-jointed, three-point arch (a technique which had already been used in

some German stations). To allow for the metallic expansion and contraction caused by heating and cooling, the arches were all hinged at the apex and free to move at the bases.

Stuffed full of objects from around the world, these exhibition buildings offered a treasure trove of eclectic design, opening an Aladdin's cave of all the world's delights in extravagant profusion. Specifically architectural features at the rebuilt Crystal Palace were a medieval court designed by Pugin and others of Greece, Rome, Pompeii, Byzantium, the Romanesque, the Alhambra, the Renaissance and Egypt, all faithfully reproduced on top of the suspended timber-plank floor, among the exotic palms and below the cast iron openweb beams and patent glazing.

The eclectic architect had it all in front of him now, and confusion was absolute.

THE LATER ECLECTICS

'How is it possible that the same architect could have designed two such contradictory buildings?' This question, which could be asked again and again through the century, is perhaps the most important

if we want to understand why buildings of the period look the way they do. It is also the most difficult to answer briefly.

Early in the century the classical taste had never really achieved exclusive power, although many followers would only produce classical designs. Later, although the mid-century force for Gothic as the one true style was most effective in its monopoly in England, its power was broken by the tussle in 1870 over the government buildings which became notorious as the Battle of the Styles. After much skulduggery, Gilbert Scott, the Ecclesiologist's leading Goth, was forced, under Prime Minister Palmerston's unremitting pressure, to abandon his principles or lose the job. The Foreign Office had to be Italian Renaissance. It was a shattering betrayal for those whose colours had been nailed to this mast, and Puginian Gothic never recovered its force as the one pure style.

But why was that so traumatic? What significance did style have, if indeed it had any at all? These questions inevitably led to: What was the essence of architecture? For more than half a century, from about 1840 to 1900, these were questions which

divided the avant-garde and rationalists from the eclecticism of the conservative establishment in bourgeois Britain or Imperial France. It also divided the architect from his patron, and the lack of force in their attempts to answer these questions helped to leave architects in a position of low repute scarcely equalled even today. In 1872 Robert Kerr called architecture 'the most unpopular profession of modern times'. The conservative eclectic clung to the idea that the one thing which separated the architect from the engineer was his freedom to choose one form rather than another, and the exercise of his taste and discrimination in knowing which forms and details are suitable for specific uses. In France the rationalists had a sounder base, and an unexpected late Gothic flowering in Viollet-le-Duc.

Viollet became heir to a strong French rationalist tradition when its more forward-looking leaders, Henri Labrouste (1801–75) and Hector Horeau (1801–72), withered in the impartial climate after 1871.

Labrouste, an architect comparable with Schinkel and Soane earlier in the century, had made his name with the

elegant and original library of Ste Gene-viève (1843–50). It had a refined classical façade and an equally fine exposed iron structure inside, but both are but facets of Labrouste's meticulously detailed pro-gramme. This building, which can be literally read as a book once one has a few clues, was much influenced by the archi-tect's friend Victor Hugo who, not long before (in *Notre-Dame de Paris*), had called the advent of the printed book the death of architecture. Two decades later, Labrouste's other masterpiece, the reading room of the Bibliothèque Nationale in Paris (1862–8), was to go much further, effortlessly throwing a tent of terracotta domes over the heads of the readers within. This superb classical interior, the rational architect's use of glass and iron, makes fascinating comparison with Wood-ward's work at Oxford, and then again with Viollet, the 'Gothic rationalist'.

Labrouste, preaching at his own private school of architecture, was also not far from Durand's aims but by mid-century these had inevitably become linked with progressive science and politics. Here was the architectural parallel of Courbet's pictorial realism, of Daumier's bitter anti-bourgeois satire, of Comte's philosophy. After the 1848 revolution and the new

French Empire, Labrouste closed his school, while Horeau continued ever more emphatically and in 1870, like Cour-bet, joined the Paris Commune, ending up in prison.

So in the 1850s, students dissatisfied with the Académie went to the less com-mitted Viollet, whose anti-eclectic stance was the last campaign for Gothic, and for Gothic now seen as the *rational* style, admired for its clarity, economy and sys-tem. But with him the Gothic really died: as the bored Académie pronounced, style is a matter of habit, and any claim to exclusiveness is outmoded.

Just as much nineteenth-century culture is epitomized by the sudden contrasts of brashness and insecurity, of earnestness and profound anxiety, so with architec-ture there is always an essential element of doubt, and this concerned style. The vague associational expressiveness and super-ficial copying helped buildings to become more jumbled and less articulate. Two design procedures developed in tandem: on the one hand geometric rules of com-position controlled the basic forms; while on the other, motifs were borrowed and applied to this form as a decorative icing. Details, taken from historical models, were applied as if this were the central

importance of architecture—each without a convincing relationship to the whole—and every part given the same emphasis. All too often this meant a loss of coherent message and a surfeit of frothy finish. 'Three-fourths of the poetry of building lies in the details,' said Street. But there is more to building than that view of poetry.

That the eclectic virtue of appropriate-ness—classical learning, Gothic sanctity and so forth—was pretty thin is seen in Bombay, one of the finest of nineteenth-century colonial cities. Here, as in Cal-cutta, Madras or Hyderabad, the designers till mid-century were army officer en-gineers. The Neo-classical Mint (Major Hawkins's Ionic of 1829) and Town Hall (Colonel Cowper's of 1825–33, Doric out-side, Corinthian within) contrasted with the visually more incongruous 'Early English' High Court and the Renaissance telegraph office. In 1874 the Old Secre-tariat was built in Venetian Gothic and the hall for Bombay University in fif-teenth-century French Decorated. The University's contemporary library, by Gilbert Scott, would have melted into fourteenth-century Flanders more appro-priately than late-nineteenth-century India.

Copyism was rampant, with forms taken, seemingly at random, from all

Left: The railway station and administration offices, Bombay, India, by F.W. Stevens. Watercolour, 1878, by Axel Herman Haig.

Right: Garnier's Paris Opéra, 1861–74.

Below: Interior of the Reform Club, London, by Barry, 1838–40.

The stylistic dilemma of the mid-nineteenth century, manifest in these three buildings, was pinpointed by the immensely successful G.G. Scott: 'Nothing is more striking [today] than the absence of creative power in architectural art . . . Everywhere we meet with reproductions . . . attempted revivals . . . nowhere with any genuine power of creating new forms . . . united to new requirements.'

possible sources. For the Bradford Town Hall competition winning local architects copied their tower directly from Palazzo Vecchio in Florence, and other prominent details from Amiens Cathedral. Prince Albert built a Swiss chalet in the grounds at Osborne for the royal children; it even had large stones on the roof and looked for all the world like a life-size musical box. Style had now become a game; and the architecture which played this game took its priorities from the doll's house.

Visual prototypes needed little research. By mid-century there was a flood of exemplars of exotica, and, of course, actual reconstruction inside the Crystal Palace. Writing about architecture, a rare literary gesture in 1800, was by 1900 filling a clutch of weekly and monthly magazines, as well as an ever-swelling stream of books. The quality of illustration improved rapidly, as engravings and drawings made by a *camera obscura* were replaced by those based on photographs, and then by the photographs themselves. Similarly, hand-coloured aquatints were replaced by magnificent full-colour lithographs. Thus, for

the first time architects had all the world's architecture in their studio. It made their task no easier, and their self-consciousness no less. The art historians had shown the merits of every age and culture, making the world accessible to the architect in his studio. How could he choose?

'How is it possible that the same architect could have designed two such contradictory buildings?'—the question was actually put by Napoleon III when he was shown Victor Baltard's scheme for the central Paris market, Les Halles. In 1843 Baltard had designed and begun construction of his masonry market building when the new Préfet for Paris, Baron Haussmann, had it demolished. He instructed the architect to prepare an iron building and to abandon all concern with style. 'All I want is a vast umbrella and nothing else.' Baltard, under this pressure, duly and with considerable charm, gave him just that.

Haussmann had answered the Emperor's question. 'The architect is the same, but the Préfet is different.' Indeed the architects were weak; they knew of no way—without such rare and strong external influence—to escape from the impasse of the eclectic use of the past. Even when looking hardest for a contemporary

style, especially in Britain, they were caught in the circular trap of believing that style was ornament, and therefore inevitably it had to be won from history.

If the professionals' self-confidence was shattered it is no wonder that their public esteem was low. There were always, of course, architects whose eclecticism was carried lightly and without an oppressive conscience; perhaps the most brilliant were two Englishmen—Charles Barry (1795–1860) up till mid-century, and Richard Norman Shaw (1831–1912) thereafter. Each designed fluently and freely without forcing a serious, slavish imitation. Barry's Whig clubs in London—his finest is the Reform of 1838–40—were Renaissance, an Italian palazzo pastiche most stylishly handled. If Barry's nearest European equivalent is Gottfried Semper (1803–79)—who contributed a fine theatre (1874–88) and two duller, identical, museums (1872–81) to the Ringstrasse in Vienna—it is only in his lack of historicism. For Semper's neo-Renaissance style is only lightly carried because, as a terribly serious rationalist at heart, he gave it little importance.

The eclectic's exuberant and showy High Renaissance style found most European favour in Paris, and is thus fairly

known as Deuxième Empire. Here its
greatest monument, L'Opéra (1861–74)
by Charles Garnier, is also the best example of the rigid and élite Beaux-Arts
education system, where great effort went
into rigorous planning, particularly of
circulation, but much less emphasis was
placed on what happened above the
ground. The Beaux-Arts buildings too
often showed off a lovely mixed salad,
whose ingredients could be varied at
will. L'Opéra has wonderful opulence
and stylishness—'a stupidly sumptuous
façade,' as the ascetic Catalan Antonio
Gaudí later wrote in his diary. Progressing
in full evening dress amidst the glittering
crowd up the great staircase of Algerian
onyx is as powerful make-believe as any
opera on stage.

Though unable to break crippling self-
criticism, which weighed the profession
down even more than it does again today,
rationalists nevertheless searched for clues
for a way forward. Rather than ask, 'In
what style shall we build?' the question
became, 'Where is today's style?'; in the last
third of the century, they changed this to,
'Where is the new architecture we are
moving towards?'

It was not a new cry: 'Should we not try
to find our own style?' Schinkel had asked
back in 1826. Then came James Fergusson,
England's leading rationalistic critic, and
the American Horatio Greenough who
kept harping on about 'function',and who
eulogized the steamships and railway
bridges just as early-twentieth-century
critics were to make architectural iconography from grain silos and aeroplanes.
However, under their noses, a modest way
out of the impasse was being suggested by
a new generation centred on William
Morris (1834–96) whose own house
(1859–60) signified a real shift of focus from
the sterile battle of styles.

THE NEW URBAN HELL
One permanent theme of nineteenth-
century culture was based on a distorted,
emotional and confused contrast—the
one Pugin specifically stated and to which
Morris returned—between a rosy past
and an awful present. The past was certainly less pure and clean; but it would be
difficult to overstate the hideousness of the
present. Here is part of Charles Dickens's
first description of Coketown from *Hard
Times* (1854), one of the best brief intro-
ductions to the nineteenth-century town:
'It was a town of red brick, or of brick that
would have been red if the smoke and ashes
had allowed it; but as matters stood it was
a town of unnatural red and black, like the
painted face of a savage. It was a town of
machinery and tall chimneys, out of which
interminable serpents of smoke trailed
themselves for ever and ever, and never got
uncoiled. It had a black canal in it, and a
river that ran purple with ill-smelling dye,
and vast piles of building full of windows

where there was a rattling and a trembling
all day long and where the piston of the
steam engine worked monotonously up
and down, like the head of an elephant in a
state of melancholy madness.'

The growth of Britain's cities, caused
both by sudden population increase and
by the huge migration into them up to the
1840s, was having catastrophic results.

By mid-century London had more inhabitants than many European countries
and most had not been born there. Suddenly, towns themselves were no longer
comprehensible, limited, static places; no
longer could one imagine them as an
entity, see them in their entirety, reconstruct them in the mind's eye, cross them
on a walk. Nor could any of the old
overall physical unity be retained. Suddenly the towns, even for the third of the
population who had lived their lives there,
were no longer a permanent, secure
background—a memory, support and
point of reference for the rhythm of urban
life.

The prevailing colour was black—black
clouds of smoke, soot and cinders everywhere. With streets lit by town gas, smoke
and industrial fog no longer stopped production: and the town expanded yet
further. In Leeds, for example, black dyes
turned the river into a poisonous sewer;
oily smudges of soft coal fell everywhere
and fine particles of iron caught on clothing and the skin; the air was full of chlorine
and acrid fumes; din was everywhere.

The urban crisis, which came to a head
in the second quarter of the century, did
not, fundamentally, concern the quality
of individual buildings. Although much
was thrown up with little concern, and
although speculators built cheap, unsafe,
non-sanitary houses with little light or

ventilation, most were probably of a better quality than earlier houses of the poor had been. But the actual evils may have seemed greater in contrast to the new facilities becoming visible in the houses of the bourgeoisie. After 1830, iron piping, improved toilets, gas for both light and cooking, and collective sewage systems all became available to a middle class within a generation of their introduction. But for nearly the whole century, the builders aimed to provide for the masses of the population without resorting to these new 'luxuries'. The problem was precipitated by the assumption that row upon row of such buildings could be piled together into vast areas without altering anything. The suddenly increased density of living led to insanitary accumulation of excreta and refuse; whole quarters were built without even a local water supply from wells; in Liverpool, a sixth of the population lived in underground cellars; in Manchester, in 1843, there was one privy—probably in an unlit cellar and foul beyond description—for every twenty-one people. The question of scale was absolutely central, for rubbish could no longer be buried or burned; no longer

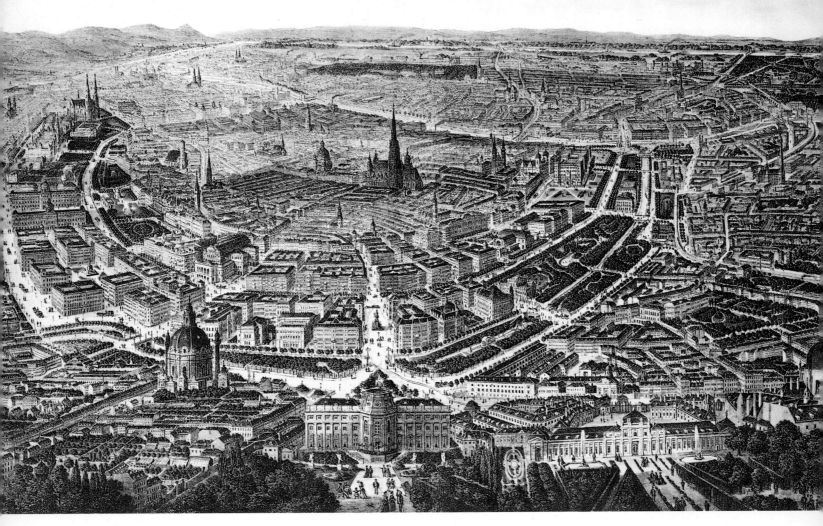

was there easy access to wells or fountains. Cholera hit England in 1831. By mid-century Glasgow was the unhealthiest and dirtiest city known, and one of the worst slums in England was in the elegant spa town of Bath.

Industrialization, this great creative force, had produced the most degraded urban environment ever seen, and now even the areas of the ruling classes were overcrowded and befouled. Long before Prince Albert died of typhoid in 1861 it was not necessary to be altruistic to be concerned about conditions; epidemics were oblivious of class distinction.

Yet for so long, in an age of such technical progress, the city as a social and political system seemed outside the circle of invention. This was finally broken in both England and France in the 1840s, when municipalities were forced to restrict the 'absolute freedom' to build, and thus modern planning was born.

Much groundwork for this had been laid by Edwin Chadwick, who, as secretary to the Poor Law Commission from 1832, instigated every one of the British Government's moves to improve condi-

tions in the towns up to 1850. In his role with the Poor Law, Chadwick was able to link social problems and physical environmental conditions in a way that had never been formalized before. In his own image, he invented the Medical Officer of Health, a new type of man who would arrive with powers to clean up a district, skilled in a fusion of medical, engineering or building and administrative techniques.

By 1835 elected local administrations in England at last had power over public services; by 1851 it was established that towns over 10,000 could build economic housing for the poor, but very few local administrations took advantage of this possibility. And the next keystone in the social development of modern architecture and the structure of modern town planning—the compulsory purchase of slums below their market value for demolition—became British law in 1866, but here the French had acted earlier. During the Second Republic, from the 1848 revolution to the 1851 restoration of the Empire, their urban legislation caught up with the British, galvanized by reports on the slum conditions in Lille and Paris.

THE NEW PLANNERS

Out of the urban hell, town planning as something distinctive from just architecture writ large was being born almost unnoticed.

The old city, with its coherent form, could not cope with the new density of living; the new city, over the coal-bed or at the rail-head, expanded without system or control. If disorder was being caused by industrialization, it was getting seriously in its creators' way, reducing industrial efficiency. That had to be 'regularized'.

The word 'regularization', and indeed the activity, was coined by Baron G.-E. Haussmann (1809–91), Napoleon III's energetic Préfet of the Seine from 1853–69. On one level Haussmann's work, which created modern Paris, can be seen—with its almost military conquest of space—as the final Napoleonic fling expressed in Baroque planning. But on another level the very different aim is clear: to give unity to the huge consumer market, the immense workshop, as an operative whole.

Haussmann built 95 new kilometres (59 miles) of road (replacing an abandoned 49 kilometres, 30 miles) in the

centre of Paris and a further 70 kilometres (43 miles) on the outskirts. He demolished 27,000 houses and built 100,000 new homes, all in flatted appartments—a form of urban family housing which became common over a wide middle-class spectrum throughout Europe including Scotland, but excepting England. His huge boulevards strode across the city with abandon. The bleak, noisy thoroughfare of Boulevard St Michel, for example, sliced through the very heart of Paris's ancient Latin Quarter which had been almost an autonomous entity since the Middle Ages. No longer a series of villages grown together, the city under Haussmann was now made visible as one functioning entity.

Certainly Napoleon III felt a need to gain public favour as well as to maintain order. Certainly the new tree-lined boule-

Three different approaches to the regularization of the urban fabric in the 1850s.

Left above: The Vienna Ring, built on the site of the old city walls, by Förster.

Above: The node of L'Etoile, cut by Haussmann through old Paris.

Top: Cerdá's plan to fill the space between the tight and squalid city of old Barcelona in Spain and the villages beyond with chamfered 'super blocks'. Unlike the Viennese emphasis on public buildings, the Parisian on efficient communication – and both on military tactics, Cerdá's Barcelona was non-hierarchical, grouping buildings and street blocks round social facilities.

vards were grand while also well suited to troop movements and cannon fire. But for Haussmann, the urban functions were reduced to production and consumption linked only by circulation, and the city had to reflect this new model. The new squares are no longer urban 'places', but are functional traffic nodes. In a circulatory system based on traffic flow between key points, these spaces in fact are visually defined only by the crowds and vehicles rather than by the surrounding buildings —a point most obvious at that most famous node: l'Etoile. With buildings too far apart to enclose or form the space, the roads and squares lose any individual quality and melt into each other.

Other attempts at regularization followed fast. In Barcelona, for example, the 1859 plan of Ildefonso Cerdá (1815–76) drove a couple of boulevards through the old city and on the site of the walls. More importantly, Cerdá laid out a chess-board plan beyond the old city, all based on what he saw as clear scientific principles. In what is only now being recognized as the most far-sighted nineteenth-century approach to the problem of city planning, Cerdá, in his *General Theory of Urbanization* (1867), argued against dominant centres and dormitory suburbs, against excessive concentration or social segregation, and for egalitarian distribution of services— parks, schools, medical assistance, workplaces, public transport systems and so forth.

The street layout of Barcelona, with its non-hierarchical grid of octagonal blocks, remains today, but the planning principles had been subverted from the first to be used—as the New York plan had been— as a basis for commercial speculation.

In London new routes such as Shaftesbury Avenue and Charing Cross Road were driven through the worst slum rookeries, opening the social wound to the healing air while also, as in Paris, dividing and ruling the potentially restless quarters. But Britain lacked the general powers of wholesale surgery on a Parisian scale. Elsewhere, too, speculation tended to defeat planning intentions, the exception being where the authority already owned sufficient land to transform the town. This was the clearest in northern European cities, Cologne, Leipzig, Lübeck, Copenhagen, and especially Vienna, where a tight ring of fortifications was now transformed into public space, a green belt dotted with civic buildings.

In Vienna a broad band of old fortifications separated the nuclear city from the new peripheral districts until, in 1857, the Austrian Emperor decided to demolish the city walls and, giving a very precise brief regarding what buildings should go where, set a competition for the planning of Vienna's new Ring. There were to be barracks to the south and north, with a great linking road for easy troop movement; there was to be a vast *place d'armes* and public buildings including the opera house, town hall, museums, markets, galleries and archives. The competition was won in 1858 (by Ludwig Förster) and eventually the Vienna Ringstrasse let the modern urban system fit over the necessarily small old town, without the frustration of London or the slaughter of Paris.

In its organization, techniques and intentions, the new city planning grew from England's mid-century sanitary and housing reforms, nourished by the differently motivated Haussmann's transformation of Paris. But simply in terms of *image*, the Americans had been undermining the Baroque townscape from a much earlier date.

In fact, right from William Penn's late-seventeenth-century plan for Philadelphia, American town plans were based on a geometrical and regular layout which was not classical and finite, not architectural and coherent, but open and limitless; not shaped, edged and centralized, but seen rather as co-ordinates which stretch, potentially, to the horizon. Here the very un-European idea of the non-central, non-finite grid town is born. It is the start of a tradition which leads directly to late-twentieth-century Los Angeles, a tradition which today Europeans still have great difficulty understanding.

When occasionally European ideas did take over, as with L'Enfant's plan for the new republic's capital in Washington, the gridiron had focuses and a hierarchy of sizes. But the scale of Washington was monstrous—much more space was given to highway than to building; the axis from the Capitol to the river was even longer than the seemingly infinite axis of that country seat of despotism, Versailles.

But, anyway, what was the use of avenues, of squares and open spaces? The utilitarian questioning of the early nineteenth century took little time to combine with the reality of new urban capitalism: 'Squares are not necessary; people live in houses not in squares. . . . A city is made up of houses, and when streets cross at right angles, houses are less expensive to build and more convenient to live in.' The 1811 report (from which this comment comes) on a plan for New York sealed the historical end of classical urban design.

Comparison with Edinburgh 'new town', for example, a grand design then at the peak of its building, shows the fundamental changes. The planned succession of enclosed and open spaces in Edinburgh was contained and sequential, reaching climaxes as its streets and axes, squares, circuses and crescents rode the Scottish topography with care and precision. In New York the decision was taken to abandon that view of the world. It was to be no longer urban design but rather a set of bland base rules. The New York State Commissioners divided the city up with a uniform abstract network, based on twelve 20 kilometre (12 miles) long, dead-straight north-south axes (avenues), and 155 identical shorter east-west axes (streets). Only one road, the Broadway, was allowed to remain, as a link with the town's history.

This utilitarian framework made no comment, other than limiting plot-size, on the eventual buildings; it was a chessboard street system, the simplest of ground rules, to be built up at any future date and offering as little hindrance as possible to any kind of building. With all the charm and romance it could muster the roads were called 'Third Avenue' or '129th Street' as appropriate; they weren't named, but given a grid reference.

European urban ideas were developing in reaction to the still unreformed city centres in the late century. Ruskin and Morris, the most vocal representatives of a traditionalist approach, while horrified by the industrial city, were equally un-

Below: A section of the New York plan of 1811. (Central Park was a later addition.)

Right: A view of Chicago towards the end of the century. The American grid-iron town, without centre, focus or edges, has a long history. It coincides perfectly with Jefferson's libertarian individualism whose other side is seen in that least obtrusive possible functional support, the American Declaration of Independence.

Right centre and bottom: Soria y Mata's proposed typical plan and section for the 'ciudad lineal' (linear city) based on efficient communication, which he put forward in 1882. A part of his plans was actually built in Madrid in 1898.

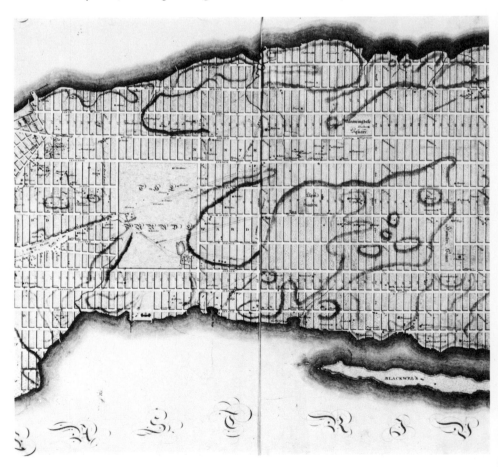

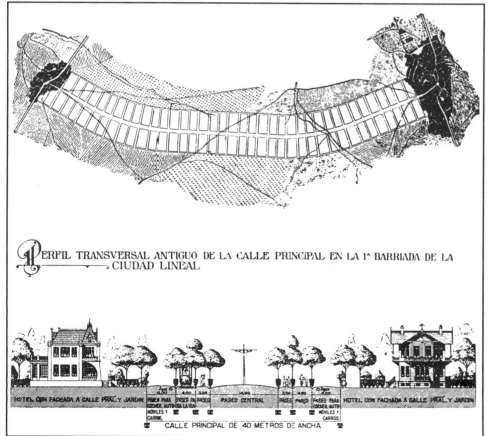

PERFIL TRANSVERSAL ANTIGUO DE LA CALLE PRINCIPAL EN LA 1ª BARRIADA DE LA CIUDAD LINEAL

HOTEL CON FACHADA A CALLE PRAL. Y JARDIN   HOTEL CON FACHADA A CALLE PRAL. Y JARDIN

CALLE PRINCIPAL DE 40 METROS DE ANCHA

inspired by the modern planning notions of Paris or America.

Morris's *News from Nowhere*, projected two centuries into the future, is set in a London returned to a cluster of convivial villages, with linking countryside in the place of industry, slum and suburban sprawl. Clearly their preferred towns are traditional: well-defined in size and shape, concentrated, with a continuous urban fabric, full of spatial and architectural variety, embracing contrast and picturesque juxtaposition. Indeed this pseudo-natural or organic beauty took on the role which hygiene and rationality fulfilled for their contemporary opponents.

In 1889 these principles were formalized in a short and easily read book, Camillo Sitte's *Der Städtebau nach seinen Künstlerische Gründsätzen* (Town Design According to Artistic Principles). Sitte (1843–1903) observed the modern monotony, the obsessive regularity and symmetry, and the vacuous spaces between unrelated island buildings. He argued that the demand for a plan, like the 1811 New York one, to be produced without knowledge of how the buildings and open space would be used, was like asking an architect for a building but refusing to tell him whether it would be used for a hospital or house, a farm or factory.

Half a century after Pugin, but with similar brevity and directness, Sitte contrasted his world with the tight medieval urban order and its asymmetrical public spaces contained by continuous walls of picturesque yet useful buildings, each one forming part of this urban context for the happy life.

Here, and in the notion of the city beautiful which he created, Sitte was in many ways reactionary. Like Morris's, his views were based on a misunderstood romantic view of the past. A simple, bucolic, pre-industrial paradise could not return, even supposing it had ever existed. But Sitte's concentration on the sense of place, and on movement by foot and

short-distance travel as the essential mode of human contact, in addition to concern for the urban context of a building, was an essential antidote. By renewing interest in old places, in towns as a total fabric rather than for their isolated monuments, Sitte provided a fruitful alternative train of thought for modern town design, and one which laid the theoretical foundation of urban conservation. A Haussmann could never again with such impunity cut so deeply, regardless of the social implications

The other European stream was rather different. It saw the town as 'a tumour, an elephantiasis, sucking into its gorged system half the life and the blood and the bone of the rural districts', as Lord Rosebery said of London in 1891. Their answer would be in new towns; towns close to the countryside, reversing the century and a

half's migration to the city. Towns with a place for industry made possible by easy road and rail communication, towns where every family would have a house, and every house a garden.

The first such proposal, formulated by Soria y Mata in Madrid in 1882, was for a linear city. Soria argued that 'the most perfect type of city possible will be that running along a single road, with a width of 500 metres, and which will stretch, if necessary, from Cadiz to St Petersburg and from Peking to Brussels.'

His rationale was based on the 'progressive' one of communication: traffic causes all the problems, rail is the most efficient means of movement, therefore the city should take the linear form of rail. The electric train would run down the centre of a tree-lined 100 metre (110 yard)

BALLOON FRAMING: THE FIRST GENERATION OF CHICAGO

'If it had not been for the knowledge of the balloon frame', said a writer of 1855, 'Chicago and San Francisco would never have arisen, as they did, from little villages to great cities in a single year.'

George Washington Snow settled in Chicago, a village of 250 people, in 1832, becoming its surveyor and drainage commissioner; he was also lumber dealer, builder, and had trained as a civil engineer. While he seems to have invented the balloon frame, it nevertheless had roots in the US East Coast wood building tradition. The essence of balloon frame is a skeleton of long matchwood sticks covered with a skin of timber clapboarding, forming a continuous structural spider's web whose surfaces also help hold it together. The studs form a cage crate whose members are fastened together by machine-made nails.

The ancient skilled craft of timber building, based on heavy sections, on morticed and tenoned joints, was suddenly replaced – thanks to industrialized mass nail production and improved machine saw cutting of wood – by the use of thin plates and studs (5 × 7.5 centimetre – 2 × 3 inch – sections) running the full height of the building, and all put together, like a box, with just nails and hammer. In the 1860s balloon framing cut the cost by forty per cent and speeded construction immeasurably. One might be tempted to argue an analogy between this New World radical carpentry and the exploitation of metal construction. But there is no evidence of a special Chicago strength; it took to iron no more enthusiastically than other US cities.

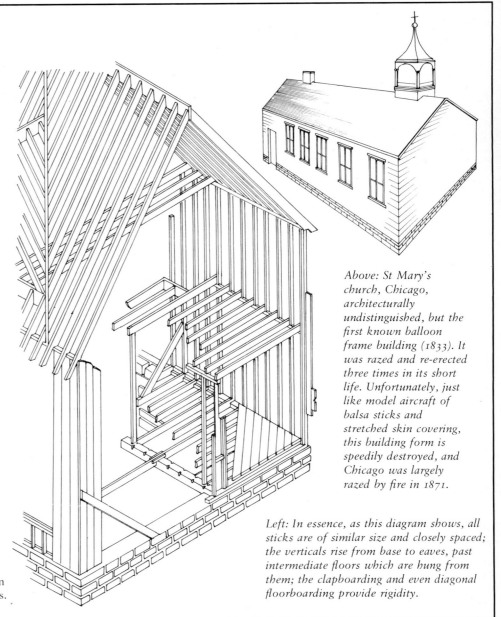

Above: St Mary's church, Chicago, architecturally undistinguished, but the first known balloon frame building (1833). It was razed and re-erected three times in its short life. Unfortunately, just like model aircraft of balsa sticks and stretched skin covering, this building form is speedily destroyed, and Chicago was largely razed by fire in 1871.

Left: In essence, as this diagram shows, all sticks are of similar size and closely spaced; the verticals rise from base to eaves, past intermediate floors which are hung from them; the clapboarding and even diagonal floorboarding provide rigidity.

Above: The Grand Hotel, Scarborough, England, by Brodrick, 1865–7, built on a spectacular slope. A stranded sea monster where the design ingenuity was all channelled into increasing the size and improving the technical efficiency of the new equipment.

wide spine. On each side, short cross streets every 200 metres (220 yards) would surround blocks of extensive gardens with small houses. Parallel green strips would then insulate the strip city from surrounding agriculture.

A little was actually built in Madrid in 1898, and in the same year Ebenezer Howard's *Tomorrow: a Peaceful Path to Real Reform* appeared. This short but highly influential book advocated, from similar motives to Soria's, cities controlled in size, expanding here not as a strip but by a system of satellites and 'mother cities', with agricultural land between. This notion of the 'Garden City' was not to imply a garden to every house, but more importantly, a city (of up to 58,000 people) set in its own rural, agricultural 'garden'.

As the century turned, the Garden City Pioneer Company Limited issued a prospectus; and by 1903 the first settlement was being built at Letchworth, the inhabitants preparing to settle down happily away from the real urban problems which remained unresolved. But in individual buildings, meanwhile, technical advances were setting the pace.

A NEW COMPLEXITY

The key buildings of the last third of the nineteenth century were dependent upon technical advance for their very existence. Earlier hotels, apartment blocks, department stores, offices, could all be housed in essentially the same building, the traditional urban masonry form, perhaps with some iron backbone, but neither too deep nor too tall.

By three quarters of the way through the century, however, came the hydraulic elevator, central heating, air-conditioning, pneumatic post systems, the telephone and, very soon thereafter, electric light; there were great improvements in services,

like catering facilities for the hotels and clubs, and then there came the steel-frame building. Because of these—and other minor technical supports—it finally became possible to operate them—the huge hotels (like Cuthbert Brodrick's in Scarborough) with their central heating, lifts and catering technology, the huge stores (like Bon Marché and Printemps in Paris), the huge commercial blocks of Chicago, Buffalo and New York.

Although Elisha Otis patented his steam elevator in New York, the hydraulic elevator appeared first in Chicago in 1870, and the electric elevator in Chicago in the 1880s. The steel-frame skeleton building was perfected in Chicago in the 1880s—Chicago, which was a fort in the early nineteenth century, a town by 1830, and sixty years later an urban area of 492 square kilometres (190 square miles) housing 1.7 million people.

But in 1871, booming, timber-built Chicago was suddenly very largely wiped out by fire. In the subsequent rebuilding the first phase of modern architecture which actually looked the part flowered in Chicago. The lead was again set by engineers, a new generation trained in the US Civil War and led by William Le Baron Jenney (1832–1907), from whose studio came the architects Burnham, Root and Sullivan. In the 1880s and 1890s, for the first time, architectural originality was flowing from America rather than from Europe; and there was a notable unity of style in the new high buildings. Contemporaries called it the Chicago Style; here the skyscraper was born.

Jenney's Leiter Building of 1879 was followed by his Home Insurance Building (1884–5), the first ever to have a complete metal skeleton. The outer wall is no longer load-bearing, and here not even self-supporting but carried on the primary structure. He developed this system further in the second Leiter Building and then the Fair Building (both 1889).

Other designers, however, with more cultural awareness, could not avoid the problem of style. Henry Hobson Richardson (1838–86), Beaux-Arts trained in

Paris, showed this at its least ludicrous and its most majestic. His Marshall Field Store (1885–8), more a massive block than a skyscraper perhaps, has the exterior of an expanded Quattrocento palazzo; the heavily moulded façade is perfectly graded according to the classical canon, getting narrower to the top with more numerous arches, and being firmly held under a strong cornice and attic. It may have been a step back technically, but it resulted in a building which was spacious, simple, resolved and grand; nothing was arbitrary, gawky or weak.

In contrast, those early tall buildings which the Modern Movement was later to find most important were those which were the least self-conscious about their form, those which were seen, quite unfairly, by a self-conscious generation, as advancing towards 'pure form', best illustrated in Chicago's Reliance Building by Burnham and Root.

More than any other building, Reliance demonstrates the idea of the skyscraper as a three-dimensional equivalent to the new American view of planning. It is an absolutely orthogonal repetitive form, and of arbitrary height. Here its history is instructive: Burnham and Root built it as a five-storey block in 1890. Five years later, John Willborn Root (1850–91)—who had been the real architect—was prematurely dead when another ten storeys were requested. Without gradation towards

Left: Richardson's masterpiece, the Marshall Field Wholesale Store, Chicago, 1885–6, was an iron skeleton clad with dignity and grandeur in arcaded masonry. This bold, almost Piranesian, monument was one of the last important Chicago buildings with walls of loadbearing masonry. Only 20 years later it was destroyed for a car park.

Left below: The refined Reliance Building, Chicago, by Burnham and Root, 1890–95, was the most advanced skyscraper of its time. Its light-coloured terracotta cladding was reduced to a minimum; its cap on top, similarly, is a thin slab; there is no cornice or entablature.

Right: Guaranty Building, Buffalo, New York, USA, by Sullivan, 1894–5. In this, his masterpiece, the most architecturally effective of all early skyscrapers, the controlled composition is clear; its tawny terracotta sheathing enriched with feathery ornament. The ground floor clarity, where columns were almost free-standing, isolated from the wall plane as the glass skin bent back, has unfortunately now been lost by solid filling on the face of the building.

the top, and with virtually no cap, the tower was extruded further from the ground. This pure example of 'multiplication', paradoxically, was also a building of great charm; a slender, remarkably modern-looking tower.

Just at that moment the skyscraper received its first true analysis in 1896 from Louis Sullivan (1856–1924) who, although a pupil of Jenney, was also inspired by Richardson's stylistic integrity. His aim was to mould the two influences into his own, very individual, position.

Sullivan described the skyscraper as a functional organism which could be divided into three zones. First, a service basement, public ground floor (for 'greater freedom of access'), and a connected mezzanine; these form the podium. The scale is large, helped by the inserted mezzanine floor. At the top the second zone, an attic floor, completes 'the circulatory system'. And, in between, there is the third, an indefinite number of office floors, seen as one whole. Indefinite is the keyword. (Sullivan's assistant from 1888–93, Frank Lloyd Wright (1867–1959), later acutely called the skyscraper 'a mechanical device to multiply by as many times as it is possible to sell over and over again the original ground area'.)

Sullivan's own masterpiece, the Guaranty Building in Buffalo (1894–5), illustrates his theme. The ground floor is a very modern podium, the columns almost free-

standing pilotis, as glass cuts back round them. The office floors are exactly the same with only the vertical thrust leading up to the great coved crown. The effect is simple, majestic and rational, and yet the whole surface is covered with lacy low relief in tawny terracotta; decoration and structure are perfectly integrated.

The less unified Carson, Pirie and Scott Building (1899–1904) was his swansong. Although he lived on for twenty more years, Sullivan's individual line was overtaken by a pompous classicism to which Burnham had succumbed by the turn of the century.

One new technique at this time did not come from anywhere near Chicago, although it hides in the foundations and cellars of the Chicago blocks. Mass concrete, used by the Imperial Romans in all their major structures, was forgotten as a material and for its structural properties for a millennium and a half, being first mentioned again around 1800. Portland cement, first patented in England in 1824, was being produced commercially by 1854 and used as the basis for concrete. Proposals for mass concrete buildings in England and France appear in the 1830s and foundations of mass concrete were becoming more common by the mid-century when the first experiments were made to combine its great crushing strength with the tensile strength of metal.

make the craftsman's task so easy but also, as the 1851 Exhibition had demonstrated, so tasteless. But mass production, if reducing quality in the object as art, was vastly increasing its accessibility.

The late-nineteenth-century street in urban western Europe and America became a positive exuberance of decorative detail. On the most ordinary houses, decorative keystones appeared, accompanied by stained glass, intricate ridge tiles and boards, string courses in glazed patterned brick and lintels with a foliage design. The bollards in the street were decorated and the lamp-posts festooned

Left: St Jean-de-Montmartre, Paris, by Baudot, begun in 1897, used concrete in the tradition of Viollet's metallic Gothic.

Below: The Teresian College, Barcelona, Spain, by Gaudí, 1888–90; a carefully calculated construction in single-skin brick parabolic arches, producing lightness and clarity.

Right above: The Red House, Bexley Heath, England, by Webb, 1859, for William Morris, fits within a tradition from Pugin which already included parsonages by Street and Butterfield. No ecclesiastical styling was needed and the asymmetrical form responds directly to designed use.

Right below: All Saints, Brockhampton, England, by Lethaby, 1902. Its walls are in local masonry and its thatched jacket blends with the countryside, sandwiching an exposed concrete vault. The expression links directly to the Morris tradition – indeed, the tapestries were by Burne-Jones and woven by Morris and Co.

By 1844 patents existed for such construction. The roof of a Parisian terrace was built in 1852 in pre-moulded concrete, reinforced with iron rods, and Joseph Monier patented reinforced concrete pipes (1868) and pre-cast panels (1869), columns, beams (1877) and bridges (1880).

In the 1880s the French engineer François Hennebique began work on reinforced concrete floors, and by 1891 Coignet had built a floor of pre-cast reinforced concrete girders in Biarritz. Hennebique replaced iron with steel, and in 1895 he built a spinning mill at Tourcoing with an uncompromising façade of exposed concrete frame and glass panels. Antonio Gaudí made the first Spanish experiments in reinforced concrete construction (at Parc Guell) but the first major reinforced concrete building was Anatole de Baudot's boldly expressed frame church St Jean-de-Montmartre, Paris, begun in 1897.

THE NEW ART

The All Saints Church, Brockhampton, Herefordshire, built by William Lethaby (1857–1931) just after the turn of the century, shows the imaginative uses to which the material was being put. Its simple forms—local masonry walls, clapboard tower and thatched roof—fit snugly into the landscape. But under the thatch, and exposed, just as boldly as Baudot's frame in its very different way, was a curved steeply pitched tunnel vault in concrete; 'formed on rough boards', as his specification noted. Here was the result of developing technology but, also, and more importantly, the outcome of a half century's maturing of ideas of honesty and simplicity held by the great Goths from Pugin on, which formed the bridge to the twentieth century. They had been developing in part in response to the machines; the tools of Midas which could

or encircled with dolphins, while the rail-
ing or street benches—even if they came
from a catalogue of one of the iron-
founders like Walter MacFarlane of Glasgow, and were thus identical to those in
Halifax, Scarborough or Bombay—were
sure to have a decorative charm. There
was pleasure to be gained from the ornamental cast iron work of Melbourne, the
timber of San Francisco and the polychrome brickwork of London.

But the machine-made abundance was
not universally welcomed. The spirit which
attacked it was held together, since Pugin
and Ruskin, by the virtues of honest,
crafted expression. This embraced Henry
Cole (who had set up the 1851 Exhibition)
and his friends Owen Jones and Gottfried
Semper. While freely admitting the influence of Pugin's theory of 'honest
design', this group were confident about
industry and its potential to create objects
of beauty-utility. Others were more wary
of industry, placing much of the blame,
inevitably social and aesthetic, on the
machine, or, more precisely, on mechan-
isms and mechanistic design which came
between the creative craftsman and his
material, between the worker and the
surface worked. Here William Morris
stands out, on the one hand for his
willingness to follow these notions through
to political philosophy and action, and on

turn of the century Voysey and Mackintosh were designing exquisite cutlery for their exquisite buildings, while the sinuous jungle growth of European Art Nouveau was returning again to the *Gesamtkunstwerk* of total design.

While Morris never really escaped from the Gothic Revival himself, one of the first effects of his teaching was to foster an atmosphere in which various domestic crafts could be revitalized. This movement was successful to such an extent that, only thirty years after the 1851 Exhibition, the pottery of William de Morgan, the glass of Powell, the designs of Christopher Dresser or Walter Crane and architecture of Arthur Mackmurdo or C.R. Ashbee could seem from another age.

Emphasizing the process of making things and the dignity of creative work,

the other as he was, simply, a more gifted and original designer than Henry Cole or Pugin.

Morris founded the firm Morris, Marshall and Faulkner in 1861, carefully subtitling it Fine Art Workmen in Painting, Carving, Furniture and the Metals. They began to produce widely—carpets, fabrics, wallpaper, furniture and glass—with Morris's motto 'I don't want art for a few, any more than I want education for a few, or freedom for a few.' From this moment stems that modern concern with the ordinary man's house—his chairs and tables, his wallpaper and pepperpot— each object worthy of a designer's creativity. Despite a later style that would be called Art Nouveau, the New Art really began here with Morris and the Arts and Crafts Movement.

This notion itself was easily diverted, however, into the bid of designers to produce *Gesamtkunstwerk*, the total, almost theatrical, environment where nothing was allowed that was not part of the designer's master plan. That fantasy world had bizarre, exciting but unhealthy Gothic consequences in the construction of aristocratic fairy castles like the Wagnerian Neuschwanstein (1869–81) for Ludwig II of Bavaria by Edvard Riedel (1813–85) and others, or the similar but more imaginative Coch and Cardiff castles (begun 1865) for the Marquis of Bute where William Burges (1827–81) designed not just the wallpaper, but the water taps and hairbrushes.

A whole generation after Morris— Godwin, Mackmurdo, Bodley and others —came to regard nothing as too small to receive the designer's attention. By the

Morris blamed the machine: 'As a condition of life, production by machinery is altogether an evil.' And this immoderation trapped him. His aim, an art 'by the people, for the people', when produced without any of the post-Renaissance machine aids turned out, of course, to be exquisitely expensive—as Morris ruefully said, for 'the swinish luxury of the rich'.

In 1877 Morris founded the Society for the Preservation of Ancient Buildings to fight the clumsy, aggressive 'restorations' of a Viollet or a Scott. But soon the 'anti-scrapes', as they were called, moved beyond that, and with Morris's close colleague Philip Webb (1831–1915) at its centre, SPAB became a meeting ground for a new generation of radical architects.

By the 1890s, there was a real spirit of hope. This group was against revivalist architecture, and a free style seemed at last to be appearing. To locate its source, we must return to that first house which Webb built for his friend in 1859 at Bexley Heath. The Red House, a product of the joint ideas of Webb and Morris, had progenitors, including notably The Grange at Ramsgate, the house Pugin built for himself only a decade earlier. Both adopt a comfortable irregularity, close in feeling to fourteenth- and fifteenth-century monastic architecture. Although built in the Gothic spirit, growing from inside outward, Webb never aped Gothic buildings. There is no attempt to fit a symmetrical façade. Like Pugin's house and Butterfield's simple country vicarages of the 1840s, perhaps its most important quality is careful unpretentiousness.

Inside, details are even bolder, often absolutely direct and plain. The materials speak for themselves—a major lesson from the Pugin–Ruskin heritage, which was also very influential in America stemming from A.J. Downing's book *Cottage Residences* of the 1840s, which began a fashion for board-and-batten timber houses with bay windows and ample verandahs.

The Red House remained a foundation stone in this revival of domestic architecture which developed its free style quietly up to the end of the century, not quite extinguished by the grand eclecticism all around.

Richard Norman Shaw (1831–1912) followed Webb as Street's chief draughtsman. He could play the Grand Manner Eclectic with the best, but produced important town houses with free seventeenth- to eighteenth-century motifs, the most sparkling of which was an office, the much

'Eschew all imitation; strive to produce an effect of repose and simplicity.' Another fifteen years later, when Charles F.A. Voysey (1857–1941) made this comment in 1892, he was emerging as the most brilliant of the Arts and Crafts architects.

Voysey's buildings are calm and graceful; they have a refreshing charm and often a radical simplicity in form—as in the forceful horizontality of a long band of window under the eaves of a high roof; the interiors are clean and light (in a way only equalled by Mackintosh in his Clydeside houses), and, finally, they entirely avoid any medievalism.

The Arts and Crafts aim, again a Pugin–Morris–Ruskin one, was for an organic architecture, and one which grew inconspicuously out of the earth. William Lethaby, for example, began his designs from consideration of the building's purpose and its location; including site planning and any local traditional techniques or local materials he could use. This was a real but quiet, and in a sense, conservative revolution.

If the 1890s was a decade of hope, by 1903 the free style was dead in England, although it still had a few years to flower in Glasgow. Lethaby had given up architecture, despite a large country house practice; Voysey's innovations were past, Lutyens had left Arts and Crafts for a grand neo-Baroque manner and Philip Webb had retired. The new vision was forgotten except by Hermann Muthesius (1861–1927), returning to his native Germany in 1902 to produce his influential book *Das Englische Haus* which was to praise these developments and channel the notion of objectivity (*Sachlichkeit*) towards the Bauhaus.

In the 1890s two Belgians, Henry van de Velde (1863–1957) and Victor Horta

lamented New Zealand Chambers (1872–3). Edward Godwin (1833–86) won the 1861 Northampton town hall competition with a 'Stones of Venice' Gothic confection, but by the following year his own house in Bristol had bare floors and plainly coloured walls. Bolder still was the amazing house he designed fifteen years later in Chelsea for his friend the painter James McNeill Whistler. It was original and challenging in its forms; its street front displayed bold asymmetry and simplicity and inside it had white and rich yellow walls, Japanese matting floors, plain curtains, a few Chinese porcelain pieces and simply framed pictures. He confidently wrote 'if asked what style your work is, say "it is my own".'

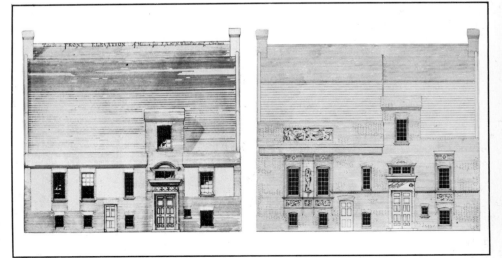

Left above: New Zealand Chambers, London, by Shaw, 1872; a personal 'Queen Anne' which, rare to commerce, looks elegant and domestic.

Left: Whistler's House, London, by Godwin, 1877. Modifications (right) were forced on the first, radically unhistorical elevation (left).

Top: Low House, Bristol, Rhode Island, USA, by McKim, Mead and White, 1886. A masterpiece of the Shingle Style, this dramatic seashore house has no hint of the past.

Above: Maison du Peuple, Brussels, by Horta, 1896. It eschews historical reference, and culminates in an auditorium under graceful iron beams enclosed only by glass, or thin, metal-framed panels.

(1861–1947), in unprecedented designs between 1892 and 1894, began a parallel architectural revolution which was part of the European Art Nouveau.

These architects were also eliminating references to past style; but rather than fitting in to the surroundings, moving towards a compromise with tradition, they were emphasizing the avant garde personality of the creative artist. Simultaneously in America, Frank Lloyd Wright, the contemporary of Mackintosh and Lutyens (and a continuous correspondent of Ashbee's) was beginning to assert an equally strong formal independence, as in the Winslow house, River Forest (1893).

Berlage, Antonio Gaudí and the men of the Sezession—Hoffman, Olbrich and even Olbrich's master Wagner—were men of the other side of the century. Even though Otto Wagner was an eminent fifty-nine when the century turned he was influenced by his younger colleagues, and changed his style fundamentally from a conventional classicism.

With the turn of the century came this change of style, a most curious and unprecedented phenomenon in design history. While it revitalized Wagner, it ossified many of his younger contemporaries. Sullivan and Lethaby, for example, lived about thirty years into the new century building little of significance; Ashbee, Voysey and Horta survived, bypassed, into the 1940s; Mackintosh had no significant new commission after 1905, and died virtually penniless twenty years later. It seems the flow of architecture had moved far from them all. When the new wave broke after 1900, England, which had provided so much of its force, was left high and dry.

The growing-up process, perhaps, was complete. In a sense, architecture reclined in a mixed state of relief and anticipation. Henry Wilson's account of Ruskin's death in 1900 sums it up:

'There came a sudden clamour outside, the door burst open and another well-known artist rushed in dancing and frantically waving an evening paper. "Ruskin's dead! Ruskin's dead!" he cried; then sinking into a chair. "Thank God, Ruskin's dead! Give me a cigarette!"'

The century was over and, with it, the architecture of the first industrial age.

THE TWENTIETH CENTURY

The twentieth century, as much as any previous age, has been preoccupied with the question of an architectural style appropriate to its time. Fashion in the late nineteenth century had been eclectic, that is to say adopting various styles for various types of building; but with the arrival of a new century, a self-conscious attempt was made to break away from that to find a new style. It did not evolve immediately, and one of the interesting features of the twentieth century is how the style known as modern architecture became predominant, and why it is now being questioned if not rejected altogether.

At the turn of the century, architecture as an intellectual pursuit was still the preserve of the rich, or the wealthy middle class. After almost eighty years of social and political upheaval the predominant client has become the public authority: either central or local government. Thus the architect has changed his role to that of the servant of society as a whole.

Even the private client, now in a subordinate position in many countries, has changed his character. Apart from the consistent stream of individuals prepared to commission private houses or art galleries—who have provided the main opportunity for architects to innovate and experiment—the main 'class' of private client is no longer the nineteenth-century 'captain of industry'. He has been replaced by the corporate client and the multi-national company keen on its image—less prepared to experiment than the private individual, but more prepared to commission outstanding buildings than most official bodies.

Charities and educational institutions—particularly universities—although small in output and financial resources as compared to the two main groupings of clients—have commissioned high-quality buildings which have had an influence quite disproportionate to their numbers.

The Unité d'Habitation at Marseilles, France, 1947–52 designed by Le Corbusier. This building became one of the most potent post-war architectural images – and, in many cases, a cracked one. Corbusier's intention was to use modern techniques to achieve a 'unit of living' – a building which combined flats with shops, recreational facilities on the roof, and leisure facilities such as a cinema and provision for children and parents: a communal view of the world. The photograph illustrates the deep window reveals necessary to control the strong Mediterranean sunlight, and the bright colours with which the reveals were painted. Unfortunately, the building's imitators concentrated more upon a visual resemblance than upon repeating the innate social idea – and frequently failed on that as well.

The changed nature of the clients has greatly changed architecture. The previously sporadic tradition of social building has become the predominant building activity: public housing, schools, town halls, swimming baths, libraries, clinics, hospitals and old people's homes. Many architects have responded to this changed emphasis by becoming socially committed, wishing to use their skills to achieve a new order. The disadvantages have become apparent only slowly. The public bodies instructed their architects through committees, committees which often proved to be remote from the intended users of the buildings. Sometimes the results of such programmes have manifestly failed to meet the occupants' needs—as was exemplified in the demolition of a huge housing

Above: A prophetic warning from Fritz Lang's 'Metropolis' film, 1925, which illustrated vividly how technology could be perverted to serve inhuman ends.

Left: By contrast, Le Corbusier's Villa Savoye, Poissy, France, 1929–31, encapsulates some of the life-enhancing opportunities of new materials and methods of construction: light, a free plan, and openness.

Below: One of two Sports Halls for the 1964 Tokyo Olympics by Kenzo Tange. The larger had the biggest suspended roof in the world, yet with far more grace and spatial subtlety than that might imply.

Right: The Sears Tower, Chicago, 1973, by Skidmore, Owings and Merrill. At the time it was the tallest building in the world: 442 m (1420 ft), with 110 storeys. Architecture replaced by technical achievement.

estate in St Louis, USA, only twenty years after its completion.

To some extent, the twentieth century has been a century of lost opportunity. The old order was removed by wars and replaced by mass popular movements such as communism, socialism and fascism. These new ideals, together with the creation of new countries, could have provided architects with the opportunity to develop a totally new approach, unshackled by the past. In almost every case the popular movements and their governments rejected the idea, sometimes immediately, and sometimes once the new regime felt secure in power. They were particularly opposed to the presumed internationalism of modern architecture, as compared to the national identity conveyed by historic styles.

The production of exciting architecture

involves risk; the number of clients prepared to take that risk has diminished. At the same time, the money available for building has had to be spread over a far larger number of projects. These two factors combine to explain the mediocrity of much modern building; and this social and political context has thus been a primary influence in the development of modern architecture.

The second major influence on modern architecture has been the love affair between architects and technology. The use of iron and steel, the development of the elevator, electricity, and some pioneering attempts at air conditioning were all initiated in the nineteenth century, but it was the twentieth century that brought them to such refinement as to permit a completely new scale of building. In 1900 people looked forward to a new century when all the evils of the old world could be conquered by science. The old empires were considered to be effete and obscurantist, with the good things of life reserved for a small section of the population. Against this, technology was the agent of equality, able to provide for everybody. The new technology of travel—particularly cars and aircraft—would provide a potent imagery used in the course of the century by many architects and thinkers—including Marinetti, Walter Gropius, and Le Corbusier. The buildings constructed for cars, aircraft, and other forms of travel were often the ones chosen to exploit modern technology as a reflection of the machines they contained. For a while, technology could do no wrong, and, moreover, life could be rearranged to suit its demands. There was a feeling that if it could be done, it had to be good—and this led to a search for superlatives such as the highest, the biggest, the fastest. All that technology could offer was encapsulated in Le Corbusier's Villa Savoye (1929); it was light, airy, free, open-plan, and released from the ground—in contrast to buildings at the turn of the century which were of solid-wall construction, mass weight, a style determined by eclecticism, decorated, and with an emphasis on the major features such as the doors and the windows and the roof. The appearance of the Villa Savoye must have seemed like a breath of fresh air, incorporating as it did all the pioneering efforts of the previous 29 years—namely new materials, a new structure, a new internal layout, and a new aesthetic.

Fritz Lang's film *Metropolis* warned that technology could be perverted, but

was out of keeping with the predominant feeling of the times. It took another twenty years at least before people realized that technology in itself was neither good nor bad: what mattered was how it was used.

As technology advanced, architecture became, increasingly, a matter of fitting together various components. This trend had begun in Victorian times, but now fewer and fewer parts of the building were made on site; more and more were available from international catalogues, ordered from far away. Thus building became to a large extent a matter of assembling a kit, with detailed co-ordination of vital importance. It was due to this development as much as anything that the individual characteristics of given countries began to be ignored, or were considered irrelevant. Although in France and Italy concrete might predominate because

it was cheap, or in north Europe and Britain brick, or in America steel, components of buildings—such as window frames—which used to be made on site, were now mass-produced and internationally distributed. This view of buildings as an assembly of a kit was confirmed by experiments in assembly-line building, or system building, which was developed particularly after the Second World War. It also happened to coincide with an influential architectural aesthetic derived from the belief that technology was so sacrosanct that materials should be used in the condition that they came in from the factory.

As building became more technical, it became increasingly the preserve of the architectural élite who could understand the technology. So, although more buildings than ever before went up, fewer and

Left: 'The Orchard', Chorleywood, England, designed by Voysey for himself in 1899. His plain, simple approach was held to presage the Modern Movement. Yet Voysey disliked Art Nouveau, 'mere eccentricity . . . the spook school', and also Modern Movement buildings, 'square box, roofless buildings . . .'

Below: Hotel van Eetvelde, Brussels, 1897–1900, by Horta. Light and airy in contrast to the prevailing fashion for cluttered and 'heavy' buildings, Horta's designs are more obviously innovative, particularly in their use of iron-work with Art Nouveau swirls and motifs.

Right: The Glasgow School of Art Library, completed 1909, is part of Mackintosh's competition-winning design for the School. There is more than a hint of Celtic mystery in this inspiring room.

fewer were built by the occupiers themselves using traditional methods. Thus the design of even simple little buildings became a cerebral exercise, and very often local characteristics were ironed out. So-called vernacular building was, if not annihilated, certainly reduced to a tiny percentage of the total building work.

The third force behind modern architecture was the aesthetic resulting from the previous two forces: decoration—even the symbolic celebration of a necessary function—was eschewed. In previous centuries, the meeting of one material with another provided the opportunity for some celebration, such as a carving or a moulding. Now that detailing had been reduced to the assembly of standard components, this celebration of decoration was omitted. Superfluous decoration, previously used to indicate perhaps the use of the building or the aspirations of its owner, was rejected on aesthetic grounds, and this to a large extent removed the function of symbolism in a building. The consequence of this is that the dual function of a building—that is to say, first, the provision of space to accommodate some use and, secondly, the embellishment of the area in which it is set—is reduced to a single function, that of clothing the building's use. With the abolition of tell-tale signs from the exterior, many modern buildings could enclose a variety of uses; factories can look like offices, or hotels, or sewage stations, or even houses or university buildings. And so, it was considered that the exterior form and shape of a building should be determined by its internal functions; for many architects this meant that the external aspect of a building was the mere clothing of what went on inside; it had no

separate reality. This aesthetic led to a modern architecture of considerable plainness and austerity, with little or no message for the general public. This is perhaps best illustrated by the problem of designing modern churches, of which a large number have been built despite social upheavals. The absence of an easily identifiable symbolism has meant that each new church has started anew, with nothing to build on, with the result that the only way churches can be identified is by the fact that they all have some peculiar shape. 'It must be a church,' people say; 'it's got a funny roof.'

By the 1970s, as a result of a revulsion against the austerity and absence of symbolism in modern architecture, fashion is changing once more, and there are stirrings of what is called post-modern architecture. The thesis that technology is good in itself is also being questioned and the plentiful cheap energy on which so many twentieth-century developments are based is no longer likely to be available in such quantities. As a result, a reconsideration of building form is taking place.

BIRTH OF THE MODERN MOVEMENT

By the turn of the century, a European-wide youthful artistic revolt against the imperial establishment was already well established. It consisted of the combination of a search for a new style and an innovation in structure and materials. The earliest manifestation of this revolt was the Arts and Crafts movement in England, which in essence probably dated back to as early as 1859. Unlike the florid styles of Victorian and, later, Edwardian buildings, the architecture of the Arts and Crafts

movement drew its inspiration from simplicity, and from the old English traditions. —particularly of steeply pitched roofs, overhanging eaves, and low gables, all arranged in a picturesque way. One celebrated exponent of this style was C. F. A. Voysey, who recommended that interiors should be painted white, furniture should be made of oak, and that there should be only one pure ornament in each room. The Arts and Crafts movement also attempted to include within its ambit not only architecture, but also sculpture, painting, furniture, fabrics, pottery, metalwork, book printing, publishing and

binding. This was an important forerunner for other movements.

Subsequent movements, mainly in the 1890s, were far less gentle. Whether known as the Art Nouveau movement, or the Sezession, or the Jugendstil, the emphasis was always on something new, youthful, and revolutionary. The Vienna Sezession was a group of designers and artists who broke away—seceded—from the Establishment, and their exhibition hall in Vienna, designed by Josef Olbrich (1899), must have been calculated to offend the stalwarts of the Austro-Hungarian empire in their neo-Baroque twilight. Two great unadorned cubic shapes stand on either side of the main entrance, which is itself topped by a gilded, wrought iron dome, known affectionately as the golden cabbage. The entrance is decorated with a

sinuous, rather decadent sculpture.

Elsewhere Art Nouveau took a different form, although like the Arts and Crafts movement in England it was an arts-wide trend most easily identifiable by its distinctive decoration. This decoration included a combination of the sinuous designs supposedly derived from nature, with formalized representations of flowers supported on long intertwined stalks. In Scotland, at least, this was linked to the Celtic revival movement—possibly another example of the new movement finding its roots in history. In many places—Paris, Glasgow, Munich or Brussels—Art Nouveau was primarily a decorative movement, and as such had some affinities with the Victorian Gothic fantasies of the previous twenty years. The façade of the Atelier Elvira, Munich, designed in 1896

by August Endell, had a stucco decoration that had more affinity with some of the illustrations of fiery dragons in contemporary fairy story publications than with nature.

In the works of three architects in particular the forms of the breakaway movements were used as an integral part of a new building style as opposed to simple decoration. In the buildings of Victor Horta (1861–1947) in Brussels not only was sinuously designed ironwork used for such necessary functions as balconies, railings, balustrades, windows and doors, but ironwork was also used openly in the structure. Horta's use of iron allowed a relatively free plan for the interior of his houses and hotels which influenced Hector Guimard (1867–1942), whose best known works are the entrances to the Paris Métro,

built between 1899 and 1904. These cast-iron and glass landmarks are not unlike some of the crazier illustrations for science fiction stories.

The buildings of Charles Rennie Mackintosh (1868–1928) are almost all concentrated in the West of Scotland and generally speaking are restricted to the limited range open to an architectural innovator—a church, schools, private houses and, most notably, the Glasgow School of Art, the commission for which was won in an open competition. Mackintosh also designed a wide range of furniture and a number of interiors including a famous series of tea rooms. The library of the School of Art (completed in 1909) synthesizes much of Mackintosh's approach, in that both interior and ex-

terior decoration are kept to a minimum except where allied to some necessary function, such as the lights, balcony, or protruding windows. On the other hand, the design of the main parts of the library is so contrived as to produce not only the indefinable atmosphere of *fin de siècle* but also a visual affinity with Art Nouveau detailing—particularly an emphasis on verticality and height reaching up into the darkness. The exteriors of Mackintosh's buildings were plain, but very much in keeping with the Scottish vernacular tradition. His effects therefore were created by the interplay of division of space, specially designed furniture and sparingly used necessary ornament; this sets him apart from the purely decorative tradition of continental Europe.

The third of these exceptional architects was Antonio Gaudí (1852–1926), whose buildings in Barcelona are highly individual products in an area of mixed cultural heritage and a traditional idiosyncracy, generally isolated from the mainstream of European architecture. His work consisted mainly of blocks of flats, a church, a park, and the unfinished Church of Sagrada Familia. In these buildings Gaudí experimented with structure, with the use of multicoloured mosaics, and in weird roofscapes, all in order to achieve a totally distinctive architecture of a wholly personal inspiration, probably deriving from the human body and from nature.

During the same years which saw these new stylistic trends, developments had also been made in terms of new materials and structure. For example, Otto Wagner (1841–1918), one of the supporters of Sezession movement in Vienna, designed between 1910 and 1912 a postal savings bank whose main booking hall had a glazed roof, supported by a light patterned metal framework supported on simple metal piers. In France the engineer François Hennebique (1842–1921) had been experimenting with reinforced concrete, a material which was subsequently used by Auguste Perret (1874–1954) in a block of flats in rue Franklin, Paris (in 1903) and again for his Garage Ponthieu, also in Paris (1906). Concrete was also the material which Tony Garnier planned for his visionary Cité Industrielle, prepared between 1901 and 1904. Garnier (1869–1948), who became City Architect of Lyons, designed several buildings in reinforced concrete, and was the first of the architect planners on the grand scale. His city of concrete was planned around factories, communications (such as the port and railways) and power (a vast dam provided cheap electricity). The houses consisted of miles of mundane little cubic, flat-roofed boxes adorned only with trellis work and plants, and separated one from another by extensive foliage. Refinements included the fact that at least one room of each house faced south, the houses were mostly two storeys only, and the entire complex was laid out according to Garnier's perception of how the inhabitants' needs might best be met.

In America, and particularly in the booming city of Chicago, where the control of the old Establishment was probably not quite so rigid as in Europe, innovation was even less hampered. The Reliance Building in Chicago and Louis Sullivan's Guaranty Building in Buffalo

Left above: Hoffman's exotic Palais Stoclet, Brussels, begun in 1905, presages Art Deco with its tower, its contrasts of solid and void, and horizontal and vertical elements.

Left below: Ward Willetts house, Highland Park, Illinois, USA, by Frank Lloyd Wright, 1902. The house clearly radiates from its central core; the overhanging eaves are a Wright motif.

Right: Garnier's proposed Cité Industrielle, 1901–4. A view of a residential quarter: no traffic, plenty of planting and little, unadorned houses.

Right below: Letchworth Garden City, England, first begun in 1904; a part designed by Barry Parker and Raymond Unwin. Greenery and peace are kept, but the houses are 'Olde Englishe', with steep pitched roofs and tall brick chimneys.

are particularly distinctive for their grid-like façades with windows the predominant visual elements. This effect is created by the steel frames of the buildings which determined the location of the window apertures (though modified in the Guaranty Building by Sullivan's brick dressing and arches). The advantage of a steel frame was that it did away with the enormously solid wall otherwise required to bear the weight of a 14-storey building.

The outstanding innovator in the Chicago area was Frank Lloyd Wright, whose most important buildings of the period, with the exception of the Larkin Office Building in Buffalo (1904) and Unity Church, Oak Park, Chicago (1906), were his houses for private clients. The interesting features of Wright's houses are first that the central part and its space was designed as the dominant feature, linking other areas such as the bedrooms and the living quarters; and secondly that the houses were no longer self-contained boxes arbitrarily placed in a landscape, but were designed so that they seemed to grow from the land. This was achieved, to use Wright's own words, by 'gently sloping roofs, low proportions, quiet skylines, suppressed heavy set chimneys, and sheltering overhangers, low terraces, and outreaching walls sequestering private gardens'. In some houses advantage was taken of the *porte-cochère* to extend the curtilage of the house over the entrance driveway. The Robie house (1909) in a tight urban location in Chicago and the more rural Ward Willetts house, Illinois (1902), are good examples of these principles in practice.

In England a significant development

was the establishment of the garden cities, originally inspired by Ebenezer Howard's publication *Tomorrow, a Peaceful Path to Real Reform* (1898). The plan for garden cities of about 58,000 souls surrounded by an agricultural belt was put into operation by the founding in 1903 of the First Garden City Limited, which began work on Letchworth Garden City in 1904. The architects were Barry Parker and Raymond Unwin, who were subsequently involved in Hampstead Garden Suburb near London (1909). There, with others such as Sir Edwin Lutyens and Baillie Scott, they developed the character already formed in Letchworth of the archetypal picturesque development, deriving much from Voysey and the Arts and Crafts movement. A comparison of a Baillie Scott house with

one of Tony Garnier's proposed dwellings in the Cité Industrielle—both for the same sort of occupant and of similar size—shows that whereas the Garnier houses are compact little cubes, each room clearly divided from the next by solid walls, the Baillie Scott house has rooms leading one into another with a continuity of space, and with an outside patio designed as an integral part of the house. It is possible that the Garden City houses were among the first manifestations of the twentieth-century national nostalgia movements which reached a peak between the wars.

In 1907 a German ex-diplomat Hermann Muthesius founded the Deutscher Werkbund on principles not dissimilar to the English Arts and Crafts movement—namely the involvement of good designers

in production; but with the significant difference that Muthesius wanted to see good designers involved in industrial production, in order to raise the standard of industrial design. In the same year, Peter Behrens (1868–1940) was appointed to design virtually everything produced by the German electrical company AEG, and this included electrical equipment, catalogues, letterheadings, packaging, and posters, as well as their buildings. Behrens's turbine hall (1908–9) was a land-mark in the development of modern architecture, in that it is largely devoid of ornament, being reduced to the elements of an enormous shed, making significant use of iron and glass. It is a solid heavy building, conveying a suitably appropriate image for turbines. In creating the climate for new ideas Behrens's work was particularly influential, since Walter Gropius, Mies van der Rohe, and Le Corbusier all spent some time working in his office.

In 1908 one of the most significant architectural essays of the century was published: *Ornament and Crime* by the Viennese architect Adolf Loos (1870–1933). It is likely that part of the inspiration behind this essay was a dislike of what Loos considered the overweening arrogance of Art Nouveau architects in demanding the right to be able to design everything. Part of the inspiration might also have derived from a reaction against the ubiquitous Baroque and neo-Baroque stucco decoration in Vienna, and part

THE WERKBUND THEATRE: ART NOUVEAU STYLING

Henri van de Velde (1863–1957) painter by training and leader of Art Nouveau, designed this theatre as part of the 1914 Cologne Werkbund exhibition. His interest in pure line, more apparent in earlier curvilinear plans for the building, shows in the treatment of the exterior – particularly of the flowing entrance façade. The powerful massing of the theatre is notable, as is the introduction of the tripartite stage inside. This allowed the producer to use all or part at any one time, thus easing scene changes and giving the opportunity to intensify dramatic impact.

Left: View from the edge of the orchestra pit up the auditorium. Doors at the back lead into the main entrance foyer, with doors on both sides in the foreground, to side foyers. The 600-seat theatre has no obstruction between audience and stage. There is an interesting contrast between the rectangularity of the ceiling and wall panels, and the flowing decoration within them.

Above: The cutaway in the drawing shows the auditorium without boxes. The theatre has a sunken orchestra pit, and movable columns on the huge semi-circular stage which were used to divide it into three when required.

Right: Stairs from the main entrance foyer down to one of the two side foyers, compensating for the change in levels caused by the raked auditorium. There are Art Nouveau touches in the sculpture, the glass in the foyer doors downstairs, doorhandles and in the attempt to mellow the rectangularity of the archway.

DAS BAUGEBIET, VOM MONTE
GENEROSO GESEHEN

Above: Bruno Taut's visionary images of glass in 'Alpine Architektur', 1919, have a semi-mystical flavour, as though glass and light in themselves could help man's condition. The proposals exploited the opportunities of new materials and the uplifting image of the Alps. Many such Expressionist schemes strove to accentuate the 'essence' of the project in physical form.

might have been a gentle attempt at poking fun. Be that as it may, Loos argued that architects should concentrate on producing buildings which were in themselves beautiful without the necessity for adornment. This theory was highly influential, and his Steiner house in Vienna (1910) demonstrated his principles in action—producing on the garden front an unadorned, and consequently a rather unattractive and lumpish, building, whose principal innovation (the absence of decoration of any sort) contrasted strangely with the classically symmetrical façade. Loos's own buildings were among the first to give greater importance to interior comfort, convenience and beauty than to the exterior, anticipating still current architectural attitudes, and if his essay can be taken as an attack on Art Nouveau, then it was apposite: few of the Art Nouveau architects who produced good

buildings between 1895 and 1905 continued to develop. By 1908 the style was already working itself out, and by 1914 there were more potent images on which to hang architectural theory.

These new images, of course, had to do with technology and transport. In 1914 in Italy the *Futurist Manifesto* was published, which proclaimed that 'everything must be revolutionized. Architecture is breaking loose from tradition. It is forcibly starting from scratch again.' Among the architects involved were Antonio Sant'Elia and Mario Chiattone. Sant'Elia's Città Nuova project contained a proposal for a gigantic development above a road/rail interchange. His fellow Futurist, Marinetti, stated: 'We declare that the world's splendour has been enriched by a new beauty, the beauty of speed. A racing motor car, its frame adorned with great pipes, like snakes with explosive breath, . . . a roaring motor car which looks as though it were running on shrapnel is more beautiful than the Victory of Samothrace.' Sant'Elia foresaw massive machine-like buildings, integrating elevators, galleries, beacons and wireless telegraphy; Marinetti became a minister under Mussolini, whose trains ran on time.

1914 was also the year of the Werkbund

Exhibition of Industrial Art in Cologne, three of whose buildings were of particular significance. The Werkbund Theatre was designed by Henri van de Velde (1863–1957), an Art Nouveau architect who had been a director of the Weimar School of Applied Arts since 1906. The theatre is symmetrical, but it retains the curves and character of Art Nouveau both in its entrance front and the way the roof steps up to articulate the seat space within the theatre, rising from its lowest point at the entrance, over the auditorium, to its greatest height above the stage. In contrast to the theatre is the model factory and office building designed by Walter Gropius and Adolf Meyer. The administration block is a severe brick rectangle flanked by two glass-enclosed stairs, which by nature of their function are permitted to be curved. The factory behind is a simple shed. This building contains several portents for the future, being austere, undecorated, and rectangular, relieved only by the stair towers, which are clad, like the rear of the building, entirely in glass. This is the first notable use of the technique known as glass curtain walling, in which a glass skin acts purely as a weather enclosure for the building, having no structural function whatsoever. Three years

Left: The Vesnin brothers' grim, battleship-like Palace of Labour proposal, 1923, exemplifies two of the Constructivist preoccupations: first to be bigger than anybody else, and second, the fascination with the paraphernalia of communications. The design is a product of architects trying not to be architects, but constructional engineers.

Right above: Nervi's aircraft hangar at Orbetello, Italy, 1939–40, is a beautiful example of an engineer turning functional requirements into elegance.

Right below: Engineer Eugène Freyssinet's hangars at Orly, France, 1916. These have a spare elegance despite their huge size. By contrast, the engineer sees no shame in a beautiful design, albeit a result, rather than a precondition.

Design, subsequently renamed the Bauhaus. In the same year, the De Stijl group of artists and architects, including architect J.J.P. Oud (subsequently City Architect of Rotterdam) and the painter Piet Mondrian, was formed in Holland. Their concern with planes of light and purity of shape together with the use of primary colours was to have an enormous influence on aesthetics. The less fortunate Sant'Elia was killed in the war leading an attack.

The war accelerated improvements in technology—notably in vehicles and aircraft—and one of the first significant combinations of a new use with a new structure, made possible by new materials, were the hangars at Orly airport, designed for airships in 1916 by the engineer Eugène Freyssinet (1879–1962). They were the first of many structures designed by engineers in the twentieth century which were to influence architectural design, and probably came as close as possible to the idea of a building or structure which could be beautiful in itself—nude and without adornment. These Orly hangars were probably the first buildings to exploit the opportunities offered by reinforced concrete and the sight of a clear, unsupported span of over 75 metres (250 feet)—a cathedral could have fitted inside it—must have been incredible to contemporaries.

The most important changes caused by the war were political, in particular the Russian Revolution of 1917 and the German Revolution of 1918. However, there were social changes in Britain and France, and the great European empires were broken up to create independent states, which would last until the follow-

later Gropius (1883–1969) succeeded Van de Velde as director of the Weimar School. The third important building was the Glass Pavilion of Bruno Taut (City Architect of Magdeburg after the War) constructed almost entirely of glass blocks and a steel frame. Taut was a strong believer in the use of glass in buildings and, after the War, designed several Expressionist, imaginary schemes using glass.

These pioneer architects and buildings were the exceptions during this period, and the increasing simplicity and austerity of their buildings must have contrasted strangely with the opulence of Edwardian drawing rooms, of new city banks, and of imperial magnificence at large. However, advances had been made: first in the use of new materials—iron and steel, and concrete; secondly in the involvement of the architect in the wider role of replanning

cities; and thirdly in the establishment of an austere style appropriate to the time, and one which was to gain greater importance after the First War had ended. But although any rigid requirements for classical façades, symmetrical layout or historically inspired details had been largely dispensed with, no single architectural theory was yet predominant.

THE FIRST WORLD WAR AND AFTER—FERMENT AND CONSOLIDATION

To some extent art and architecture managed to transcend the First World War. Le Corbusier remained in Switzerland, corresponding with engineer friends in Paris. In 1917, when most of the attention of the western world was on the Western Front, Walter Gropius was appointed as head of the Weimar School of

ing war. For a short time after the war the revulsion against the old order (which had caused the war and its horrendous loss of life) led to a way of thinking which rejected the old empires (and their style and methods of doing things) in favour of the new world—a world which would make full use of developments in technology in order to further social aims. It was the beginning of the age of mass popular movements. Consequently, Tony Garnier's vision of the architect involved in socially useful work was partly realized. Indeed, in the early days after the war, a number of prominent German architects, including Gropius, Mies van der Rohe and Taut, were actively involved in socialist politics, presaging a significant feature of twentieth-century architectural life. For example, for two years (1928–30) the Bauhaus was under the control of the Marxist Hannes Meyer. City architects were appointed to several European cities to carry out works for the people—housing estates, schools and similar works—and some of the pioneering works of this period were produced by City Architects in Rotterdam, Vienna, Frankfurt, Magdeburg and Hilversum. In Britain, the government coined the phrase 'Homes fit for heroes' as its first explicit commitment to providing the masses with decent housing, and a Commission produced a group of typical house types and layouts which provided a basic design, influential virtually until the end of the following war.

A new grim purposefulness was in the air and nowhere more so than in Russia where the visionaries, by exploiting technology to its fullest extent, hoped to drag

the country through several centuries of development within a few years. The birth of this new nation of enormous size seems to have generated a demand for self-confidence and self-expression, to the extent that one may infer the intention of many early Russian buildings of the period to be the biggest, the best, the most far advanced, and the most prepared to use modern methods. Thus the project by Leonid, Alexander and Victor Vesnin for the Palace of Labour (1923) included a hall for 8,000 spectators, a restaurant which could accommodate 6,000 at one sitting, museums, a library and a variety of other functions including a radio station. The top of the building was to be decorated like the bridge of a battleship, with air funnels, radio masts, wires and a square

tower. The chances are that had it been built, it would have been very unlovely when seen from the street.

The Russian architects, generically known as Constructivists, declared war on art and style and identified architecture with construction—in particular making the construction and technology of a building its most important visual characteristic. Indeed, a number of Constructivist projects such as Tatlin's Monument to the Third International (1919–20) and Lissitzky's Lenin Tribune (1920) displayed a harsh engineering aesthetic. The Constructivists' theories were to become an integral part of the Modern Movement, to the extent that the 'honest expression' of a building's structure is still regarded as a virtue. Yet Le Corbusier, whilst appearing to endorse this view with comments like 'A house is a machine for living in', also states later on in his book *Vers une Architecture*: 'Architecture is lowered to the level of its utilitarian purposes: boudoirs, WC's, radiators, ferro-concrete, vault or pointed arches, etc. etc. This is construction, this is not architecture. Architecture only exists when there is poetic emotion.'

The identification, however, of architecture with structure meant that the influence of engineers always remained strong. Freyssinet continued building concrete bridges (notably the Elorn Estuary bridge in 1926), harbours and water tanks. In Switzerland, Robert Maillart was responsible for a number of outstandingly slender and beautiful bridges, whose innovation was that the track along the top was an integral part of the structure, instead of being laid upon it. In Britain the engineer Owen Williams designed a pioneering concrete and glass factory (Boots at Beeston, Nottinghamshire), two famous newspaper offices, and some social services buildings; and in Italy the new Fiat works in Turin, designed by Mattei Trucco in 1927, showed a strong engineering influence—particularly in providing the structure for a car-testing track actually on its roof. The continuing interest in engineering led to a revival of admiration for Gustave Eiffel, the influence of whose metal structures might arguably be seen in the John Hancock building in Chicago (Skidmore Owens Merrill, 1970), and in the adulation shown for the beautiful concrete structures of the Italian engineer Pier Luigi Nervi.

But as far as the pioneers were concerned, the first influence was the De Stijl group from Holland which had got off to an early start in 1917. Its inspiration lay in an artistic preoccupation with the interplay of flat planes and primary colours, and the group was engrossed by the question of whether architecture as a physical medium could reproduce the harmonies and values of painting. Buildings designed according to its precepts include the housing schemes by J.J.P. Oud (1890–1963) in Rotterdam which were very severe, plain in impact and entirely devoid of ornamentation, the house designed by Gerrit Rietveld in Utrecht in 1924, and the Restaurant Aubette in Strasbourg, designed in 1928 by Theo Van Doesburg, the leader of the De Stijl group.

The other predominant 'style' of the pioneers immediately after the war was termed Expressionism, and many notable architects claimed allegiance to it until its replacement by the so-called 'International Style' from about 1927. Expressionist architecture denied any absolute rules save the total independence of the creative spirit to do what it thought best, and it was thus dubbed antirational or irrational. In practice, the buildings which were termed Expressionist were modern in the sense that they eschewed historic styles and made full use of new techniques where appropriate, but they also tried to express something else as well—perhaps the character or the use of the building. Most of the resulting buildings were of great individuality and interest, having a 'fantastic' common denominator, good examples being Peter Behrens's Hoechst Dye Works headquarters, the entrance hall of which is an amazing concatenation of many coloured bricks, Hans Poelzig's Grosses Schauspielhaus in Berlin

(1919), in which the ceiling has been transformed into a stalactite-encrusted dome above a circular stage, and Erich Mendelsohn's Einsteinsturm, designed between 1919 and 1921 to be Einstein's workshop and laboratory. Mendelsohn's drawings are every bit as Expressionist as his buildings and illustrate some of his design criteria—the streamlining of shapes, the dramatic profile, the contrast between rectangle and curve, and the contrast between vertical and horizontal. His sketch for the Schocken store is as sleek as a new car.

Although in each of these buildings there is little or no applied decoration, the impact of the form is very decorative indeed, and is a long way from designing everything down to the bare minimum as was being practised by the De Stijl group. Two contemporary buildings in Northern Europe which have particularly close affinities with Expressionist ideals are P.V.J. Klint's Grundtvig Church in Copenhagen (1913–26) which is an enormous brick church whose west front is reminiscent of organ pipes, the whole being strongly allied to historic Danish church

Left: Klint's Grundtvig Church, Copenhagen, 1920. Northern Europe seemed set to develop a speciality in the imaginative use of brick. Although the form of the church is traditional, the west front simulates massed organ pipes; the interior is not dissimilar to Behren's Dye Works entrance in the way that richness is created by brickwork.

Right: Mendelsohn's Einsteinsturm, Potsdam, East Germany, completed 1920. It contains a telescope, laboratories, a study and sleeping quarters. Owing to the shortage of concrete it was built in brick and covered in concrete, instead of being mass-concrete. Mendelsohn called it a 'mystical building'.

Below: De Klerk's Eigen Haard housing scheme, Amsterdam, 1913–19. Brick combined with a romantic roofscape, sinuous curves, and bay windows. The subtleties of this Expressionism did not survive the puritan, geometric shapes of Dudok.

forms; and the unusual Eigen Haard housing scheme designed by Michel de Klerk in Amsterdam and completed in 1921. This building also uses brick—the vernacular material—and is a highly romantic assembly of elaborately curved pantile roofs, projecting windows, towers and patterned brickwork.

The next phase consolidates the influence of the moderns. When Walter Gropius took up his position as the successor to Van de Velde as Director of the Weimar School of Applied Arts, it was re-christened the Weimar State Bauhaus (or School of Building). The intention was to end the divorce between art and craft and

to achieve buildings and their furnishings designed by a team of artists/craftsmen as part of a collective effort to unify the whole. Students at the Bauhaus were therefore instructed in materials, in their usage and in their opportunities. In 1923 Gropius held an exhibition of Bauhaus work, to justify his ideas to a public rather wary of modern innovations, but in 1925 increasing local opposition forced him to remove the Bauhaus from Weimar to Dessau. The new campus in Dessau, designed by Gropius, became one of the first large public demonstrations of the new architecture. The workshops block was enclosed in a refined glass curtain wall

and was linked to the teaching block on the other side of the road by an administration block in the form of a bridge raised on stilts. There was no extraneous detail on this building, the effect being achieved by a contrast between white painted solids and black horizontal window openings, and horizontal balconies on a dormitory block. It is a factory-like, austere building, a public demonstration of the belief that building, refined to its bare essentials, could be beautiful.

From 1918, the expatriate Swiss architect, Charles-Édouard Jeanneret (1887–1966), under the pseudonym Le Corbusier, had been writing essays in the publication *L'Esprit Nouveau*, and in 1923 they were published collectively in his book *Vers une Architecture*. The book is an anti-humbug manifesto, full of exhortations such as 'A great epoch has begun. There exists a new spirit.' The underlying message of the book is that each previous generation whose architecture is admired had developed an architecture appropriate to the times, whereas the buildings in which most people were living in the 1920s were totally unsuited to their age. It was a matter of restating the problem and making the best use of modern materials. Le Corbusier said, 'Architecture is the masterly, correct and magnificent play of masses brought together in light', and he extolled the virtues of pure form, in the juxtaposition of the primary forms of spheres, cubes, rectangles and cylinders. In this Le Corbusier was not alone: in 1923 Walter Gropius said, 'We want a clear, organic architecture, whose inner logic will be radiant and naked, unencumbered

Left: The Schröder house, Utrecht, Netherlands, by Rietveld, 1924. A cubist, intellectual exercise in contrasting planes and colours, thus totally different from the emerging International Style, with its emphasis upon a complete and unified exterior.

Below: The purpose-designed Bauhaus buildings, Dessau, East Germany, 1925, by Gropius. The curtain-walling on the right encloses the workshops, whilst the two-storey bridge crossing the road houses the administration, linking the workshops to the teaching block on the left. A block of student flats is beyond the bridge.

Right: Inside the first floor of the Villa Savoye, Poissy, France, 1929–31 by Le Corbusier. The all-encircling façade conceals the existence of this outdoor terrace. The glazed doors open into the living area. The main living quarters are L-shaped, enclosing the terrace. The ramp on the right goes up to the rooftop solarium, as well as down to the ground-floor entrance.

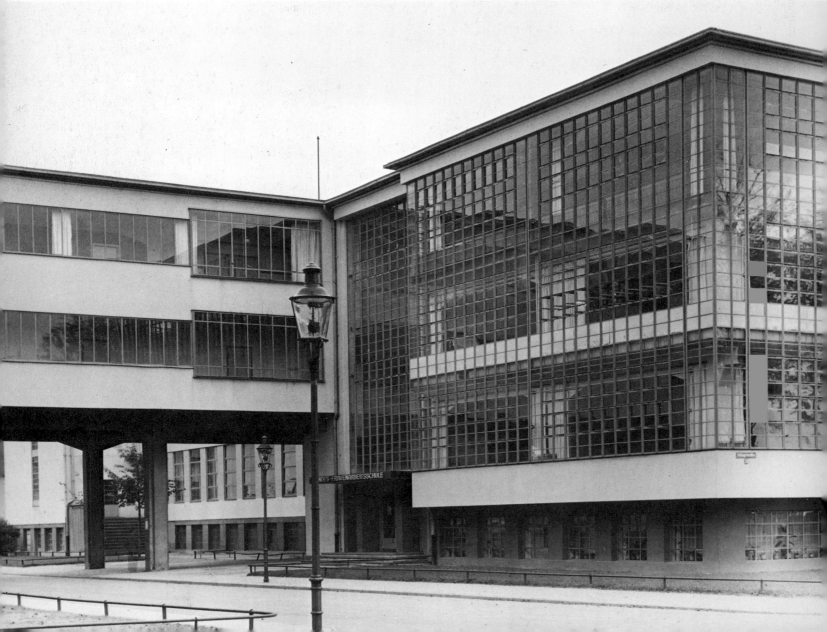

by lines, façades and trickery: we want an architecture adapted to our world of machines, radios and fast motor cars, an architecture whose function is clearly recognizable in relation to its form.' As became clearer over the years, Le Corbusier's buildings created magic out of the 'magnificent play of masses in light', whereas the 'inner logic' of Gropius's buildings rarely achieved this. Gropius's real importance in architecture was as a teacher and theorist, both in Germany before 1928 and thereafter in the USA.

Le Corbusier's other major preoccupation was continuing the investigation of the production of houses in order to identify the minimum base of the house (commonly known as the Dom-ino house), and consequently the possibility of producing houses on a production line, like cars. To this end he designed a prototype

house capable of mass-production, which he christened 'Citrohan' as a pun on the French mass produced car 'Citroën'. The major innovations in his approach are exemplified in the luxurious Villa Savoye at Poissy, which was designed in 1929. The building is liberated from the ground by being lifted up on free-standing columns (called *pilotis*); the house has a flat roof with a garden or solarium, a free internal plan, and the outdoors and the indoors are integrated within the all-embracing form. Le Corbusier has freed the structure from the external walls, and the floors and walls are all able to extend beyond the supporting columns. This is clearly demonstrated by the long strip windows, which would have collapsed if inserted in load-bearing walls. The Villa Savoye also creates pleasure from the contrast between the rectangular and the

cylindrical. Even after forty years of experimentation with modern materials and new forms, the Villa Savoye still delights with its freedom of internal planning, its openness and its light.

Back in the old world, as it were, the revivalist, escapist and nationalist movements were gaining momentum. At the one end of the market, banks and commercial buildings were still adopting a ponderous style with classical connotations, while at the other end, particularly in pubs and consumer-orientated buildings, there was a continuing revival of traditional historic details. Some revivalist construction was excellent, and it is worth mentioning Sir Edwin Lutyens, who was by far the finest of the Establishment architects in England. His particular forte since the beginning of the century had been the country house, some of the best planned to stand within gardens designed by Gertrude Jekyll, and he was adept at creating a beautiful sequence of varying spaces which slip comfortably into the country house way of life. Many of the other more traditional buildings at this time were limited purely to making use of classical details on entrance façades.

1925 was the year of the Paris Arts Décoratifs Exhibition, whence the term Art Deco, this new 'style' being a direct descendant of previous decorative styles and deriving a great deal from Art Nouveau. It is interesting to note how most decoration in Art Deco buildings is not applied, but achieved largely by a manipulation of the form of the building, and by the inter-relationship of everything to do with it, such as the design of the lettering, lights, lamps, railings, carpets, ceilings, plasterwork and hoardings. Contemporary with the Jazz Age, the style was subsequently often identified with it, since certain of the effects display the same frenzied, frenetic energy. Art Deco became a full-blown consumer style, widely used throughout Europe in shop interiors, restaurants, pubs, showrooms, hotels, and notably in the rash of new factories—with particular emphasis on artefacts such as furniture, ornaments, light fittings and radios.

It is difficult to put a rigorous dividing line between the geometrics of the De Stijl group (Van Doesburg's Aubette restaurant, for example) and some Art Deco interiors. These concentrate very much upon the effective use of lines—parallel lines, the dividing of surfaces into shapes by such lines and various motifs such as the sunburst motif—with the result that an Art Deco shop in Paris would derive its character from the inter-action of the design of the lampshades, the mirrors, the wall surfaces, the furniture, the ceiling and the shop front.

In America, too, factory building had also been developing apace—notably

Albert Kahn's factories for the Ford Motor Company—but the Art Deco style as such was mainly reserved in the American form of 'Moderne' for the decoration of the entrances and the tops of skyscrapers. The skyscraper decoration fad could be seen as the last flowering of Victorian eclecticism, insofar as some skyscrapers, such as the Chicago Tribune Building by Raymond Hood, were decorated with Gothic forms, whereas others such as the sunburst-capped Chrysler building or Radio City chose more modern forms. One might wonder at the tremendous efforts put by architects into a highly stylized capping for the high blocks, since after all the result would only ever be appreciated from a distance, so far were they from street level. But the spirit of the time appears to have been less concerned with the style of the top of the skyscrapers, than with their sheer scale—the tallest characteristically became the most famous (the Empire State Building).

Left above: The Alfa Romeo showroom, Paris, by Robert Mallet-Stevens, 1925, exemplifies an earlier angular Art Deco.

Left below: The Hoover factory, London, by Wallis Gilbert, 1932–5, blends impure, popular Art Deco with borrowings from Egypt, the Aztecs, and Mendelsohn.

Right: Dudok's Hilversum Town Hall, Netherlands, 1928–30, whose brick geometrics were very influential.

Below: The Woolwich Odeon, London, 1937, designed by George Coles. The Odeon house-style was distinctively 'moderne'.

CIAM AND ITS ADHERENTS

In 1927, the Deutscher Werkbund organized a new exhibition in Stuttgart, the most important part of which was the housing estate at Weissenhof, which the vice-chairman of the exhibition, Ludwig Mies van der Rohe (1886–1969), was asked to design. In fact Mies chose to design only one large block of flats himself, and called together some of the most outstanding forward thinkers of Europe to design the remainder, and thus to Weissenhof came Le Corbusier (France), J.J.P. Oud and Mart Stam (Holland), Josef Frank (Austria), and Walter Gropius, Peter Behrens, Hans Poelzig, Bruno Taut, Hans Scharoun, Ludwig Hilbersheimer and Max Taut (Germany)—among others —all to contribute to an estate which was designed for permanent use. Today the Weissenhof estate still remains a permanent exhibition of the different approaches these various architects brought to modern buildings. The differences are striking. Some of the houses were built on steel-frame construction, and some of reinforced concrete. Some are exciting, making inventive use of new materials, and some are plain and simple. However, two common features stand out: first the fact that most of them were designed with mass-production in mind, and secondly the uniformity of their external appearance; an austere approach, allowing for effect upon the plane, form and shadow. The similarity between these buildings is so strong that it was encapsulated a few years later in a book by Philip Johnson and Henry-Russell Hitchcock entitled *The International Style*.

The Weissenhof exhibition was also a public demonstration of an explicit social commitment—the putting of architectural skills to the service of the public and particularly to the service of the poor. No monuments these, but houses for the people—and some of the participants of Weissenhof, notably Oud in Rotterdam, were already in charge of very large housing programmes. The fact that it had been planned as an estate was a portent for the future, in that architects became particularly interested in the wider interests of town planning, as a logical development of an interest in designing for people. Although as long ago as 1923, Le Corbusier had published designs for a city for three million people, novel features of which had included building high to release the land at ground level for park plans and traffic segregation, nothing had actually come of this.

The following year, 1928, many of the architects involved at Weissenhof formed the Congrès Internationaux d'Architecture Moderne (CIAM) which created an international climate of architectural ideas lasting certainly until the late 1950s. Among the many aims for which CIAM stood was the involvement of architects in town planning or 'putting architecture back on its real plane, the economic and social plane', and secondly the enthronement of the machine: 'The most efficacious production is derived from rationalization and subsidization.'

The pattern books of this modern era, particularly appropriate to buildings of the International Style, were the glossy architectural magazines which exercised a tremendously powerful influence. They contained beautiful black-and-white photographs of new developments, which were taken so as to enhance the contrast between the man-made artefact and the natural world. In many cases, they gave false impressions of the buildings by showing them gleaming white against an artificially darkened sky, and by presenting them as though they were sculptures in space. The influence of these glossy magazines had considerable dangers, not least in that it was impossible to tell from the black-and-white photographs how far colour was integral to the buildings involved, as it certainly was to many Modern Movement buildings. That the photographs were exciting is not in dispute: but that they failed to show buildings in their settings may well have been responsible for the fact that architects of many subsequent buildings took no account of location.

It would be wrong to suppose that the pioneers were solely concerned with housing, and that they were preoccupied with

concrete or steel with concrete infill panels. Erich Mendelsohn (1887–1953) designed several department stores, including the Schocken store in Stuttgart, notable not only for its streamlined styling, but also the projecting semi-circular glass-enclosed staircase, perhaps derived from Gropius's factory at the 1914 Werkbund exhibition. In 1928 Brinkman, van der Vlugt and Mart Stam designed the Van Nelle Tobacco Factory in Rotterdam, which is notable principally for its use of curtain walling of glass as well as its rather spare detailing. Although much later, the Peter Jones department store in London

Left above: Asplund's Stockholm exhibition building, 1930. Lightweight and airy, it featured curves, hoods, glass and plenty of colour.

Left below: Mies van der Rohe's Barcelona Pavilion, 1929. With its cool, uncluttered spaces, it makes Asplund's building seem almost vulgar. The impression of luxury is conveyed by opulent spaciousness and the quality of materials.

Right: Entrance to the block of flats by Mies van der Rohe as part of the Weissenhof development, Stuttgart, West Germany, 1927: the International Style achieved at last.

Below: Beaudouin and Lods's École de Plein Air, Suresnes, France, 1935. It is a series of self-contained classrooms in the form of glass pavilions whose walls could fold back to allow open-air teaching.

(1938) by Crabtree, Slater, Moberley and Reilly, is a further development of curtain walling, except in this case it is curved to follow the street line, thus adding distinction to the building.

Another contemporary style was that of Willem Dudok (1884–1974), City Architect of Hilversum, whose Town Hall (1928) adapted the International Style into a geometric play of brick rectangles with a slender tower as a key central focus. The Hilversum Town Hall was extremely influential in northern Europe and particularly in Britain, where it represented the closest the Establishment was prepared to go towards accepting the Modern Movement. A spate of imitations was built and in 1935 Dudok was awarded the Royal Gold Medal of the Royal Institute of British Architects.

However, the brave new world that the Weissenhof exhibition and the formation of CIAM seemed to herald was not to take place, principally for political and economic reasons. The last building of the heroic period could probably be said to be the German Pavilion at the Barcelona International Exhibition designed by Mies van der Rohe in 1929. It was an extraordinary building of extremely luxurious austerity and purity, and it was impossible to tell from the outside the function, purpose or nationality of the building. Even the entrance was not obvious. It was totally devoid of the obvious characteristics of the International Style such as the long horizontal windows or contrast between black and white. Instead, the Pavilion consisted of a thin flat roof supported on thin cross-shaped steel columns. The space beneath the roof was enclosed by slabs of polished marble or glass panels, not to create rooms but merely to divide up the space into different sections according to need. This glittering interior was reflected by the use of water. It was the ultimately cool, minimum, classy design.

In the wide world outside architecture, however, Europe was in trouble. Mussolini had been entrenched in Italy for a number of years, and Hitler was on his way to power, aided by the worldwide depression and the recurrent collapses of the German economy. In Spain governments became unstable, and civil war was imminent. In Russia the revolutionary fervour had died down, and by 1929–30 Stalin was rejecting the modern Constructivists' ideals, in favour of a solid, established architecture in keeping with the solidity of the new state. Although France remained relatively unaffected until the war, it is notable how few commissions came to its most eminent architect— namely Le Corbusier—and his followers.

Two areas in Europe—Scandinavia and Britain—managed to stay relatively independent of these trends and American architecture remained completely unaffected by them. In Sweden the transition from traditional architecture to modern architecture is best seen in the works of Gunnar Asplund (1885–1940), whose Stockholm City Library (1924–7) is a severe, solid, symmetrical building in brick, displaying no traces of the new materials, of the International Style, nor of Expressionism. By contrast, his Stockholm exhibition in 1930 contained large, light, slender buildings of steel and glass with a semi-circular glass-covered staircase tower, contrasting with brightly coloured sun-blinds. The Modern Movement had arrived. The entrance to the Gothenburg Law Courts, designed later, displays affinities with the International Style (lack of decoration, severity of form and horizontal windows). More or less contemporary with this is Sven Markelius's Haslingborg Concert Hall, which is very much influenced by that style (contrasting white rendered walls and glass, banded horizontal windows, contrasts between round and flat surfaces). Possibly Asplund's most notable building is the Stockholm Forest Crematorium (1935–40), situated on the top of an artificially heightened hill, the dominant features of which are a great marble cross, and a plain covered courtyard at the entrance where a flat-roofed portico is supported on slender, equally spaced, concrete columns.

In neighbouring Finland, the key architect was Alvar Aalto (1898–1976), who brought the influence of the International Style to that country during the 1930s. His tuberculosis sanatorium (1933) in Paimio displays a lightness of glass and concrete structure, complete with long strip windows and decorative use of balconies and railings; yet the plan of the sanatorium

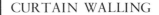

CURTAIN WALLING

A curtain wall is an enclosing wall: in modern buildings, it signifies a wall – or skin of a building – which carries no structural weight. A framed building – whether steel or concrete – removes the load from the outer walls and redistributes it evenly throughout the building. As a result, the skin – or curtain wall – has its function reduced to that of a weather shield. The drawing shows the structure of the building separate from the enclosing skin. Glazing techniques have improved dramatically since the war eliminating the need for mullions between panes of glass.

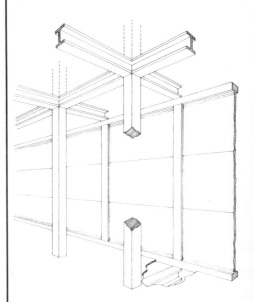

Right: The Peter Jones store, London, under construction, showing the steel frame, its lower portions already encased in concrete. Completed in 1939, the store was designed by W. Crabtree with Professor C.H. Reilly. Much of the store's character, when completed, lay in the rhythm of the deep mullions.

places more importance on the windows of the rooms being able to face south, than on conformity to some rigid rectangularity. In his later buildings, Aalto demonstrated that it was possible to interpret modern architecture with greater freedom of expression than the severe avant-garde appeared to admit, and he placed particular emphasis on natural materials. Thus he gave the puritanism of the Modern Movement a human face.

Left: The Casa del Fascio at Como, Italy, by Terragni, completed 1936. The International Style survived in Italy despite the Fascists– who in this case were even the clients.

Right: Willis Faber Dumas offices, Ipswich, England, by Foster Associates, 1975. The building occupies the entire site, with a top-lit central light-well, and curving glass skin. Tinted for solar control, the skin is hung from the top, the lower panes being attached to the upper by corner patches. Translucent silicone between panes of glass replaces mullions.

Below right: Laurel Racetrack, Maryland, USA, designed by Bennett and Brandt, 1974. Curtain walling can provide spectators with an environmentally controlled, but uninterrupted view. The glass wall is again hung from the top, stiffened by fins at right angles to the window.

Britain was the lucky recipient of those continental architects forced to leave their native countries—principally Chermayeff, Gropius, Breuer and Mendelsohn. Although most of them moved on to other countries, they were responsible for some buildings in Britain; Gropius, for example, established a partnership with Maxwell Fry who was possibly the only comparable British architect of the time.

Meanwhile, internationalism of style was out of keeping with the two fascist governments' preoccupation with their own culture and history. Hitler did not like the mass housing schemes of the Modern Movement, calling Ernst May's housing developments in Frankfurt 'cultural bolshevism'. Despite Gropius's plea to Goebbels, questioning whether Germany could afford to reject modern architecture which was in its functional usefulness 'very German', conditions were such that the Bauhaus decided to close in 1933. After this date the favoured architecture of the Thousand-Year Reich was the monumental type designed by Albert Speer—heavy, sterile, overpowering masses of stone decorated as much as anything else with flags of the swastika and with eagles. Mussolini in Italy was less rigid, and one of the purest Modern Movement buildings is the Casa del Fascio at Como (1936), designed by Giuseppe Terragni, but a neo-classical style was more popular with the Fascists, tending to represent itself by the use of semi-circular headed windows, although concrete and plainness nevertheless prevailed.

In France, an important building of this last decade was Le Corbusier's hostel for Swiss students at Paris University, which already showed significant departures from the accepted International Style aesthetics in the use of a curved solid wall indicating the presence of the staircase as well as a glass curtain wall. He also designed a Salvation Army hostel in Paris which refined certain modern techniques

Above: Nazi Stadium Zeppelinfeld, Nürnberg, West Germany, begun 1934, by Albert Speer. Although it is not classical in any pure sense, there are many classical echoes, and it skilfully overwhelms human beings.

Left: The EUR building, near Rome, begun 1938, by Marcello Piacentini. Planned as a permanent exhibition of Fascist achievement, the entire complex was never finished.

Right: A military tower in Jersey, part of the Nazi-erected coastal defences of the Channel Islands. Wholly utilitarian, virtually indestructible, yet not without some grace.

even further. The firm Beaudoin and Lods designed some housing estates (including the first point block in 1933) and the Maison du Peuple at Clichy in collaboration with Jean Prouvé, a manufacturer of steel and aluminium panels who had already exerted considerable influence over architects in the previous ten years and would continue to do so long after the Second World War. In general, however, Modern Movement French architects lacked the backing of City Architects'

Departments that existed in Holland and Germany. The school at Villejuif (1931–3) by André Lurçat is exceptional in that he consulted educationalists, teachers and doctors while preparing his plans, and perhaps the apotheosis of what the Modern Movement had been trying to achieve is represented by Beaudoin and Lods's École de Plein Air at Suresness (1935–6). If, as Victor Hugo had said, the only enemy was darkness and ignorance, which led to illness and crime, here was the answer: a school—a socially useful building—whose glass walls could fold back, permitting openness, light, fresh air and health. The 1937 Paris International Exhibition more or less turned away from this stream of architecture and there were few further architectural developments until after the war.

A look at British architecture during this period illustrates very clearly the battle of styles that was taking place. The Dudok influence permeated town halls, and later hospitals and schools; buildings with Classical or Georgian styling were still being designed and constructed as headquarters of companies, city offices, or country houses; Art Deco styling was used for factories, some shops and particularly cinemas; most public authority housing in high-density areas was of neo-Georgian blocks of four-storey flats grouped around courtyards; the greatest amount of building was in the suburban detached or semi-detached houses whose aesthetic was divided between the neo-traditional (Tudorbethan) or the Art Deco with its sunburst motif; a considerable influence was being exerted by the new underground stations being designed for London Transport by Charles Holden, some of which, such as Southgate or Arnos Grove station, were almost space age in appearance; and finally, there were a few, isolated Modern Movement buildings. These tended to be private houses by architects such as Connell, Ward and Lucas, blocks of flats such as Highpoint in London designed by Tecton, and rare buildings such as the Impington Village College in Cambridgeshire by Walter Gropius and Maxwell Fry, or the De La Warr Seaside Pavilion, Bexhill, by Chermayeff and Mendelsohn.

Cinemas in Britain provided the most widespread use of the Art Deco style. Films, like buildings, are image-makers. Because cinemas were governed by commercial pressures, both the image and speed of construction were extremely important. Probably the largest chain of cinemas in Britain was the Odeon chain

which was founded by Oscar Deutsch, and mostly designed by architect Harry Weedon, or other architects working in conjunction with him. Deutsch maintained that although he could not solve the problems of the poor, he could provide them with some hours of comfort each week. The cinemas were plush (the interior design was conceived as a unity by Mrs Deutsch) and speedily built. Three-thousand seat structures, usually built on a steel frame, and faced with faience tiles, were started and completed within seven months; and although each Odeon was different, each had sufficient of the brand image to make it clearly identifiable and welcoming wherever it was located.

The Second World War effectively brought to an end this period of architectural development, and virtually nothing of note was designed or built in Europe during that time. Perhaps the only exceptions were the buildings constructed by Germany along the Atlantic Wall which, apart from being quite spectacular in themselves, helped to continue the development in the use of reinforced concrete. After the war, many of the considerable technological innovations made during the war were evident in the development of prefabricated buildings, the greatly increased speed of construction, the wider use of engineering and the further development of technology. Furthermore, this war was the agent of even greater social changes than its predecessor. Throughout Europe the balance tipped firmly towards social buildings—that is to say, buildings commissioned by governments and local authorities. Another consequence of the

war was that after 1946 what had previously been called Western architecture became, to all intents and purposes, worldwide architecture.

The USA is something of a special case. Apart from the buildings of Richard Neutra and the exile Rudolf Schindler (whose Lovell Beach House in California (1926) was a pioneering example of the Modern Movement, using concrete and glass to provide a free-flowing and airy structure) the principal interest still rested with Frank Lloyd Wright, who had, as it were, gone into abeyance for most of the twenties and thirties. However, between 1935 and 1937 he built what is probably his most famous house, Falling Water, Bear Run, Pennsylvania, which consists of a series of floors cantilevered out over a waterfall. Development in technology had enabled him to abandon the pitched roof of his previous houses and to execute a design—namely layers of concrete interspersed with layers of glass—that so fits into the landscape as to make it appear as though it were growing from it. His other notable building of the period, the Johnson

Wax Building, Racine, Wisconsin (1936–9), has several innovations: the junction between the curved red-brick wall and the roof is replaced by glass tubing which acts as the clerestory into the offices within, and the structure of the offices themselves is a very forest of tapering concrete columns, mushroom shaped.

It was to America that some of the most distinguished exiles from Europe finally came: Marcel Breuer, Walter Gropius, Mies van der Rohe, Erich Mendelsohn. Walter Gropius went to teach at Harvard, and subsequently founded the Architects Collaborative which was responsible, among many buildings, for the Harvard Graduate Centre. The most influential of these exiles, however, was to be Mies van der Rohe. In 1938 he began a twenty-year stint as Director of the School of Architecture at the Illinois Institute of Technology; his campus buildings for the IIT, begun in 1946, illustrate his approach. The components of the buildings have been refined as much as possible, in keeping with Mies's saying 'Almost nothing'. They consist of what are really a series of rectangular

boxes, constructed of brick, glass, and steel, formally laid out. There is virtually no symbolism in these buildings, distinguishing the function of one from another, the assumption being that everybody on the campus would already know the purpose of each building. The only exception was the School of Architecture itself, which is purely a steel and glass building raised from the ground and reached by a flight of steps, which gives it a rather more imposing air than some of the others. This clear-span structure had already been tested in his Farnsworth House, Plano, Illinois (1945–50) which is a country holiday house consisting entirely of a steel-framed rectangle, partly enclosed with glass, approached up a double flight of steps and apparently suspended in air from its steel frame. Not a cheap house, nor even a homely house, but one nevertheless that was refined to the minimum of what was necessary, and no more: almost nothing. An interesting comparison can be made with his skeleton steel-framed high buildings, such as the Lakeshore Drive Apartments or the 1956 Seagram Building in New York (in association with Philip Johnson) in which the towers would appear to have been reduced to almost nothing in terms of decorative effect. However, this is not actually the case, since the metal beams running down the side of the building are not in fact those which hold up the structure, for those are inside, encased in concrete as fire regulations demanded. They are beams used as window mullions, which are at the same time supposed to be informative as to the nature of the structure within. The effort devoted to the external appearance was justified by Mies on the grounds that the use of the building would change, and that its interior should be designed to permit this. Therefore architectural skills should be concentrated on those aspects which would not change—such as the exterior.

Also of considerable importance at this time was the construction of Philip Johnson's own glass house, New Canaan, Connecticut, in 1949. Johnson was one of the two authors who in 1932 had christened the new architecture the 'International Style'. His own house, in contrast to Mies's Farnsworth house, is a steel-framed rectangle sitting on a brick plinth on the top of a rise, with a doorway in each wall. There is an off-centre brick tower which contains the services. The house is set in private parkland, approached by a sinuous path, which sometimes reveals and sometimes conceals it;

it is as though the house is the climax of this private parkland and, at the same time, the place where shelter is provided in inclement weather. The setting is quite beautiful, and as an expression of refinement the house would be difficult to beat. It is negative, in the way that what matters in this building to those who are outside is the inside, or what is happening there, while to those who are inside what matters is the view outside. The building and its components have been reduced to a minimum. The building might be com-

Far left: 'Falling Water' house, Pennsylvania, USA, by Frank Lloyd Wright, 1936. The building almost grows out of the landscape.

Bottom: Architecture Faculty building, Illinois Institute of Technology, Chicago, USA, by Mies van der Rohe, 1946. This is a pure, impersonal steel and glass temple, with as much below ground as visible above it.

Below: Philip Johnson's own glass house in New Caanan, Connecticut, USA, 1949. Another kind of shrine, with the building's presence reduced to a minimum.

pared with Palladio's Villa Capra which has a similar setting, but which offers a more positive contribution to the landscape by way of porticoes, steps and statues.

An architectural critic prior to becoming an architect, Philip Johnson was more aware of the issues than most. In an illuminating address to Harvard students in 1954 he outlined what he called the seven crutches of modern architecture; and by doing so exposed many of the underlying myths of the Modern Movement.

'The most important crutch in recent times is not valid now: the Crutch of History. In the old days you could always rely on books.

The Crutch of Pretty Drawing: it's a wonderful crutch because you can give yourself the illusion that you are creating architecture while you're making pretty drawings. Architecture is something you build and put together.

The Crutch of Utility: they say a building is good architecture if it works. Merely that a building works is not sufficient. You expect that it works. If the business of getting the house to run well takes precedence over your artistic invention the result won't be architecture at all: merely an assemblage of useful parts.

The Crutch of Comfort: after all, what is architecture for but the comforts of the people living there? But when that is made into a crutch for doing architecture, environmental control starts to replace architecture.

The Crutch of Cheapness: anybody that can build a $25,000 house has indeed reason to be proud, but is he talking about architecture or his economic ability?

The Crutch of Serving the Client: serving the client is one thing, the art of architecture is another.

The Crutch of Structure: structure is a very dangerous thing to cling to. You can be led to believe that clear structure clearly expressed will end up being architecture by itself. You say "I don't have to design any more. All I have to do is make a clear structural order."

I like Corbusier's definition of architecture. The play of forms under the light. And, my friends, that's all it is. You can embellish architecture by putting the toilets in. But there was great architecture before the toilet was invented . . .' (Abridged.)

An important building contemporary with the glass house was the house built by Charles Eames for himself at Santa Monica in California, which is a steel-framed building, constructed entirely from prefabricated units as they were available from manufacturers' catalogues. For this reason it could be termed a prefabricated house, suitable for mass-production. One interesting point is that in order to ensure that the glass plane of the studio window is perceived as a plane, the glass is wired so that it can be clearly seen. This 'case-study house', as Eames called it, showed that houses *could* be assembled from a kit of parts, but also that this route was more likely to be followed by architects trying to prove a social or technological point than by those trying to build homes. The factory aesthetic is a very personal taste.

In all these buildings, traditional symbolism has either been designed out altogether, or replaced by the symbolism of the components from which the buildings are constructed. Traditional features like doors, entrances, roofs, eaves, and windows have more or less disappeared, to the extent that unless a doorway is signified by a canopy or approach of steps, it can sometimes only be discovered by pressing a variety of glass panels to see which one opens.

Back in Europe, the principal task was reconstruction. In the countries dominated by Russia—notably Eastern Europe—which by this time was far from being avant-garde in its architectural approach, many of the historic towns and cities were, and still are being, restored with considerable care. Restoration was also carried out in towns like Augsburg and Munich. However, there are other towns such as Rotterdam, and notably in England such as Coventry and central Bristol, where advantage was taken of the bomb damage to reorganize the layout of the cities, rezone their activities and do away with all the small streets and narrow alleys. Some

Right: Eames's house and studio, Santa Monica, California, USA, 1949: a creative use of out-of-the-catalogue components.

SYSTEM BUILDING

System building was introduced to speed the rate of construction and reduce the cost. It consisted of preparing prefabricated, mass-produced components which could be easily erected on site. The system shown here is 'heavy', using concrete panels which were manufactured on site. Other systems – particularly used for schools immediately after the Second World War – included 'light', large span steel structures, which offered a variety of wall panels to clip into a standard steel framework. This permitted considerable flexibility in the location of internal partitions.

Left: The half-complete building shows how the system comes together. The stacked panels awaiting erection are mostly external wall panels, with window embrasures cast in.

Below: Each manufacturer had his own system. Here a Wates precast, load-bearing panel is being lowered into position to be fixed as the drawing on the left indicates.

Right: Precast wall and floor panels are locked together and laid in concrete. Wall panels are storey-height and include cast-in electric conduits, and fixing blocks for skirting. One crane and a 6-man erection team could erect 5½ dwellings per week. Wall panels are fixed upright with adjustable props (not shown) until set – within 24 hours. The system can be used for buildings of 21 or more storeys.

Levelling bolt

Wedge-shaped wall edge in mortar bed

Steel lengths passed through horizontal and vertical 'hoops'

twenty years later, those countries which had proceeded with wholesale redevelopment began to realize the value of the conservation which had been practised in the less adventurous countries.

Redevelopment meant planning, and for a time the United Kingdom led the world with its planning legislation. It began with the 1944 Bomb Damage Act, followed by an Act in 1946 providing for the setting up of new towns, and completed by the 1947 Town and Country Planning Act. An increasingly elaborate system of controls affecting buildings, the location of various activities, and the future of the country, dates from this Act. The British New Towns Act (1946) provided the first formal opportunity for architects to indulge in the town planning dreams with which they had been preoccupied since Tony Garnier's Cité Industrielle in 1904. The initial aim was to

provide self-sufficient towns for about 50,000 people with their own industry, and a staggering range of planning and financial powers was given to their non-elective governing bodies. In these new towns. the opportunities were taken to devize new forms of layout, full traffic segregation, pedestrianization of the central areas and rear servicing of shops. The whole concept breathed efficiency, but whether it breathed humanity is open to debate. The programme was adopted nationwide, and in 1968 was expanded to the concept of a major new city—Milton Keynes.

Austerity, scarcity, and the rationing of building materials all combined to make prefabrication of building components a matter of some importance. Perhaps the best example of success is in Britain, where the Hertfordshire County Council's architects re-analysed the functions within

a school, and translated them into a prefabricated design which could be mass-produced and erected quickly and cheaply, consisting of steel columns and lattice-beams, with separate standardized wall panels. Despite the standardization, the components were small enough to permit a wide variety of choices in each school, and this method of construction meant that internal partitions could be moved according to the need—if not removed altogether—thus allowing the teachers to select the right type of space for any given activity. This flexibility was innovatory as compared to the traditional classroom design of existing schools.

Mass-production of houses was considered to be equally if not more important, and the new generation of architects, planners and sociologists were largely convinced by Le Corbusier's image of towers in a park providing the healthiest

and safest environment. Indeed, some of the plans produced during the war (such as the County of London Plan in 1943) had included sketches of a possible 'mixed development' which consisted of some tower blocks interspersed with houses and lower blocks of flats surrounded by grass. The major trendsetter for this type of building was Le Corbusier's Unité d' Habitation at Marseilles, the first of several such buildings, which was begun in 1947. As its title suggests, this was conceived as a complete living unit as opposed to a mere block of flats, and it included shops on the seventh floor, a running track, a gymnasium, and a school on the roof. Each flat had a double-height living-room and each went right through the block from east to west to provide a double view. The roof was designed to have the character of a concrete garden, and so the ventilation towers are sculpted into decorative cloverleaf shapes. Many different flat sizes are provided in the Unité, to avoid the criticism justifiably attracted by its poor imitations that such blocks cater for only one type of family, and over 1,600 people were housed in it. In keeping with the five

Left above: Le Corbusier's Unité d'Habitation, Nantes, France, 1946–52: flats, shops, crèche, sports-track, restaurant, laundry, theatre and nursery school in one.

Left below: Roehampton housing, London 1955–60, by County Council architects. Traces of the Corbusian façade remain, but these are flats not integrated living units.

Right: Hunstanton School, Norfolk, England, by Peter and Alison Smithson, 1952. A British descendant of Eames's house, it helped to spread the factory aesthetic.

Below: Ithaca Gardens apartments, designed in 1951–4 by Harry Seidler, one of Australia's most celebrated modern architects. The forty privately owned flats, with token communal facilities, overlook Sydney harbour.

principles enunciated some twenty years before, the Unité is liberated from the ground on stilts, which taper downwards like legs, rather than upwards like columns. The façade is relieved of monotonous regularity by the interposition of the seventh floor containing the shops, and the central access tower, and by the fact that the flats are set back from the façade both in order to provide a balcony, and in order to give some shade from the strong Mediterranean sun; the concrete reveals are brightly painted. A portent for the future can be noted in the use of raw concrete (*béton brut*) in its naked state, as it appears once its wooden shuttering is removed, displaying all the whorls and grain of that shuttering. A significant difference between this block of flats and most of its imitators is that it was designed in accordance with Le Corbusier's Modulor system of proportions, based on the human body. The idea of proportion relating to building is a very ancient one, but is one which nearly all other modern architects have largely disregarded.

The Unité in Marseilles had two important effects: first it provided the impetus for many subsequent 'towers in the park', and secondly it provided the inspiration for architects to use building materials as found. In many respects, the first was a social disaster. For reasons of shortsightedness or lack of money, none of the subsequent tower blocks contained the same social services as the Unité, and few of them were designed as carefully. Indeed the image was purely one of towers in a park, and that came to mean in many Western cities that any old tower would be satisfactory as long as it was surrounded by grass. Consequently the fringes of towns such as London, Paris, Munich, or Milan, are dotted with little blocks of a generally shoddy quality. The green parkland at the base of the towers was overtaken by a growth in car ownership so that, far from standing in green parkland, many of these towers stand in grey car-park land. Perhaps the most important mistake was that officialdom failed to distinguish between families who would appreciate tower blocks, and families for whom they were not suitable—particularly those with young children. Officialdom also proved inefficient at maintaining the communal areas—halls, elevators, staircases, exteriors, which provide a lifeline to each flat. The consequence of all this was that those who could choose where they wished to live moved out, and those who had no choice remained: thus social distinctions became frozen in built form.

The second effect was an increasing fashion among architects for using materials as they came. Mention has been made of the Charles Eames house, and of the Unité at Marseilles. Le Corbusier designed another building—the Maison Jaoul at Neuilly (1954–6)—in which the concrete was even more roughly marked. These buildings led, or coincided with, the Brutalism movement which erupted in England in the early 1950s, allied with the names Peter and Alison Smithson, and with the commentator Reyner Banham. The seminal building was a school designed by the Smithsons at Hunstanton in Norfolk which makes an explicit feature of each part of the structure and the services, elevating the water tower to the status of a monument.

At about this time, the term 'honesty of expression' was extended to encourage the design of buildings as a collection of functions in built form, so that the onlooker could stand on the outside and be able to distinguish the restaurant from the offices, and the offices from the council chamber, and the council chamber from the lavatories, and the lavatories from the lift tower, and so forth. Consequently, the impact of the building was no longer that of a complete, total form—as the Villa Savoye had been—but a collection of forms put together sometimes with ingenuity, and sometimes without. Moreover, it was frequently impossible to discern from the outside a hierarchy of

In 1951 the United Kingdom held its Festival of Britain exhibition, with its attendant completion of the showpiece Lansbury neighbourhood redevelopment in East London. The exhibition displayed to the public many of the aesthetic and constructional possibilities of the new materials and a new architecture, and the link was made between advanced design and technological and industrial experiment which unfortunately became lost afterwards. None of the Festival buildings were allowed to survive, save the Royal Festival Hall, designed by Robert Matthew with the London County Council, but it is possible to look back and discern a 1950s 'style'—which was often a combination of brick building with very thin concrete boxed window frames, lintels and porch canopies. The hallmark is the very thinness of these details.

space within which the onlooker could infer the most important functions or purposes of the building; for example, where offices are wrapped around a new council chamber in a town hall, it is the offices which comprise the view to the street, no matter what protrudes from the roof that lies behind them.

The alternative to this approach was to combine all the components of the building into a pure single form, as did Mies van der Rohe, sometimes covering the building with mirror glass, so that the external interest would derive from the reflection of other buildings; this approach never considered that an entire city of mirrored glass buildings would be glittering but very sterile. These approaches seemed to aim at achieving decoration by any other means; in some cases trees or creepers, or in other signs, notices and neon lights, were called on to help make interesting what were really very plain buildings.

Contemporary with the development of these trends was the completion of some interesting buildings on the Continent. In 1949 Aalto completed the Civic Centre at Säynatsälo which provides a variety of communal uses such as municipal offices, a library and a council chamber grouped around an open courtyard which takes advantage of the change in levels to provide for steps rising up into it. The building is of a nice red brick and dark stained timber, and on all sides the pine trees are dominant. It is a very fine, human building. In Denmark Arne Jacobsen, who had won his International Style spurs between the wars, and who was soon to display his kinship with the new severity of his

Rødovere Town Hall (1955) and again with his St Catherine's College, Oxford (1969 onwards), produced between 1950 and 1955 a row of small pretty houses, in Soholm, each one differentiated from its neighbour, each with a garden, a pitched roof, and a clearly defined chimney. Unfortunately, this approach to housing was not influential. In 1950, Montuori Associates made an Expressionist use of concrete with their booking hall at Rome's main railway station, approaching the design in a way which had clear affinities with Eero Saarinen's later airports in America.

Above left: Jacobsen's Søholm houses, Denmark, 1950–5. They showed that modern, plain architecture could be pleasing to look at and friendly in scale.

Below: Aalto's Civic Centre at Säynatsälo, Finland, 1950–52. A modest, high-quality courtyard development which – unlike many subsequent civic grandiosities – does not seek to dominate its setting.

Right: The Lever building, New York, by Skidmore, Owings and Merrill, 1952. Imitations and descendants of this tower and podium block exploded the scale and character of many old cities.

MODERN ARCHITECTURE ENTHRONED

By 1952, the post-war depression seemed to have ended: far more money was available, trade was on the increase, technological developments proceeded apace, and architects duly prospered. The creation of new countries from the old empires led to demands caused by a new national pride for government and university buildings throughout the world. In the already developed world, social expectations were rising so fast that the buildings built between the wars were often no longer fit for their purpose. The rise in car ownership, and the extent to which the Western economy depended on transport, was unexpected, and not only did motorways linking city to city become a common feature, but also the more detailed design of cities themselves became severely affected. Control of the external spaces around buildings seemed to be removed from the architects, and handed over to the traffic engineer. As a consequence, for about a decade genuine urban design was in decline; new buildings were designed as independent and individual sculptures in space. The exceptions were those public spaces provided as part of a commercial development. The Lever Building in New York (Skidmore, Owings and Merrill, 1951) was the forerunner of many schemes in which the tower blocks were associated with a podium and attendant public space. A particularly dramatic example of this is the garden between the two gigantic towers of the World Trade Center in New York (Yamasaki, 1975).

Most types of modern development now had to provide car parking as an integral part of the design, and the period witnessed great experimentations with materials and with form. Buildings became higher and higher, and new materials were exploited to their design limits. Plastics, glass-reinforced plastic, chipboard, plywood, suspended structures, and high-tension cables joined more traditional materials—some of which were used in totally new ways—and many architects whose training had concentrated on the virtues of originality and experimentation made use of them in untried situations. The consequence was many building failures.

Town-planning theories of the time encouraged a belief in a finite 'end-state' when a given community would be complete. In pursuit of this the incremental approach to rebuilding was abandoned in favour of comprehensive redevelop-

ment, first of the bomb-damaged areas, and subsequently of anywhere that did not live up to the new glossy twentieth-century image. In the name of progress, the centres of many historic communities were gutted and then filled with new megastructures entitled 'central area redevelopment schemes' in which the obvious components—shops, access, car parking, offices and occasionally flats—were rearranged inside high-energy monoliths with a resulting loss of the less tangible factors that made historic centres so attractive.

With the arrival of the boom years in the sixties and seventies, buildings became higher, and often nastier, and the freedom from constraint was generally abused with the construction of what came to be called accountants' architecture: namely, buildings which did no more than enclose lettable or sellable space. During the same period, there was considerable experimentation with new materials and new forms, and an overwhelming preoccupation with how to deal with change. In Japan a group of architects calling themselves Metabolists produced ideas, and

indeed buildings, based on the principle of extendability and flexibility; the most famous of these was the Nagakin Capsule Tower in Tokyo (1972) by Kisho Kurokawa, in which 140 boxes—each one a prefabricated living unit—were driven to the site and stacked around two service cores. Some went even further: why have a building at all? The British Archigram group devised schemes for a 'plug-in city' which presupposed that technology could provide everything that people needed for living. The idea consisted of an enormous covered space with service points—electricity, gas, water, etc.—provided everywhere. People just needed to plug in their machinery. Concurrently Buckminster Fuller was achieving the status of a guru with his geodesic domes, which are made of standardized parts and capable of covering large areas with the greatest efficiency. The most famous dome was that constructed for the Montreal Expo in

1967. Fuller had previously been developing prototypes for industrialized housing, including the autonomous living package, and the prototype for the machine-based 'Dymaxion' house. This particular, rather anti-architecture, trend led to the investigation of inflatable structures, and eventually suspended structures, the leading innovator of which was Frei Otto, who designed, among many other projects, the Olympic Stadium in Munich (1972) whose membrane roof covered an area of 34,000 square metres (366,000 square feet). A suspended form of construction, for a permanent and most elegant building, had also been used by Kenzo Tange for the Tokyo Olympics sports hall (1964).

Public reaction against the general standard of modern buildings was inevitable. A desire developed to preserve everything that was historic, in case its replacement would be worse. The strength of a European-wide conservation lobby led to architects being forced to take account of location; and this constraint was followed by the fuel crisis which for the first time since the beginning of the century brought an awareness that fuel might run out, or at least become extremely expensive, making energy-consuming buildings a liability. The consequence of these two forces has been both good and bad. Buildings became lower, better thought-out in relation to their settings, and in some cases new developments made excellent use of existing buildings on the site. The negative result was that planning control in historic areas became so severe that many architects lost their nerve, and new development was being reduced to either a pastiche of historic forms, or an anodyne imitation. The demand for participation in design grew at the same time, permitting architects to have a closer relationship with the consumers of these buildings, thus breaking down the bureaucratic barrier which had come between them. As was to be expected, where such

Left above: Fuller's American Pavilion Dome for the Montreal Expo, 1967. Fashion in enclosure since then has moved on from domes to tent-like, suspended structures.

Left: Archigram's Plug-In-city – an influential vision of high technology whizz, conceived in the early 1960s.

Right: Kurokawa's Nakagin Capsule Tower in Tokyo, 1972, is literally a block of prefabricated apartment capsules plugged into a service and life core. Its panache raises it above the purely utilitarian.

experiments took place—such as the Byker housing redevelopment scheme in Newcastle (architect Ralph Erskine, 1975 onwards), the results have been highly original and interesting. After all, such a relationship is merely the one that has traditionally existed between the architect and his client over the centuries.

In the field of mass housing, sociologists and politicians discovered that life in the towers and blocks of flats was often unsatisfactory and led to loneliness; so new schemes were designed with gallery access, called 'streets in the air'. The first major scheme of this type was the Park Hill scheme in Sheffield (City Architects' Department, 1960) although it was subsequently refined and made more human in the schemes by Darbourne and Darke, particularly in their Marquess Road scheme, London. The continuing transition from large to small was encouraged by the demolition in 1972 of part of Minoru Yamasaki's award-winning 1951 Pruitt Igoe housing scheme in St Louis on the grounds that it was no longer habitable. Since that time public authority housing schemes have been smaller; many of them in Europe now provide tenants with gardens, some schemes allow tenants to participate in their design, and there is more of good landscaping, colour and intimate scale. Mass housing, for a large part, has ceased to be monumental.

One major characteristic of this period has been the re-emergence of interest in symbolism in buildings. It happened gradually, with the standard rectangular shape for buildings being broken down into more interesting forms, and with the increasing use of colour. Possibly Robert Venturi in America was the leader of this trend, and his private houses in America from the early 1960s onwards display an increasing number of historic 'signs'— such as pitched roofs or an emphasized front doorway. A connection with this approach is also discernible in the houses of the American Robert Stern and the Spaniard Ricardo Bofill. This was not a matter of reviving historic styles, but rather of finding out from the public the symbolism by which they recognize features of buildings. Particularly in private houses, the use of symbols, and in some cases historic details, has increased so much that this trend is now being christened 'post-modern architecture'; the title itself draws a distinction between modern architecture with its austere, machine and factory symbolism and the more extrovert polychromatic styles of

TRUMAN'S BREWERY: A TWENTIETH-CENTURY SYNTHESIS

This development by Arup Associates in 1977 encapsulates many of the problems which Western architects are now having to face: an increasing scarcity of greenfield sites, with consequent emphasis on inner-city locations; cramped sites including preserved buildings which must be retained; planning pressure to respect the existing scale; redevelopment within existing sites because the labour force does not wish to move out of town; and finally, the possibility of upgrading a poor inner-city environment.

This development is located in London's East End on a restricted site in Spitalfields. The existing eighteenth-century Director's and Brewer's houses on the site are both protected. Opposite, across Brick Lane, are further historic buildings: the Vat House,

Stables, and Engineers' house. Otherwise, the surrounding environment consists of slum tenements long overdue for demolition.

The new Truman building is in two distinct halves: a brick podium up to the level of the cornice of the elder buildings: and a stepped development of glazed offices above.

The brick podium is all that can be seen from Quaker Street, thereby maintaining the three-storey scale and style of the Brewer's house.

It encloses the amenity floor (second floor) over double height storage tanker bays and workshops. Three storeys of offices sit above. The paved entrance courtyard is a completely new space, with specially designed railings.

Left: The Quaker Street façade is slightly curved, following existing street lines, its blind arcades of brick reminiscent of late Georgian industrial architecture. The rear curtain wall shows on the right, indicating the location of floors of administrative offices above the rear, double-height servicing and loading yard and workshops.

Below: Typical view in one of the three office floors. Largely open-plan with circulation round the perimeter to get the views. Lighting, with air supply and extraction, operated from within the 1.2 m (4 ft) deep ceiling coffers. Subsequent Arup buildings have developed the coffer ceilings so as to create a greater sense of identity within large open-plan offices.

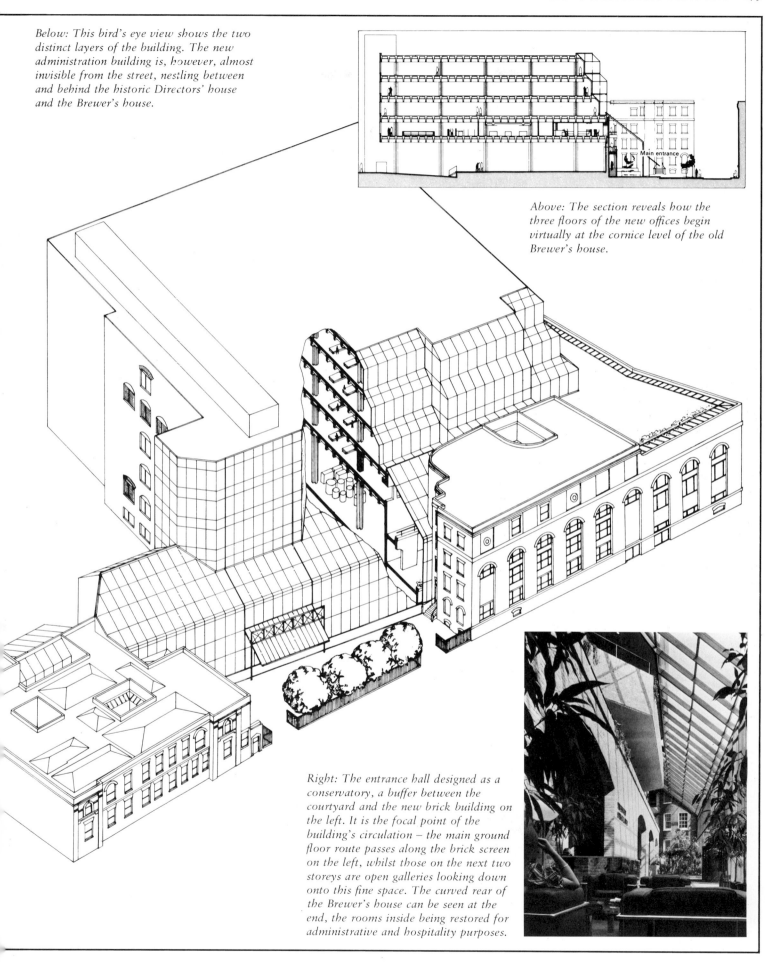

Below: This bird's eye view shows the two distinct layers of the building. The new administration building is, however, almost invisible from the street, nestling between and behind the historic Directors' house and the Brewer's house.

Above: The section reveals how the three floors of the new offices begin virtually at the cornice level of the old Brewer's house.

Main entrance

Right: The entrance hall designed as a conservatory, a buffer between the courtyard and the new brick building on the left. It is the focal point of the building's circulation – the main ground floor route passes along the brick screen on the left, whilst those on the next two storeys are open galleries looking down onto this fine space. The curved rear of the Brewer's house can be seen at the end, the rooms inside being restored for administrative and hospitality purposes.

post-modern architecture. Such a distinction, however, ignores the large number of beautiful Expressionist buildings constructed throughout the period of modern architecture, and is therefore unlikely to stand up to full analysis.

The private house market continues to provide the opportunity for individualists to produce strange and interesting buildings, far too numerous throughout the West to specify here. One offshoot is perhaps represented by the sunken houses of Bruce Gough located in Oklahoma farmlands, whose relationship with nature and natural materials is reflected in the current interest in hand-made houses in America, self-built timber houses and a return to the traditional. During the sixties, there was a brief boom in houses pieced together from junk, like Drop City, assembled by drop-outs from parts of cars. The slightly more intellectual branch saw the gradual return of symbolism in housing mentioned above. In an unconscious way, this was probably reflected in an increasingly popular 'vernacular' style of building, using traditional forms such as pitched roofs and traditional materials in order to create a homely feeling. In Britain in particular, very successful private villages were developed by Span

(architect, Eric Lyons). The mainstream, however, used modern materials in a normal way, continuing the experiments on the outdoor/indoor relationship begun in the private houses of the 1930s, and of course using the increasing refinements of technology. One or two opted to follow the path of high technology, and a recent descendant of the Charles Eames house is the house in London designed for himself by Michael Hopkins (1977). Of particular note is the work of the so-called New York Five (Peter Eisenman, Michael Graves, John Hejduk, Richard Meier, Robert Siegel/Charles Gwathmey), who have produced a series of very pure Modern Movement houses of concrete and glass, the main interest of which lies in how they have made use of modern technology to extend the scope of the original Modern Movement, and also how they play with the idea of space.

As far as cities are concerned, the predominant buildings are offices, hotels and shops. The general run of these buildings is pretty poor, and those that stand out tend to have been designed for a specific owner-occupier. Some were towers, notable ones including the Pirelli Building in Milan (Gio Ponti with Nervi, 1959), a tall, tapering block whose slenderness as com-

pared with the normal run of office blocks made it popular, the Torre Velasca, also in Milan (BBPR, 1961) whose upper floors are corbelled out in a rather precious reminiscence of medieval towers, the extendable monument Kenzo Tange built in Koufu for the Yamanashi Broadcasting Institution, in which the office floors are suspended between vertical tubes which contain the services, and possibly the curved glass, intestine-shaped towers which Karl Schwanzer designed for the BMW headquarters in Munich. *The Economist* complex in London, designed by the Smithsons (1964), represented a major

change, since it is small-scale and grouped around stairs and a piazza so as to fit in with the locality. This sensitive approach has been adopted by other developments, perhaps the most sophisticated example being the Willis Faber Dumas Building in Ipswich (Foster Associates, 1975) which is a four-storey kidney-shaped building occupying its entire site, with a curved glass wall following the street line. International companies such as Olivetti and IBM consistently choose good design for their

Left above: Park Hill, Sheffield, England, 1960. A massive city housing redevelopment scheme, which introduced 'streets in the sky' to overcome social isolation.

Left below: The Tucker House, New York, 1975, by Venturi and Rauch. A new symbolism – amalgamating old with new.

Right: The Smith House, Darien, Connecticut, USA, by Richard Meier, 1965–7. Modern Movement – US style: intellectual games with space, the gleaming white mass-concrete of the 1930s returns married to even higher technology.

Below: The mid-1970s version of a city housing scheme: Byker in Newcastle, England, by Erskine, begun in 1975. Every effort is being made to soften and humanize mass rehousing.

headquarters in the countries in which they are involved. This period has also seen an increasing sophistication in glass curtain-wall technique as in buildings like the IBM headquarters in Johannesburg (Arup Associates) or the blue glass Pacific Design Centre (Pelli, 1976) known locally as the 'Blue Whale'. Hertzberger's Centraal Beheer Offices in Appeldoorn (1975) represent a significant effort by an insurance company to have their building designed to promote the wellbeing of employees.

Monuments were built to art, to sport and to culture. Because they were monuments, substantial freedoms were allowed the architects, so that most of the buildings tended to be Expressionist in character, such as the Sydney Opera House (Utzon, 1973), the Berlin Philharmonic Concert Hall (Hans Scharoun, 1963), the auditorium of which is designed to convey the impression of a valley in which the orchestra plays, Frank Lloyd Wright's Guggenheim Museum in New York, which consists more or less of a massive white spiral ramp, Eero Saarinen's two

Left: Ponti's Pirelli building, Milan, Italy, 1958, much admired for its elegant tapering. It seems very dated alongside the pluralist 1970s buildings.

Below: Pelli's Pacific Design Centre, Los Angeles, California, USA, 1976, reduces architectural form to glass-clad moulding.

Right above: Hertzberger's Centraal Beheer, Apeldoorn, Netherlands, 1976, is an insurance office broken up into identifiable compartments for greater worker satisfaction.

Right below: The atrium of Portman's Embarcadero Center, Regency Hyatt Hotel, San Francisco, California, USA, 1976: an environment so controlled that it seems not far removed from that forecast by Fritz Lang. (see page 246).

marvellously expressive airports in America—Kennedy and Dulles (both completed in 1962)—which convey the feeling of excitement that air travel should engender, Charles de Gaulle airport at Roissy, which sacrifices architectural appearance in favour of the creation of space-age environment, and the Palazzo dello Sport in Rome (1969) by Nervi, the impact of whose soaring vaulting gives the same feeling as medieval cathedrals. The exceptions are the National Theatre in London (Lasdun) which is straight Brutalist/Modern Movement in the use of exposed concrete, and the Centre Georges Pompidou in Paris (Piano and Rogers, 1976) which is purely Constructivist, although rather gayer and brighter and more colourful than the serious-minded Vesnins would have tolerated.

The main commercial impact of the period has been made in hotels, most of which provide an international standard of packaged comfort, restaurants and large new shopping complexes. Two developments stand out: the enormous

Abramovitz, with initial ideas by Le Corbusier in 1947) followed by a subsequent complex almost twenty years later in Vienna. Frank Lloyd Wright designed a strange, ship-like building for Marin County, and a number of concrete Brutalist town halls were constructed in Japan, perhaps the heaviest being the Kurashiki Town Hall, by Kenzo Tange (completed 1960). A more sophisticated but nevertheless heavy City Hall was built by Kallman McKinnell Knowles (1964–9) in Boston, and curved glass towers designed by Viljo Revell won the competition for Toronto

Left: The Sydney Opera House, Australia, a 1957 competition-winning design by Jörn Utzon. On a reclaimed spit of land in Sydney Harbour, the Opera House is most famous for its silhouette and exterior.

Below: Hans Scharoun's Berlin Philharmonic Hall, completed in 1963, is most notable for its interior. The hall is designed like a valley in which the audience is arranged in serried tiers which converge onto the orchestra at the bottom. The curved roof, dotted with pinpoint lights, acts as a sky.

Right: The Centre Pompidou, Paris, 1976, a competition-winning design by Piano and Rogers. Rogers has referred to it as a 'setting for things to happen', in preference to the more finite term 'building'. Architecture is reduced to the role of providing a backcloth and back-up services. The new building for Lloyds of London by Rogers demonstrates how this approach to architecture is evolving.

complexes designed by John Portman in America such as the Peach Tree Plaza in Atlanta, which are high-technology, consumer-orientated, dream worlds; and the vernacular revival of holiday villages, such as Port Grimaud and its many imitators on the Mediterranean coast. Ersatz though these schemes are, their Mediterranean, picturesque character has proved very popular.

In recognition of their newly increased power, the authorities throughout the world built themselves new town halls, city halls and government offices. The trend was really set pre-war, with the Rio de Janeiro Ministry of Education (1937–43) designed by a number of architects including Lucio Costa, Oscar Niemeyer and, as consultant, Le Corbusier; a building which included a sheer dark curtain wall on one side, and deep concrete *brise-soleils* (sunshades) on the sunny side. After the war, the first off the mark was the United Nations itself, with its headquarters in New York (Harrison &

City Hall. Despite competitions and interesting schemes, Britain produced very few significant buildings for this type of client. Perhaps the most important exception is the Hillingdon Civic Centre (1977) designed by Robert Matthew, Johnston Marshall & Partners. Its importance lies in that despite its being a massive, expensive building, it seeks to conceal its shape behind the form of a cluster of pitched red roofs, and pleasantly detailed brick. A better result of integration between a new town hall and an ancient city was achieved in Bensberg Town Hall by Gottfried Böhm

(1967) whose white concrete form is so designed as to match the way the ancient town rises up on a hill.

Some of the best buildings of the sixties and seventies have been those designed for traditional patrons, like universities, museums and the Church. So much good work has been done for universities throughout the world that it is possible only to mention a few of the more notable schemes. The American architect Louis Kahn produced externally austere buildings for Yale University and, later, the University of Pennsylvania, and apart from his Yale

Art Gallery, his most notable buildings were the Richard Medical Research Buildings at Pennsylvania (1957–61) and the Salk Institute for Biological Studies in La Jolla (1965). The Medical Research Buildings exemplified Kahn's distinction between what he called the 'served' spaces as opposed to the 'service' spaces: the service towers are encased in brick and are designed in a vertical, slender way, whereas the main glazed laboratories display a horizontal emphasis. Paul Rudolph's complicated Yale Arts and Architecture Building in Newhaven, Connecticut (1963),

uses the different approach of separating the functions one from another to make their purpose visible from the outside. Most notable American architects worked on university buildings during this period —Eero Saarinen (MIT Chapel, 1963), Marcel Breuer, Philip Johnson, Louis Kahn, Paul Rudolph and many more. In Canada, Andrews, Page & Steele produced Scarborough College, of Toronto University, a stepped building which followed the contours of the site. In Britain, the combination of an enlightened client and plenty of money produced a fine collection of buildings from a range of about thirty good-to-excellent architects or firms, of which particular note should be taken of the ziggurat block for East Anglia University by Denys Lasdun, and the influential buildings of James Stirling (initially with James Gowan). Their engineering tower for Leicester University (1963) made a worldwide impact. This building was admired because, although the separate function of the tower was differentiated clearly so that looking from the outside the lecture rooms, stairs, offices, the work floor and the laboratory are all separate and identifiable, there is nevertheless, an overall sense of unity, conveyed by the use of glazing and red tiles. In an age used to heavy and poorly detailed buildings, the Leicester engineering tower appears small, neat and jewel-like. A subsequent Stirling building—the history faculty library in Cambridge—consisted of a red brick L-shaped administration block enclosing a triangular waterfall of patent glazing which covered the library itself. Claiming inspiration from historic forms, Stirling had little truck with the contemporary architecture of the day:

I consider 99% of modern architecture to be boring, banal and barren and usually disruptive and unharmonious when placed in older cities. In England the Government—either local authorities or central government—are politically concerned to build the greatest number of the common good, be it schools, houses, factories, etc. Private enterprise developers are concerned with building the biggest quantity of square footage (i.e. offices) at the least cost to maximise profits. Both see shoebox style modern architecture with its stripped down puritan aesthetics and repetitive expression as very suitable for building to the lowest cost. I believe that the shape of the building should indicate—perhaps display— the usage and way of life of its occupants, and it is therefore likely to be rich and varied in appearance and its expression unlikely to be simple.

Other interesting university buildings in Europe included residential buildings for the University of Urbino by Giancarlo de Carlo which fit in well with this historic hill-town, and the medical faculty building at the University of Louvain near Brussels (Lucien Kroll, 1969–74) which was designed in partnership with the students and other users of the building. Even builders were allowed to improvize, but the final result indicates that in this case full participation by the users was no substitute for coherent design.

The Church remained a patron, but had very few cathedrals built, one notable exception being Sir Basil Spence's Coventry Cathedral (1962); much more frequent were small churches and chapels. There are interesting examples throughout Europe and in America, too many to enumerate, although note should be taken of Aalto's church at Vuoksenniska (from 1957) and of the Spaniard Félix Candela's

Below: Engineering Faculty Tower, Leicester University, England, 1963, by Stirling and Gowan; glass-roofed workshops are behind. The parts of the building are clearly separated – lecture theatre, rooms, administration, circulation – yet unified by red tile and glass. A developing Stirling 'aesthetic' can be seen in the History Library, Cambridge, and the Florey Building, Oxford.

Right: Richards Medical Research Building, Pennsylvania University, USA, by Kahn, 1957–61. Most notable for its group of service towers, whose verticality contrasts with the horizontal 'served' areas, which are the principal parts of the building.

Right below: Kurashiki Town Hall, Japan, 1960, by Kenzo Tange. Acclaimed for the way in which the concrete beams project in the traditional manner of Japanese timber buildings. For all that, a heavy-lidded, if not inscrutable building.

in which justice is carried out.

In 1957, Lucio Costa's plan for a new capital of Brazil 1,000 kilometres (620 miles) inland was selected as the competition winner, and most of the buildings in Brasilia were designed by a former pupil of his, Oscar Niemeyer. The designs are monumental and picturesque, use being made of heavy, oversailing flat roofs to provide shade, supported on delicate, almost Gothic, inverted arches. A favourite view of the city, the Assembly Building, with its horizontal block capped with two domes—one the right way up and the other inverted, and the twin glass and concrete towers of the Secretariat beyond—convey an impact similar to that of science-fiction magazines: cold hard shapes of the future. Brasilia's problem is that these buildings are monuments, isolated from each other by a great deal of empty space, while the real life of the city is relegated to acres of shanty towns only a few kilometres away.

The third capital is Dacca in Bangladesh. The Assembly Building, begun by Louis Kahn in 1962, was constructed partly of brick and partly of concrete. Like Chandigarh, this development is a monument, but its impact is different and picturesque, probably the result of the different method Kahn has adopted to shield the Assembly from the direct sun—namely brick screen walls pierced with enormous holes, giving the visual effect of cloisters from within.

Although not a capital, the fourth architecturally important city of the period is Milton Keynes in England. Its importance is, first, that a number of eminent

splendid Church of the Miraculous Virgin, Mexico City (1954), which has strong affinities with Gaudí's work, particularly in the use of hyperbolic paraboloids, with the major difference that Candela uses concrete rather than stone. Perhaps the most influential were Le Corbusier's La Tourette monastery at Evreux (1954–9) and his Pilgrimage Church at Ronchamp (1950–5).

The apotheosis of monument design has occurred in new cities, of which there are four important ones during this period. The first is the new capital of the Punjab in India, Chandigarh, designed by Le Corbusier and begun in 1950. The Capitol consists of a series of buildings laid out as part of an interconnecting plan involving buildings, planting, walkways, and reflecting pools using landscape and architectural variety to achieve an overall effect. The buildings are monuments, and the spaces between are almost intolerable in the Indian climate. The buildings themselves are in concrete, and much is made of the *brise-soleils* and their patterns, and much again of the enormously heavy concrete canopy above the Courts of Justice. This latter building is designed almost as a piece of scenery in that its visible parts—the concrete canopy which isolates the roof heat from the internal spaces and the multi-patterned *brise-soleils*—conceal from view, if not completely obscure, the actual function of the building, that of being concrete chambers with glass walls

architects from Britain and Europe have been asked to contribute to the housing developments; secondly, the city as a whole is planned around a very high car ownership; and thirdly, the central area of the city and many of the factories are designed by the city's own architectural staff, which is wholly committed to the ideal of high technology and the Modern Movement. It is likely that the new city centre will be the largest and purest rectangular glass shopping centre in the world. Milton Keynes is being designed at a time when the ecological and fuel crisis is known, and account is being taken of earlier mistakes in house planning and town planning. It will be interesting to see whether this new city is to be taken as the last gasp of the old movement, which began in 1947 based on Modern Movement architectural aesthetics, or the first cry of the new, which has tempered the original ideas with some human reality. It is a building for people, not government.

Every age looks for special heroes, and there is thus a constant demand to identify the architects of the post-war generation who have the stature of Mies van der Rohe or Le Corbusier. It is probably too early to make such judgements. However, the contrasting works of Alvar Aalto and Kenzo Tange are so consistent in their

Left above: The General Assembly, Chandigarh, India, 1951 onwards, by Le Corbusier. The administration block appears behind, to the left. Each major function is separate in its own monument, linked by a pattern of lakes and piazzas.

Left below: Twin towers of the Secretariat, and shallow dome of the Senate in Brazilia, 1957–60 by Oscar Niemayer; again, an administrative centre in free-standing monuments. It is a futuristic image, but one which relegates ordinary people to shanty towns five miles away.

Below: The new shopping centre of Central Milton Keynes, England, 1979, in rectilinear steel and glass, designed by the Development Corporation architects. In many respects the Centre has the repetitive aridity of inter-war Fascist buildings, despite its social function. Here the individual blocks are subservient to the arcades which link them together.

variety, and so well considered that they would be likely candidates for such an accolade. The sheer inventiveness of Tange's buildings, in particular, designing with western tools within an eastern tradition, comprise an immense achievement.

If the architectural history of the twentieth century has been a search for a style appropriate to its time, the final question must be whether this has been reached. Probably there is no single architectural style as such, but a number of them: instead of a style, what matters is the architect's approach. In the nineteenth century, much has been made of whether a building should be a purely naked construction, or whether it should be decently dressed. In the twentieth century, naked construction has been tested and found wanting. Although people have been eager to accept what technology offers so as to

improve their conditions of living, they have been less eager to forfeit those elements and symbols which make life pleasant. The current worldwide recession has reduced the number of buildings being built, and also influenced the size of schemes so that many of them are now small. If the world economy improves, and large schemes become viable once more, it seems unlikely that the sort of scheme that would have been built ten years ago will return. The politicians, the public, and architects themselves are gradually realizing that there is no real substitute for architecture—not functionalism, not socialism, not Brutalism—not in systems, not in materials by themselves, not in inflatables, nor necessarily in technology. Difficult as it is to design a good building, standards of expectation are rising. More and more people will not be put off with less.

GLOSSARY

ABACUS Slab which forms the top part of a column, above the CAPITAL (see fig. 13).

AISLE The lateral division of a building (usually of a church or a basilica) parallel to its main axis; it is generally separated from the nave by piers or columns (see figs 10,11).

AMBULATORY Corridor around the main body of a building; normally referring to the semi-circular or polygonal passage within the apse around the sanctuary in a church (see fig. 10), which may have radiating chapels off it.

APPLIED COLUMN See COLUMN: ATTACHED COLUMN.

APSE Large semi-circular or polygonal recess; usually referring specifically to the apse at the east end of a church (see fig. 10).

ARCADE Series of arches supported by columns or piers. An arcade attached to a wall is called a BLIND ARCADE.
    Also a vaulted covered shopping street with a glazed roof (sometimes called a *galleria*).

ARCH Curved structure of masonry spanning an opening. The shape of most arches is made up of one of more circular arcs (see figs 1–9).
    CONTAINING ARCH see RELIEVING ARCH.
    CORBELLED ARCH (fig. 1) Primitive arch formed of courses of horizontal masonry, each projecting beyond the course below.
    DIAPHRAGM ARCH Stone arch spanning the nave of a church which has no stone vault but a wooden roof.
    ELLIPTICAL ARCH (fig. 2) Arch formed of a half-ellipse with its centre on the springing line.
    FOUR-CENTRED ARCH (fig. 3) Pointed arch of composite curve with arcs projected from two centres on the springing line and two below this line.
    HANGING ARCH Arch used upside-down.
    HORSESHOE ARCH (fig. 4) Round-headed arch with its centre above the springing line.
    OGEE ARCH (fig. 5) Arch formed of two S-shaped double curves.
    POINTED ARCH Arch formed of two arcs centred on the springing line which meet in a point at the apex. In an EQUILATERAL ARCH (fig. 6) the centres are at the springing points; in a taller LANCET ARCH (fig. 7) the centres fall outside the supporting walls; while in a lower DROP ARCH (fig. 8) the centres fall within the walls.
    RELIEVING (or CONTAINING) ARCH Arch formed in the substance of a wall to relieve the part below it from the weight above; often used over a lintel or straight-topped opening.
    STRAINING (or STRAINER) ARCH Transverse arch constructed in the interior of a building to give stability to opposite walls.
    TRANSVERSE ARCH Arch spanning the nave of a church, separating one bay of a vault from the next (see fig. 11).
    TRUE ARCH (fig. 9) Arch built up of wedge-shaped blocks (VOUSSOIRS), as opposed to a CORBELLED ARCH. The arch must be supported on CENTRING during construction until the KEYSTONE is placed in position, thus locking together the voussoirs, whose shape and weight acting upon one another ensure the stability of the structure.

ARCHITRAVE The lowest division of the classical ENTABLATURE (see fig. 13); also used to define any horizontal block of masonry resting on columns.

ASHLAR Masonry regularly dressed in large square blocks to a fine finish.

ATRIUM Inner court or hall in a Roman house. Also the enclosed forecourt leading to the main doors of an early Christian church.

ATTACHED COLUMN See COLUMN.

ATTIC A low storey at the top of a building below the roof space; a term properly used of a lower storey above the ENTABLATURE of an Order.

BALLOON FRAME Simply constructed wooden frame, with closely spaced vertical members running from SILL to EAVES and with horizontal members nailed to these (see p. 234).

BAPTISTRY Building, within a church or separate from it, for baptism.

BARREL VAULT See VAULT.

BAR TRACERY See TRACERY.

BASE In classical architecture the moulded area at the bottom of the SHAFT immediately above the PLINTH.

BAY The principal division of an interior or exterior elevation, generally defined by the main vertical features, e.g. columns, pillars or pilasters, by windows, or by ceiling beams etc. (see figs 10, 11)

BEAM One of the principal load-bearing horizontal members of a building.
    TIE-BEAM Beam spanning the full width of a building, which connects the principal rafters and prevents the walls from spreading. See also HAMMER BEAM.

BLIND ARCADE See ARCADE.

BOSS Ornamental projection at the intersection of ribs or beams of a vault or ceiling (see fig. 18).
    HANDLING BOSS Projection left in a dressed block of stone for ease of handling.

BOX FRAME Type of timber frame common in vernacular architecture (see illustration on p. 15).

BRACING Application of diagonal members (braces), as in a TRUSS, to give rigidity (see fig. 12).

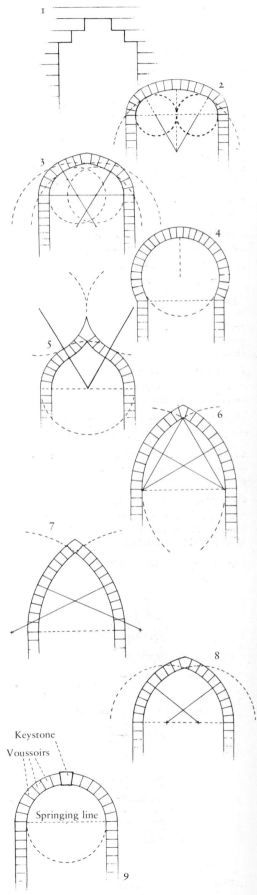

Keystone

Voussoirs

Springing line

BUTTRESS A projection of masonry or brickwork from a wall to give additional strength, particularly where the wall supports a vault (see fig. 11).

FLYING BUTTRESS Buttress standing free from the wall it strengthens, giving support by a half-arch at the point of main stress (see illustration on p. 15).

CAMPANILE Bell-tower, generally free-standing.

CANTILEVER Beam or arch projecting outward beyond its point of support and counter-balanced by the fixing of the inner part of the member. A double cantilever projects on both sides. The cantilever principle is used in the medieval JETTY and also often in reinforced concrete structures.

CAPITAL The head of a column or pilaster (see fig. 13).

CENTRING Structure, usually of wood, to support an arch or vault under construction.

CHANCEL The CHOIR and SANCTUARY in the eastern part of a church (see fig. 10).

CHANTRY Small privately endowed chapel, where masses were said for the repose of the soul of the founder, whose tomb was generally contained in the chantry or was close by.

CHAPTER HOUSE Building or room for meetings of the chapter (assembled clergy) of an abbey, cathedral etc.

CHOIR The eastern limb of a church; strictly the part with stalls for singers (see fig. 10).

CLADDING Material used to cover the main structural material of a building, for protection or decoration.

CLAPBOARD Overlapping horizontal boards used as a cladding material over a timber-framed wall; known also in Britain as WEATHERBOARDING.

CLEAR-SPAN STRUCTURE See SPAN.

CLERESTORY The upper storey of a building pierced by windows, usually above the aisles (as in a church), admitting light to the nave or main hall (see fig. 11).

CLOISTER Quadrangular covered walk, open towards an inner court, in monasteries etc.

COFFERING Decoration of a ceiling with recessed panels, generally square or polygonal in shape.

COLONNADE A range of COLUMNS supporting a straight ENTABLATURE.

COLUMN A vertical supporting member, normally circular in plan and including base, shaft and capital (see fig. 13).

Columns or semi-columns partly sunk into a wall or built up against it are described as ATTACHED or ENGAGED, as opposed to free-standing.

See also MUSHROOM COLUMN.

CONCH Plain semi-dome of an APSE or NICHE.

CONFESSIO CRYPT used in the Middle Ages for burials of martyrs or saints or for their relics, generally surrounded by a corridor.

CONTAINING ARCH See ARCH.

CORBEL Bracket projecting from a wall used as a support (see fig. 12). Corbelling, i.e. allowing each successive course of masonry to project beyond the one below it and support the one above it, is used to construct a primitive arch (see fig. 1) or dome.

CORNICE Horizontal moulded projection terminating a building; in classical architecture the top division of an ENTABLATURE (see fig. 13).

CORTILE Internal courtyard, generally enclosed by ARCADES.

COURSE Horizontal range of stones or bricks of uniform height in a wall.

CROSS VAULT See VAULT.

CROSSING Space in a church where NAVE and TRANSEPTS intersect (see fig. 10).

CRUCK Pair of large curved timbers used as a frame to support a cottage (see illustration on p. 15).

CRYPT Underground chamber beneath a church, generally extending under the CHANCEL.

CUPOLA Generally used of a small dome or domed roof; also the inside ceiling of a dome.

CURTAIN WALL In medieval architecture the connecting wall between two towers or buttresses, or internally between two piers.

In twentieth-century architecture a non-load-bearing wall, generally of glass or metal (see p. 264).

CURTILAGE Area attached to a house as part of its enclosure.

DENTILS Ornaments resembling teeth used in the moulding of a classical CORNICE (see fig. 13).

DIAPHRAGM ARCH See ARCH.

DOMICAL VAULT See VAULT.

DORMER Upright window projecting through the slope of a roof with its own separate roof.

DOWEL Headless pin used to hold two pieces of masonry or timber together.

DRESSED MASONRY Masonry either finished as smooth ASHLAR or decorated with MOULDINGS or sculptured decoration.

DROP ARCH See ARCH: POINTED ARCH.

DRUM Of a column: one of the cylindrical blocks of stone of which the shaft of a column is generally made up.

Of a dome: cylindrical or polygonal wall beneath a dome or cupola.

EAVES Lower edges of a sloping roof; generally used where they overhang the sides of the building.

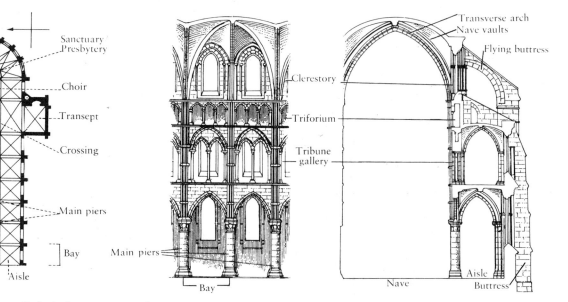

10 Plan of a church (Langres Cathedral)

11 Elevation and cross-section of a church (Laon Cathedral)

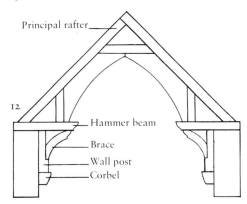

Principal rafter

12

Hammer beam

Brace

Wall post

Corbel

ELEVATION An exterior or interior vertical face of a building, or a drawing of this (see fig. 11).

ELLIPTICAL ARCH See ARCH.

ENGAGED COLUMN See COLUMN.

ENTABLATURE The horizontal structure supported by columns or pilasters in classical architecture (see fig. 13); used also of any main horizontal masonry member.

EQUILATERAL ARCH See ARCH: POINTED ARCH.

FAN VAULT See VAULT.

FERRO-CONCRETE Concrete with steel reinforcement.

FILIGREE VAULT See VAULT.

FLÈCHE Slender spire rising from a roof.

FORMWORK Structure made to contain concrete while it is setting, also called SHUTTERING.

FOUR-CENTRED ARCH See ARCH.

FRAME The structural skeleton of a building made up of members of timber, iron, steel, reinforced concrete etc. (See p. 15 for illustrations of box frame, cruck frame and concrete frame; see also BALLOON FRAME, SPACE FRAME.)

FRIEZE The middle division of a classical ENTABLATURE (see fig. 13); also any broad horizontal band decorated with sculpture.

GABLE Upper part of an end wall shaped by the pitch of the roof, or (e.g. a stepped gable) projecting decoratively beyond the line of the roof.

GALLERIA Iron and glass vaulted shopping street, particularly in Italy.

GALLERY In general, a long, narrow enclosed or partly enclosed interior space. Used specifically of the storey above the aisle of a church (see TRIBUNE GALLERY); of an open raised gallery in a church, hall or theatre (e.g. organ gallery, minstrels' gallery); of the upper room extending the full width of an Elizabethan or Jacobean house (the long gallery); of a connecting passage-way, generally only partly enclosed; or of a room or building used to display works of art.

GROIN VAULT See VAULT.

HALF-TIMBERING Building with timber frame (generally exposed) and infill of LATH AND PLASTER, brick or other material.

HALL CHURCH Church with NAVE and AISLES of approximately equal height, therefore having no CLERESTORY.

HAMMER BEAM (fig. 12) Horizontal beam projecting inwards supported on a bracket and itself supporting the main roof structure.

HANDLING BOSS See BOSS.

HORSESHOE ARCH See ARCH.

HÔTEL French town mansion.

HYPERBOLIC PARABOLOID Form of double-curved SHELL developed from the parabolic arch. It has been found particularly useful in modern architecture because it can be constructed with straight members.

INFILL Material used (often as panels) to fill spaces between structural members in a frame construction.

JAMB The straight side of a window, door or archway.

JETTY Upper part of a building projecting over the lower part (see illustration on p. 15).

JOISTS Parallel horizontal timbers on which floorboards are laid and to which ceiling laths are attached.

KEYSTONE The central stone or VOUSSOIR at the top of a true arch, the last to be placed in position (see ARCH: TRUE ARCH and fig. 9).

LAMINATE Material made from thin layers of wood glued together.

LANCET Narrow pointed arch or window. See also ARCH: POINTED ARCH.

LANTERN Small structure on top of a dome or roof to admit light and for decoration.

LANTERN STEEPLE Openwork structure on top of a church tower.

LANTERN TOWER Tower open to view from the ground and lit by an upper tier of windows; often used over the CROSSING of a church.

LATH AND PLASTER WORK INFILL for walls made of horizontal strips of thin wood (laths) covered with plaster.

LIERNE Subsidiary decorative (non-structural) vaulting rib (see fig. 18).

LIERNE VAULT See VAULT.

LINTEL Beam or stone placed horizontally over an opening to support the weight of the wall above.

LOG CONSTRUCTION Type of timber structure with solid walls formed of logs laid horizontally in courses.

LOGGIA A covered space with one or more sides open and bounded by ARCADES or COLONNADES.

LOMBARD BANDS Shallow stone bands carved with geometrical decoration or formed of small decorative COLONNADES.

MACHICOLATION Projecting parapet supported on CORBELS on a fortified wall. There were openings in the floor between the corbels to drop missiles on attackers.

MARTYRIUM Generally circular shrine built as a memorial and containing the tomb or relics of a Christian martyr.

METOPE Space between the TRIGLYPHS on the FRIEZE of the Doric Order (see fig. 13), sometimes decorated with painting or sculpture.

MEZZANINE A low intermediate storey between two higher ones.

MIHRAB Prayer-niche in a mosque; orientated towards Mecca.

MODULE A measure of proportion adopted for an individual building on which all other dimensions are based; also, more generally, a standard basic unit of measurement. In classical architecture the basic module is usually the measure of half the diameter of a column at its base then divided into thirty parts or minutes.

MOULDING Contour or profile given to many features of masonry, often enriched with carving.

MULLION Slender post or upright member forming the division between the lights of a window.

MUSHROOM COLUMN Column of reinforced concrete with a wide flat capital that enables the reinforcement to be continuous with the structure of the floor supported above.

MUTULE Thin projecting block below a Doric CORNICE (see fig. 13).

NAVE The main body of a church, for the assembly of the congregation (see figs 10, 11).

NET VAULT See VAULT.

NICHE Shallow recess in a wall, generally arched at the top and often used to accommodate a statue, vase or other ornament.

NODDING OGEE OGEE ARCH curved forward at its apex in front of the plane of the wall.

OCTAGON Eight-sided building, or an eight-sided LANTERN.

OCULUS Round window or opening.

OGEE ARCH See ARCH.

OPUS RETICULATUM See RETICULATE.

ORDER Generic term for COLUMN and ENTABLATURE in classical architecture (see fig. 13 and p. 43).

ORIEL WINDOW Projecting bay window, generally supported on a wide CORBEL or bracket.

PANTILES Roof tiles curved in an S-shape so as to overlap one another and thus protect the joints from the wet.

PEDIMENT Low-pitched triangular GABLE in classical architecture used above a PORTICO; or similar feature above doors, windows etc. (see fig. 13).

PENDENTIVE Concave triangle of masonry which descends into a corner formed by the angle of two walls where a dome is placed over a straight-sided area. A similar form is used in a FAN VAULT.

PERISTYLE A court surrounded by a COLONNADE, or the colonnade itself.

PIAZZA An open area or square surrounded by buildings.

PIER A strong pillar of masonry (or concrete), often of composite shape with attached shafts or columns and generally supporting an arch (see figs 10, 11).

PIER (SEASIDE) Iron or wooden promenade projecting into the sea.

PILASTER Shallow flattened column attached to a wall.

PILOTIS Concrete pillars (which may taper to the base) supporting a building, leaving the space beneath it free.

PIN JOINT Pinned joint in a metal arch, allowing for expansion and contraction or other movement in the structure.

PITCHED ROOF Roof that slopes down from the ridge to the side walls.

PLATE TRACERY See TRACERY.

PLINTH In classical architecture the square member forming the bottom division of the base of a column. Used also for any projecting base beneath the wall of a building.

POINTED ARCH See ARCH.

PORTE-COCHÈRE Porch large enough to admit a wheeled vehicle.

PORTICO Range of columns forming a porch in front of a building.

PORTICUS Covered entrance porch of an early church where the tombs of important people were placed.

POST-AND-PLANK CONSTRUCTION Type of timber structure in which the walls are built up of horizontal planks held by grooves in the main posts.

PRESBYTERY The part of a church east of the CHOIR where the priests officiate at the high altar (see fig. 10). Strictly speaking the presbytery is between the choir and the SANCTUARY, but is normally used as synonymous with the sanctuary.

RELIEVING ARCH See ARCH.

RENDERING Plastering of an external wall.

RETICULATE (or *OPUS RETICULATUM*) Masonry constructed like a net of diamond-shaped or polygonal stones, or square stones placed diagonally.

RETROCHOIR The chapels and other space behind the high altar in a large church.

REVEAL The side of a window or door opening between the framework and the outer surface of the wall.

REVETMENT Masonry used as a facing material.
    Also retaining wall, usually sloping, to hold back earth or sometimes water.

RIB Projecting band of masonry on a ceiling or vault, generally marking the lines of the structure (see figs 18–20).

RIB VAULT See VAULT.

ROTUNDA Building or room of circular plan, often domed.

RUBBLE Unworked masonry of rough, irregular stones generally not laid in courses.

RUSTICATION Marking the joints of masonry with grooves or channels to make them conspicuous. There are numerous variants, but most commonly only the edges of the blocks are worked to a smooth finish and the faces are left rough or are roughened.

SACRISTY Room attached to a church where sacred vessels and vestments are kept.

SALONE, SALOON Central hall of a mansion or palace.

SANCTUARY The part of a church where the high altar is placed (see fig. 10).
    Also used in non-Christian architecture of a temple or place sacred to a god.

SCREENS PASSAGE Passage in a medieval house entered by the main door and dividing the screen of the hall on one side from the kitchen, buttery and pantry on the other.

SERVICE CORE In skyscrapers a central structural concrete core, housing elevators and other services; the floors are cantilevered out from the core.

SHAFT The body of a column (see fig. 13) or pillar; or a vertical moulding, generally circular, applied to a wall, pier or vault.

SHELL CONSTRUCTION Structure formed of thin panels of concrete or wood, curved, generally in a double curve, to give structural strength.

SHINGLES Wooden tiles used for covering roofs or as a cladding on walls.

SHUTTERING See FORMWORK.

SILL The horizontal timber or stone below a door or window, or (a ground sill) below a wall.

SLAB CONSTRUCTION Use of the concrete slab in a continuous structure with the vertical members that support it, generally MUSHROOM COLUMNS.

SOLID-WALL CONSTRUCTION Using walls of masonry, brickwork, concrete, logs etc. which both enclose the interior and bear the load of the building.

SPACE FRAME Rigid structure, generally of steel members arranged in three-dimensional trusses, having great strength in proportion to its weight and able to cover very large spaces.

SPAN Breadth of the opening of an ARCH.
    A CLEAR-SPAN STRUCTURE is one where the space is covered with a single unsupported span.

SPUR WALL Short projecting wall.

STALACTITE VAULT In Islamic architecture a vault formed of corbelled motifs with concave geometrical carving, resembling natural stalactites.

STAR VAULT See VAULT.

STRAPWORK Mannerist masonry or plaster decoration of interlaced bands.

STRINGCOURSE Projecting horizontal band or moulding set in a wall.

STUCCO A type of plasterwork, usually used in imitation of stone.

STYLOBATE The continuous base beneath a COLONNADE (see fig. 13).

TABERNACLE Niche or receptacle over an altar, or canopy with rich ornamentation.

TIE-BEAM See BEAM.

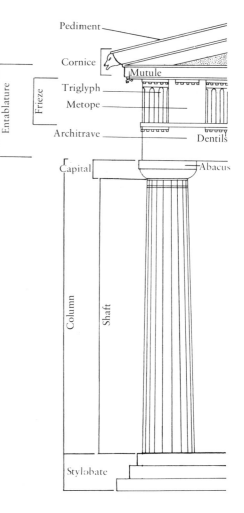

13 Main features of the Doric Order (Temple of Zeus, Olympia)

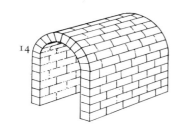

14

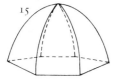

15

16

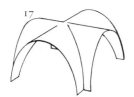

17

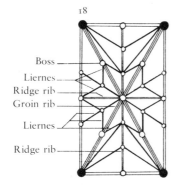

18

Boss
Liernes
Ridge rib
Groin rib
Liernes
Ridge rib

19

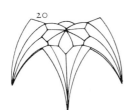

20

TRACERY Patterns of thin intersecting bars of masonry in the upper part of a window, or used to decorate a wall or vault. This BAR TRACERY was preceded by PLATE TRACERY, where the window openings were cut into a solid plate of masonry in the window head.

TRANSEPT Part of a cruciform church at right angles to the body or nave (see fig. 10); or in an aisled building at right angles to the aisles.

TRANSOM Horizontal cross-bar in a window.

TRANSVERSE ARCH See ARCH.

TRAVERTINE Compact form of calcareous tufa, much used in Rome.

TRIBUNE GALLERY Storey above the aisle of a church, with an arcade dividing it from the nave (see fig. 11).

TRIFORIUM Arcaded passage within the thickness of the wall over the pier-arches of a church, at the height of the aisle roof, below the clerestory (see fig. 11).

TRIGLYPH Grooved ornament in a Doric FRIEZE (see fig. 13).

TRIUMPHAL ARCH Commemorative arch developed in Roman architecture. The characteristic triple form has a large central arch with two smaller ones flanking it. Its application to the church façade and interior became an important motif in Christian architecture.

TRUE ARCH See ARCH.

TRUSS Timber or metal members forming the principal supports of a roof, bridge etc., framed together to give support to one another and prevent spreading or distortion.

TUFA Light porous calcareous or volcanic stone.

TUNNEL VAULT See VAULT.

TYMPANUM The space between the lintel of a door and the arch or pediment above it.

UNDERCROFT A subterranean vaulted apartment or chapel.

VAULT An arched structure covering an interior space (see figs 14–20).
  BARREL (or TUNNEL) VAULT (fig. 14) A continuous arch, springing from opposite walls of the central body of a building. It is generally semi-circular, but may also be pointed.
  CROSS VAULT GROIN or RIB VAULT formed by intersecting vaults.
  DOMICAL VAULT (fig. 15) Vault or dome formed of sections of a hemisphere, rising directly from a straight-sided, square or polygonal bay, separated by groins.
  FAN VAULT (fig. 16) Type of vault, peculiar to late Gothic in Britain, which is composed of curving conical PENDENTIVES meeting, or nearly meeting, at the top of the vault. The masonry is covered with decorative panels and ribs which radiate

from the base of the pendentive to form a fan shape.
  FILIGREE VAULT Vault decorated in intricate pierced patterns.
  GROIN VAULT (fig. 17) Vault formed by the intersection at right angles of two barrel vaults, the lines where the surfaces join forming a sharp curved edge known as a groin.
  LIERNE VAULT (fig. 18) RIB VAULT with additional non-structural ribs, known as liernes, joining the structural ribs.
  NET VAULT Vault decorated with an intricate pattern of straight and curved ribs.
  PENDANT VAULT Elaborate vault where the structure supports hanging BOSSES.
  RIB VAULT (fig. 19) Vault where the main loads are all carried by a structure of ribs, with webs of masonry used to fill the spaces between these. The main ribs in a CROSS VAULT are the groin ribs, which follow the diagonal lines formed by the intersection of two vaults, and the longitudinal and transverse ridge ribs, which are placed at the apex of the vault. A decorated BOSS normally covers the main points of intersection of the ribs.
  STAR VAULT (fig. 20) Vault whose ribs form the shape of a star.
  TUNNEL VAULT See BARREL VAULT.

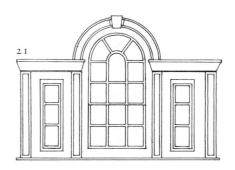

21

VENETIAN WINDOW (fig. 21) Window with three openings, the central wider one arched. It was much used by Palladio, his followers and imitators.

VOLUTE A spiral scroll; particularly that which forms part of the Ionic capital.

VOUSSOIR See ARCH: TRUE ARCH and fig. 9.

WALL PLATE Principal beam of a timber-frame wall, which supports the roof truss or the joists for an upper-storey floor.

WATTLE Interlaced thin laths (or rods) and twigs used as a building material and covered with mud or clay as in wattle-and-daub construction.

WEATHERBOARDING See CLAPBOARD.

WEB Masonry used to fill the space between the ribs of a vault.

WESTWORK West end of an early medieval church, consisting of entrance hall, upper chamber and a tower; most common in German architecture.

FURTHER READING

Wherever possible the date of the latest edition has been given
except in those cases when the first date of publication is of historical interest

GENERAL BOOKS

Copplestone, T. (ed.) *World Architecture*
Feltham 1969

Fletcher, Sir B. *A History of Architecture*
(18th edn revised by J.C. Palmes) London
and New York 1975

Girouard, M. *Life in the English Country
House* London and New Haven, Conn. 1978

Harris, J. and Lever, J. *An Illustrated
Glossary of Architecture, 850–1830* London
1969; Salem, New Hampshire 1979

Kidson, P., Murray, P. and Thompson, P.A.
History of English Architecture London 1979

Kubler, G. and Soria, M. *Art and
Architecture in Spain and Portugal and their
American Dominions, 1500–1800*
Harmondsworth and New York 1959

Mainstone, R.J. *Developments in Structural
Form* London and Cambridge, Mass. 1975

Norberg-Schulz, C. *Meaning in Western
Architecture* London and New York 1975

Pevsner, Sir N., Honour, H. and Fleming, J.
A Dictionary of Architecture Harmondsworth
1975; New York 1976

Pevsner, Sir N. *A History of Building Types*
London and Princeton 1976

Pevsner, Sir N. *An Outline of European
Architecture* Harmondsworth 1973; New
York 1960

Raeburn, M. *An Outline of World
Architecture* London and New York 1978

Rasmussen, S.E. *Experiencing Architecture*
London 1959; Cambridge, Mass. 1962

Zevi, B. *Architectura in Nuce* Venice 1960

Zevi, B. *Architecture as Space* (tr.) New
York 1975

INTRODUCTION

Brunskill, R.W. *Illustrated Handbook of
Vernacular Architecture* London and Salem,
New Hampshire 1978

Giedion, S. *Space, Time and Architecture*
(5th rev. edn) London and Cambridge, Mass.
1967

Gimpel, J. *The Cathedral Builders* London
and New York 1961

Hodgkinson, A. (ed.) *Handbook of Building
Structure* London and New York 1974

Laugier, M-A. *Essai sur l'Architecture* Paris
1755 (Translated as *An Essay on Architecture*
Los Angeles 1977)

Lavedan, P. *French Architecture* (tr.) London
1979

Mercer, E. *English Vernacular Houses*
London and New York 1975

Palladio, A. *I quattro libri dell'architettura*
Venice 1570 (Translated as *The Four Books
of Architecture* London and New York 1965)

Ragon, M. *Histoire mondiale de
l'architecture et de l'urbanisme modern*
Paris 1971–8

Riegl, A. (1858–1905) *Historische Grammatik
der bildenden Künste* (published
posthumously) Cologne 1966

Rudofsky, B. *Architecture without Architects*
London 1972; New York 1969

Semper, G. *Der Stil in den technischen und
tektonischen Künsten* Munich 1860–3

Summerson, Sir J. *The Classical Language of
Architecture* London 1963; Cambridge, Mass.
1966

Vitruvius *The Ten Books on Architecture*
(tr.) London and New York 1960

Wright, F.L. *Writings and Buildings* (selected
by E. Kaufman and B. Raeburn) London and
New York 1978

Zevi, B. *The Modern Language of
Architecture* (tr.) Seattle 1978

GREEK ARCHITECTURE

Berve, H., Gruben, G. and Hirmer, M. *Greek
Temples, Theatres and Shrines* London and
New York 1963

Coulton, J.J. *Greek Architects at Work*
London 1976; Ithaca, New York 1977

Lawrence, A.W. *Greek Architecture*
Harmondsworth 1973; New York 1975

Martin, R. *Manuel d'architecture grecque 1:
Matériaux et techniques* Paris 1965

Plommer, W.H. *Ancient and Classical
Architecture* London and New York 1956

Tomlinson, R.A. *Greek Sanctuaries* London
1976; New York 1977

Ward-Perkins, J.B. *Cities of Ancient Greece
and Rome* New York 1974

Wycherley, R.E. *How the Greeks Built Cities*
London 1962; New York 1976

Wycherley, R.E. *The Stones of Athens*
Princeton 1977

ROMAN ARCHITECTURE

Boethius, A. and Ward-Perkins, J.B. *Etruscan
and Roman Architecture* Harmondsworth
1970; New York 1969

Brown, F.E. *Roman Architecture* London and
New York 1961

Chevallier, R. *Roman Roads* London and
Berkeley 1976

Clavel, M. and Lévêque, P. *Villes et
structures urbaines dans l'occident romain*
Paris 1971

Crema, L. *L'Architettura romana* Turin 1959

Gazzola, P. *Ponti romani* Florence 1963

Grant, M. *Cities of Vesuvius* London 1971;
New York 1978

Grant, M. *The Roman Forum* London and
New York 1970

MacDonald, W.L. *The Architecture of the
Roman Empire* Vol. 1, London and New
Haven, Conn. 1965

McKay, A.G. *Houses, Villas and Palaces in
the Roman World* London and Ithaca, New
York 1975

Percival, J. *The Roman Villa: A Historical
Introduction* London and Berkeley 1976

Picard, G. *Living Architecture: Roman* (tr.)
London 1966

Robertson, D.S. *Greek and Roman
Architecture* Cambridge 1943; New York
1969

Ward-Perkins, J.B. *Roman Architecture* New
York 1977

Wheeler, R.E.M. *Roman Art and
Architecture* London 1964; New York 1965

THE MIDDLE AGES

Bowie, T. (ed.) *The Sketchbook of Villehard
de Honnecourt* Bloomington, Indiana 1968

Branner, R. *Gothic Architecture* London
1964; New York 1961

Branner, R. *St Louis and the Court Style*
London 1965

Braunfels, W. *Monasteries of Western
Europe* London 1972; Princeton 1973

Conant, K.J. *Carolingian and Romanesque
Architecture, 800–1200* Harmondsworth and
New York 1974

Frankl, P. *Gothic Architecture*
Harmondsworth and Baltimore 1962

Gall, E. *Cathedrals and Abbey Churches of
the Rhine* London 1963

Grodecki, L. *L'Architecture ottonienne* Paris
1958

Harvey, J. *The Cathedrals of Spain* London
1957

Kidson, P. *The Medieval World* London 1967

Kraus, H. *Gold Was the Mortar: Economics
of Cathedral Building* London and Boston 1979

Krautheimer, R. *Early Christian and
Byzantine Architecture* Harmondsworth and
New York 1975

Mango, C. *Byzantine Architecture* New York
1976

Panofsky, E. (ed.) *Abbot Suger on the Abbey
Church of St Denis and its Art Treasures*
Princeton 1979

Shelby, L. (ed.) *Gothic Design Techniques; the fifteenth-century design booklets of Mathes Roriczer and Hanns Schmuttermayer* Chicago 1977

Stoddart, W.S. *Art and Architecture in Medieval France* New York 1972

Webb, G. *Architecture in Britain: The Middle Ages* Harmondsworth 1965; New York 1975

THE RENAISSANCE

Ackerman, J.S. *The Architecture of Michelangelo* Harmondsworth 1971; New York 1961

Ackerman, J.S. *Palladio* Harmondsworth 1966; New York 1977

Alberti, L.B. *De re aedificatoria . . .* Florence 1485 (Translated by J. Leoni as *The Architecture of L.B. Alberti* London 1726; reprinted London 1955)

Bialostocki, J. *The Art of the Renaissance in Eastern Europe* Oxford and Ithaca, New York 1976

Blunt, A. *Art and Architecture in France, 1500–1700* Harmondsworth 1973; New York 1977

Blunt, A. *Artistic Theory in Italy, 1450–1600* Oxford 1945; New York 1956

Burns, H. *Andrea Palladio, 1508–1580* London 1975

Bruschi, A. *Bramante* London and New York 1977

Gilbert, C. (ed.) *Renaissance Art* London and New York 1973

Girouard, M. *Robert Smythson and the Architecture of the Elizabethan Era* London 1966

Heydenreich, L.H. and Lotz, W. *Architecture in Italy, 1400–1600* Harmondsworth and New York 1974

Lotz, W. *Studies in Italian Renaissance Architecture* Cambridge, Mass. 1977

Partner, P. *Renaissance Rome, 1500–1559* London 1976; Berkeley 1977

Shearman, J. *Mannerism* Harmondsworth 1967; New York 1978

Summerson, Sir J. *Architecture in Britain, 1530–1830* Harmondsworth 1970; New York 1969

Wittkower, R. *Architectural Principles in The Age of Humanism* London 1962; New York 1971

BAROQUE, ROCOCO AND CLASSICISM

Berger, R.W. *Antoine Le Pautre* New York 1969

Blunt, A. *Borromini* Harmondsworth 1979

Braham, A. and Smith, P. *François Mansart* London 1973; New York 1974

Coope, R. *Salomon De Brosse and the Development of the Classical Style in French Architecture, 1565–1830* London and University Park, Pa. 1972

Downes, K. *Hawksmoor* London 1980

Downes, K. *Vanbrugh* London and New York 1977

Hautecoeur, L. *Histoire de l'architecture classique en France* Paris 1943–55

Hibbard, H. *Bernini* Harmondsworth 1965; New York 1966

Hibbard, H. *Carlo Maderno and Roman Architecture, 1580–1630* London and University Park, Pa. 1972

Hitchcock, H-R. *Rococo Architecture in Southern Germany* London 1968

Otto, C.F. *Space into Light: the churches of Balthasar Neumann* London and Cambridge, Mass. 1979

Thornton, P. *Seventeenth-Century Interior Decoration in England, France and Holland* London and New Haven, Conn. 1978

Whinney, M. *Wren* London 1971

Wittkower, R. *Palladio and English Palladianism* London and New York 1975

Wittkower, R. *Studies in the Italian Baroque* London 1975

THE FIRST INDUSTRIAL AGE

Benevolo, L. *History of Modern Architecture* Vol. 1, London 1971; Cambridge, Mass. 1977

Clark, Sir K. *The Gothic Revival* London and New York 1974

Collins, P. *Changing Ideals in Modern Architecture, 1750–1950* London and Salem, New Hampshire 1965

Drexler, A. (ed.) *The Architecture of the Ecole des Beaux Arts* London and Cambridge, Mass. 1977

Dyos, H.J. and Wolff, M. (eds.) *The Victorian City: Images and Realities* London 1977–8; Boston 1978

Eastlake, Sir C.L. *History of the Gothic Revival* (2nd rev. edn of 1872 edn) Leicester and New York 1970

Fergusson, J. *A History of Architecture in All Countries* London 1865–73

Girouard, M. *Sweetness and Light: 'Queen Anne' Movement, 1860–1900* Oxford and New York 1977

Girouard, M. *The Victorian Country House* London and New Haven, Conn. 1979

Hitchcock, H-R. *Architecture: 19th and 20th Centuries* Harmondsworth and New York 1977

Hitchcock, H-R. *Early Victorian Architecture in Britain* London 1973; New York 1972

Klingender, F.D. *Art and the Industrial Revolution* London 1947. Revised and extended by A. Elton, London 1968; New York 1970

Muthesius, S. *The High Victorian Movement in Architecture, 1850–1870* London 1972

Pevsner, Sir N. *Pioneers of Modern Design* Harmondsworth 1970; New York 1961

Pugin, A.W.N. *Contrasts* London 1836

Pugin, A.W.N. *The True Principles of pointed or Christian Architecture* London 1841

Ruskin, J. *Stones of Venice* London 1851–3

Ruskin, J. *Seven Lamps of Architecture* London 1849

Summerson, Sir J. *Four Studies in Evaluation* London and New York 1970

Viollet-le-Duc, E. *Entretiens sur l'architecture* Paris 1863–72

THE TWENTIETH CENTURY

Banham, R. *Age of the Masters* London and New York 1975

Banham, R. *Architecture of the Well-tempered Environment* London 1973; Chicago 1969

Banham, R. *Theory and Design in the First Machine Age* London 1970; New York 1967

Bayer, H. and others *Bauhaus 1919–28* London and New York 1976

Blake, P. *The Master Builders: Le Corbusier, Mies van der Rohe, Frank Lloyd Wright* London 1960; New York 1976

Benevolo, L. *A History of Modern Architecture* Vol. II, London 1971; Cambridge, Mass. 1977

Benton, C. and T. *Form and Function: a source book for the history of architecture and design, 1890–1939* London 1975

Cooke, P. and others *Archigram* London 1972

Howarth, T. *Charles Rennie Mackintosh and the Modern Movement* London and New York 1977

Jencks, C. *The Language of Post-modern Architecture* London and New York 1977

Jencks, C. *Le Corbusier and the Tragic View of Architecture* Harmondsworth 1973; Cambridge, Mass. 1974

Jencks, C. *Modern Movements in Architecture* Harmondsworth and New York 1973

Joedicke, J.A. *A History of Modern Architecture* London and New York 1959

Le Corbusier *Towards a New Architecture* (tr.) London and New York 1970

Mumford, L. *The City in History* London and New York 1961

Richards, J.M. *An Introduction to Modern Architecture* London 1961; New York 1947

Sharpe, D. *A Visual History of Twentieth-Century Architecture* London and Boston 1972

Watkin, D. *Morality and Architecture* Oxford 1977; New York 1978

ACKNOWLEDGMENTS

The following abbreviations have been used: T = top; B = bottom; R = right; L = left

The drawings on pages 15, 43, 50, 58–9, 67, 69, 70–71, 83, 89, 110–11, 115, 131, 135, 143, 151, 167, 172, 186–7, 196, 215, 223, 234, 252, 264 and 279 were specially commissioned from Studio di Grazia, Rome.

The illustrations on the pages listed were kindly provided by the following sources:

A.C.L. Brussels: 243B; Aerofilms: 125T, 199B; Agencja Autorska, Warsaw: 122L; Agence Top (Rozine Mazin): 125T; Alinari: 65T, (Brogi) 74B, 79T, 127T; American School of Classical Studies, Athens 49B, 53B; Heather Angel: 197; Archigram: 276B; Archives d' Architecture Moderne, Brussels: 252B; Archivio SAGEP: 151; © Arch. Phot/S.P.A.D.E.M., Paris 1980: 218T. 219T, 231B, 238T, 263B (Studio Chevojon); Artia (Karel Neubert): 120; Arup Associates: 278T, 278B, 279; Lala Aufsberg: 165; James Austin: 94T, 102, 104B, 107B; Australian Information Service: 273B; Australian Tourist Commission: 240B; Bavaria-Verlag: 20, 209; BBC Hulton Picture Library: 229T; Belgian State Tourist Office: 155T; John Bethell: 6, 36T, 49T (Bernard Cox), 84 (Bernard Cox), 87T, 109 (Bernard Cox), 146, 147B, 172T (Bernard Cox), 175B, 185T, 185BR, 189, 220T; The Benedictine Abbey, Rohr: 176; Bibliothèque Nationale: 150T; Bildarchiv Foto Marburg: 19, 34B, 86, 94B, 95L, 108L, 115L, 187BR, 224B, 250T, 252T, 258B; J. Bottin: 88, 104T; Brecht-Einzig Limited: 286; British Library: 11B, 42B, 56B, 57B; Trustees of the British Museum: 133L; Bulloz: 72B, 153, 220B; Dr Harald Busch: 121TR, 122R; Canadian High Commission: 276T; Cement and Concrete Association: 25B, 255B; Centraal Beheer: 283T; Centro di Studi d'Architettura Andrea Palladio, Vicenza: 142; Chicago Historical Society: 236T; Nicola Coldstream: 125B; Country Life: 242BL; Courtauld Institute of Art, London: 8, 150B, 156, 159T, 178R, 186 (P. Smith), 206 (Professor John Shearman); Dalton Howarth & Partners: 216B; James Davis: 16 (Private Collection), 123; Deutsche Fotothek, Dresden: 257T; Deutsches Archäologisches Institut, Rome: 79B (Bardo Museum, Tunis); Dissing & Weitling, Hellerup: 274T (Strüwing Reklamefoto); John Donat: 246C, 259, 263T, 265T, 272B, 280T; Charles Eames: 270; Explorer: 96T (R. Lanaud), 105 (M. Cambazard); Finlands Arkitekturmuseum, Helsinki: 274B; Werner Forman Archive: 32B, 40–41, 60–61; Fototeca Unione: 63B, 70; French Government Tourist Office: 143T, 285; Germanisches Nationalmuseum, Nürnberg: 13B; Keith Gibson: 249; Giraudon: 87B (Lauros), 116L (Lauros), 193B, 225 (Lauros); Gladstone Pottery Museum, Longton, Stoke on Trent: 21B; South Glamorgan County Council: 240T; Greater London Council Photograph Library: 261B; Gruen Associates: 282B; Sonia Halliday Photographs: 42, 44B, (F.H.C. Birch), 52L, 57T, 83 (Jane Taylor), 116R; Claus & Liselotte Hansmann: 48T; Robert Harding Associates: 58 (Nigel Cameron), 59 (Nigel Cameron); F. L. Harris: 12, 93, 100B, 138T, 173, 174T, 192R, 195; Hedrich-Blessing: 27T, 250B; Lucien Hervé: 288B; Hirmer Fotoarchiv: 51T, 95R; Historisches Museum der Stadt Wien: 230T; Hoechst Aktiengesellschaft: 21T; Hofstetter Dia: 177TL, 177TR; Michael Holford Library: 45R (Gerry Clyde), 97, 101L, 101R (Gerry Clyde), 127B; Angelo Hornak: 4, 68, 80–81, 141B, 147T, 167R,

208T (Soane Museum), 221, 260B, 275; Martin Hürlimann: 18L; I.C.P.: 241; I.G.D.A.: 17 (Barengo-Gardin), 184B, 196 (Beaujard/Titus), 44T, 72T, 76 (Bevilacqua), 114 (Dagli Orti), 205 (A.F. Kersting), 277 (Leigheb), 264 (Mariani), 85, 28B (Marzari), 164L (Moretti), 2, 39T, 53T, 56T, 65B, 69, 96B, 152B (Pubbli-aer-foto), 126B (Quiresi), 237 (Sandak), 180T (Schmidt-Metz), 168T (S.E.F.), 248B (Splendid Color), 91L (Titus), 145 (Tomsich); India Office Library: 226; Instituto Municipal de Historia de Barcelona: 231T; Elton Collection/Ironbridge Gorge Museum Trust: 214; John Lewis Partnership Archives: 265BL; Johnson Wax: 15TL; A.F. Kersting: 103, 106, 107T, 110T, 110B, 111TL, 111B, 112T, 115R, 121TL, 124B, 133R, 134, 158, 160–161, 162T, 172B, 174B, 177B, 179T, 181, 183T, 184T, 190T, 191B, 192L, 207B, 210, 215, 218B, 219B, 239T, 248T; Lucinda Lambton Library: 212B; Siegfried Lauterwasser: 284B; Letchworth Museum: 251B; Library of Congress, Washington D.C.: 191T, 236B, 243T, 266T; G. Mairani: 144B; David Wharry: 171L; The Mansell Collection: 46R (Anderson/Museo Laterano, Rome), 67, 77T (Alinari), 138B (Anderson), 139B (Anderson), 155B, 162B, 166 (Anderson), 167L, 168B; Eric de Maré: 188B, 211B, 213, 239B; Leonard von Matt: 34T, 63BL, 74T, 179B, 199T; Metropolitan Museum of Art, New York: 24B detail from Robert Campin (also called Master of Flémalle and Master of the Merode Altarpiece), active between 1406–1444, *The Annunciation with Donors and St Joseph*, oil on wood, (The Cloisters Collection, Purchase), 51B (Rogers Fund, 1903); Oscar de Milliano: 23B; Milton Keynes Development Corporation: 289; Ann Münchow: 92B; National Film Archive: 246T; National Monuments Record: 111TR, 190B, 242T; National Museum of Wales: 78B; National Tourist Organisation of Greece: 54B, 55BR; National Westminster Bank Limited: 25T; Courtesy of New York Historical Society, New York City: 233T; New York Public Library Astor Lenox & Tilden Foundation, Eno Collection: 232; Norwegian Embassy: 27B; Office du Livre, Fribourg: 43T, 47, 75L, 170, 178; C. E. Östman-F. Hubalek: 124T; A. Ottar & K. Mallory: 267; Alexander Paul: 194; Ann & Bury Peerless: 288T; Pennsylvania Historical Society, Philadelphia: 208B; Photoresources: 77B; Pictor: 284T; Picturepoint: 113; Pilkington Brothers Glass Limited: 265BR; Pitkin Pictorials: 216T; Pirelli Limited 282T; John Portman & Associates: 283B; Mauro Pucciarelli: 140; Michael Raeburn Collection: 17T, 35R, 39B, 260T; Reform Club: 277B; Royal Institute of British Architects Library: 23T, 159B, 254; Rijksdienst voor de Monumentenzorg, Zeist: 163B; Roger-Viollet: 224T, 227T, 266B; Musée Rolin, Autun: 1; Jean Roubier: 163T; Royal Commission on Ancient Monuments, Scotland (Crown Copyright): 203T, 211T; Royal Netherlands Embassy: 257B, 258T; The Royal Pavilion, Art Gallery and Museums, Brighton: 24T; Salmer: 89, 200–201; Sandak: 175T, 188T, 269B; Scala: 33T, 36B, 73B, 82, 90, 100T, 118T, 118B, 119, 121B, 128–129, 130, 132, 135, 136, 137, 139T, 141T, 144T, 149T, 152T, 157T, 157B, 164R, 169; Scarborough Grand Hotel: 235; H. Schmidt-Glassner: 35L, 91R, 182, 183B; Toni Schneiders: 22, 64, 112B, 256; Sears Roebuck: 247; Edwin Smith: 13T, 30, 31T, 31B, 66T, 66B, 185BL; Peter Smith: 187T, 187BL; Alison & Peter Smithson: 273T; Society for the Preservation of New England Antiquities, Boston: 18R; Brian Souter: 15TR; Stadtbildstelle Augsburg: 154; Nico van der Stam: 261T; Staatliche Museen Preussicher

Kulturbesitz, Berlin (FRG) Kupferstichkabinet: 38 detail from Albrecht Dürer, *Die Drahtziehmühle*; Staatliche Museen Berlin (GDR) Kupferstichkabinet: 207T; Dr Franz Stoedtner/Heinz Klemm: 262B; Ezra Stoller © ESTO: 37R, 269T, 281T; Sveriges Arkitektur Museum, Stockholm: 262T; Wim Swaan: 171R; C. Tadgell: 143B; Kenzo Tange: 246B, 287B; Toledo Museum of Art, Ohio: 32T; Adolfo Tomeucci: 63BR, 71; Adrian Turner/Bardo Museum, Tunis: 78T; University of Pennsylvania, Fine Arts Library: 26, (News Bureau/Lawrence S. Williams Inc) 287T; Foto Vasari: 255T; Venturi & Rauch: 280B; Versailles Museum: 180B; Victoria & Albert Museum: 222T, 222B, 242BR; Monumenti e Musei e Gallerie Pontificie, Vatican: 198R; Edward & Winifred Ward: 228T; Wates System: 271T, 271B; Wawel State Collections of Art, Cracow, (Lukasz Schuster): 136B; Weidenfeld Archives: 46L, 73T; Yale University Library: 28T; Yan/Jean Dieuzaide: 98; ZEFA: 99, 193T; Joseph Ziolo: 117 (Toni Schneiders), 204B (Candelier-Brumaire), 224–245 (Babey, Basel), 272T (Phedon Salon); Vision International: 281B (Steve Herr).

In addition the illustrations on the following pages were taken from the sources listed:

10: *The Sketchbook of Villehard de Honnecourt* P.XXXIX; 11TL: P. Le Muet *Traité des cinq Ordres d'Architecture . . . traduit du Palladio . . .* Paris 1645, Pl.4; 11TR: G. Semper *Der Stil in den technischen und tektonischen Künsten oder praktische Aesthetik* Munich 1860–63, Vol.I, Tafel I; 33BL: M.A. Laugier *Essai sur l'Architecture* Paris 1755, frontispiece; 37L: *Zeitschrift für Kunstgeschichte* Leipzig 1937, Vol.6, Abb.9; 45L F. Krauss *Die Griechische Tempel* Berlin 1959 (By courtesy of the Deutsches Archäologisches Institut and De Gruyter Verlag); 48B; A. Mallwitz *Mitteilungen des Deutsches Archäologisches Institut Athenische* Abb. 77 (1962), 167, fig. 2 (By courtesy of the Deutsches Archäologisches Institut and Gebrüder Mann Verlag); 52R: H. Krackfuss *Didyma I*, 3, Berlin 1941; 53C: J. J. Coulton *Greek Architects at Work* London 1977, p. 118, fig. 51 (By courtesy of Elek Books Ltd); 54T: Ecole Française d'Athènes *Délos* Vol. XXVII, p.3, fig. 2 (By courtesy of the Ecole Française d'Athenes); 55T: *Annual of the British School at Athens* No. 57, 1962, p.112 (By courtesy of the British School at Athens); 55BL: *Praktika Tis en Athenais Archaiologike Etaireia* 1972, p. 261, fig. 5 (By courtesy of Alexander Cambitoglou); 75R: T. Wiegand *Baalbek II* Berlin 1923, Abb. 17 (By courtesy of De Gruyter Verlag); 108R: *The Sketchbook of Villehard de Honnecourt* P. LXII; 195T: B. and T. Langley *Gothic Architecture improved by rules and proportions etc.* 1747, pl. LII; 202: *New Lanark*, colour lithograph drawn by L. Clark (London 1825); 203: J. Bentham *Works* Edinburgh 1842, Vol.4; 204T: C.N. Ledoux *L'Architecture* Paris 1804, p.15; 212T: *Illustrated London News* Nov. 3 1849, p.304; 217: A.W.N. Pugin *Contrasts* Edinburgh 1898, pl. 9; 229B: G. Doré *London: A Pilgrimage* London 1862, p.120; 233B A. Soria y Hernadez *The Problem of Land in Spain* Madrid 1926; 251T: T. Garnier *Une Cité Industrielle* Paris 1918, Vol.II, p. 74; B. Taut *Alpine Architecture* 1919, Blatt 17.

INDEX

Page numbers in italic refer to illustrations.
The various forms of 'Saint' (San, Santo, St etc.) are given in each case as S.